KV-638-221

Operational Research

MILTON KEYNES LIBRARY
555 SILBURY BOULEVARD
CENTRAL MILTON KEYNES MK9 3HL
TEL: 663130

Operational Research

D. J. White

Department of Decision Theory
University of Manchester

BUCKS COUNTY LIBRARY

mil CRA 5726

R
519·5
WHI

JOHN WILEY & SONS

Chichester · New York · Brisbane · Toronto · Singapore

Copyright © 1985 by John Wiley & Sons Ltd.

All rights reserved.

No part of this book may be reproduced by any means, or transmitted, or translated into a machine language without the written permission of the publisher.

Library of Congress Cataloging in Publication Data:

White, D. J. (Douglas John)
    Operational research.

    Includes bibliographies and index.
    1. Operations research.   I. Title.
T57.6.W586   1985   658.4'03'4   85–608

ISBN 0 471 90717 0 (cloth)
ISBN 0 471 90718 9 (paper)

British Library Cataloguing in Publication Data:

White, D. J.
    Operational research.
    1. Operations research
    I. Title
    001.4'24   T57.6

ISBN 0 471 90717 0 (cloth)
ISBN 0 471 90718 9 (paper)

Printed and Bound in Great Britain.

Contents

Preface

The formal institution of Operational Research as a recognized sphere of scientific activity is attributed to A. P. Rowe at the Air Ministry Research Station, UK, between 1937 and 1939 (see Williams [19]). Of course the basic approach of Operational Research to finding solutions to problems probably goes back to the earliest times when men could articulate and reason about such problems. For example, Hudson [8] cites the resolution of an industrial dispute over kosher food in King Nebuchadnezzar's civil service, in which a controlled dietary experiment led to the demonstration that one of two options was the better, and this was implemented. The reader may wish to consult Trefethen [17] for more details on the history of Operational Research.

It would, of course, be naive to suggest that any mode of thought, or any approach which relates to problems which groups or individuals face, constitutes an Operational Research study *per se*, although it may contribute to a resolution of the problem. For example, statistical analysis would contribute to a resolution of Nebuchadnezzar's problem but, unless it is coupled with a study of the decisions which have to be taken, and, hence, with the formulation of the problem in the first instance, it is not, in itself, Operational Research (Morse [13] says that statistics is not to be equated with Operational Research). In this text, while appreciating the role that these two aspects play in Operational Research, we will not discuss them and will, in essence, concentrate on the quantitative content of modelling in Operational Research, and on the decision element, which is taken to be fundamental to the identity of Operational Research. We will also take the view that research, and not just search (e.g. for information of a cataloguing kind), is essential in this identity. Indeed, Johnson [9] emphasizes the essential need for Operational Research to remain research-oriented, which is particularly important in the light of trends in Operational Research to being dominated by the computer and information processing needs of industrial operations and, for example, giving scant attention to the need to examine carefully the approaches open to tackling problems, giving scant attention to problem formulation, and giving even less attention to the fundamental object of scientific endeavour, viz. measurement.

There are, of course, many definitions of Operational Research and we will not dwell unduly on this. We might well ask ourselves, in being consistent with our Operational Research philosophy, what the value of precise or less precise definitions might be, and this might lead to another Operational Research study, that is if we know what Operational Research is, of course. Clearly the definition of Morse [12] who says that Operational

Research is what Operational Researchers do and what appears in Operational Research journals (although he does give, subsequently, other definitions in Morse [13] and Kimball *et al.* [10]) does not appear to be too helpful. One would naturally wish to avoid the situation referred to by Chow [3] who cites the inclusion of Operational Research under the heading of 'Medical and Surgical' in the 1957 edition of the *Directory of Newspapers and Periodicals*. Other references to the definitions may be found in Rhinehart [15], Bevan [1], Hamilton [7]. We will take the view that Operational Research is 'the science of (prescriptive) decision making' (although this may involve a study of actual (descriptive) decision making which may be important, for example, in the context of problem formulation). This is the definition of Rhinehart and it involves science (inclusive of measurement) and decision (this will become clearer in the problem formulation chapter). In taking this stand it becomes no longer an exclusively operational activity and encompasses all spheres of prescriptive decision making (e.g. see Ornea *et al.* [14] on operational, technological and investment hierarchies). Nor does it restrict itself to institutional decision making, although the profession of Operational Research is essentially geared to such because of the resource factors involved. On an individual plane Siegel [16] faced the problem of finding the initials of a Colonel Lewis. He used the telephone directory and chose the letter which was most common, viz. C, and then, given C, the next most common letter was H. He used, correctly as it turned out, these initials, viz. C. H. Of course, a deeper study of gains or losses from the use of particular letters might have been rather more demanding. However, a probability model for his research, and a decision element, did exist.

We will not involve ourselves with what science is or is not, or with its limitations, which, in Operational Research, it clearly has. We must be as scientific as we can within the limitations imposed by the context of the study. Eilon [6], Dando *et al.* [5], White [18] discuss such aspects.

A view is taken by some that an activity is not Operational Research, or good Operational Research, unless it results in implementation. In this sense we refer to the practice of Operational Research and not to, for example, the development of techniques of Operational Research. Clearly the objective of practical Operational Research is to secure appropriate implementation, but poor recommendations can be implemented, and good recommendations fail to be implemented, for a range of reasons. In this text we will not consider the implementation issue and the objectives will be quite restricted. Naturally implementation, as with any innovational activity, is of fundamental importance. The readers will find the references White [18], Wysaki [20], Cain [2] and Marett *et al.* [11] useful.

Also, although we take a mathematician's viewpoint throughout, this is not intended to minimize the place of other disciplines in the effective conduct of Operational Research. Notably, one should take note of the place of psychology in Operational Research (see Creelman *et al.* [4]) since it plays a role in problem formulation, development of solution (e.g. see the convoy size and aircraft colour problems of Chapter 1), in team activities and, of course, in implementation.

In this text we concentrate on certain mathematical aspects of Operational Research. Chapter 1 introduces elements of the military origins of Operational Research, and at the same time introduces an element of modelling which not only leads on to a specific consideration of Operational Research techniques in Chapter 2, but also is used to highlight certain aspects of Operational Research to which we return later on more specifically in Chapter 4 on problem formulation.

Chapter 2 covers a selection of techniques, some of which relate to dynamic problems and have common characteristics, and others of which relate to some techniques for solving problems. In the latter group an emphasis is put on heuristic programming, which is a rapidly growing area in the light of inferences drawn from modern complexity theory, and which is geared, in our case, to solving problems which may be formulated as mathematical programmes, but for which efficient algorithms may not exist. The fact that, for example, our dynamic problems may be tackled in different ways, is emphasized. The content of this chapter is intended as a basis for model building and no detailed study of algorithms in general is given, for example, for mathematical programming formulations. The text does not intend to substitute for specialist texts in each of the areas covered, and the models developed are used later on to illustrate the themes in later chapters. Some numerical and analytic results are, very selectively, included to illustrate particular points.

Chapters 3, 4, 5 and 6, cover parametric and sensitivity analysis, problem formulation, combined use of techniques, and measurement respectively. This author believes that, as fundamental as measurement is to Operational Research, it has not yet been given the serious attention in Operational Research that it should have been, and that certain currently popular areas such as entropy, fuzzy sets, and flexibility have been improperly incorporated into the Operational Research area. The readers must judge for themselves, of course.

In Chapter 4 on problem formulation special attention is given to recent developments in multi-objective interactive methods, based on mathematical programming, which amplify the author's subject–object system dichotomy.

The text is essentially intended as a single mini-course on Operational Research. Students specializing in Operational Research will naturally study texts devoted to specific topics briefly covered in this text for the purposes of this text. Nonetheless, the modest integration of several features of Operational Research provided by the text may be of use to them.

Not all techniques are covered. For example, although reference is made to branch and bound, it is not studied (it is interesting to ask if this is an algorithm or an heuristic method). Nor do we deal with forecasting, and so on, which are important in any diet of Operational Research which purports to produce a rounded individual.

At the end of each topic a reference list is provided for further reading, or for the purposes of following up the exercises, which are based, in many cases, on actual papers, and hence, perhaps, have a little more authenticity than traditional class exercises in some cases.

Finally, some small licence has been taken in the writing of the text, which derives from the limited background of the students which the author has taught on a related course. In places, both discrete and continuous formulations are used, partly because, except in special cases, solutions require discrete methods, and partly because some students do not have adequate knowledge of integration. Instead of using functional notation such as $g(.)$, $v(.)$, $\theta(.)$, the use of $g(s)$, $v(x)$, $\theta(y)$, is made for functions, with the arguments explicitly included. Where a random variable arises the differentiation between it and its realized value is not made. Thus we refer to r as a random variable and its value at the same time instead of, for example, to R as the random variable and r as its realized value.

REFERENCES

1. Bevan, R. W., Trends in operational research, *Operations Research*, **6,** 441–447, 1958.
2. Cain, H., The intangibles of implementation, *Interfaces*, **9,** 144–147, 1979.
3. Chow, W. M., Incidental intelligence, *Operations Research*, **6,** 130, 1958.
4. Creelman, G. D. and Wallen, R. W., Place of psychology in operations research, *Operations Research*, **6,** 116–121, 1958.
5. Dando, M. R., Defrenne, A., and Sharp, R. G., Could operational research be a science?, *Omega*, **5,** 89–92, 1977.
6. Eilon, S., How scientific is operational research?, *Omega*, **4,** 1–8, 1975.
7. Hamilton, O. W., Industrial operations research, *Operations Research*, **1,** 145, 1953.
8. Hudson, M. G., Letter to the Editor, *Operational Research Newsletter*, September, 1983.
9. Johnson, E. A., Long range future of operational research, *Operations Research*, **8,** 1–23, 1960.
10. Kimball, G. E. and Morse, P. M., *Methods of Operations Research*, Wiley, 1951.
11. Marett, P. G. and Watson, H. J., A survey of management science implementation problems, *Interfaces*, **9,** 124–128, 1979.
12. Morse, P. M., Trends in operations research, *Operations Research*, **1,** 159–165, 1953.
13. Morse, P. M., Statistics and operations research, *Operations Research*, **4,** 2–18, 1956.
14. Ornea, J. C. and Stillson, P., On the optimum solution in operations research, *Operations Research*, **8,** 616–629, 1960.
15. Rhinehart, R. F., Threats to the growth of operations research in business and industry, *Operations Research*, **2,** 229–233, 1954.
16. Siegel, G. J., The application of the operations research approach in making a decision of no great importance, *Operations Research*, **1,** 446, 1953.
17. Trefethen, F. N., *A History of Operations Research, in Operations Research for*

Management, Vol. I., J. F. McCloskey and F. N. Trefethen (Eds.), John Hopkins Press, 1954.

18. White, D. J., *Decision Methodology*, Wiley, 1975.
19. Williams, E. C., Reflections on operational research, *Operations Research*, **2,** 441–443, 1954.
20. Wysaki, R. K., O.R./M.S., implementation research, a bibliography, *Interfaces*, **9,** 37–41, 1979.

CHAPTER 1

Introduction

1.1 MILITARY OPERATIONAL RESEARCH

The formal initiation of Operational Research was given in the Second World War and arose from a study of the effectiveness of military operations, primarily in the Royal Air Force. In fact (see Williams [86]) A. P. Rowe is credited with its inception at the Air Ministry Research Station at Bawdsey in 1937–9, although Blackett is said to have done so in all armed forces (see Solandt [71]).

We will therefore commence with a look at some simplified studies of some military problems. Some of these were actually studied during the war, and some have appeared since the war, but must certainly have been perceived during the war. The reasons for a look at these are that they are historically important and that they capture the central spirit of Operational Research and raise questions which are no less relevant to Operational Research now, and to which, in the intervening years, some answers have been derived.

As with any scientific endeavour we will have the central phases of a study, viz. observation, experiment, hypothesis formation, prediction, and, in our case, action. In this introductory section we will look at some very simplified problems so as not to obscure the central Operational Research activity, viz. modelling and aid to action. We will discuss a few salient points about the problems studied, but will not enter into details of the observation, experiment and hypothesis formation phases. These are, naturally, extremely important, but can be very detailed. The best thing to do on this is to look at some of the literature on military Operational Research, notably the work of Blackett [12] and Waddington [78]. The early issues of *Operational Research*, which provide a fine insight into Operational Research, contain various supplementary papers. The readers would find it of interest to look at Laurent [51], Robbins [65], Lundquist [55], Solandt [71], Blackett [11], Brothers [15], Boldyreff [13]. In addition, the following articles will be of interest, viz. Larnder [50], Stansfield [72], Waddington [78], Jones [42], Falconer [23].

The illustrations chosen all have an elementary probability basis, and, indeed, much of the early Operational Research did. Much present Operational Research tends to ignore the probability element, but it is nonetheless important in all Operational Research studies to some degree, more explicitly so in some cases than others (e.g. in queueing, to which the will turn

2

later on). Having said this, because so many of the military operations repeated themselves, to some degree, the results assume a more deterministic form if we replace probability by proportion of times, and, to begin with, readers may prefer this interpretation.

Let us now look at a few studies.

Optimal Convoy Size Problem

One of the more significant Operational Research studies carried out during the war was that of convoy sizes and associated escorts. We will deal with this briefly, and further reference will be found in Blackett [12], Waddington [78], White [82], Hitch [39].

Let us consider a convoy of x merchant ships, with an escort of z protective vessels, placed around the convoy at a density of y per mile, and a U-boat somewhere in the surrounding sea, as indicated in Figure 1.1. A statistical study suggested that, for a given value of escort density y, the proportion of ships which were sunk in a convoy was inversely proportional to convoy size x, as given in Figure 1.2.

As has been stated, Operational Research is, ideally, an experimental science. At the same time, although the data on which Figure 1.2 was based was very limited, there are clearly limitations to experimentation in wartime since decisions need to be made reasonably quickly. On the other hand, it is just possible that the value of f is really quite random, independent of

| × : U-boat |
| • : Convoy |
| — : Escorts |

Figure 1.1

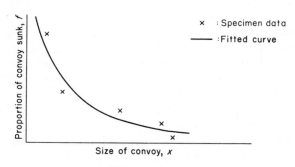

× : Specimen data
——— : Fitted curve

Proportion of convoy sunk, f

Size of convoy, x

Figure 1.2

convoy size, and that the apparent relationship is quite spurious, just as one might get ten heads in ten tosses of a coin without the coin being in any way biased. In view of the importance of the decision being made, some independent confirmation of the hypothesis was needed. Scientists then came up with an explanation of the hypothesis, which was accepted. Blackett [12] stresses the importance of explanation (or equivalently synthesis, as discussed in White [82]) in Operational Research, and, indeed, our whole process in Operational Research is a synthesis of various known, or at least accepted, hypotheses combined to produce a composite prediction.

The primitive hypotheses given were as follows (see White [82] p. 119):

 (i) the probability, p, of a U-boat seeing a convoy is independent of convoy size, at least within the feasible range of convoy sizes;
 (ii) the probability of a U-boat, having spotted the convoy, being able to penetrate the escorts, is a function, $q(y)$, of escort density, y;
(iii) once the U-boat has penetrated the escort, there is a fixed number of ships, d, it can sink, determined by its attacking capacity.

Combining these hypotheses, the proportion of ships expected to be sunk is given by

$$f(x, y) = pq(y)d/x.$$

The result is now self-evident when y is fixed, and convoy sizes were increased and, indeed, proportional losses were reduced.

It was not possible, after the event, to demonstrate that the reduced proportion of losses was due wholly, or indeed in part, to this change, since so many other things also changed. In addition to this there are other decision makers involved, viz. the enemy, who will, after a while, change their strategy, e.g. introduce improved detection methods, increase capacity of U-boats to sink convoys, and so on. We will return to the question of who are the decision makers when we get on to 'problem formulation' in Chapter 4.

Hitch [39] takes the analysis a little further in his examination of whether certain objectives are really the ones to use, and again we will return to this later in Chapter 4. The objective implicit in the preceding analysis is proportion of a convoy sunk. This of course ignores the fact that the convoy escorts can sink U-boats, and that sinking U-boats is bound to affect the fates of future convoys. The substitute objective is the ratio of convoy ships sunk to U-boats sunk. Let us call this g, and let c, u be, respectively, the number of ships in all convoys sunk and U-boats sunk, and w be the size of the U-boat population. It is assumed that $q(y) = q/y$, and that $u = rwy$, where q, r are constants, r depending on total convoy population. We then have, for some constant, k, depending on total convoy population,

$$c = k(pqd/y)w$$
$$u = rwy$$
$$g(y) = c/u = (kpqd/r)y^2.$$

4

This suggests that this objective is optimized when y is as large as is possible. Thus both objectives combined lead to larger convoys and larger escort densities, with similar objections, in the case of y, to those in the case of x. There were other objections raised by Hitch. For example the effectiveness (e.g. speed) of a convoy in transporting men, equipment, etc., reduces as the fleet size increases, and this factor was not taken into account. It is not clear, therefore, that optimizing the objectives stated is compatible, for example, with a higher level objective such as the probability of winning the war. We will turn to hierarchical objectives in Chapter 4. This also raises the question of multiple objectives, to which we will return later on in Chapter 4.

Finally, Jones [42] also discusses the convoy size problem in the context of the trade-off between escorts and merchant ships, arguing that the former should be proportional to the perimeter of the convoy, and the latter proportional to the area covered by the convoy, and hence the ratio of escorts to merchant ships minimized when the convoy is as large as possible.

Aircraft Colour Problem

The following problem, which we briefly mention, is discussed in more detail in Blackett [12] and Waddington [78]. A study of the extent to which U-boats had been submerged, at the time of attack by aircraft, gave rise to the estimated curve given in Figure 1.3. The Whitley aircraft, which were the subject of the study, were darkish in colour, and the U-boats were able to see them from some distance and to take action to submerge. The question arose as to whether painting the underneath of the aircraft would lead to a significant increase in the effectiveness of attacks. It was estimated, by psychologists, that, with the aircraft speeds then existing, an aircraft would be able to get about 12 seconds closer to the U-boat before being spotted, dependent, of course, on general visibility conditions. In such a case, all those U-boats which would have been submerged for at most 12 seconds

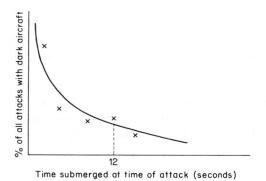

Figure 1.3

at the time of the attack would now be caught on the surface and would be likely to be sunk. About 34% of all U-boats fell into this category.

Three important points came from this. First, this was a clear case in which psychologists played a role, emphasizing the multidisciplinary nature of Operational Research. Secondly, it was clear that changing the colour would help, but this is a qualitative assessment, and does not enable a decision to be made as to the worthwhileness of using scarce resources for this exercise, instead of for other exercises. Blackett [12], in a more general context, states that the qualitative statement, increased effort implies a reduction in losses, does not enable us to reach a decision as to how much effort to use in a given context. The unambiguous numerical representation of the effects of decisions is an important feature of Operational Research, and we will return to this later on in Chapter 6. Finally, as with other situations, the Royal Air Force is not the only decision maker, because the enemy can also make decisions. As indicated by Waddington [78], a feature of the change of strategy by the Royal Air Force in the instance of U-boat attacks, was the move by the U-boats to fighting it out on the surface instead of trying to escape. This changes the nature of the problem radically. We will come back to the decision maker problem later on in Chapter 4, and also to the 'quantification' problem in Chapter 6.

Depth Charge Problem

Another area of considerable research effort was in the determination of depth charge strategies against U-boats. A full account of this work is given in Waddington [78], and reference is given in Blackett [12], Abrams [1]. Depth charges are released in sticks containing several depth charges. When they are released from an aircraft they follow the path of the aircraft, hit the water, sink, and then explode. If the distance between the depth charge and submarine at the time of explosion is less than or equal to a critical amount, α, referred to as the lethal radius, it is estimated that the U-boat is likely to be sunk. Of course this is not always the case, and, in any event, U-boats may be damaged, and hence disabled to some extent, for larger distances. Nontheless, the idea of lethal radius is a central one. Waddington discusses many aspects of the problem, viz. lethal radius, depth of U-boat, aiming errors, orientation of stick relative to the U-boat, and stick spacing (i.e. distance between individual charges in a stick).

We will present a simple analysis, which captures some of the essence of the problem, bearing in mind that the real problem is somewhat more complex. We will assume that we have a single depth charge which is to be dropped vertically above the U-boat. In what follows, s will be the distance, unknown, of the U-boat, below sea level ($s = 0$). The U-boat will be assumed to be stationary. We will make assumptions about the probability distribution of the position of the submarine.

It is of interest to note that Abrams [1], discussing Blackett's involvement

6

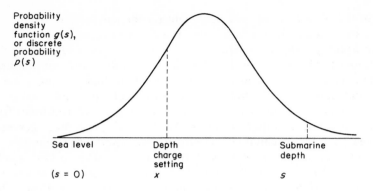

Figure 1.4

with the depth charge problem, mentions that, prior to analysis, depth charges had been set to go off at between 50 and 150 feet below sea level, whereas, at the point of attack, statistics indicated that U-boats were likely to be much closer to the surface. A subsequent change to 25 feet doubled the effectiveness of the attacks.

For our problem, Figure 1.4 gives the probability distribution. Initially, we will assume that s is discrete, taking values, $0, 1, 2, \ldots$. Let us make the following assumptions:

(i) the submarine is stationary during the depth charge attack;
(ii) $p(s)$ is the probability that the submarine is at depth s when the attack takes place;
(iii) x is the depth charge setting (non-negative);
(iv) $d(z)$ is the damage done if the difference in the position of the submarine and the depth charge at time of explosion is z $(=x-s)$;
(v) the objective is to choose x to maximize the expected value of $d(z)$.

Let $f(x)$ be the expected value of $d(z)$ for a given x. Then

$$f(x) = \sum_{s=0}^{\infty} p(s)d(x-s).$$

The problem then reduces to:

$$\text{maximize } [f(x)]$$
$$\text{subject to } x \geqslant 0.$$

Let

$$d(z) = k_0 - kz^2, \qquad k_0 > 0, \qquad k > 0,$$

as an approximation. Then

$$f(x) = \sum_{s=0}^{\infty} p(s)(k_0 - k(x-s)^2)$$

$$= k_0 - k \sum_{s=0}^{\infty} p(s)(x-s)^2$$

$$f'(x) = -2k \sum_{s=0}^{\infty} p(s)(x-s)$$
$$= -2k(x-\mu)$$

where

$$0 \leqslant \mu = \sum_{s=0}^{\infty} sp(s) = \text{expected value of } s,$$
$$f''(x) = -2k < 0.$$

Hence, setting $f'(x) = 0$ gives a unique maximum providing the solution is non-negative. We have, if we allow x to be continuous,

$$x^* = \text{optimal } x = \mu$$

and the maximal expected damage is

$$f(x^*) = k_0 - k \sum_{s=0}^{\infty} p(s)(\mu - s)^2$$
$$= k_0 - k\sigma^2$$

where σ^2 is the variance of s.

Note, if we can predict the position of the submarine, $\sigma^2 = 0$, and the maximal damage is k_0. Thus $k\sigma^2$ is the increase in damage for a perfectly predictive system. This is another important aspect of Operational Research, viz. determining the pay-off from reducing uncertainty.

Let us now look at the continuous form of the above problem. The assumptions are as before, but the discrete probability, $p(s)$, is replaced by a probability density function $g(s)$ (so that $g(s)\,\delta s$ is the approximate probability of the submarine being between s and $s + \delta s$). Then $f(x)$ becomes

$$f(x) = \int_{s=0}^{\infty} g(s)d(x-s)\,ds.$$

In the quadratic case for $d(z)$

$$f(x) = \int_{s=0}^{\infty} g(s)(k_0 - k(x-s)^2)\,ds$$
$$= k_0 - k \int_{s=0}^{\infty} g(s)(x-s)^2\,ds$$
$$f'(x) = -2k \int_{s=0}^{\infty} g(s)(x-s)\,ds$$
$$= -2k(x-\mu)$$

where

$$0 \leqslant \mu = \int_{s=0}^{\infty} sg(s)\,ds = \text{expected value of } s,$$
$$f''(x) = -2k < 0.$$

8

The solution is as before, viz.

$$x^* = \mu$$
$$f(x^*) = k_0 - k\sigma^2$$

where

$$\sigma^2 = \int_{s=0}^{\infty} g(s)(\mu - s)^2 \, ds.$$

Let us now suppose that the assumptions are as before (for either discrete or continuous case), with the exception that the objective $f(x)$ is changed. This is important, since one of the basic problems in OR is to determine appropriate objectives. We will deal with the general problem of objectives later on in Chapter 4.

Let us suppose that some critical damage level, δ, is specified and that the problem is:

(v)′ to choose x to maximize the probability that the damage, $d(z)$, is greater than or equal to δ.

Let us now look at the values of s for which $d(z) \geqslant \delta$. From Figure 1.5 it will be seen that

$$d(z) \geqslant \delta \rightleftarrows \underline{z} \leqslant z \leqslant \bar{z}$$

where $\underline{z}$, $\bar{z}$ depend upon δ.
This is equivalent to

$$\underline{z} \leqslant x - s \leqslant \bar{z}$$

which is equivalent to

$$x - \bar{z} \leqslant s \leqslant x - \underline{z}.$$

Then the probability, $f(x)$, that the damage is greater than or equal to δ,

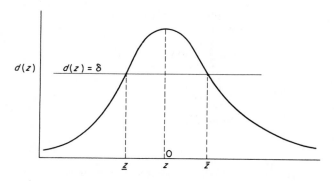

Figure 1.5

given x, is the probability that s is in the latter range, given x. Hence

$$f(x) = \int_{s=x-\bar{z}}^{x-\underline{z}} g(s)\, ds \quad \text{in the continuous case}$$

$$= \sum_{s=x-\bar{z}}^{x-\underline{z}} p(s) \quad \text{in the discrete case.}$$

The problem then reduces to:

$$\text{maximize}\,[f(x)]$$
$$\text{subject to } x \geq 0.$$

Let

$$p(s) = 1/(S+1), \qquad 0 \leq s \leq S$$
$$= 0 \qquad \text{otherwise.}$$

Assume that $\bar{z}, \underline{z}$ are integer. To simplify the analysis, assume that

$$d(z) = k_0 - kz^2, \qquad k_0 > 0, \qquad k > 0.$$

Then

$$d(z) = \delta \rightleftarrows k_0 - kz^2 = \delta$$
$$\rightleftarrows z = \pm\sqrt{((k_0 - \delta)/k)}$$
$$= \pm\alpha$$

where

$$\alpha = \sqrt{((k_0 - \delta)/k)}.$$

Hence

$$\bar{z} = \alpha, \qquad \underline{z} = -\alpha$$

$$f(x) = \sum_{s=x-\alpha}^{x+\alpha} p(s).$$

Then consider the following cases.

Case 1: $2\alpha \leq S$ (see Figure 1.6)

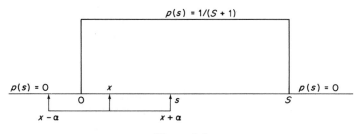

Figure 1.6

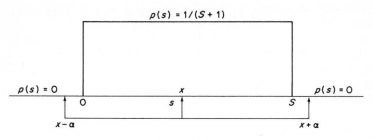

Figure 1.7

It is clear that, since we can choose x so that

$$0 \leqslant x - \alpha < x + \alpha \leqslant S,$$

this will give us the maximal possible value of $f(x)$, viz.

$$f(x) = (2\alpha + 1)/(S + 1),$$

and this is true for any such x.

Case 2: $2\alpha > S$ (see Figure 1.7)

In this case we can choose x so that the range $0 \leqslant s \leqslant S$ is included in $x - \alpha \leqslant s \leqslant x + \alpha$, and any such x will give

$$f(x) = 1.$$

It is to be noted that this formulation is identical with maximizing the probability of sinking the U-boat if α is the lethal radius referred to originally.

Search Problem

One of the very important and frequent problems tackled was that of search, in which the objective was to detect U-boats, aircraft, ships, etc. This problem has been studied under a range of different circumstances, and reference is given to these in Blackett [12] and Waddington [78] where many details may be found of actual studies. In this section we will mention a few, very simple, models developed by Koopman [45–48], as exemplifying some of the earlier thoughts on this type of problem. This is very ancient history and, since those early days, the subject has grown enormously, and the interested reader can refer to Stone [73, 74], Dobbie [19], and Haley [36]. Nonetheless the ideas are as important today as then, and quite simple to follow, but, as indicated by Koopman, need to be extended in the context of a rather more complex setting than the simple models portray.

In [45] Koopman looks at the problems involved when searcher and target have specific relative movement patterns. We mention this for completeness sake, but do not pursue it.

In [46] Koopman looks at the problem of detecting targets, under a range of assumptions.

The simplest problem is one in which a target is known to be in a given region and n independent attempts are made to locate it, e.g. n aerial photographs. If the attempts are independent, and g is the probability that the target will be located on any specific attempt, then the probability that it will be located within the n attempts is

$$p(n) = 1 - (1 - g)^n.$$

The probability that it will be located on the nth attempt is

$$q(n) = (1 - g)^{n-1}g.$$

The expected number of attempts to locate it is then

$$\hat{n} = \sum_{n=1}^{\infty} nq(n) = 1/g.$$

A continuous variant arises when the area is monitored (e.g. photographed) continuously in time, and, if $\gamma \delta t$ is the probability that it will be located in time $[t, t + \delta t]$, given that it has not been located up to time t, then the probability of detection within a time interval t is

$$p(t) = 1 - e^{-\gamma t}.$$

This may be obtained, formally, from the previous formula by setting $n = t/\delta t$, $g = \gamma \delta t$, and letting $\delta t \to 0$.

Both g and γ depend on the circumstances such as visibility, distance of target from observer, mode of observation, etc.

The dependence on distance is sometimes described in terms of the so-called inverse cube law of sighting. It assumes that the observer is at a height h above the ocean on which target is cruising, that the observer detects the target by seeing its wake, and that the instantaneous probability of detection γ in the continuous case, or g in the discrete case, is proportional to the solid angle subtended at the observer by the wake. In the discrete and continuous cases, we have

$$g = kh/s^3 \quad \text{or} \quad \gamma = kh/s^3$$

k being different in both cases, and where s is the lateral distance between observer and target.

Koopman also considers the problem of searching, along a path of length l miles, for a target known to be somewhere in a specified region of m square miles. It is assumed that the target probability density function is uniform over the area, that on any small part of the path a target within a distance $w/2$ either side is detected, but never outside the area, that the path can be thought of as a large number of adjacent pieces, the direction of each being random and independent of each other, and that, for such small pieces, w is small with respect to the length of the piece, so that the overlap between the successive pieces is small. If we now consider each segment, with n segments in all, the area of each piece within which a target, if there, can be detected is wl/n. Hence the probability that the target is detected in this segment is wl/nm. Hence the probability that the target is detected in the whole path is

$$p(n) = 1 - (1 - wl/nm)^n.$$

If n is large $p(n)$ tends to

$$p = 1 - e^{-wl/m}.$$

This approximation needs to be treated with caution. If the target is stationary, then if, at any time, the target has not been located, the probabilities of detection at the next step will change, since they will be conditional on not having found the target. If the target is allowed to move quickly, possibly into an area already searched, then the approximation will be a better one.

Note that this assumes that, if a target is in a given small segment, it will be detected for certain. If q is the probability that, given the target is in a very small segment, it will be detected, we obtain, respectively

$$p(n) = 1 - (1 - qwl/nm)^n, \qquad p = 1 - e^{-qwl/m}.$$

The objections to the exponential form remain similar to those given earlier on. However, if the target is stationary, but we are allowed to search previously searched areas, then little difficulty arises.

In [47] Koopman looks at the optimal use of search effort. To fix our ideas let us suppose that the target is at some point s on a given line, where s is measured from some origin. To make things easy let us assume that s can only take values $0, \pm 1, \pm 2, \ldots$. Let $q(s)$ be the probability that the target is at s and x_s be the amount of effort (e.g. men, time, etc.) to be expended in searching for the target at s. Koopman assumes that the probability of finding the target at s, given that it is at s, is $(1 - e^{-\gamma x_s})$. If b is the total effort available and we wish to use this to maximize the probability of finding the target, this becomes the following problem:

$$\text{maximize} \left[f(x) = \sum_{s=-\infty}^{\infty} q(s)(1 - e^{-\gamma x_s}) \right]$$

$$\text{subject to} \sum_{s=-\infty}^{\infty} x_s = b$$

$$x_s \geqslant 0, \quad \text{for all } s.$$

This is in 'mathematical programming form', to which we will turn later on in Chapter 2. Let us now spend a little time on the solution of this problem as an illustration of some of the later work we will consider in Chapters 2 and 4, where the use of Lagrange multipliers will be emphasized as a tool for handling constraints. In addition, since Operational Research models will be either discrete or continuous in form, as with the depth charge problem, we will consider both forms. Part of this arises from the different solution procedures which may be used, and part arises from the fact that some students are not quite as able as others when dealing with continuous problems.

If we now treat s as a continuous variable, and let $q(s)$, $x(s)$ be density functions for position and effort respectively, the problem takes the following form:

$$\text{maximize} \left[f(x) = \int_{s=-\infty}^{\infty} q(s)(1-e^{-\gamma x(s)}) \, ds \right]$$

$$\text{subject to} \int_{s=-\infty}^{\infty} x(s) \, ds = b$$

$$x(s) \geq 0 \quad \text{for all } s.$$

As with the previous models, the term γx_s (and $\gamma x(s)$) in the expression for $f(x)$ may be modified to reflect not only the effort x_s (or $x(s)$), but also particular conditions which might exist at s, in which case γx_s (or $\gamma x(s)$) would become $\gamma_s x_s$ (or $\gamma(s)x(s)$).

Let us briefly look at the way in which we might get a solution, first of all for the discrete case $s = 0, \pm 1, \pm 2, \dots$. This form is fairly simple when seen against the reality of most problems when s has three dimensions. Even so it can still pose problems, and it is here that the theory of mathematical programming becomes important. For this problem we can use the ideas of Lagrange multipliers, introduced later on in Chapter 4, but extended to Kuhn–Tucker multipliers (see Mangasarian [56]), and there will exist weighting factors λ, $\{\mu_s\}$, $\mu_s \geq 0$ for all s, such that if

$$l(x, \lambda) = f(x) - \lambda \sum_{s=-\infty}^{\infty} x_s + \sum_{s=-\infty}^{\infty} \mu_s x_s$$

then the optimal solution satisfies

$$\partial l(x, \lambda)/\partial x_s = 0, \quad \text{for all } s$$

$$\sum_{s=-\infty}^{\infty} x_s = b$$

$$\mu_s x_s = 0 \quad \text{for all } s.$$

providing only a finite number of $\{x_s\}$ are non-zero.

In fact we can get stronger results because we can use the full strength of duality theory, but we will not do so. It is to be noted that the resource availability constraint has been set as an equality constraint since it is clear that all the resource will be used up. However, later on in Chapter 4, we will deal with equalities and inequalities.

From the above we obtain, setting $\gamma = 1$ for simplicity,

$$q(s)e^{-x_s} - \lambda + \mu_s = 0 \quad \text{for all } s.$$

Taking logs, we obtain

$$x_s = \log(q(s)/(\lambda - \mu_s)) \quad \text{for all } s.$$

If $x_s > 0$, then $\mu_s = 0$, and

$$x_s = \log(q(s)/\lambda)$$
$$= \log(q(s)) - \log(\lambda).$$

Then

$$b = \sum_{s=-\infty}^{\infty} x_s = \sum_{s:x_s>0} x_s = \sum_{s:q(s)>\lambda} (\log(q(s)) - \log(\lambda)).$$

Koopman suggests the following method for solving this problem:

(i) choose a value of $\lambda^0 \leqslant \min_s[q(s)]$, with $\lambda^0 \geqslant 0$;
(ii) evaluate $x_s(\lambda^0) = \log(q(s)) - \log(\lambda^0)$ for all s;
(iii) evaluate $\sum_{s=-\infty}^{\infty} x_s(\lambda^0)$;
(iv) if the sum in (iii) is equal to b, stop, and the solution is optimal;
(v) if the sum in (iii) is less than b, decrease λ until the sum in (iii) equals b, and the solution is then optimal;
(vi) if the sum in (iii) is greater than b, increase λ until the sum in (iii) equals b, setting $x_s(\lambda) = 0$ if $\lambda > q(s)$, since this would give $x_s(\lambda) = \log(q(s)/\lambda) < 0$, contrary to hypothesis.

Koopman actually deals with the continuous case of $q(s)$ and $x(s)$, but the analysis is similar, using integrals instead of summations.

In analysing this problem we have introduced the weighting factor idea for constraints, via the Lagrange, or Kuhn–Tucker approach. This approach is important not only computationally, but also from the point of view of examining the effects of constraints and their violation. Later on, in Chapter 4, we will deal with the problem of constraints as a special aspect of problem formulation, and the weighting factor approach is important, although not infallible.

Later on, in Chapter 4, we will deal with the question of multiple decision makers and will make reference to game-type situations. This is relevant to the search problem in that the seeker and the target may each have decisions which they can take. The models become much more complex. Gal [30] provides a useful introduction to these.

Firing Salvos Problem

Another serious area of study was in the firing of salvos of ammunition at a target. One of the problems, studied by Walsh [81], concerns the determination of an optimal design feature to maximize the probability of killing a target with a salvo of n rounds of ammunition.

We will deal first of all with the discrete problem, and then generalize to the continuous case. We will assume that everything is in one dimension (see

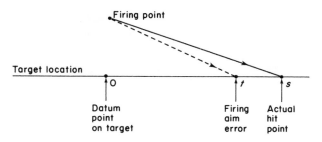

Firing point

Target location

O

Datum
point
on target

t

Firing
aim
error

s

Actual
hit
point

Figure 1.8

Figure 1.8). The following assumptions are made:

(i) a salvo of n rounds is to be fired;
(ii) each round of the salvo will have the same firing aim probability distribution of error $t = 0, \pm1, \pm2, \ldots$;
(iii) the probability that the aiming error is t, is $q(t)$ and is fixed;
(iv) the probability that, given t, the actual hit point will be at s, is x_{ts}, and it is $\{x_{ts}\}$, t, $s = 0, \pm1, \pm2, \ldots$; which has to be designed, and each round in the salvo has the same probabilities;
(v) the expected value of s given t is equal to t;
(vi) the target will be killed with a probability $r(s)$ if the hit point of a given round is at s.

The problem is to choose $x = \{x_{ts}\}$ to maximize the probability of a kill by the salvo. The formulation is as follows.

For a given round, the probability of a kill is, given t,

$$\sum_{s=-\infty}^{\infty} x_{ts} r(s).$$

Hence the probability of at least one round killing the target is

$$1 - \left(1 - \sum_{s=-\infty}^{\infty} x_{ts} r(s)\right)^n.$$

The problem is then:

$$\text{maximize} \left[f(x) = \sum_{t=-\infty}^{\infty} q(t)\left(1 - \left(1 - \sum_{s=-\infty}^{\infty} x_{ts} r(s)\right)^n\right)\right]$$

subject to

$$\sum_{s=-\infty}^{\infty} x_{ts} = 1, \quad \text{for all } t.$$

$$\sum_{s=-\infty}^{\infty} s x_{ts} = t, \quad \text{for all } t.$$

$$x_{ts} \geq 0, \quad \text{for all } t, s.$$

As before we may solve this, because it has certain analytic properties, by using the multiplier method, as for the search problem. Let

$$l(x, \lambda) = f(x) + \sum_{t=-\infty}^{\infty} \lambda_t \sum_{s=-\infty}^{\infty} x_{ts} + \sum_{t=-\infty}^{\infty} \sum_{s=-\infty}^{\infty} \mu_{ts} x_{ts} + \sum_{t=-\infty}^{\infty} \nu_t \sum_{s=-\infty}^{\infty} s x_{ts}.$$

Then the solution is given by:

$$\partial l(x, \lambda)/x_{ts} = 0, \quad \text{for all } t, s$$

$$\sum_{s=-\infty}^{\infty} x_{ts} = 1, \quad \text{for all } t$$

$$\sum_{s=-\infty}^{\infty} s x_{st} = t, \quad \text{for all } t$$

$$\mu_{ts} x_{ts} = 0, \quad \text{for all } t, s$$

$$\mu_{ts} \geq 0, \quad \text{for all } t, s.$$

For the case $n = 1$ these become

$$q(t)r(s) + \lambda_t + \mu_{ts} + s\nu_t = 0, \quad \text{for all } t, s$$

together with the other constraints.

If the error in aim is, for example, always 0, the above becomes, putting $x_{0s} = x_s$, $\mu_{0s} = \mu_s$, $q(0) = 1$, $\nu_0 = \nu$, $\lambda_0 = \lambda$, for simplicity,

$$r(s) + \lambda + \mu_s + s\nu = 0, \quad \text{for all } s.$$

If $x_s > 0$, then $\mu_s = 0$. Thus if $x_s > 0$, we have

$$\lambda = -r(s) - \nu s.$$

In the simple case when, for each feasible value of (ν, λ) the above equation has two solutions, say s^1, s^2, we can calculate the corresponding x_{s^1}, x_{s^2} from the equations

$$\sum_{s=-\alpha}^{\infty} x_s = 1, \qquad \sum_{s=-\infty}^{\infty} s x_s = 0,$$

and check that the solutions are non-negative, and (λ, ν) varied until they are, and at the same time $\mu_s = -r(s) - \lambda - s\nu \geq 0$, for all s. The latter condition is achieved if we restrict (λ, ν) to values for which $r(s) + \lambda + \nu s \leq 0$, for all s, i.e. for a given ν, $\lambda \leq \min_{s=-\infty}^{\infty} [-r(s) - \nu s]$.

Note that, for $n = 1$, the problem becomes a simple linear programming problem, which can be solved by appropriate means, providing the ranges of t, s are finite.

This is, of course, what one would expect, and, indeed, can easily be obtained from first principles. The weighting factor method is, of course, more general.

The continuous form, which may also be tackled in a similar manner using weighting factors. The formulation, using density functions, is:

$$\text{maximize} \left[f(x) = \int_{t=-\infty}^{\infty} q(t) \left(1 - \left(1 - \int_{s=-\infty}^{\infty} x(t, s) r(s) \, ds \right)^n \right) dt \right]$$

subject to

$$\int_{s=-\infty}^{\infty} x(t, s) \, ds = 1, \quad \text{for all } t$$

$$\int_{s=-\infty}^{\infty} sx(t, s) \, dt = t, \quad \text{for all } t$$

$$x(t, s) \geq 0, \quad \text{for all } t, s.$$

It is important to draw a distinction between the constraints on $\{x_{st}\}$ for this problem, and the constraints on $\{x_s\}$ in the search problem. The former are 'hard' constraints in that they must be satisfied. The latter are 'soft' constraints in that they reflect value judgements as to the worthwhileness of setting the resource level at b. We will deal with these in Chapter 4.

Redundancy Problem

Problems of design of redundancy were also of significant interest, and are discussed by Gordon [34]. Any system will have components of various kinds, and the effectiveness of the system's operations will depend on the effectiveness of the components. If components fail, the system may fail to operate, or at least to perform effectively. A fail may mean not responding to a signal when it is there, or responding to a signal when it is not there. Let us assume, for the purposes of simplicity, a fail means ceases to function during the life of a particular operation, and that only the first failure type may arise. One way of guarding against this is to put in redundant components, which take over when a failure arises. To put in redundant components is expensive, and takes up space. In addition to this, if we have different types of component, which will have extra ones fitted in?

Let us look at a simple problem (see Figure 1.9). The assumptions are as

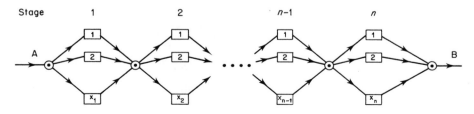

Figure 1.9

. follows:

   (i) the system consists of n types of component in series;

  (ii) at each stage, i, in the series, x_i identical components are placed in parallel, each component being independent of the others;

 (iii) the stage i will be operational providing at least one component type i is working;

 (iv) the system as a whole will be operational providing all its stages are operational;

  (v) the probability, $q(i)$, of a component type i not failing during the operation, is identical, and independent, for each component at stage i;

 (vi) each component type i costs $c(i)$;

(vii) there is a total amount of cash, b, available for the system.

The problem is to choose the number of repetitions, x_i, of each component i, to maximize the probability that the system will operate during the specified period subject to the cash constraint. This probability is referred to as the reliability of the system (Gordon [34]).

If $x = (x_1, \ldots, x_i, \ldots, x_n)$, then the problem reduces to:

$$\text{maximize} \left[f(x) = \prod_{i=1}^{n} (1 - (1 - q(i))^{x_i}) \right]$$

subject to

$$\sum_{i=1}^{n} c(i)x_i \leqslant b$$

$$x_i \text{ integer and} \geqslant 1, \quad \text{for all } i.$$

This is again in mathematical programming form, but now the $\{x_i\}$ are integers. Many problems may be cast into integer mathematical programming form, but they are not easy to solve, even with existing optimization procedures in Chapter 2. Such problems may be tackled by heuristic methods, which we will discuss later on. It is also to be noted that, whereas we were able to assume an equality resource constraint for our continuous search problem, we have only been able to assume an inequality resource constraint for the integer redundancy problem since it does not necessarily follow that an optimal solution uses up all the resource.

The weighting factor method will give some results but not all we may want. Thus let

$$l(x, \lambda) = f(x) - \lambda \sum_{i=1}^{n} c(i)x_i + \sum_{i=1}^{n} \mu_i x_i$$

and consider the following equations and inequalities:

$$\partial l(x, \lambda)/\partial x_i = 0, \quad \text{for all } i$$

$$\lambda \left(\sum_{i=1}^{n} c(i)x_i - b \right) = 0$$

$$x_i \geqslant 1, \quad \text{for all } i$$
$$\mu_i x_i = 0, \quad \text{for all } i,$$
$$\lambda \geqslant 0, \qquad \mu_i \geqslant 0, \quad \text{for all } i.$$

If we are prepared to let x_i be continuous variables, because of the analytic conditions of this problem, the above equations and inequalities will solve the problem. This might then give a starting point for determining the optimal integer solutions. We will turn to this when we study heuristic and sensitivity analyses in Chapters 2 and 3.

However, even if we do not accept this, the method is useful for generating the optimal solutions for a range of actual expenditure values c. Thus, if we set:

$$l(x, \lambda) = f(x) - \lambda \sum_{i=1}^{n} c(i) x_i$$

and let $\{x_i(\lambda)\}$ give the maximal value of $l(x, \lambda)$ over the integers $\geqslant 1$, then $\{x_i(\lambda)\}$ will solve the following problem (see Everett [22]):

maximize $[f(x)]$

subject to

$$\sum_{i=1}^{n} c(i) x_i = c(\lambda) = \sum_{i=1}^{n} c(i) x_i(\lambda)$$

x_i integer and $\geqslant 1$ for all i.

In this case λ may be positive, negative or 0.

A similar result applies for the inequality resource constraint, but with $\lambda \geqslant 0$.

Thus by varying λ we can solve a series of possible resource level problems. These may not, however, include the specific value of b, as a possible value of $c(\lambda)$, with which we began. However, such a b is unlikely to be a rigid constraint.

We will return to this later on when we get to Chapter 4.

1.2 THE OPERATIONAL RESEARCH PROCESS

Any Operational Research study will involve two interlinked conceptual systems, viz. the 'subject' system, and the 'object' system (see White [82, 83]).

The subject system is identified with the decision makers on whose behalf the analysis is being carried out; the object system is identified with the system about which the decisions are being made.

In the simplest case we have a single decision maker and a simple, non-decision-making, system being controlled. Thus, in the convoy problem, at its simplest level, the decision maker (subject system) may be an admiral, and the system being controlled (object system) might be the convoy, assuming that any decision making by the enemy is implicitly allowed for. If we add a little more complexity, we may explicitly recognize the decision making of the enemy, but, from the admiral's point of view, the enemy is still part of his object system, although the extent to which the enemy's activities can be controlled may be limited. We may even have the case when subject and object system are essentially the same, but only particular attributes used to describe parts. Thus any individual may make decisions, as a subject system, about his own physical welfare, as an object system.

The essential point about the dichotomy described above is that the study is being carried out on behalf of some individual, or group, in terms of the behaviour of some activities which are to be controlled. The purpose of the study is to bring together both systems in order to guide the subject system towards a good, or preferably, optimal, decision. Consider Figure 1.10. Let us suppose that the subject system (let us assume it is a single decision maker for ease of presentation) has available a set of options, X. He can examine the behaviour of his object system in terms of $x \in X$, and, for ease of analysis, let $f^1(x)$, $f^2(x)$ be this behaviour, which may be described in probabilistic terms.

In the simplest form of study, the decision maker is simply presented with a listing of $\{(f^1(x), f^2(x))\}$ for each $x \in X$. For example, in the redundancy problem, the decision maker is merely given a list of

$$\{(f^1(x), f^2(x))\}, \qquad x \in X$$

where: $x = (x_1, x_2, \ldots, x_n)$ specifies the numbers of each component,
$f^1(x)$ specifies the corresponding reliability,
$f^2(x)$ specifies the corresponding cost,
X may be any set of $\{x\}$ with upper bounds on x_i, $i = 1, 2, \ldots, n$.

The decision maker may then be left to choose his most preferred x on the basis of the pairs $\{(f^1(x), f^2(x)\}, x \in X$. This is called the open form of analysis. It has very limited use when X contains a very large number of options, and some problems (e.g. sequential problems) do contain very many options, as we shall see later in Chapter 4.

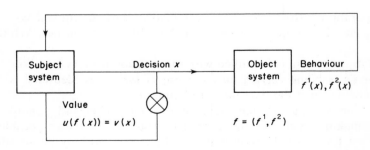

Figure 1.10

Let us now look at the subject system, i.e. the decision maker. If we can express his preferences between pairs $\{(f^1(x), f^2(x)\}$ in some manner, we may use this information to some advantage. Thus, suppose we can determine some measure of value, say $u(f^1, f^2)$, for pairs $\{(f^1, f^2)\}$, such that (f^1, f^2) is preferred to $(f^{1'}, f^{2'}) \rightleftarrows u(f^1, f^2) > (f^{1'}, f^{2'})$.

In this case the problem has become completely formalized, and reduces to:

$$\text{maximize } [v(x)]$$
$$\text{subject to } x \in X$$

where

$$v(x) = u(f^1(x), f^2(x)).$$

This is referred to as the closed form of analysis, and is very powerful, but often very difficult to achieve. Later on we will describe some attempts to obtain a balance between the two approaches.

Thus in any Operational Research study we have to examine the two conceptual systems, model them some how, validate the models, and, ultimately, arrive at some decision. There are various identifiable phases involved (see Ackoff [2], [3]), viz.

(1) formulating the problem (of the subject system);
(2) constructing the model (of the object system);
(3) testing the (total) model;
(4) deriving the solution;
(5) testing and controlling the solution;
(6) implementing the solution.

Sometimes it may be difficult, in a given study, to identify each of the phases explicitly, but any complete study should involve all phases in some form. The fact that the phases are listed in a sequence does not mean that they will be executed in that sequence, and, indeed, the process may be cyclic. Thus a solution offered at phase (4) might be so unsatisfactory as to suggest that the problem may have been incorrectly formulated, and a reformulation tried.

The above format is not the only one, and the reader may refer, for example, to Tocher [77], Bonder [14], each of whom emphasize different aspects. Müller-Merbach [59] also gives a framework for Operational Research, involving fourteen components.

Like any scientific discipline, the true Operational Research process involves:

observation
hypothesis formation
experimentation
prediction

again in a cyclic manner. All the early Operational Research, and much of present Operational Research, has been true to this spirit to some extent, although experimentation, in the pure sense, has not been very evident, for various reasons, such as time, resources, controllability, and reversibility considerations. In this text we will not deal with these, very essential, ingredients, nor with the concomitant statistical analysis so important to hypothesis formation and validation. We will, essentially, deal with phases (1), (2), and (4). Material on the remaining phases may be found in White [82] and some of the references given there. We will, however, spend some time on a vital ingredient of scientific method, viz. measurement, which has implications for phase (4).

As a discipline evolves, it generates techniques of various kinds, and certainly Operational Research is no exception. Indeed, many feel that 'techniques' are way ahead of their current needs. Some practitioners feel that 'techniques' are irrelevant to their needs. Let us now look briefly at the nature of the techniques and at their role in Operational Research.

1.3   THE TECHNIQUES OF OPERATIONAL RESEARCH

Operational Research is a problem-oriented discipline. Hence it is not surprising that the world may be viewed in terms of classes of problem situations which one might recognize. This has led to the development of what one might term problem-oriented techniques.

Thus, if we look back at the first section dealing with military problems, the original involvement with simple search problems has now given birth to a whole theory of search (e.g. see Stone [74]) where problems are characterized by a searcher and a target, with various objectives and under various environmental conditions.

Ackoff [2] discusses a whole range of types of problem situation, to which the reader may refer. In this text we will look at four classes of problem-oriented techniques, with certain purposes in mind, viz. queueing, inventory, maintenance and defective products. We will not deal in depth with these. There are many standard texts which deal with them at various levels, and we merely mention Lee [52], Conolly [17], Lewis [53], Love [54], Arrow *et al.* [5], Whitin [85], Sherif *et al.* [68], Pierskella *et al.* [62], Jardine [41] and Gollers *et al.* [33]. Silver [69] gives a review and critique of inventory studies, and Aggarwal [4] gives a review also. Assad *et al.* [6] give a very useful research bibliography on a whole range of Operational Research techniques.

There are many general texts on Operational Research techniques, but we mention merely Wagner [80], which is fairly comprehensive, and Elmaghraby *et al.* [20]. Other classes of problem, which have given rise to major research areas are scheduling (see French [29], Rinnooy Kan [64], Graves [35] and Baker [7]), location (see Halpern [37], Francis *et al.* [27, 28] and Handler *et al.* [38]), bidding (no book, but see Ropfkof [66]), networks (Shapiro [67]), portfolio (see Markowitz [58] and Elton *et al.* [21]) and sports (see Ladany *et al.* [49]), travelling salesman (no book, but see Bellmore [10]). We will not consider these in the same way as we will the other techniques, but will use them for specific illustration purposes, particularly in mathematical and heuristic programming.

Queueing problems are essentially characterized by streams of customers (people, jobs) 'arriving' at some 'service' mechanisms. The circumstances governing these situations may be quite varied in terms of arrival patterns, service patterns, number of channels, rules of service, and so on. The objective is to study how the queues behave, with a view to determining acceptable facility levels and service rules.

Inventory problems are characterized by streams of demands to be satisfied by some supplies. Again, we may have a variety of circumstances in terms of demand patterns, supply mechanisms, replenishment mechanisms, and so on. The objective is to study the effects which different rules and capacity levels, etc., have on the effectiveness in meeting the demand.

Maintenance problems are characterized by failure, deterioration and maintenance and repair of systems of various kinds. Again we may have a variety of circumstances in terms of failure or deterioration patterns, maintenance and repair facilities, and in terms of the uses of the system. Thus medical care is a form of maintenance. The objective is to study the effectiveness of maintenance policies and capacities in terms of their effect on the systems being served.

Defective product problems are characterized by the production of products which are subject to defects, and where the problem is to get an appropriate balance between production costs and defect levels. Again, we may have a variety of circumstances in terms of the patterns of defective product, and the means of coping with this. The objective is to study the effectiveness of different means in terms of the service to the customers, whatever or whoever these may be.

We have chosen these with various purposes in mind, but, as has been indicated, there are many other classes of problem which have been studied, e.g. location, scheduling, network, portfolio, bidding and so on, all of which have been treated in some depth. Many of the points we will make about the above problem classes will apply to other problem classes.

While passing, it is to be noted that the classes are not strictly exclusive. For example, see Karush [43], Foster [26], who show how an 'inventory' problem may be looked at as a 'queueing' problem.

The classes of problem chosen also exhibit, in a simple manner, the classical Operational Research objective of getting a compromise between the various conflicts in a problem.

Many of the models developed within the four groups mentioned are special to the particular problems, and analytic solutions are sought, or at least some properties of optimal solutions are sought. This is not always possible, and one has to seek more general methods of solution which are not restricted to particular types of physical problem. We have thus seen the development of many, fairly general, solution-oriented techniques. Again, these will be found in various general texts such as that of Wagner [80]. In this text we will consider five, with certain purposes in mind, viz. mathematical programming, dynamic programming, heuristics, simulation, analogues, and Las Vegas (or optimal stopping). We will not deal in depth with these. Again there are many standard texts which deal with these at various levels, and we merely mention Wagner [80]. There are few books on heuristics (e.g. see Pearl [61]) and none on Las Vegas. The former topic appears extensively in the literature, and a good starting paper is that of Müller-Merbach [60]. The Las Vegas technique is not extensively mentioned, and can be found in White [82]. It does, however, cast a different perspective on the problem of getting solutions, and, for this reason, we include it. There is no book on analogues, and no extensive work done on these. However, they do provide another point of view, and have historical interest, and we include them. Again see White [82] for a discussion of them. Tocher [76] is a useful introduction to simulation.

Let us say a few words as to why these particular solution techniques have been chosen.

First of all, a very large number of problems can be cast into mathematical programming form. This is not necessarily the correct way to solve the problem since, as powerful as the mathematical programmes may be, some problems are just too large to solve, within the limits of reasonable expenditure, this way. They do have positive attributes, viz.

 (i) where optimal solutions (relative to the formulation) are required, appropriate algorithms will give them;
 (ii) they at least give a precise statement of the problem (relative to the formulation);
(iii) the precise statement in (ii) may be used as a base for examining ways of getting good solutions (e.g. heuristics), for examining the behaviour of solutions in response to parametric variations, and for getting particular information of value.

Secondly, a very large number of problems involve a sequence of decisions, and the concept of a decision rule. Dynamic programming is a natural way of studying these, since it explicitly recognizes the interdependence of the decisions in the sequence. The computational problem can be burdensome, but the above points (i), (ii) and (iii) apply.

Thirdly, in view of the difficulties of solving many problems using mathematical programming or dynamic programming algorithms, it is natural to look for methods which lack the capability of getting optimal solutions, but make up for this in their relative ease of application. Heuristic methods which, in this text, will be restricted to methods for getting good solutions for precisely stated problems, and not extended to the more general sense (see Müller-Merbach [60], Reitman [63], Silver et al. [70]), provide a useful, and growing, approach to the solution of the problems.

Similarly, simulation provides a means of looking at problems involving sequences of decisions usually, but not wholly, in a probabilistic framework, which does not usually give optimal solutions, but allows many details to be included which, although they may also be included in, say, a dynamic programming formulation, would certainly defeat any attempt to solve the problem in this form.

Fourthly, in principle, in all approaches to solving problems, we must terminate the calculations when we feel the cost of doing further calculations will not lead to at least as high an improvement in the value of the solution obtained by doing so. This applies in all the other cases, even when applying a standard optimization algorithm. Clearly, in general, one tries to learn how the solution is improving as we proceed, and we use this experience to terminate at a suitable point. We will not deal with the general problem of this kind (some comments may be found in White [82]) and will restrict ourselves to the Las Vegas sampling technique, for which the precise mathematical formulation is required, but no mathematical optimization algorithm theory. Its philosophy is close to intuitive behaviour of decision makers in practice, but in a formalized manner.

Finally, the symbolic mathematical models, or simulation models we use are not the only form of modelling we may have. We may also have analogue models. The use of the words is a matter of definition. The symbolic model is self-evident. Simulation models are look-alike physical models, which represent the problem being studied by some other physical system, e.g. the computer. They differ from the real thing in scale, e.g. time scale, and the actual events are equivalent numbers. They are called ionic models. The analogue models referred to are actually physical models whose behaviour, in some respects, is identical with that of the problem being studied. In this text the behaviour we will capture is that of minimum or maximum seeking, and the physical principle used is that of systems, under certain conditions, seeking a position of minimal potential energy. We do not put these forward as approaches which are in any way competitive with other approaches. They do fit in with the historical classical views on Operational Research whereby one tries to find an existing system, which behaves in a similar way to the one we are studying, and from which we might learn. It is compatible with the modern view as epitomized by cybernetics (see Beer [9]), and it is not without interest to natural scientists concerned with Operational Research. Ackoff [2] gives a useful discussion of modelling.

We have separated these techniques into those which characterize the problem and those which characterize the solution method. They are, of course, related in that, for a problem in a given class, we might have a special model, developed specifically for that problem, which might give analytic solutions, or we might actually formulate the problem in such a way that one of the standard solution techniques may be used. Correspondingly, for any given solution technique, problems within different classes may be

26

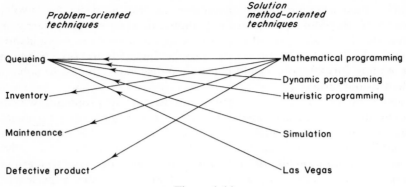

Problem-oriented
techniques

Solution
method-oriented
techniques

Queueing — Mathematical programming

Dynamic programming

Inventory — Heuristic programming

Maintenance

Simulation

Defective product

Las Vegas

Figure 1.11

amenable to that technique. Thus, symbolically, we have Figure 1.11 as an illustration, where we have put in a few of the possible links. The big question is: which of the available techniques should be used for the particular problem which may be faced, in the light of the circumstances surrounding the study? We make no pretence to answer this. We will examine a few cases to see what might be gained, or lost, in taking particular approaches. No distillation of experience, in a communicable form, exists as yet, although some simple studies have been carried out on particular categories of problem (e.g. the universal travelling salesman problem, quadratic assignment problems, and so on) (see Golden *et al.* [32], and Gilmore [31]). In the final analysis, the researcher must, in the light of his own knowledge, judge; but he should be aware that there is a problem. This sort of problem is referred to as the secondary problem, as distinct from the primary problem which is the subject matter of the study (e.g. queueing problem) (see White [82]).

It goes without saying that, in some cases, a combined use of techniques may be appropriate and we will briefly examine this.

The techniques referred to are not the only techniques which are of relevance to Operational Research. For example the wide variety of statistical and computing techniques available are clearly relevant and very important. Thus the process of validating a particular assumption about arrival patterns, in a queueing problem, requires statistical techniques. The process of eliciting information from people may require psychological technique as might the process of implementation (see Huysmans [40] for the latter). These are all important, but the central view taken in this text is that of formulating and solving problems, and for this reason the types of technique chosen have been chosen. Naturally this must be supplemented by wider-based material.

There is, however, one particular class of techniques involving problem formulation (to some extent) and solution which have developed rapidly in the last decade. For this refer back to section 1.2 dealing with the subject system. There are many circumstances in which a decision maker may be clear about the objectives he is attempting to achieve but not about his preferences as a whole over these objectives. Techniques have been developed which allow a combined decision maker–optimization interaction to take place, which allows the operational researcher to learn about the decision maker's preference bit by bit and to make some use of his solution procedure techniques at the same time, thus producing a procedure which is between the open and closed forms. We refer to such procedures as multi-objective interactive programming techniques, and we will spend some time on them in Chapter 4.

Let us now look at the role of techniques of various kinds in the general Operational Research process. White [82] discusses these in detail but we will briefly say a little here.

As has been stated, as a subject area progresses, it naturally develops its own techniques to tackle the problems arising within its domain. This has its dangers in that the inexperienced operational researcher may try to force his view of the world, in terms of techniques, on the problems he encounters and seeks. Thus he may try to force everything into linear programming form, or concentrate his efforts on queueing situations, even to the extent of applying models which may not be valid for his circumstances. While this may be true, it does depend on the quality of the Operational Researcher, and the fault cannot be laid at the feet of the techniques. For inexperienced operational researchers it is obviously of value to be able to accelerate their capacity to identify and solve problems. To this end the continual categorization and study of classes of problems which has taken place will certainly provide a framework within which this process may be accelerated. Even if the problems eventually tackled do not fit exactly with any of the known formulations, the capacity to develop new models, and solution procedures, must be facilitated by the knowledge of the existing techniques, and some insight must be obtained (see Tocher [77]). And even if an existing model is not an exact fit, it might actually be used, in a 'sensible' manner, to facilitate the study (e.g. the use of queueing models to facilitate simulation). Thus, within the general Operational Research process, techniques of various kinds must form an integral part in this process.

Readers may wish to consult Byrd [16], Taha [75], and Köenigsberg [44] on the value, for example, of queueing theory.

We will devote the next chapter to a study of some techniques, in the light of the previous remarks.

1.4 EXERCISES

1. Solve the depth charge problem when we have a probability density function $g(s) = g/s$, $0 < \underline{s} \leq s \leq \bar{s}$, and $d(x-s) = k_0 - k |x-s|$, $k > 0$, $k_0 > 0$:

(a) to maximize the expected damage;
(b) to maximize the probability of the damage being $\geq \delta$.

28

2. Solve the depth charge problem when $d(x-s) = k_0 - k(x-s)^2$, $k_0 > 0$, $k > 0$, when the depth charge descends at a constant speed u, and the submarine has a uniform speed of submersion of v, and everything takes place in a vertical line, to maximize expected damage. Do this for the general probability density function $g(s)$ for the distance the submarine is submerged when the depth charge is dropped and assume that the depth charge is dropped at sea level.

3. Suppose you have m guns and n targets, that the value of destroying target j is v_j, and that q_{ij} is the probability that gun i aimed at target j will destroy it. Formulate the optimization problem of aiming the m guns to maximize the expected total target destruction value. Reduce the problem to a problem of maximizing a single objective function with no constraints, using the multiplier method (Manne [57]).

4. (a) A target is known to be in one of n locations, $i = 1, 2, \ldots, n$. The initial probability that it is in location i is p_i. Show that the procedure which locates the target in the expected smallest number of steps, assuming the locations may be searched one at a time and that a target in a location is always located by a search in that location, is to search in order of decreasing values of p_i.

(b) Now suppose that it takes a time t_i to search location i, and that a search will only reveal the truth with probability $1 - q_i$. Show that:

(i) if the objective is to minimize the expected time of finding the target, and each location is searched until the truth is known, the optimal procedure is to search in order of decreasing values of $p_i(1-q_i)/t_i$;

(ii) if the objective is to find the location in which the target is, in the minimal expected time, the optimal procedure involves first searching the location with the highest value of $p_i/(1-q_i)t_i$ or not at all (Bellman [8] p. 90).

It is not necessary to use the dynamic programming formulation.

5. A target is known to be in one of two locations. The probability that, if a time x is devoted to searching either location and the target is in the location, it will be found, is $1 - e^{-kx}$. The initial probabilities of the target being in either location are p, q respectively and a total time T is available for search. Formulate and solve, analytically, the problem of determining how much time to devote to each location to maximize the probability of finding the target. Use the multiplier method if you wish, but this is not necessary and is complicated (Koopman [48]).

6. (i) For the initial quadratic depth charge problem discussed in the text examine how the problem of errors in depth charge setting may be handled and how the worth of reducing these errors and reducing the uncertainty in submarine position might be evaluated.

(ii) Also, how would you examine the worth of improving the effectiveness of the depth charges? (Waddington [78] discusses, for example, the problem of changing the depth charge explosive.)

(iii) How would you examine whether concentration on error reduction or depth charge effectiveness would be a better way of using resources?

(iv) Waddington also discusses the arguments as to whether the damage function is of the form $d(z) = k_0 - k |z|$ or $k_0 - kz^2$. How would you examine this question? (Forget the errors in depth charge setting.) Use the expected damage format.

7. As has been indicated in the text, the effectiveness of a convoy is increased by increasing its size. Suppose that a total number of convoy ships has to be divided into convoys of size x and that it is required, in the light of losses and effectiveness, to maximize the overall transport effectiveness and that, for a convoy of size x, its effectiveness (e.g. speed) takes the form k/x. Build a model to solve this problem and solve it, assuming that escort density, y, is fixed.

8. For the aircraft colour problem, construct a model for determining the expected damage to a submarine attacked by the aircraft if you are given the probability density function, $g(r)$, for the distance r at which the dark aircraft is first seen, allowing a gain of 12 seconds for a light-coloured aircraft. Assume that the submarine dives vertically and that the aircraft drops its depth charge immediately above it, with a pre-set explosion depth x. Make use of the depth charge analysis.

9. (i) A bomber squadron has to carry a fixed total load of bombs on a mission. Aircraft will be lost both through icing up and as a result of enemy attacks. Without a de-icer an aircraft can carry a load of b_0 bombs. With a de-icer an aircraft can only carry a load of b_1 bombs. The probability of an aircraft being lost due to icing, without a de-icer, is α. The probability of an aircraft being shot down is β. If the objective is to deliver the fixed total load of bombs and to minimize the expected number of aircraft lost, find the optimal decision as to whether or not de-icers should be used in terms of the parameters of the problem.

(ii) Suppose now that the whole squadron, or what is left of it after each mission, is to be used for a long sequence of missions, and the objective is to maximize the expected number of bombs to be delivered over all the missions. What is the solution to the problem now?

(iii) Comment on the objectives given in (i) and (ii) (Jones [42]).

10. A total of b warheads has to be targeted on one of two targets. For target i the expected damage, if x warheads are targeted on it, is:

$$f(x) = 1 - (1 + k_i \sqrt{x}) e^{-k_i}/x, \qquad i = 1, 2$$

(see Curran et al. [18]).

Examine the solution to the problem of deciding how many warheads to

30

target on each target to maximize the expected damage in terms of the parameters of the problem. Treat the problem as a continuous problem.

11. Later on, in Chapter 4, we will consider mean (i.e. expectation) variance analysis in a multi-objective framework. For the problem of Exercise 1 find expressions for the mean and variance of damage as a function of x.

1.5 REFERENCES

1. Abrams, J. W., Military applications of operations research, *Operations Research*, **5**, 434–440, 1957.
2. Ackoff, R., *Scientific Method: Optimizing Applied Research Decisions*, Wiley, 1962.
3. Ackoff, R., The development of operations research as a science, *Operations Research*, **4**, 265–295, 1956.
4. Aggarwal, S. C., A review of current inventory theory and its applications, *International Journal of Production Research*, **12**, 443–482, 1974.
5. Arrow, K. J., Karlin, S., and Scarf, H., *Studies in the Mathematical Theory of Inventory and Production*, Stanford University Press, 1958.
6. Assad, A. and Golden, B., Research bibliography of survey articles in management science and operations research, *Management Science*, **28**, 425–438, 1982.
7. Baker, K., *Introduction to Sequencing and Scheduling*, Wiley, 1974.
8. Bellman, R., *Dynamic Programming*, Princeton University Press, 1957.
9. Beer, S., *Decision and Control: The Meaning of Operational Research and Management Cybernetics*, Wiley, 1966.
10. Bellmore, M. and Nemhauser, G. L., The travelling salesman problem: a survey, *Operations Research*, **16**, 538–558, 1968.
11. Blackett, P. S., Operational research—recollections of problems studied, 1940–45, H. G. Thursfield (Ed.), *Brassey's Annual, Armed Forces Year Book*, pp. 88–106, Macmillan, 1953.
12. Blackett, P. S., *Studies of War*, Oliver & Boyd, 1962.
13. Boldyreff, A. W., A decade of military operations research in perspective—a symposium, *Operations Research*, **8**, 798–860, 1960.
14. Bonder, S., Needs in operational research education, 27th International Operations Research Society Meeting, 1970.
15. Brothers, L. A., Operations analysis in the United States Airforce, *Operations Research*, **2**, 1–16, 1954.
16. Byrd, J., The value of queueing theory, *Interfaces*, **8**, 22–26, 1978.
17. Conolly, B., *Lecture Notes in Queueing Systems*, Wiley, 1975.
18. Curran, R. T., Jacquette, S. C., and Politzer, J. L., Damage calculations for unreliable warheads, *Naval Research Logistics Quarterly*, **26**, 545–550, 1979.
19. Dobbie, J. M., A survey of search theory, *Operations Research*, **16**, 525–537, 1968.
20. Elmaghraby, S. and Moder, J., *Handbook of Operations Research*, Van Nostrand—Reinhold, 1978.
21. Elton, E. J. and Gruber, M. J. (Eds.), Portfolio theory, 25 years after, *Studies in the Management Sciences*, Vol. 11, North-Holland, 1979.
22. Everett, H., Generalised Lagrange multiplier method for solving problems of optimum allocation of resources, *Operations Research*, **11**, 399–417, 1963.
23. Falconer, N., On the size of convoys, Department of Decision Theory, Manchester University, 1976.
24. Fishman, G. S., *Principles of Discrete Event Simulation*, Wiley, 1978.

25. Firstmann, S. I. and Gluss, B., Optimum search routines for automatic fault location, *Operations Research*, **8**, 512–523, 1960.
26. Foster, F. G., A unified theory of stock, storage and queue control, *Operational Research Quarterly*, **10**, 121–130, 1959.
27. Francis, R. L. and Goldstein, J. M., Location theory: a selected bibliography, *Operations Research*, **22**, 400–410, 1974.
28. Francis, R. L. and White, J. A., *Facility Layout and Location: An Analytical Approach*, Prentice-Hall, 1974.
29. French, S., *Sequencing and Scheduling*, Ellis Horwood, 1982.
30. Gal, S., *Search Games*, Academic Pres, 1980.
31. Gilmore, P. C., Optimal and sub-optimal algorithms for the quadratic assignment problem, *Society for Industrial and Applied Mathematics, Journal of Applied Mathematics*, **10**, 305–313, 1962.
32. Golden, B., Bodin, L., Doyle, T., and Stewart, W., Approximate travelling salesman algorithms, *Operations Research*, **28**, 694–711, 1980.
33. Gollers, R. and Kleibohm, K., *Theoretische Analyse und Praktische Anwending von Modellen der Optimalen Ausschussvergobe unter Berucksichtigung des Edv-Einsatzes*, Westdeutscher, 1980.
34. Gordon, R., Optimum component redundancy for maximum system reliability, *Operations Research*, **5**, 229–243, 1957.
35. Graves, S. C., A review of production scheduling, *Operations Research*, **29**, 646–675, 1981.
36. Haley, K. B., Applications of search theory, *European Journal of Operational Research*, **7**, 227–231, 1981.
37. Halpern, J. (Ed.), Special issue on locational decisions, *European Journal of Operational Research*, **6**, 1981.
38. Handler, G. Y. and Mirchandani, P. B., *Location on Networks: Theory of Algorithms*, Massachussetts Institute of Technology Press, 1979.
39. Hitch, C., Sub-optimisation in operations problems, *Operations Research*, **1**, 87–99, 1953.
40. Huysmans, J. H. B., *The Implementation of Operations Research*, Wiley, 1970.
41. Jardine, A. (Ed.), *Operational Research in Maintenance*, Manchester University Press, 1970.
42. Jones, R. V., The Blackett Memorial Lecture, *Journal of the Operational Research Society*, **9**, 779–791, 1982.
43. Karush, W., A queueing model for an inventory problem, *Operations Research*, **5**, 693–703, 1957.
44. Köenigsberg, E., Queueing theory: two nations, *Interfaces*, **11**, 94–95, 1981.
45. Koopman, B. O., The optimum distribution effort, *Operations Research*, **1**, 52–63, 1953.
46. Koopman, B. O., The theory of search I: kinematic bases, *Operations Research*, **4**, 324–346, 1956.
47. Koopman, B. O., The theory of search II: target detection, *Operations Research*, **4**, 503–531, 1956.
48. Koopman, B. O., The theory of search III: the optimum distribution of searching effort, *Operations Research*, **5**, 613–626, 1957.
49. Ladany, S. P., Machol, R. E., and Morrison, D. P. (Eds.), Management science in sports, *Studies in Management Science*, Vol. 4, North-Holland, 1977.
50. Larnder, H., The origin of operational research, in *Operational Research '78*, Haley, K. B., (Ed.), North-Holland, 1979 (also in *Operations Research*, **32**, 465–475, 1984).
51. Laurent, A., Bombing problems, *Operations Research*, **4**, 395–396, 1956.
52. Lee, A., *Applied Queueing Theory*, Macmillan, 1966.
53. Lewis, C. D., *Scientific Inventory Control*, Butterworth, 1981.

32

54. Love, S., *Inventory Control*, McGraw-Hill, 1979.
55. Lundquist, N. H., *Swedish Military Journal*, **84,** No. 3, 1955.
56. Mangasarian, O., *Non-Linear Programming*, McGraw-Hill, 1969.
57. Manne, A. S., A target assignment problem, *Operations Research*, **6,** 346–351, 1957.
58. Markowitz, H., *Portfolio Selection*, Wiley, 1959.
59. Müller-Merbach, H., Phases or components, *Interfaces*, **12,** 61–65, 1982.
60. Müller-Merbach, H., Heuristics and their design: a survey, *European Journal of Operational Research*, **8,** 1–23, 1981.
61. Pearl, J., *Heuristics*, Addison-Wesley, 1984.
62. Pierskella, W. P. and Voelker, J. A., A survey of maintenance models, the control and surveillance of deteriorating systems, *Naval Research Logistics Quarterly*, **23,** 353–388, 1976.
63. Reitman, W. R., Heuristic decision procedures, open constraints and the structure of ill-defined problems, in *Human Judgments and Optimality*, Shelly, M., Bryans, G. (Eds.), Wiley, 1964.
64. Rinnooy Kan, A. H. G., *Machine Scheduling Problems: Classification Complexity and Computations*, Nijhoff, Netherlands, 1976.
65. Robbins, J. J., Military applications of operations research in Sweden, *Operations Research*, **4,** 347–352, 1956.
66. Ropfkof, M. H. and Stark, R. M., Competitive bidding: a comprehensive bibliography, *Operations Research*, **27,** 1979.
67. Shapiro, J. F., *Mathematical Programming*, Wiley, 1979.
68. Sherif, Y. S. and Smith, M. L., Optimal maintenance models for systems subject to failure—a review, *Naval Research Logistics Quarterly*, **28,** 47–74, 1981.
69. Silver, E. A., Operations research in inventory management: a review and critique, *Operations Research*, **29,** 628–645, 1981.
70. Silver, E. A., Vidal, R. V., and De Werra, D., A tutorial on heuristic methods, *European Journal of Operational Research*, **5,** 153–162, 1980.
71. Solandt, O., Observation, experiment and measurement, *Operations Research*, **3,** 1–14, 1955.
72. Stansfield, R. G., Harold Larner—founder of operational research, *Journal of the Operational Research Society*, **34,** 1–7, 1983.
73. Stone, L. D., The process of search planning: current approaches and continuing problems, *Operations Research* **31,** 207–233, 1983.
74. Stone, L. D., *Theory of Optimal Search*, Academic Press, 1975.
75. Taha, H. A., Queueing theory in practice, *Interfaces*, **11,** 43–49, 1981.
76. Tocher, K. D., *The Art of Simulation*, English Universities Press, 1963.
77. Tocher, K. D., *The Role of Operational Research*, British Steel, 1961.
78. Waddington, C. H., *O.R. in World War II, Operational Research against the U-boat*, Elek Science, 1973.
79. Waddington, C. H., Operational research, *Animal Breeding Abstracts*, **19,** 409–415, 1951.
80. Wagner, H., *Principles of Operational Research*, Prentice-Hall, 1969.
81. Walsh, J. E., Optimum ammunition properties for salvos, *Operations Research*, **4,** 204–220, 1956.
82. White, D. J., *Decision Methodology*, Wiley, 1975.
83. White, D. J., *Fundamentals of Decision Theory*, North-Holland, 1976.
84. White, D. J., *Dynamic Programming*, Oliver & Boyd, 1969.
85. Whitin, T. M., *The Theory of Inventory Management*, Princeton University Press, 1953.
86. Williams, E. C., Reflections on operational research, *Operations Research*, **1,** 441–443, 1953.
87. Williams, H. P., *Model Building in Mathematical Programming*, Wiley, 1978.

CHAPTER 2

Selected Techniques

2.1 QUEUEING

As has been indicated in Chapter 1, queueing is concerned with the servicing of arrival streams of customers, with the objective of finding an optimal, or acceptable, balance between the behaviour of queues, in terms of numbers in the queue, or waiting time in the queue, and the cost of providing the service. The original developments in this area are credited to A. K. Erlang (see Brockmeyer [6]) who began his studies on telephone exchange problems in Denmark. Bhat [4] discusses the development in queueing theory up to 1969. Queueing problems can take various forms, and variations may be found in terms of the following characteristics:

 (i) arrival patterns: deterministic, negative exponential; bulk arrivals, etc.;
 (ii) service channels: single, multiple, subject to failure or close-down, etc.;
(iii) service mechanism: first come–first served, priorities for different customers, etc.;
(iv) service time: deterministic, negative exponential, bulk service, etc.

In Chapter 1 several general texts have been given covering a wide range or circumstances. In this text our aims are modest and we will, largely, confine ourselves to negative exponential arrivals and service. We will not here even deal with the manner in which such patterns are derived but leave it to the reader to consult the appropriate texts.

As we shall see, there is some similarity between queueing, inventory, maintanance, and even reject allowance, problems, the common feature being the dynamic nature and the need to control this behaviour. This is best seen by reference to Morse [22] which, although quite dated, is still very useful. Historically it is also important since it is the first volume in the Operations Research Society special publications series.

Queues abound in life and, indeed, this has been taken to be a characteristic feature of British life during the world wars (see Taha [31]). For those interested in the humorous side of things, a glance at Ellis [11], which is taken from *Punch* (**232**, p. 407, 1957), is worthwhile, where a description of the London Transport Board's attempts to look at bus scheduling, in the light of queue formation, is given.

Let us now develop some simple formal models.

Consider two successive arrivals, with an inter-arrival time s, given in Figure 2.1. The inter-arrival time, s, will, in general, be a random variable,

34

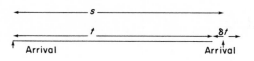

Figure 2.1

and we will want to specify its probability behaviour. This is done by considering the probability density function, $g(t)$, for which, if δt is small,

$$\text{probability } (t \leqslant s \leqslant t + \delta t) = g(t)\delta t + \text{second order terms.}$$

For the negative exponential case

$$g(t) = \lambda e^{-\lambda t}.$$

If we now consider any point in time, and wish to find the probability that an arrival takes place in the next interval of time δt, this is

$$\lambda \delta t$$

independent of when the previous arrival occurred (see Exercise 5). λ is called the arrival rate.

In many cases the arrival rate will depend upon the number, n, in the system, i.e. queue (waiting to begin service) and being served (if any). λ is then replaced by $\lambda(n)$.

We may likewise treat the service time, when an item is being served, to obtain a service rate, μ, which becomes $\mu(n)$ when it depends on the number in the system.

We are now in a position to develop a simple model to study the queue behaviour. Consider Figure 2.2, depicting the situations at times t and $t + \delta t$. Let us consider the probability, $P_n(t + \delta t)$, of there being n in the system at time $t + \delta t$. The numbers in the system at time t are $n+1$, n, $n-1$, plus $n+2$, $n+3, \ldots, n-2, n-3, \ldots$. However, the probability of moving from any of this latter group to n are at least as small as $\alpha(\delta t)^2$, α a non-negative number, since they require at least two events to take place (e.g. one arrival, one service, with move from n at t to n at $t + \delta t$), and each event has a

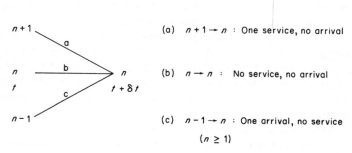

Figure 2.2

probability $\lambda(n)\delta t$, or $\mu(n)\delta t$, plus higher order powers of δt. We ignore all these events since we are only concerned with terms up to the first power of δt.

The three possible transitions, (a), (b), (c), are given in Figure 2.2. The probabilities of these are, respectively:

(a) $\mu(n+1)\delta t(1-\lambda(n+1)\delta t) \rightarrow \mu(n+1)\delta t + \text{second order terms};$
(b) $(1-\mu(n)\delta t)(1-\lambda(n)\delta t) \rightarrow 1-(\lambda(n)+\mu(n))\delta t + \text{second order terms};$
(c) $\lambda(n-1)\delta t(1-\mu(n-1)\delta t) \rightarrow \lambda(n-1)\delta t + \text{second order terms}.$

We then derive the balance equations.

$$P_n(t+\delta t) = P_n(t)(1-(\lambda(n)+\mu(n))\delta t) + P_{n+1}(t)\mu(n+1)\delta t + P_{n-1}(t)\lambda(n-1)\delta t.$$

From this we have

$$\frac{P_n(t+\delta t)-P_n(t)}{\delta t} = \mu(n+1)P_{n+1}(t) + \lambda(n-1)P_{n-1}(t) - (\lambda(n)+\mu(n))P_n(t).$$

Taking limits as $\delta t \rightarrow 0$, we have

$$P'_n(t) = \mu(n+1)P_{n+1}(t) + \lambda(n-1)P_{n-1}(t) - (\lambda(n)+\mu(n))P_n(t).$$

Now in certain cases, as $t \rightarrow \infty$, $P'_n(t) \rightarrow 0$, $P_n(t) \rightarrow P_n$ where P_n is now the stationary, or steady state, probability of there being n in the system at any time. P_n satisfies

$$(\lambda(n)+\mu(n))P_n = \mu(n+1)P_{n+1} + \lambda(n-1)P_{n-1}.$$

The steady state equations will be true for all $n \geq 0$. When $n = 0$, we have $\mu(0) = 0$, $P_{-1} = 0$ and we have the special equation

$$\lambda(0)P_0 = \mu(1)P_1.$$

We also have

$$\sum_{n=0}^{\infty} P_n = 1.$$

If the above equations have a solution, we will have a steady state solution. The general solution is then:

$$n \geq 1 \quad P_n = \left(\frac{\lambda(0)\lambda(1)\ldots\lambda(n-1)}{\mu(1)\mu(2)\ldots\mu(n)}\right)P_0$$

whence, first P_0 may be found, and then P_n.

It is easily seen that this satisfies the steady state equation. Thus, substituting, we have:

$$n \geq 2$$

The left-hand side of the steady state equation becomes

$$\frac{(\lambda(n)+\mu(n))\lambda(0)\lambda(1)\ldots\lambda(n-1)}{\mu(1)\mu(2)\ldots\mu(n)}P_0.$$

The right-hand side becomes

$$\frac{\mu(n+1)\mu(0)\mu(1)\ldots\mu(n)}{\mu(1)\mu(2)\ldots\mu(n+1)}P_0+\frac{\lambda(n-1)\lambda(0)\lambda(1)\ldots\lambda(n-2)}{\mu(1)\mu(2)\ldots\mu(n-1)}P$$

$$=(\lambda(n)+\mu(n))\left(\frac{\lambda(0)\lambda(1)\ldots\lambda(n-1)}{\mu(1)\mu(2)\ldots\mu(n)}\right)P_0.$$

We see that the expressions are identical.

$$\underline{n=1}$$

The left-hand side of the steady state equation becomes

$$(\lambda(1)+\mu(1))\frac{\lambda(0)}{\mu(1)}P_0.$$

The right-hand side becomes

$$\frac{\mu(2)\lambda(0)\lambda(1)}{\mu(1)\mu(2)}P_0+\lambda(0)P_0=\left(\frac{\lambda(1)+\mu(1)}{\mu(1)}\right)\lambda(0)P_0.$$

We see that the expressions are identical.

Saaty [28] is a useful source of formulae.

Some Special Cases

(i) *Single Server, Single Arrival Stream, Both Negative Exponential*

We have

$$\underline{n\geqslant0}\quad\lambda(n)=\lambda$$
$$\underline{n\geqslant1}\quad\mu(n)=\mu$$
$$\underline{n=0}\quad\mu(0)=0.$$

In this case, for $n\geqslant1$, and trivial for $n=0$,

$$P_n=\rho^nP_0$$

where

$$\rho=\frac{\lambda}{\mu}<1$$

is called the traffic intensity factor.

Then

$$(1+\rho+\rho^2+\ldots)P_0=1$$

i.e.

$$P_0=(1-\rho).$$

Hence

$$n \geq 0 \quad P_n = \rho^n(1-\rho).$$

These results are only true if $\rho < 1$.

The expected number, $\hat{n}$, in the system, is given by

$$\hat{n} = \sum_{n=0}^{\infty} nP_n = (1-\rho) \sum_{n=0}^{\infty} n\rho^n = (1-\rho)\rho \sum_{n=0}^{\infty} n\rho^{n-1} = (1-\rho)\rho \frac{d}{d\rho} \left(\sum_{n=0}^{\infty} \rho^n \right)$$

$$= (1-\rho)\rho \frac{d}{d\rho} \left(\frac{1}{1-\rho} \right) = \rho/(1-\rho).$$

The expected waiting time in the system for a customer arriving at random is

$$\hat{w} = \frac{(\hat{n}+1)}{\mu} = \frac{1}{(1-\rho)\mu} = \frac{1}{(\mu-\lambda)}.$$

As a check against the average waiting time, w^*, given later on in this section,

$$w^* = \hat{n}/\hat{\lambda} = \rho/(1-\rho)\lambda = 1/(\mu-\lambda) = \hat{w}.$$

In Exercise 1 of the Queueing exercises we will consider the use of the general equations for multi-server queues. Material on this will be found in many of the standard references. Ovuwarie [24] gives a survey and bibliography for this general area.

(ii) A Simple Queue with Discouragement (see Cox *et al.* [8])

Single server and single arrival stream as for (i), but arrival rates are influenced by the number in the system, so that, for example:

$$n \geq 0 \quad \lambda(n) = \lambda/(n+1)$$
$$n \geq 1 \quad \mu(n) = \mu$$
$$n = 0 \quad \mu(0) = 0.$$

In this case for $n \geq 1$, true also for $n = 0$,

$$P_n = (\rho^n/n!)P_0$$

where

$$\rho = \lambda/\mu.$$

Then

$$P_0(1+\rho+\rho^2/2!+\ldots)=1$$

i.e.

$$P_0 = e^{-\rho}.$$

Hence

$$\underline{n \geqslant 0} \quad P_n = \rho^n e^{-\rho}/n!.$$

Then

$$\hat{n} = e^{-\rho} \sum_{n=0}^{\infty} n\rho^n/n! = \rho e^{-\rho} \sum_{n=0}^{\infty} \rho^n/n! = \rho.$$

Then

$$\hat{w} = (\hat{n}+1)/\mu = (\rho+1)/\mu = (\lambda + \mu)/\mu^2.$$

As a check against the average waiting time, w^*, given later on in this section;

$$\omega^* = \hat{n}/\hat{\lambda}$$

$$= \hat{n} \Big/ \sum_{n=0}^{\infty} P_n \lambda(n) = \hat{n} \Big/ \sum_{n=0}^{\infty} \lambda \rho^n e^{-\rho}/(n+1)!$$

$$= \rho^2 \left(\frac{e^\rho}{\lambda}\right) \Big/ \underset{n=0}{\overset{\infty}{\kappa}} \rho^{n+1}/(n+1)! = \rho^2(e^\rho/\lambda)/(e^\rho - 1) = \rho^2/\lambda(1 - e^{-\rho}) \neq \hat{\omega}.$$

It is seen that the two expressions are not identical, and this arises because arrival rate and waiting time are not independent.

If we re-interpret $\lambda(n)$ so that the arrival rate is fixed at λ, but $1/(n+1)$ is the probability that an arrival will actually join the system, viz. we may use the expected waiting time conditional on joining the system, $\hat{w}(J)$. This is discussed later on in this section. For this problem it is true that

$$w^* = \hat{w}(J)$$

since $\lambda(n+1) = \lambda q(n)$, where $q(n)$ is the probability, $1/n+1$, of joining the system.

(iii) Single Arrival Stream, Infinite Number of Servers (Cox et al. [8])

In this case

$$\underline{n \geqslant 0} \quad \lambda(n) = \lambda$$

$$\underline{n \geqslant 1} \quad \mu(n) = n\mu$$

where μ is the service rate of a single server.

$$\underline{n = 0} \quad \mu(n) = 0.$$

Then, for $n \geqslant 1$, true also for $n = 0$,

$$P_n = \frac{\rho^n}{n!} P_0$$

$$P_0\left(1 + \quad + \frac{\rho^2}{2!} + \dots\right) = 1$$

i.e.

$$P_0 = e^{-\rho}.$$

Then

$$\underline{n \geqslant 0} \quad P_n = \frac{\rho^n}{n!} e^{-\rho}.$$

As for (ii),

$$\hat{n} = \rho$$

Also

$$\hat{w} = 1/\mu.$$

Since arrivals and waiting are independent we may use the formula $w^* = \hat{w} = \hat{n}/\hat{\lambda} = \rho/\lambda = 1/\mu$.

One of the key 'laws' in queueing theory relates waiting time to arrival rate and number in the system, to which reference has been made in the cases we have studied. The law is true for many, but not all, queueing systems. We will now briefly study this and, for further discussion, see Morse [22] (p. 75), Little [21], Jewell [16], Eilon [10], Kohlas [18] and Heyman [14].

Waiting Time in the System

Let us consider a long period of time T and let there be N customers who are, at some time, in the system during this time. Let $\{w_1, w_2, \ldots, w_N\}$ be the waiting times of each customer, including service time. Ignoring the time spent in the system before time 0, and after T, as being small, with respect to T, the average waiting time per customer is defined as

$$w^* = (w_1 + w_2 + \ldots + w_N)/N.$$

the average arrival rate is defined as

$$\lambda^* = N/T.$$

From these

$$\lambda^* w^* = (w_1 + w_2 + \ldots + w_N)/T.$$

Now consider Figure 2.3. Each individual will contribute to the cumulative waiting time of all customers during time T. This cumulative waiting time is

$$W = \int_0^T n(t)\, dt = \frac{T \int_0^T n(t)\, dt}{T}$$

$$= Tn^*$$

where n^* is the average number of customers in the system at any time t in the time period T.

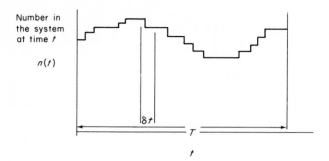

Figure 2.3

Thus the contribution to the cumulative waiting time per unit time is

$$\frac{W}{T} = n^*.$$

Now

$$W \cong (w_1 + w_2 + \ldots + w_N).$$

Hence

$$n^* \cong \lambda^* w^*$$

This is an identity if we exclude the time in system before time 0 and after T, and becomes exact as $T \to \infty$, if we include end effects also.

Let us now look at the problem, not in terms of the long run behaviour, n^*, λ^*, w^*, but in terms of the steady state probabilities and expectations $\hat{n}$, $\hat{\lambda}$, $\hat{w}$, defined as follows, assuming, for the moment, that all customers join the system.

$$\hat{n} = \sum_{n=0}^{\infty} n P_n$$

$$\hat{\lambda} = \sum_{n=0}^{\infty} \lambda(n) P_n$$

$$\hat{w} = \sum_{n=0}^{\infty} w(n) P_n$$

where: $\lambda(n)$ is the arrival rate when we have n in the system; $w(n)$ is the expected waiting time when we have n in the system.

Let:

$t(n)$ be the total period in the time interval T during which we have n in the system.

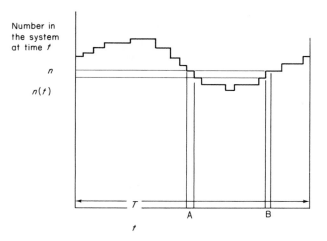

Figure 2.4

Then, returning to Figure 2.3, we have Figure 2.4:

$$A + B = t(n)$$

$$n^* = \frac{\sum\limits_{n=0}^{\infty} nt(n)}{T} = \sum_{n=0}^{\infty} n\left(\frac{t(n)}{T}\right) \rightarrow \sum_{n=0}^{\infty} nP_n = \hat{n}$$

as $T \rightarrow \infty$.

Now let N_n be the number of arrivals in this period T when there are n in the system, so that:

$$N_n = (TP_n)\lambda(n), \quad \text{if } T \text{ is large.}$$

Then

$$\lambda^* = \frac{N}{T} = \left(\sum_{n=0}^{\infty} N_n\right) \bigg/ T = \sum_{n=0}^{\infty} \lambda(n)P_n = \hat{\lambda}$$

$$w^* = (w_1 + w_2 + \ldots + w_N)/N = \left(\sum_{n=0}^{\infty} N_n w(n)\right) \bigg/ N, \quad \text{if } N \text{ is large,}$$

$$= \left(\frac{T}{N}\right) \sum_{n=0}^{\infty} \lambda(n)w(n)P_n$$

$$= \left(\sum_{n=0}^{\infty} \lambda(n)w(n)P_n\right) \bigg/ (N/T)$$

$$= \left(\sum_{n=0}^{\infty} \lambda(n)w(n)P_n\right) \bigg/ \left(\sum_{n=0}^{\infty} \lambda(n)P_n\right).$$

Thus $w^* \neq \hat{w}$ in general.

If $\lambda(n)$ is independent of n, and equal to λ;

$$w^* = \sum_{n=0}^{\infty} w(n)P_n = \hat{w}.$$

Note that, in the general case, we will always have:

$$w^* = \hat{n}/\hat{\lambda}.$$

As it is defined, $\hat{w}$ takes no account of the fact that some customers might not join the system. If $q(n)$ is the probability that a customer arriving at random, and finding n in the system, joins the system, and $P_n(J)$ is the probability that there are n in the system for a customer arriving at random and joining the system, we have:

$$P_n(J) = q(n)P_n \bigg/ \sum_{n=0}^{\infty} q(n)P_n.$$

If $\hat{w}(J)$ is the expected waiting time of those who join the system, we have:

$$\hat{w}(J) = \sum_{n=0}^{\infty} w(n)P_n(J) = \sum_{n=0}^{\infty} w(n)q(n)P_n \bigg/ \sum_{n=0}^{\infty} q(n)P_n.$$

If $\lambda(n) = \lambda q(n)$, then we see that:

$$\hat{w}(J) = w^*.$$

For more general problems this is not the case.

If $q(n) = 1$, for all n, we obtain:

$$\hat{w}(J) = \hat{w}$$

and, if $\lambda(n) = \lambda$, for all n, we obtain:

$$\hat{w}(J) = \hat{w} = w^*.$$

From an Operational Research point of view there is the question of whether $\hat{w}$ (or $\hat{w}(J)$) or w^* is the appropriate measure of performance. w^* might be appropriate for a company concerned with average customer service in the long run; $\hat{w}$ (or $\hat{w}(J)$) might be appropriate for a customer looking at his own individual waiting time on an expected basis. Note, also, it may be shown that $\lambda^* = 1/$expected inter-arrival time.

Little's paper actually defines $\hat{\lambda}$ to be equal to $1/$(expected inter-arrival time), and, under specified conditions, he shows that $\hat{n} = \hat{\lambda}\hat{w}$, but it is to be noted that his $\hat{\lambda}$ is effectively the same as that defined in this section, and effectively the same as λ^*.

The above analysis has been carried out in the context of the number in the system. A similar analysis will produce corresponding results for the number in the queue and, indeed, the number actually being served.

We have so far been concerned with steady state or long-run behaviour.

In some cases transient behaviour is much more important to study. Let us briefly look at this.

Transient Behaviour

For some problem situations sudden changes in the circumstances surrounding a problem require that we investigate the behaviour of the system in the relatively near future. For other problems repeated interjections into the system are made which again require a study of the ensuing behaviour in the relatively near future. Thus, if at the beginning of each week, we were re-allocating resources, the effect of a change at any specific queueing point for that week would be important. Erikson [12] discusses the problem of queueing at petrol pumps when shortages of petrol arise. Customers tend to fill up with their petrol tanks rather more full than they are usually. This increases the arrival rate λ, and increases the service rate μ, and hence influences queueing behaviour. Erikson's analysis is actually steady state, but, at least for temporary shortages, a transient analysis might be important.

For negative exponential problems of the kind we have discussed, we can study the transient behaviour directly. We choose $\delta t = \delta$, to be of an appropriate size, and our equations, for $t = k\delta$, $k = 0, 1, 2, \ldots, K$, are, with $P_n(t) = P_{nk}$:

$n \geqslant 1, 0 \leqslant k < K$

$$P_{nk+1} = (1 - (\lambda(n) + \mu(n))\delta)P_{nk} + \mu(n+1)\delta p_{n+1k} + \lambda(n-1)\delta P_{n-1k}$$

$n = 0, 0 \leqslant k < K$

$$P_{0k+1} = (1 - \lambda(0)\delta)P_{0k} + \mu(1)\delta P_{1k}.$$

To begin with we have:

$$P_{n_0 0} = 1 \text{ if we begin with } n_0 \text{ in system,}$$

$$P_{n0} = 0 \text{ for all other } n.$$

For non-negative exponential situations, but where the time of the next arrival still depends only on the time elapsed since the last arrival, it is easy to formally modify these equations to allow for this.

These equations will, in general, still be difficult to solve, but they might be more meaningful than steady state analysis in some cases. In Donaldson *et al.* [9], some discussion of the numerical solution of these equations is given. Pegden *et al.* [25], Cox *et al.* [8], also discuss transient solutions for the negative exponential case. Bhat *et al.* [5] discuss general approximation techniques, some of which may be useful for transient analysis. Neuts [23] discusses some general matrix approaches to queueing problems.

So far, the queueing problems we have looked at are passive in the sense that no actual decision making takes place while the queues operate. The vast majority of queueing theory, in its classical form, is of this kind, and allows one merely to determine what the facility levels, or mechanisms, ought to be. Modern interests in queueing are of the more active kind looking at actual decisions made at the time queueing takes place. We will confine ourselves to some simple ideas, and the reader can consult Sobel [30] and Prabhu *et al.* [26].

Decision Making in Queues

In the classical queueing theory area, the central piece of work is due to Cobham [7] on priority systems of queueing. In this work it is assumed that:

(i) there are L arrival streams, $l = 1, 2, \ldots, L$;
(ii) arrival stream l is negative exponential with arrival rate λ_l, $l = 1, 2, \ldots, L$;
(iii) the service time of arrival stream l is general with probability density $f_l(t)$, (not strictly necessary, but assumed for simplicity) and service rate μ_l, $l = 1, 2, \ldots, L$;
(iv) any member of arrival stream l in the queue at any time has priority over any other customer in the queue at that time in arrival streams l' if $l' > l$, with the exception of any customer being served at that time, $l = 1, 2, \ldots, L - 1$;
(v) we have a single service facility.

It is shown that if $\hat{w}_l$ is the expected time that a customer in arrival stream l will have to wait in the queue, then, providing $\sigma_l < 1$, $1 \le l \le L$,

$$\hat{w}_l = \tfrac{1}{2} \int_0^\infty t^2 f(t) \, dt / ((1 - \sigma_{l-1})(1 - \sigma_l)), \quad \text{for} \quad 1 \le l \le L,$$

where

$$f(t) = \sum_{l=1}^{L} \lambda_l f_l(t)$$

$$\sigma_l = \sum_{r=1}^{l} \lambda_r / \mu_r, \quad 1 \le l \le L$$

$$= 0, \quad l = 0$$

$$\mu_l = 1 \Big/ \int_{t=0}^{\infty} t f_l(t) \, dt.$$

Using these results we can see the effects of different priorities on various classes of customer. Jaiswal [15] gives a coverage of priority queues in general.

In discussing our techniques, we have made reference to solution techniques, in particular to dynamic programming, which may in principle be applied to this problem and which will be discussed in section 2.5. Let us assume that for simplicity, $L = 2$, that for a customer of class l, the cost of waiting per unit time in the queue is c_l, and that all costs have to be discounted by a factor α, $0 \leqslant \alpha < 1$ (see Chapter 6 for a discussion of this). Let us assume that we wish to decide, as soon as the facility becomes available, which class of item to service next in order to minimize the expected discounted cost over a finite time period $T = K\delta$, $\delta = \delta t$, δt small. Finally, let us assume that the services are negative exponential. More complicated problems can be dealt with, although the analysis is more demanding. Note that α is relative to the time interval δt.

Let, at time $t = k\delta$, measured from the end of the time horizon, there be n_l customers of type l in the queue, $l = 1$, 2, and customer type m being served, $m = 1$, 2, or 0, where 0 indicates that the system is empty. It is clear that the minimal discounted expected cost to the end of the time horizon depends only on k, n_1, n_2, and m. Let this be, as a function of the current state (n_1, n_2, m),

$$f_k(n_1, n_2, m)$$

discounted to $t = k\delta$ as time origin.

If $m = 1$, or 2, no decision arises, and the immediate contribution to cost is, in terms of waiting time in the queue,

$$(n_1 c_1 + n_2 c_2)\delta.$$

Let us assume that $n_1 > 0$, $n_2 > 0$, and $m = 1$. Then the new state at the beginning of the next period is:

$(n_1, n_2, 1)$ with probability $1 - (\lambda_1 + \lambda_2 + \mu_1)\delta$ to a first order
$(n_1 + 1, n_2, 1)$ $\lambda_1 \delta$ approximation
$(n_1, n_2 + 1, 1)$ $\lambda_2 \delta$
$(n_1, n_2, 0)$ $\mu_1 \delta$

The 'principle of optimality' (see Bellman [3]) states that 'an optimal policy has the property that, whatever the initial state and decision are, the remaining decisions must constitute an optimal policy with regard to the state resulting from the first decision'. Thus the expected discounted cost from the time $(k-1)\delta$ to the end must be optimal, and, by definition, this is, discounted to time $k\delta$,

$$\alpha f_{k-1}(n_1, n_2, 1) \text{ with probability } 1 - (\lambda_1 + \lambda_2 + \mu_1)\delta$$

$$\alpha f_{k-1}(n_1 + 1, n_2, 1) \text{ with probability } \lambda_1 \delta$$

$$\alpha f_{k-1}(n_1, n_2 + 1, 1) \text{ with probability } \lambda_2 \delta$$

$$\alpha f_{k-1}(n_1, n_2, 0) \text{ with probability } \mu_1 \delta.$$

We then have:

$$f_k(n_1, n_2, 1) = \delta(n_1 c_1 + n_2 c_2) + \alpha((1 - (\lambda_1 + \lambda_2 + \mu_1)\delta)f_{k-1}(n_1, n_2, 1)$$
$$+ \lambda_1 \delta f_{k-1}(n_1 + 1, n_2, 1) + \lambda_2 \delta f_{k-1}(n_1, n_2 + 1, 1)$$
$$+ \mu_1 \delta f_{k-1}(n_1, n_2, 0)).$$

Table 2.1

State at time $t = k\delta$	Decision	Contributed cost	New state	Probability
$n_1, n_2, 0$	serve class 1	$((n_1-1)c_1+n_2c_2)\delta$	$(n_1-1, n_2, 1)$	$1-(\lambda_1+\lambda_2+\mu_1)\delta$
			$(n_1, n_2, 1)$	$\lambda_1\delta$
			$(n_1-1, n_2+1, 1)$	$\lambda_2\delta$
			$(n_1-1, n_2, 0)$	$\mu_1\delta$
	serve class 2	$(n_1c_1+(n_2-1)c_2)\delta$	$(n_1, n_2-1, 2)$	$1-(\lambda_1+\lambda_2+\mu_2)\delta$
			$(n_1+1, n_2-1, 2)$	$\lambda_1\delta$
			$(n_1, n_2, 2)$	$\lambda_2\delta$
			$(n_1, n_2-1, 0)$	$\mu_2\delta$
	serve no one	$(n_1c_1+n_2c_2)\delta$	$(n_1, n_2, 0)$	$1-(\lambda_1+\lambda_2)\delta$
			$(n_1+1, n_2, 0)$	$\lambda_1\delta$
			$(n_1, n_2+1, 0)$	$\lambda_2\delta$

Let us now consider the case $n_1 > 0$, $n_2 > 0$, $m = 0$. We may now make decisions as to which class of customer, if any, to serve. We have Table 2.1. We can then set up our equations as follows:

$$f_k(n_1, n_2, 0) =$$

$$\min \begin{bmatrix} \underline{\text{serve class 1}} & ((n_1-1)c_1-n_2c_2)\delta \\ & + \alpha((1-(\lambda_1+\lambda_2+\mu_1)\delta)f_{k-1}(n_1-1, n_2, 1) \\ & + \lambda_1\delta f_{k-1}(n_1, n_2, 1) + \lambda_2\delta f_{k-1}(n_1-1, n_2+1, 1) \\ & + \mu_1\delta f_{k-1}(n_1-1, n_2, 0)) \\ & = g_k^1(n_1, n_2, 0), \text{ say} \\ \underline{\text{serve class 2}} & (n_1c_1+(n_2-1)c_2)\delta \\ & + \alpha((1-(\lambda_1+\lambda_2+\mu_2)\delta)f_{k-1}(n_1, n_2-1, 2) \\ & + \lambda_1\delta f_{k-1}(n_1+1, n_2-1, 2) + \lambda_2\delta f_{k-1}(n_1, n_2, 2) \\ & + \mu_2\delta f_{k-1}(n_1, n_2-1, 0)) \\ & = g_k^2(n_1, n_2, 0), \text{ say} \\ \underline{\text{serve no one}} & (n_1c_1+n_2c_2)\delta + \alpha((1-(\lambda_1+\lambda_2)\delta)f_{k-1}(n_1, n_2, 0) \\ & + \lambda_1\delta f_{k-1}(n_1+1, n_2, 0) + \lambda_2\delta f_{k-1}(n_1, n_2+1, 0)) \\ & = g_k^0(n_1, n_2, 0), \text{ say} \end{bmatrix}$$

We may likewise set up similar sets of equations for the remaining initial states.

The calculations proceed backwards by:

(i) setting $f_0(n_1, n_2, m) = 0$, for all n_1, n_2, m;

(ii) calculating $f_1(n_1, n_2, m)$ for all n_1, n_2, m, using the equations and (i);

(iii) calculating, in general, $f_k(n_1, n_2, m)$ for all n_1, n_2, m using the equations and knowledge of $f_{k-1}(n_1, n_2, m)$ for all n_1, n_2 and m.

The analysis gives not only the discounted expected costs, $\{f_k(n_1, n_2, m)\}$, for all k, n_1, n_2 and m, but also the optimal decisions at each point in time. At each stage we calculate the optimal decision as a function of n_1, n_2 and m. This gives us a decision rule $\theta_k(n_1, n_2, m)$ as a function of n_1, n_2 and m at beginning of interval k from the end.

The infinite horizon solution may be obtained by letting $K \to \infty$, in which case we replace $f_k(n_1, n_2, m)$ by $f(n_1, n_2, m)$, the infinite horizon discounted costs beginning in condition (n_1, n_2, m).

The advantage of the dynamic programming formulation is that it is not restricted to inflexible priority rules, as is Cobham's approach, and will give an optimal answer for the stated problem. It is also formally easily extendable to many queueing situations. However, it is very costly to solve.

Later on in Chapter 4 we will discuss the advantage of closed form analysis when the number of options open to the decision maker is large. When we are dealing with dynamic problems the number of decision rules can be very large. Thus if, in the above problem, we assume that

$$0 \leqslant k \leqslant K$$
$$0 \leqslant n_1 \leqq N_1$$
$$0 \leqslant n_2 \leqslant N_2$$

the number of decision rules, dependent on the time of taking the decisions, is $(2^{N_1+N_2}3^{N_1 N_2})^K$. Thus, for example, the thought of simulating all these is daunting. Some other aid is needed to ensure that a proper coverage of the possibilities is obtained. We will return to this point later on.

An alternative approach to solving this problem is via a mathematical programming approach which we discuss in section 2.5. Let

$$x_{kn_1 n_2 mj} = 1 \quad \text{if service } j(1, 2, \text{ or } 0) \text{ is to be used in circumstances}$$
$$k, n_1, n_2, m$$
$$= 0 \quad \text{otherwise.}$$

We then obtain

$$\sum_{j=0}^{2} x_{kn_1 n_2 mj} = 1 \quad \text{for all } k, n_1, n_2 \text{ and } m$$

$$x_{kn_1 n_2 mm} = 1 \quad \text{for all } k, n_1, n_2 \text{ and } m \neq 0.$$

We also have expressions relating the $\{x_{kn_1 n_2 mj}\}$. One of these, obtained from the equation for $f_k(n_1, n_2, 0)$, is, if $w_{kn_1 n_2 m}$ is the expected discounted cost arising from using $\{x_{kn_1 n_2 mj}\}$

$$w_{kn_1 n_2 0} = x_{kn_1 n_2 01} g_k^1(n_1, n_2, 0) + x_{kn_1 n_2 02} g^2(n_1, n_2, 0) + x_{kn_1 n_2 00} g^0(n_1, n_2, 0)$$

where $\{g_k^i(n_1, n_2, 0)\}$ are specified on the right-hand side of the expression for $f_k(n_1, n_2, 0)$, replacing $f_{k-1}(n_1, n_2, m)$ by $w_{k-1 n_1 n_2 m}$ throughout.

There are many more equations.

The objective function, with $x = \{x_{kn_1n_2mj}\}$, $w = \{w_{kn_1n_2m}\}$, is $f(x, w) = w_{Kn_1^K n_2^K n_3^K}$ where (n_1^K, n_2^K, m^K) is the starting condition.

We wish to minimize $f(x, w)$ subject to the constraints. Note that the optimal $f(x, w)$ is equal to $f_K(n_1^K, n_2^K, m^K)$.

The optimal $x_{kn_1n_2mj}$ is equivalent to $\theta_k(n_1, n_2, m)$ in the dynamic programming formulation, i.e. $j = \theta_k(n_1, n_2, m)$.

Again the formulation is a difficult one to handle but, like the dynamic programming formulation, it will give an optimal answer for the stated problem. It has no advantage over the dynamic programming formulation in this case, since the formulations are essentially equivalent computationally. For other problems this is not the case, particularly for deterministic problems, since dynamic programming, in such cases, will result in calculations for states which do not actually arise.

In making the above comments it should be pointed out that, for the mathematical programming formulation, one can relax the conditions that $x_{kn_1n_2mj}$ be 0 or 1 to the continuous form of lying between 0 and 1, and this will allow the use of standard linear programming procedures, although it is doubtful if such an approach will be efficient. This point applies equally well to similar subsequent material, for example in inventory formulations.

Although the dynamic and mathematical programming approaches have some advantages, they do depend heavily on the objectives involved in the formulation of the problem. The same point applies to other stochastic problems which we will meet later on. In our example the objective was stated in terms of expected weighted waiting times (where the costs c_1, c_2, represent the weighting factors). However, if, for example, the expected (mean) waiting time and variance of the waiting time is important, the analysis becomes considerably more difficult (see White [32, 33] and Sobel [30], for a discussion of mean-variance analysis in Markov decision processes, which our formulation really is, and where Sobel gives a method of calculating means and variances for infinite horizon discounted problems, the ideas of which may also be adapted to finite horizon problems). We will turn to the question of problem formulation in Chapter 4.

It is to be noted that, if we move away from a simple objective function such as the one we have used, then the linear programming approach is, at present, somewhat superior in some cases, for example for finding efficient solutions (see Chapter 4).

2.2 INVENTORY

As has been stated in Chapter 1, inventory problems are characterized by supply and demand. There are many variations in this problem area, for example

(i) the demand may be deterministic or probabilistic, and dependent, or independent, of time;

(ii) there may be many commodities;

(iii) supplies may have zero lead time, probabilistic lead time, and an order may be delivered in parts;

(iv) demands may be for quantities of particular sizes, e.g. 0 or 20, etc.;

(v) inventory may deteriorate with time in stock.

Again the objective of this section is modest and the reader may care to consult one of the texts cited in Chapter 1 for a more general coverage of the area.

We will begin with the simplest of problems, viz. the classical economic order quantity problem of Wilson [23]. We make the following assumptions, concerning a single commodity:

(ii) the demand for the commodity is uniform throughout the year, at an annual rate of s;

(ii) for each non-zero order placed there is a fixed order cost, a, independent of the size of the order;

(iii) the cost of purchase is c per unit purchased;

(iv) the cost of holding one unit of commodity in stock for one year is h, this cost being incurred on a *pro rata* basis for any fraction of a year held;

(v) orders are instantaneously supplied;

(vi) the objective is to minimize the average annual total cost over a long time period.

The problem is cast in the form of a purchase problem, but the problem of producing the commodity using one's own facilities is similarly analysable.

Let x be the size of the order placed. We will assume that all orders are of the same size. For this problem it can be established that an optimal solution exists which is of this form. This is not true for all inventory problems, even for uniform demand cases. We will also assume that x is a continuous variable, whereas for many problems x is integer, and suitable modifications have to be made to solve the problem in this form.

Figure 2.5 forms the basis of the analysis, where T is the cycle length i.e. time between orders.

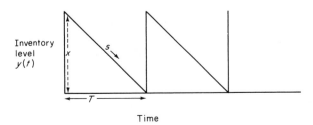

Figure 2.5

The fixed cost per cycle is a.

The purchase cost per cycle is cx.

The inventory cost per cycle is $h \int_0^T y(t)\, dt = \frac{1}{2}hxT$, where $y(t)$ is the inventory level at time t.

Hence the total cost per cycle is:

$$a + cx + \tfrac{1}{2}hxT.$$

Then the average annual cost in the long run is:

$$f(x) = (a + cx + \tfrac{1}{2}hxT) \text{ (number of cycles per year)}$$
$$= (a + cx + \tfrac{1}{2}hxT)/T$$
$$= a/T + cx/T + \tfrac{1}{2}hx$$
$$= as/x + cs + \tfrac{1}{2}hx$$
$$f'(x) = -as/x^2 + \tfrac{1}{2}h$$
$$f''(x) = 2as/x^3 > 0.$$

Hence the minimal value of $f(x)$ is given by $f'(x) = 0$, i.e.

$$x^* = \sqrt{(2as/h)}$$
$$f(x^*) = cs + \sqrt{(2ash)}.$$

There are many variants of this simple problem, for example problems in which quantity discounts (see Donaldson et al. [6]) or quantity premiums apply, and see Muhlemann [13] for a problem with more general holding costs. In the former case it is not true that an optimal solution exists with equal order quantities. This point is important for many inventory problems, thus adding more complexity to the analysis of the problem. None the less the classical Wilson analysis is valuable in showing how basically conflicting aspects can be put together in one overall model. We will make use of this model to illustrate other aspects of the Operational Research process later on, but, in this section, will look at a few more complex variations of this problem.

Further useful references relating to the economic order quantity problem are Crowe [5] (who discusses the variety of symbolic representations of the same problem and also gives a very useful reference list), Gardner [7] (who discusses the validity of such models when the costs depend upon more than one item, raising the problem of separability of many items into individual items).

In the simple model, we have assumed that demand is uniform throughout the year. Let us now assume that, to keep the problem simple, the following conditions apply:

(i) the time period is broken into unit intervals, $k = 1, 2, \ldots, K$;
(ii) the initial inventory is y_1;
(iii) orders may be placed only at the beginning of each interval;

(iv) the demand in interval k is s_k and is uniform in this interval and must be satisfied from any order placed at the beginning of interval k and/or from any inventory existing at the beginning of interval k;

(v) the cost structure is as for the simple model;

(vi) the objective is to minimize the total cost over the K intervals.

In this problem we cannot assume that the orders are of equal size, and the most straightforward approach is via mathematical programming. Let x_k be the quantity ordered at the beginning of interval k. We then have the following constraints, to ensure that all orders will be met, where y_k is the inventory at the beginning of interval k before an order is placed for that interval:

$$y_2 = y_1 + x_1 - s_1$$
$$y_3 = y_2 + x_2 - s_2$$
$$\vdots \qquad \vdots \qquad \vdots$$
$$y_k = y_{k-1} + x_{k-1} - s_{k-1}$$
$$y_K = y_{K-1} + x_{K-1} - s_{K-1}$$
$$y_{K+1} = y_K + x_K - s_K$$

(y_{K+1} is the inventory at the end of interval K)

$$y_k \geqslant 0, \qquad 2 \leqslant k \leqslant K + 1$$
$$x_k \geqslant 0, \qquad 1 \leqslant k \leqslant K.$$

Note that $\{s_k\}$, $1 \leqslant k \leqslant K$, are all fixed.

Let us now look at the total cost in interval k. This is

$$a\tau(x_k) + cx_k + \tfrac{1}{2}h(y_k + x_k + y_{k+1}) = a\tau(x_k) + cx_k + h(y_k + x_k - \tfrac{1}{2}s_k)$$

where $\tau(x_k) = 1$ if $x_k > 0$, and $\tau(x_k) = 0$, if $x_k = 0$.

The total cost over k invervals is then given by

$$f(x) = \sum_{k=1}^{K} (a\tau(x_k) + cx_k + h(y_k + x_k - \tfrac{1}{2}s_k))$$

where $x = (x_1, x_2, \ldots, x_K)$.

The problem then reduces to:

$$\text{minimize } [f(x)]$$
subject to the stipulated constraints.

It is now in standard mathematical programming form with the exception of the terms $\{\tau(x_k)\}$. Apart from the $\{\tau(x_k)\}$ terms it is a linear programme, but the $\{\tau(x_k)\}$ terms can make for difficulty in getting a solution. It is possible to convert to a standard mathematical programme in 0–1 variables by replacing $\tau(x_k)$ by z_k where

$$z_k \geqslant x_k/M, \qquad z_k = 0 \text{ or } 1, M \text{ large}.$$

The use of $\tau(x_k)$ is not in standard mathematical programming form.

An alternative method is to use the dynamic programming formulation. At the beginning of interval k, let the inventory be y. The minimal total cost to the end of interval K depends only on k and y. Let this be $f_k(y)$.

If x is the quantity ordered, the cost in interval k is as given previously.

The inventory level at the beginning of interval $k+1$ is $y_{k+1} = y + x - s_k$. The Principle of Optimality (see section 2.1) says that all decisions in the remaining intervals must be optimal. Hence, by definition, the minimal total cost in the remaining interval is $f_{k+1}(y + x - s_k)$.

Note that, in this formulation, we move from k to $k+1$, whereas, in the queueing formulation we move from k to $k-1$. It is merely a matter of how we label the intervals. Either will do. For this problem the approach chosen is the natural one.

We may now put the pieces together, noting that x is free, subject only to $x \geqslant 0$, and $y_{k+1} \geqslant 0$ i.e. $y_k + x_k - s_k \geqslant 0$, to give the following equations:

$\underline{1 \leqslant k \leqslant K}$

$$f_k(y) = \min_{x \geqslant s_k - y} [a\tau(x) + cx + h(y + x - \tfrac{1}{2}s_k) + f_{k+1}(y + x - s_k)]$$

$$x \geqslant 0$$

$\underline{k = K+1}$

$$f_{k+1}(y) = 0.$$

It is to be noted that, as with the queueing problem, these equations have to be solved for all k and for all y, in some suitable region. This involves considerable calculation, but the $\{\tau(x)\}$ terms do not create any problems as they do with a mathematical programming approach.

For this problem we begin with $f_{K+1}(y) = 0$, for all $y \geqslant 0$, and work backwards, finally calculating $f_1(y_1)$, where y_1 is given. At the same time we determine the optimal decision rules, $\{\theta_k(y)\}$, which tell us which value of x to take for a given y. The actual sequence of optimal decisions is then

$$x_1 = \theta_1(y_1), \qquad x_2 = \theta_2(y_2) = \theta_2(y_1 + x_1 - s_1), \ldots, \qquad x_{k+1} = \theta_{k+1}(y_{k+1})$$

$$= \theta_{k+1}(y_k + x_k - s_k), \qquad x_k = \theta_K(y_k) = \theta_K(y_{K-1} + x_{K-1} - s_{K-1}).$$

It is to be noted that, in the dynamic programming equation, we have dropped the subscript k from y_k and x_k without loss of generality. Thus dynamic programming deals with general levels of x_k, y_k, not with particular levels, except for starting conditions.

Let us now return to the simple problem. In that problem we assumed that the demand was known for certain, and we did not include any penalty costs for shortages, and no shortages were allowed. Let us modify the problem to allow for these aspects, and make the following assumptions:

(i) orders are placed every T units of time, and are always such as to increase the existing inventory to a level x;

(ii) the costs are as for the simple problem, assuming the demand is

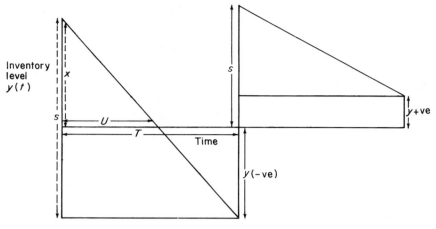

Figure 2.6

uniform over T, but, in addition, there is a penalty cost, r, for each unit of demand not supplied, with no backlog allowed;
(iii) the probability density function for demand, s, in period T is $g(s, T)$;
(iv) supplies are instantaneous.

To simplify the problem we assume that the initial inventory is no greater than x, and hence is immediately increased to x. The following Figure 2.2.2 is useful in the analysis.

For each cycle of length T we have the following expected costs.

There is a fixed cost a, providing the order quantity is >0. Since we are assuming a probability density function, the probability that the demand is >0 is 1. Hence the expected fixed cost is a.

The size of the order at the end of period T will be x if the demand s is $\geq x$ and s if the demand s is $\leq x$. Hence the expected order cost per cycle is

$$c\left(x\int_{s=x}^{\infty} g(s, T)\, \mathrm{d}s + \int_{s=0}^{x} sg(s, T)\, \mathrm{d}s\right).$$

The inventory holding cost depends upon whether or not there is a shortage. If the end inventory, y, is $-ve$, the inventory holding cost for the cycle is (see Figure 2.6)

$$\tfrac{1}{2}hxU = \tfrac{1}{2}hTx^2/s.$$

If the end inventory, y, is non-negative, the inventory holding cost for the cycle is (see Figure 2.6):

$$\tfrac{1}{2}h(x+y)T = \tfrac{1}{2}h(2x - s)T.$$

Hence the expected inventory holding cost per cycle is, assuming $x>0$,

$$\tfrac{1}{2}hT\left(x^2\int_{s=x}^{\infty} \frac{1}{s} g(s, T)\, \mathrm{d}s + \int_{s=0}^{x} (2x - s)g(s, T)\, \mathrm{d}s\right)$$

Shortage penalties will only arise if $s > x$. the expected shortage cost per cycle is:

$$r \int_{s=x}^{\infty} (s-x)g(s, T)\, ds.$$

Then the expected cost per unit time, being equal to the expected cost per cycle divided by T, is given by:

$$f(x, T) = \left(a + c\left(x \int_{s=x}^{\infty} g(s, T)\, ds + \int_{s=0}^{x} sg(s, T)\, ds \right) \right.$$
$$\left. + r \int_{s=x}^{\infty} (s-x)g(s, T)\, ds \right) \Big/ T$$
$$+ \tfrac{1}{2} h\left(x^2 \int_{s=x}^{\infty} \frac{1}{s} g(s, T)\, ds + \int_{s=0}^{x} (2x-s)g(s, T)\, ds \right).$$

The problem is to choose (x, T) to minimize $f(x, T)$.

There is no guarantee that the above formulation will give the optimal solution within the class of all ordering policies which might be used, and hence such a formulation may well result in sub-optimal solutions. Bellman [2] indicates this in the special case when $T = 1$, and $h = 0$. Bellman uses the dynamic programming formulation, which is much more general, but often much harder to solve. Let us assume that $T = 1$, and suppress the T for simplicity. The analysis can be done for each T and optimal solutions over T found. Let us assume that we are optimizing over K time intervals, as with the queueing problem we looked at, and we will number the intervals $k = 1, 2, \ldots, K$, moving backwards. We will also discount, with factor α, as for the queueing problem. We may set $\alpha = 1$ if we wish.

If y is the initial inventory at the beginning of interval k, then the minimal expected discounted cost to the end of the interval 1 depends only on k and y. Let this be $f_k(y)$. If the decision is to increase the inventory level to x, the expected cost is as given in the previous analysis for the interval k. The inventory level at the end of the interval is $y = x - s$ if $s \leq x$, $y = 0$ if $s > x$. The principle of optimality says that all our subsequent decisions are optimal, and hence the expected cost to the end of interval 1, discounted to the beginning of interval k, is $\alpha f_{k-1}(y)$. We then have the equations given below.

$1 \leq k \leq K$

$$f_k(y) = \min_{x \geq y} \left[q(x, y) + \alpha \int_{s=0}^{x} f_{k-1}(x-s)g(s)\, ds + \alpha \int_{s=x}^{\infty} f_{k-1}(0)g(s)\, ds \right],$$

$k = 0$
$$\forall y \geq 0,$$

$$f_0(y) = 0, \quad \forall y \geq 0$$

where

$$q(x, y) = a\tau(x-y) + c(x-y) + \tfrac{1}{2}h\left(x^2 \int_{s=x}^{\infty} \frac{1}{s} g(s)\, ds + \int_{s=0}^{x} (2x-s)g(s)\, ds \right)$$
$$+ r \int_{s=x}^{\infty} (s-x)g(s)\, ds$$

$$\tau(x - y) = 1 \quad \text{if} \quad x > y$$
$$= 0 \quad \text{if} \quad x = y.$$

The problem is solved by working backwards, and eventually calculating $f_K(y_K)$ if y_K is the initial inventory at beginning of interval K from the end, and calculating the optimal decision rules $\{\theta_k(y)\}$, which tell us the optimal x level at the beginning of interval k if the inventory level there is y.

If we let $K \to \infty$, we can obtain the limiting infinite horizon equation obtained by replacing $f_k(y)$ by $f(y)$, the infinite horizon discounted minimal expected cost for an initial inventory level of y.

As with the queueing problem we can cast this problem in a general mathematical programming form, although this is exactly equivalent to the dynamic programming formulation computationally. To keep matters simple we assume that all variables are integer, and replace the density function, $g(s)$ by the discrete probability $p(s)$. Then let x_{ki} be the level up to which the inventory is adjusted at the beginning of interval k if the initial inventory level is i at that time. If w_{ki} is the expected discounted cost to the end of interval 1, from the beginning of interval k, beginning with initial inventory i, we have the following equations:

$\underline{i \geq 0, 1 \leq k \leq K}$

$$w_{ki} = q(x_{ki}, i) + \alpha \sum_{s=0}^{x_{ki}} p(s) w_{k-1 x_{ki}-s} + \alpha \sum_{s=x_{ki}+1}^{\infty} p(s) w_{k-10}$$

$w_{ki} \geq 0$, and $x_{ki} \geq i$ and integer, for all k, i.

The objective function to be minimized is

$$f(x, w) = w_{Ki_K}$$

where i_K is the inventory at the beginning of interval K.

Again the optimal value of $f(x, w)$ is equal to $f_K(i_K)$, and the optimal $\{x_{ki}\}$ are equal to $\{\theta_k(i)\}$ in the dynamic programming formulation. As with the linear programming approach to queueing theory problems, we should stress that, although this is inefficient for the simple single objective function used, once we move away from this, linear programming may well be quite useful, for example, for multi-objective problems (see Chapter 4).

The reader may wish to consult Yaspan [24] who gives an interesting unification of some simple inventory problems. Hollier et al. [10] give a classification of inventory systems, and Lockett et al. [12] discuss the use of formal inventory models. Tinarelli [21] gives a useful up-to-date survey.

2.3 MAINTENANCE

As has been indicated in Chapter 1, maintenance is concerned with systems subject to failure or deterioration of some kind and with the maintenance and repair of these systems. We use the term maintenance to subsume the term repair in this text. The basic problem is to obtain a balance between the effects of failure and deterioration and the costs of control. Needless to say, there are a variety of maintenance problem situations which involve, for example, problems of: when and what to inspect; what sort of minor or major repairs to carry out when something has been found to be at fault; whether or not to use opportunity maintenance (i.e. if a fault is found at one point in the system, is it economic to replace or repair other items at that time, even though they may still be effective, in order to avoid having to strip the system down again later?); whether or not to use preventive or breakdown maintenance. In addition the question of resources, equipment population, and so on add extra dimensions to the problems.

In this text we will deal with some simple models only, enough for us to hinge later developments on. For a thorough coverage of the area the reader will find the references [1], [3–5] and [7], useful.

It is of interest to note that maintenance studies were of extreme importance during the Second World War. Waddington [8] describes some of the work relating to aircraft maintenance and effectiveness. The problems discussed do not relate so much to the optimal maintenance procedures, but to the effect of the number of flying hours on maintenance requirements, and hence on the eventual hours available for flying. Thus, increasing the hours flying over one interval increases the time out of action in the next interval due to maintenance requirements. There is therefore a maximal flying hours level achievable (see Exercise 2). Just as much as queueing and inventory have been shown to be related (see Inventory Exercise 8), the same applies to maintenance vis-à-vis. these two areas.

We will begin with a simple analytic model. The following model is a simple one to reflect the costs of minor and major repairs and of routine maintenance (inspections plus minor adjustments, lubrication, etc.) and its influence on the frequency of major breakdowns for a single piece of equipment.

We make the following assumptions:

(i) the routine maintenance policy is to carry out x inspections (and minor repairs, adjustments, etc.) per unit time;

(ii) the average time required in such activities is $1/m$, per inspection, etc.;

(iii) major repair requirements arise at a rate $\lambda(x)$ per unit time, on average, dependent on x;

(iv) the average time for such a major repair is $1/\mu$, independent of x (a more general model would make μ depend on x);

(v) the routine maintenance cost is M per unit time on average (a more general model would make the cost consist of a fixed cost per inspection (plus minor repairs, etc.), plus a cost per unit time);

(vi) the major repair cost is on average R (a more general model would make R depend on x) per unit time;

(vii) when operating, the equipment produces a product which has a profit

value of V per unit time (this aspect may also be made more general);
(viii) the problem is to choose x to maximize the net revenue per unit time (product output value – maintenance costs – repairs costs (major)), denoted by $f(x)$.

We calculate $f(x)$ as follows. The average time lost per unit time due to major repairs is equal to

(the average number of major repairs per unit time)(the average major repair time) $= \lambda(x)/\mu$.

The average time lost per unit time due to routine maintenance is equal to

(the frequency of routine maintenance)(the average routine maintenance time) $= x/m$.

Hence, since the average proportion of time in a time unit during which the equipment is operating is

$$(1 - \lambda(x)/\mu - x/m)$$

we see that the average revenue per unit time is

$$(1 - \lambda(x)/\mu - x/m)V.$$

Let us now look at the costs. The average major repair cost per unit time is

(the average number of major repairs per unit time)(the average major repair time)(the average major repair cost per unit time)

i.e.

$$(\lambda(x)/\mu)R.$$

The average minor repair cost per unit time is

(the average number of routine maintenance operations per unit time)(the average routine maintenance operation time)(the average routine maintenance cost per unit time)

i.e.

$$(x/m)M.$$

Combining these, we obtain:

$$f(x) = V - \lambda(x)(V+R)/\mu - x(V+M)/m.$$

From this we have

$$f'(x) = -\lambda'(x)(V+R)/\mu - (V+M)/m$$
$$f''(x) = -\lambda''(x)(V+R)/\mu.$$

If $\lambda(x)$ is convex $(\lambda''(x) \geq 0)$ and decreasing in $x(\lambda'(x) < 0)$, then the optimal x is given by:

$$\lambda'(x) = -\left(\frac{\mu}{m}\right)\frac{(V+M)}{(V+R)}$$

providing this has a solution.

If $\lambda'(x) < -(\mu/m)[(V+M)/(V+R)]$ for all x, then $f'(x) > 0$ for all x and the optimal solution is to make x as large as possible.

If $\lambda'(x) > -(\mu/m)[(V+M)/(V+R)]$ for all x, then $f'(x) < 0$ for all x and the optimal solution is to make x as small as possible.

Let us consider a special case:

$$\lambda(x) = \lambda/x.$$

Then

$$f''(x) \geqslant 0$$

and

$$f'(x) = 0 \rightleftarrows x = \sqrt{\left(\left(\frac{\lambda m}{\mu}\right)\left(\frac{V+R}{V+M}\right)\right)}$$

which gives the optimal solution.

This problem is a very simple one in concept. It is easily generalizable to the case when we have more than one machine to be serviced, in which case the machines are not serviced until the maintenance crew is free to do so. This may, in some circumstances, be tackled by using the queueing results of section 2.1 (see Queueing Exercise 1(iv)). Exercise 1 for this section gives an obvious extension of the simple model.

This model is an analytic model, but usually such models are not really possible and numerical optimization or simulation models are used. Let us illustrate this with a simple inspection decision problem which is a variant of the initial model. In that model the inspections and minor operations were carried out regularly and no information was used to determine exactly what actions to carry out and when the next inspection should take place, subject, of course, to action when a breakdown occurs. Let us modify this as follows. We make the following assumptions, based on White [9]:

(i) there is a single machine whose state at any time (of degradation) is described by some indicator y;

(ii) inspections may take place at the beginning of each of a succession of K unit intervals, at a cost a;

(iii) the actions allowed at such times are either to do nothing or to restore the machine to its best state $y = 0$;

(iv) in the event of a major breakdown, state $y = y^0$, the system is restored to state $y = 0$ in the interval in which it occurs;

(v) the cost of any maintenance action in (iii), (iv) is $c(y)$;

(vi) if the machine is in state y immediately after any action taken at the beginning of an interval, and is in state z, l intervals later, with no intermediate actions taking place, there is an expected total net income $r^l(y, z)$;

(vii) if the machine is inspected and found to be in state y, with no further action unless needed for a major breakdown, the probability that it will be in state z, l intervals later, is $p^l(y, z)$;

(viii) the machine begins in state $y = 0$ with k intervals to go, and it is required to find an inspection–maintenance policy which will maximize the expected discounted net income over the K intervals, where $\alpha \leq 1$ is the discount factor.

We may now formulate the problem as a dynamic programming problem in much the same way as we have done with the previous problems, defining $f_k(y)$ to be the minimal expected discounted cost over the next k intervals given that the machine has just been inspected and found to be in state y.

$1 \leq k \leq K$
$\overline{\quad y \neq 0}$

$$
f_k(y) = \max \begin{bmatrix} \text{I} & -a - c(y) + f_k(0) \\[2ex] \text{II} & \max_{1 \leq m \leq k} \left[\sum_{l=1}^{m} \alpha^l p^l(y, y^0)(r^l(y, y^0) - c(y^0) + f_{m-l}(0)) \right. \\[2ex] & \left. \quad + \sum_{z \neq y^0} \alpha^m p^m(y, z)(f_{k-m}(z) - a)) \right] \\[2ex] \text{III} & \sum_{l=1}^{k} \alpha^l p^l(y, y^0)(r^l(y, y^0) - c(y^0) + f_{k-l}(0)) \end{bmatrix}
$$

I caters for the decision to restore the machine to state 0;

II caters for the decision to inspect again m intervals later, providing a major breakdown has not occurred;

III caters for the decision not to inspect again unless a major breakdown occurs at some time.

$1 \leq k \leq K$
$\overline{\quad y = 0}$ As for the above, but omitting I.

$\overline{k = 0}$

$$f_0(y) = 0 \quad \text{for all } y.$$

We wish to find $f_K(0)$, and the corresponding decision rules $\{m = \theta_k(y)\}$ to determine m for each y and k. The calculations work backwards from $f_0(y) = 0$, for all y, to $f_K(0)$.

The infinite horizon case may be treated likewise, replacing $f_k(y)$ by $f(y)$, providing, for example, all the costs are bounded and $\alpha < 1$.

It is also possible to formulate this as a mathematical programming problem as we did, for example, for the invertory problem, but, as with that problem, to no real advantage, unless, as with the earlier material of this chapter, we move away from simple expectation optimization.

A little later on we will look at problem formulation, in Chapter 4, and examine the interactions between different sorts of decision. In particular we will examine the interactions between maintenance and replacement, since a proper balance between the two is essential. A probabilistic model is to be found in Hastings [2]. For our purposes we will content ourselves with a simple deterministic problem. Returning to our initial problem, let us now assume that the major breakdown rate is a function of the age t of the equipment as well as a function of the inspection frequency x. Let us also assume that we may now also consider when to replace the equipment and let y be the replacement period. Then $f(x)$ is replaced by $f(x, y)$, the average return per year if the inspection frequency is x and the replacement interval is y. If p is the purchase price of a new piece of equipment and $s(y)$ is the trade-in value of a piece of equipment of age y, $f(x, y)$ is given by:

$$f(x, y) = \sum_{t=1}^{y} (r(x, t) - p + s(y))/y$$

$$r(x, t) = V - \lambda(x, t)(V + R)/\mu - x(V + M)/m$$

and

$\lambda(x, t)$ is the breakdown rate in year t for a given inspection frequency x.

If we discount, instead of taking average annual returns, $f(x, y)$ becomes instead

$$f(x, y) = \left(\sum_{t=1}^{y} \alpha^{t-1} r(x, t) + \alpha^y (s(y) - p) \right) \Big/ (1 - \alpha^y).$$

2.4 DEFECTIVE PRODUCT

In this section we will deal with a class of problems in which decisions about products have to be made in the light of the fact that actual production runs may contain products defective in some way. The only text is that of Gollers *et al.* [3], although various applications appear in the journals and we will discuss a few.

The basic conflict is one of making due allowance for the possibility of defective items, but in such a way that the overall costs, involving the allowances and eventual rejection, are acceptable or optimal.

Let us begin with the classical machine setting problem. The following problem is taken from Donaldson *et al.* [2].

A piece of equipment is used to manufacture an item to a size within a given tolerance range. Thus the size, s, must satisfy $s_0 - \delta \leqslant s \leqslant s_0 + \delta$, where δ is the tolerance range, and s_0 is the centre of the range. It is known that, approximately, the probability distribution of finished size is Normal with

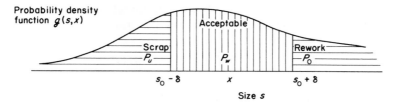

Figure 2.7

mean x and variance σ^2. σ^2 is fixed but x can be chosen at will. It costs c to produce an item initially. If the item is above size, it can be reduced to a size within the tolerance range, at a cost a, with no further risk of being undersize. If the item is below size, it is scrapped, and the production process commenced again. Two problems may be recognized:

(1) the problem of determining x to ensure that the probability of an undersize item on the first production operation is at a specified level α;
(2) the problem of determining x to minimize the expected cost of eventually producing the required item within the tolerance range.

This problem has some similarity to the depth charge problem of Chapter 1.

Let us first of all look at the general problem where $g(s, x)$ is the probability density function of size s given the expected size x. Figure 2.7 will help the analysis.

We allow s to range from $-\infty$ to ∞, although the probabilities will be zero for much of this range.

The probability that an item will be undersize, and scrapped, is:

$$P_u = \int_{s=-\infty}^{s_0-\delta} g(s, x)\, ds.$$

The probability that an item will be oversize, and reworked, is:

$$P_0 = \int_{s=s_0+\delta}^{\infty} g(s, x)\, ds.$$

The probability that an item will be within size is:

$$P_w = \int_{s=s_0-\delta}^{s_0+\delta} g(s, x)\, ds.$$

Problem (1) is solved by finding x to satisfy:

$$P_u = \alpha.$$

For problem (2), we let $f(x)$ be the expected cost of eventually producing the item within the specified tolerance range if the expected size is x. Then:

$$f(x) = c + aP_0 + P_u f(x)$$

each term corresponding, respectively, to the initial cost, the expected cost arising from the item being oversize on the first run, and the expected cost arising from having to do the operation again.

Assuming that $P_u \neq 1$, we then have:

$$f(x) = (c + aP_o)/(1 - P_u)$$

and x is to be chosen to minimize $f(x)$.

For the Normal probability density function, we have:

$$g(s, x) = \frac{1}{\sqrt{(2\pi)}\sigma} e^{-(s-x)^2/2\sigma^2}$$

$$P_u = \int_{s=-\infty}^{s_0-\delta} \frac{1}{\sqrt{(2\pi)}\sigma} e^{-(s-x)^2/2\sigma^2} \, ds.$$

Letting $t = (s - x)/\sigma$, we have

$$P_u = \frac{1}{\sqrt{(2\pi)}} \int_{t=-\infty}^{(s_0-\delta-x)/\sigma} e^{-t^2/2} \, dt = \Phi((s_0 - \delta - x)/\sigma)$$

where Φ is the cumulative probability function for the standard Normal distribution with variance 1 and expectation 0.

Similarly:

$$P_o = \frac{1}{\sqrt{(2\pi)}} \int_{t=(s_0+\delta-x)/\sigma}^{\infty} e^{-t^2/2} \, dt = 1 - \Phi((s_0 + \delta - x)/\sigma)$$

$$P_w = \frac{1}{\sqrt{(2\pi)}} \int_{t=(s_0-\delta-x)/\sigma}^{(s_0+\delta-x)/\sigma} e^{-t^2/2} \, dt = 1 - P_u - P_o$$

$$= \Phi((s_0 + \delta - x)/\sigma) - \Phi((s_0 - \delta - x)/\sigma).$$

For the case $s_0 = 1$, $\delta = 0.1$, $\sigma^2 = 0.01$, $\alpha = 0.05$, $c = 2$, $a = 1$, we have, for problem (1):

$$\Phi(9 - 10x) = 0.05.$$

For problem (2) we have:

$$f(x) = (3 - \Phi(11 - 10x))/(1 - \Phi(9 - 10x)).$$

Table 2.2 gives some values for $\Phi(t)$, for specified t values.

Table 2.2

t	-1.65	-1.5	-1.4	-1.3	-1.0	-0.5	-0.25	0.0	0.25	0.5	0.6	0.7
$\Phi(t)$	0.05	0.067	0.081	0.097	0.16	0.31	0.40	0.50	0.60	0.69	0.73	0.76

Problem (1) is solved directly by:

$$x^* = (9 - \Phi^{-1}(0.05))/10 = 1.065.$$

Problem (2) is solved by trial and error, interpolating values of $\Phi(11-10x)$, $\Phi(9-10x)$ from Table 2.2. The approximate optimal solution is $x^* = 1.04$, $f(x^*) = 2.47$.

Let us now consider the following problem, based on White [9, 10], known as the production overage problem.

A manufacturer produces special items, from time to time, for special customers (e.g. special sheet sizes for shipyards, etc.) The cost of organizing and setting up for production is quite heavy. If, at the end of the production run, the number of items which are satisfactory is below the requirement, then the process has to be set up again to provide the deficit. This procedure is repeated until the required number of good items, at least, is obtained. Any excess good items are assume to have no value and are scrapped. It is required to determine a production policy (decision rule) which enables us to determine at any stage, once the deficit to date is known, how many items to produce in order to minimize the expected sum of production and set up costs.

Let the initial order be for Y items. At any stage (end of production run) the outstanding number of good items to be produced may take any value, y, $0 \leqslant y \leqslant Y$. A decision rule, $\theta(y)$ will specify how many items, n, to produce, for a given outstanding quantity y.

For each decision rule, $\theta(y)$, the expected cost of eventually producing the outstanding quantity, y, depends only on the rule $\theta(y)$ and y. Let the expected cost be:

$$f(y).$$

We have:

$$f(0) = 0.$$

We suppress the rule $\theta(y)$ but note that cost depends on $\theta(y)$. Let:

a be the set up cost for any production run;
c be the extra cost per unit in the production run;
$p(n, s)$ be the probability that if the production run is n units long, s units will be good (acceptable).

Let us suppose we have y outstanding items to produce for a customer, and put in n items into the production run. The initial cost is:

$$a + nc$$
$$n = \theta(y).$$

Let us suppose that s good items will be produced. This occurs with probability $p(n, s)$. The outstanding number of items to be produced for the customer at the end of the run is $(y - s)$. The expected cost of using the decision rule, $\theta(y)$, to satisfy this outstanding requirement is, by definition:

$$f(y - s).$$

Since this occurs with probability $p(n, s)$ $(n = \theta(y))$ we then obtain, by summing over all possible values of s:

$$f(y) = a + \theta(y)c + \sum_{s=0}^{\theta(y)} p(\theta(y), s)f(y-s), \qquad 1 \leq y \leq Y.$$

When $s = 0$, we obtain $p(\theta(y), 0)f(y)$ on the right-hand side, and taking it on to the left-hand side we obtain:

$$f(y) = (a + \theta(y)c + \sum_{s=1}^{\theta(y)} p(\theta(y), s)f(y-s))/(1 - p(\theta(y), 0)), \qquad 1 \leq y \leq Y,$$

assuming that $p(\theta(y), 0) \neq 1$. We also have $f(y-s) = 0$ if $y \leq s$.

We calculate $f(0)$ $(= 0)$, $f(1)$, $f(2), \ldots$, and finally $f(y)$, working backwards.

Consider the following example.

Let $Y = 2$, $a = c = 1$, and $p(n, s)$ $(n \leq 5)$ be given as in Table 2.3. Consider

Table 2.3

		1	2	s 3	4	5
$p(n, s)$	1	0.70	0.30	0.00	0.00	0.00	0.00
	2	0.40	0.30	0.30	0.00	0.00	0.00
	3	0.30	0.30	0.20	0.20	0.00	0.00
n	4	0.20	0.20	0.20	0.20	0.20	0.00
	5	0.10	0.20	0.20	0.20	0.20	0.10

the following decision rule $\theta(y)$:

y	1	2
$\theta(y)$	4	5

Then, for this decision rule:

$$f(1) = \frac{a + \theta(1)c}{1 - p(\theta(1), 0)} = \frac{1+4}{1-0.2} = 6.25$$

$$f(2) = \frac{a + \theta(2)c + p(\theta(2), 1)f(1)}{1 - p(\theta(2), 0)} = \frac{1+5+0.2 \times 6.25}{1-0.1} = 8.05.$$

There are several approaches to solving this problem. Although we have not used them, each of these approaches is relevant to some of the queueing, inventory and maintenance dynamic problems discussed earlier on. We merely use this particular problem class to make the points. Later on we will return to them when we consider a qualitative comparison of techniques.

Explicit Enumeration of Decision Rules and Solving Using the Equation

This has already been discussed. However, there are a large number of decision rules which might be used. If we assume that $\theta(y) \geqslant y$, for all y, then if we limit $\theta(y)$ to 2y at most (so that $2y \geqslant \theta(y) \geqslant y$), the number of decision rules is $\prod_{y=1}^{Y}(y+1)$, since for each y, we have $(y+1)$ choices. The number of decision rules can be quite large. We will return to this later on.

Explicit Enumeration of Decision Rules and Using Simulation to Evaluate $f(y)$

The number of decision rules can be quite large, as above. In addition the simulation time can be quite large since, for each decision rule, we will have to run many simulations to get a proper estimate of $f(y)$. We will return to this later on.

Dynamic Programming

If $\theta(y)$ is an optimal decision rule then our equations are true for this decision rule. Since we can choose n to be optimal, and for simplicity, restricting $n \geqslant y$, our equations become:

$$f(y) = \min_{n \geqslant y}\left[\left(a + nc + \sum_{s=1}^{n} p(n, s)f(y-s)\right)\bigg/(1-p(n, 0))\right], \qquad 1 \leqslant y \leqslant Y.$$

Using the example given we have:

$$f(1) = \min_{n \geqslant 1}[(1+n)/(1-p(n, 0))] = \min \begin{bmatrix} n = 1: & 2/0.3 = 6.7 \\ 2: & 3/0.6 = 5.0 \\ 3: & 4/0.7 = 5.7 \\ 4: & 5/0.8 = 6.3 \\ 5: & 6/0.8 = 6.7 \end{bmatrix} = 5.0, \qquad \theta(1) = 2.$$

$$f(2) = \min_{n \geqslant 2}[(1+n+p(n, 1)f(1))/(1-p(n, 0))]$$

$$= \min \begin{bmatrix} n = 2: & 4.5/0.6 = 7\frac{1}{2} \\ 3: & 5.5/0.7 = 7\frac{6}{7} \\ 4: & 6/0.8 = 7\frac{1}{2} \\ 5: & 7/0.9 = 7\frac{7}{9} \end{bmatrix} = 7\frac{1}{2}$$

$$\theta(2) = 2 \text{ or } 4.$$

Mathematical Programming

This method proceeds by identifying specific decision variables $x_1, x_2, \ldots, x_y, \ldots, x_Y$, and formulating the problem rather like a linear program, but with non-linearities.

Let $x_1, x_2, \ldots, x_y, \ldots, x_Y$ be the production run lengths when the outstanding quantities are $1, 2, \ldots, y, \ldots, Y$, respectively, and $v_1, v_2, \ldots, v_y, \ldots, v_Y$ be the expected costs for outstanding quantities $1, 2, \ldots, y, \ldots, Y$ respectively, using the above decisions. We then have the constraints, assuming $x_y \geqslant y$, all y:

$$x_y \text{ integer}, \quad y = 1, 2, \ldots, Y$$

$$x_y \geqslant y, \qquad y = 1, 2, \ldots, Y$$

$$v_1 = (a + x_1 c)/(1 - p(x_1, 0))$$

$$v_2 = (a + x_2 c + p(x_2, 1)y_1)/(1 - p(x_2, 0))$$

$$\vdots$$

$$v_y = \left(a + x_y c + \sum_{s=1}^{x_y} p(x, s) v_{x_y - s} \right) \Big/ (1 - p(x_y, 0))$$

$$\vdots$$

$$v_Y = \left(a + x_Y c + \sum_{s=1}^{x_Y} p(x, s) v_{x_Y - s} \right) \Big/ (1 - p(x_Y, 0))$$

$$v_y = 0 \quad \text{if} \quad y \leqslant 0.$$

The problem is to choose $x_1, x_2, \ldots, x_y, \ldots, x_Y;\ v_1, v_2, \ldots, v_y, \ldots, v_Y$ to minimize $f(x, v) = v_Y$, subject to the specified constraints.

In general this is quite a complex problem to solve without, effectively, recognizing the structure in the dynamic programming formulation. Indeed, the calculations are identical. Note also that $\{x_y\}$, $1 \leqslant y \leqslant Y$, in effect, specifies a decision rule $\theta(y)$ and the mathematical programming formulation allows all decision rules to be incorporated, as does the equivalent dynamic programming formulation. As with earlier material in this chapter, the linear programming approach has no value as long as we have the simple expected total cost objective function. If, however, we separate out the contributions to this as separate objectives, and wish to use efficient solution ideas (see Chapter 4), the matter is somewhat different, as it is with other formulations (e.g. setting probability levels for certain contingencies).

2.5 MATHEMATICAL AND DYNAMIC PROGRAMMING

The four techniques discussed so far have been referred to as problem characterization techniques, because they deal with approaches to classes of physical problems. In treating these we have also used some of the solution method techniques, viz. mathematical programming and dynamic programming. These latter techniques are more widely applicable than just to the problems discussed and we will now spend some time looking at them from the modelling point of view. This will be a limited exercise and, for information on the modelling, algorithmic, and applications side of these topics, the following references are a useful sample of the many available, viz. Williams [67–69], Dantzig [8], Hadley [29], Vajda [56], Geoffrion [21], [22] Shapiro [52], Zangwill [70], Hu [34], Garfinkel *et al.* [20], Lasdon, *et al.* [38], Bellman [2], Nemhauser [48], White [61, 62], Howard [33], Norman [49], Bertelè *et al.* [5], Ellis *et al.* [13], Hammer [31], Fabozzi *et al.* [15], McClure *et al.* [43], Morris [47] Dreyfus *et al.* [10], Cullinan-James *et al.* [7], Geoffrion *et al.* [23].

2.5.1 Mathematical Programming

Mathematical programmes take the following form:

$$\text{maximize (or minimize) } [f(x)]$$

$$\text{subject to } x \in X$$

where $X \subseteq \mathbb{R}^n$, and where we allow $n = \infty$, to cater for infinite streams of decisions $x = (x_1, x_2, \ldots, x_k, \ldots)$:

x is a potential decision to be taken
f is the objective function
X is the feasible-set of such decisions.

The usual way of specifying X is in terms of constraints on x which have to be satisfied. These constraints may assume the form of equalities or inequalities. In addition, the components of x may be continuous or they may be integer. Many integer problems allow the components to be only 0 or 1, and such problems are referred to as 0–1 problems, or bivalent problems, or as Boolean problems.

The constraints determining X will take the form:

$$g_i(x) \leqslant b_i \quad \text{or} \quad g_i(x) = b_i \quad \text{or} \quad g_i(x) \geqslant b_i$$

for specified sets of $\{i\}$.

These are all equivalent forms, and we leave this as an exercise.

The common form of mathematical programme is the linear programme. In this case f and $\{g_i\}$ are all linear in $x = (x_1 \ldots x_n)$, and $\{x_j\}$ are continuous variables. The minimization form is as follows:

$$\text{minimize } \left[f(x) = \sum_{j=1}^{n} c_j x_j \right]$$

subject to

$$\sum_j a_{ij} x_j \geqslant b_i, \qquad i = 1, 2, \ldots, p$$

$$x_j \geqslant 0 \quad \text{and continuous, for} \quad j = 1, 2, \ldots, n.$$

68

This is a standard form, but the inequalities can be ≤, or replaced by equalities.

We will consider a linear programme taken from Baligh *et al.* [1], to which we will return later on in Chapter 4. The reader should also refer back to the previous mathematical programming models, some of which are in linear form, but with integer variables.

Let us make the following assumptions for a hospital patient scheduling problem:

(i) there are n classes of patient, with $i = 1, 2, \ldots, n$, denoting patient class;
(ii) each class is divided into paying and non-paying patients;
(iii) each patient in class i requires r_{ij} units of service type j, $j = 1, 2, \ldots, m$;
(iv) each unit of service type j requires a_{kj} units of resource type k, $k = 1, 2, \ldots, l$;
(v) there are t_k units of resource type k available in a given time period;
(vi) there is an upper limit, u_i, on the number of patients in class i to be treated;
(vii) there is a lower limit, l_i, on the number of patients in class i to be treated;
(viii) there is a lower limit, v_i, on the proportion of non-paying patients to be treated, in each class i;
(ix) the paying patients pay p_j for each unit of service type j;
(x) there is a unit cost c_k for resource type k;
(xi) there are fixed costs and subsidies a,b respectively;
(xii) there is a minimal profit level e;
(xiii) there is a weighting factor w_i for each class of patient i, reflecting the importance of this class of patient to the hospital;
(xiv) the objective is to maximize the weighted sum of all the patients treated, subject to the specified constraints.

The problem is formulated as a linear programme as follows.

Decision Variables

Let:

x_i be the number of paying patients to be treated in class i
y_i be the number of non-paying patients treated in class i.

We have specified a standard linear programme as one in which the decision variables are continuous. Clearly we cannot have 0.5 of a patient. However, we are usually dealing with large numbers of patients, and the treatment of x_i and y_i as continuous will usually give us a perfectly acceptable approximation, when rounded up or down to the solution we seek. In cases when x_i, or y_i, is 0 or 1, the situation is fundamentally different.

Constraints

We will identify them with the sequence of assumptions:

(v) $\sum_{i=1}^{n}\sum_{j=1}^{m} r_{ij}a_{kj}(x_i + y_i) \leq t_k,\ k = 1, 2, \ldots, l;$
(vi) $x_i + y_i \leq u_i,\ i = 1, 2, \ldots, n;$
(vii) $x_i + y_i \geq l_i,\ i = 1, 2, \ldots, n;$
(viii) $(1 - v_i)y_i - v_i x_i \geq 0,\ i = 1, 2, \ldots, n$ (from $y_i \geq v_i(x_i + y_i)$);

$$(\text{xii}) \sum_{i=1}^{n}\left(\sum_{j=1}^{m} r_{ij}p_j - \sum_{j=1}^{m}\sum_{k=1}^{l} r_{ij}a_{kj}c_k\right)x_i - \sum_{i=1}^{n}\left(\sum_{j=1}^{m}\sum_{k=1}^{l} r_{ij}a_{kj}c_k\right)y_i + b - a \geq e.$$

We add the non-negativity constraints:

$$x_i \geq 0, \qquad i = 1, 2, \ldots, n$$
$$y_i \geq 0, \qquad i = 1, 2, \ldots, n.$$

Objective Function

$$f(x, y) = \sum_{i=1}^{n} w_i(x_i + y_i).$$

The problem is to maximize $f(x, y)$ subject to the stipulated constraints.

For the above problem, it is relatively easy to identify the decision variables. For other problems this is not so. The following problem is typical of a whole range of problems where decisions are identified with combinations of things which may be simultaneously achieved. The following is based on Gilmore *et al.* [24, 25].

We make the following assumptions:

(i) material is stocked in lengths of 136″;
(ii) the demand is for material of lengths 48″, 35″, 31″ only;
(iii) the number of pieces of length 48″, 35″ and 31″ demanded are, respectively 1000, 1800, and 1200;
(iv) each raw material length may be cut into combinations of the required length, with any residual being scrapped;
(v) it is required to supply the demands using a minimal total amount of material.

Before formulating the problem we list the combinations of length available from the raw material whose residual pieces have length less than 31″, since there is no advantage in having residuals of greater than or equal lengths in the formulation. These are given in Table 2.4.

Let:

a_{ij} be the number of times length i occurs in combination j, $j = 1, 2, \ldots, n$

b_i be the number of pieces of length i required, $i = 1, 2, \ldots, m$

$\{a_{ij}\}$, $\{b_i\}$ are given in Table 2.4, with $n = 9$, $m = 3$.

Table 2.4

		Cutting combinations j								Peices
Length	1	2	3	4	5	6	7	8	9	demanded
48″	2	2	1	1	1	0	0	0	0	1000
i 35″	1	0	2	1	0	3	2	1	0	1800
31″	0	1	0	1	2	1	2	3	4	1200
Residual	5	9	18	22	26	0	4	8	12	

Decisions

Let x_j be the number of times combination j is used, $j = 1, 2, \ldots, n$. x_j is an integer, but again, if x_j is reasonably large, it may be treated as a continuous variable, and rounded off.

Constraints

$$\sum_{j=1}^{n} a_{ij}x_j \geq b_i, \qquad i = 1, 2, \ldots, m$$

$$x_j \geq 0, \qquad j = 1, 2, \ldots, n.$$

Objective function

$$f(x) = 136 \sum_{j=1}^{n} x_j.$$

The problem is to minimize $f(x)$ subject to the specified constraints.

Hinxman [32] gives a survey of trim loss type problems of this kind, and assortment problems, and Eisemann [12] discusses a two-machine trim problem. The cutting-stock problem is also related to covering and partition problems in which all the a_{ij} are 0 or 1, and $a_{ij} = 1$ means that item i is included in column j, e.g. if j corresponds to a bus route, and i corresponds to a location, then $a_{ij} = 1$ means that location i is on bus route j. In this case we may be seeking a set of routes, which, between them, cover all the locations, in some optimal way (see, for example, Garfinkel *et al.* [90]).

A further class of problems susceptible to a mathematical programming formulation are the routing problems. The travelling salesman problems form a subclass of these and are of the following form, viz. a travelling salesman is required to visit m towns, exactly once and return to his starting point. How should he sequence his visits to minimize the total distance travelled? It is assumed that he may start anywhere and we may as well assume it is town 1. One formulation is as follows, where d_{rs} is the distance between town r and town s.

Decisions

Let x_j be the number of the town which is in position j in the sequence, $j = 1, 2, \ldots, m+1$.

Constraints

$x_{m+1} = x_1 = 1$

$(x_i - x_j)^2 \geqslant 1,$ $i \neq j, i, \quad j = 1, 2, \ldots, m+1$ (forces different towns to different positions)

$1 \leqslant x_i \leqslant m,$ $i = 1, 2, \ldots, m+1$, and integer.

Objective Function

$$f(x) = \sum_{j=1}^{m} d_{x_j x_{j+1}}.$$

The problem is to minimize $f(x)$ subject to the specified constraints.

If x_j is the position of the jth town, adding town $j = m+1 \equiv 1$, we may express $f(x)$ in the form:

$$f(x) = \sum_{i=1}^{m} \sum_{\substack{j=1 \\ j \neq i}}^{m+1} d_{ij} \gamma(x_j - x_i)$$

where

$$\gamma(z) = 0 \quad \text{if} \quad z \neq 1 \text{ or } m-1$$
$$= 1 \quad \text{if} \quad z = 1 \text{ or } m-1.$$

The constraints become

$$1 \leqslant x_j \leqslant m+1, \quad j = 1, 2, \ldots, m+1$$
$$(x_i - x_j)^2 \geqslant 1, \quad i \neq j, \quad i, j = 1, 2, \ldots, m+1$$
$$x_1 = 1, \quad x_{m+1} = m+1$$
$$d_{im+1} = d_{i1}, \quad 1 = 2, 3, \ldots, m.$$

Alternatively, we can replace $f(x)$ by:

$$f(x, z) = \sum_{i=1}^{m} \sum_{\substack{j=1 \\ j \neq i}}^{m+1} d_{ij} z_{ij}$$

and add the constraints

$$z_{ij} \geqslant 1 - (1 + (x_i - x_j))^2, \quad i = 1, 2, \ldots, m, \quad j = 1, 2, \ldots, m+1, \quad j \neq i$$
$$z_{ij} \geqslant 0 \quad i = 1, 2, \ldots, m, \quad j = 1, 2, \ldots, m+1, \quad j \neq i.$$

If $x_j \neq x_i + 1$, then z_{ij} assumes a minimal value of 0. If $x_j = x_i + 1$, z_{ij} assumes a minimal value of 1.

72

An alternative formulation is given in Wagner [58] (see also Miller *et al.* [46] for mathematical programming formulations, and Bellmore *et al.* [3] for a survey).

Decisions

Let:

$$x_{ij} = 1 \text{ if town } j \text{ immediately follows town } i$$
$$= 0 \text{ otherwise.}$$

Constraints

$$\sum_{\substack{j=1 \\ j \neq i}}^{m} x_{ij} = 1, \qquad i = 1, 2, \ldots, m$$

$$\sum_{\substack{i=1 \\ i \neq j}}^{m} x_{ij} = 1, \qquad j = 1, 2, \ldots, m$$

$$u_i - u_j + m x_{ij} \leq m - 1, \qquad 2 \leq i, j \leq m$$
$$x_{ij} = 0 \text{ or } 1, \qquad 1 \leq i, j \leq m, \quad u_i, u_j \text{ unsigned.}$$

Objective Function

$$f(x) = \sum_{i=1}^{m} \sum_{j=1}^{m} d_{ij} x_{ij}.$$

This formulation has the advantage of being in linear form.

The problem is to minimize $f(x)$ subject to the specified constraints. The purpose of the $\{u_i, u_j, x_{ij}\}$ inequalities is to ensure that no cycles exist other than the one containing all towns. The fact that a cycle cannot occur is demonstrated as follows. Suppose, by renumbering if necessary, we have a cycle $2 \to 3 \to 4 \to k \to 2$ (we might have $k = 2$, or $3, \ldots$ of course). Then we have:

$$u_2 - u_3 + m \leq m - 1$$
$$u_3 - u_4 + m \leq m - 1$$
$$\vdots$$
$$u_{k-1} - u_k + m \leq m - 1$$
$$u_k - u_2 + m \leq m - 1.$$

Adding these we obtain:

$$(k-1)m \leq (k-1)(m-1), \quad \text{therefore} \quad k \leq 1.$$

Hence we can have no cycle containing 2. Nor can we have a cycle excluding 2 since this implies we also have a cycle including 2.

We still have to prove that every feasible route may be realized by appropriate $\{u_i, x_{ij}\}$. Let $u_2 = u$, $u_i = i - 2 + u$, $i \geq 2$. Then, if $x_{ij} = 1$, $i, j \neq 1$, we require $u_i - u_j + m \leq m - 1$, i.e. $u_i - u_j \leq -1$, which is true since $u_i - u_j = -1$. If $x_{ij} = 0$, $i, j \neq 1$, we require $u_i - u_j \leq m - 1$, and this is satisfied since $u_i - u_j = i - j \leq m - 1$.

Note that some sequencing problems may be formulated as travelling salesman problems. Thus, if we have n jobs and the cost of following job i by job j is d_{ij}, and we wish to sequence the jobs to minimize the total costs, we merely add dummy job $n + 1$, with $d_{n+1j} = d_{jn+1} = 0$, and the problem becomes a travelling salesman problem (see Day et al. [9] for a review of sequencing research).

A further class of problems to which mathematical programming has been applied is that of location–allocation problems. Halpern [30] provides a very good coverage of a range of such problems. See also Francis et al. [17, 18], Elshafei et al. [14], Golden et al. [28], Lea [39] and Kraemer [36].

As a point of historical interest, Bishop Absalon used a location approach to locate the city of Copenhagen (see Krarup et al. [37]).

The following problem is taken from this (see Benito-Alonso et al. [4]). the following assumptions are made:

(i)   a region is divided into n different regions, $i = 1, 2, \ldots, n$;
(ii)   nurseries are to be established in some of the regions;
(iii) if a nursery is established in region i, there are upper and lower limits to its size, viz. u, l respectively;
(iv) there is a fixed cost, a, for building a nursery of size l;
(v)   there is an additional cost c for every place provided above the minimal size l;
(vi) there is a distance factor d_{ij} associated with allocating a child from region i to a nursery in region j;
(vii) there is a weighting factor, w_i, for each child in region i for whom a nursery place is not available;
(viii) the demand for places in region i is a_i;
(ix) there are three objectives, viz.
      $f^1 =$ total distance associated with a specific location–allocation plan;
      $f^2 =$ the total cost associated with a specific location–allocation plan;
      $f^3 =$ the total weighted deficit of all children for whom a place is not available associated with a specific location–allocation plan.

We return to this later when we consider multi-objective problems. Let us now formulate the problem as a mixed integer-continuous variable mathematical programme, again noting that one of the decision variables is really integer (viz. number of children), but may be treated as a continuous variable for approximation purposes.

74

Decisions

Let:

x_{ij} be the number of children in region i allocated to a nursery in region j

$x_j = 1$ if a nursery is built in region j

$ = 0$ otherwise

y_i be the unmet demand in region i

s_j be the additional places provided above the minimal size of nursery in region j.

Constraints

$$\sum_{j=1}^{n} x_{ij} + y_i = a_i, \qquad i = 1, 2, \ldots, n$$

$$\sum_{i=1}^{n} x_{ij} = lx_j + s_j, \qquad j = 1, 2, \ldots, n$$

$$s_j \leqslant x_j(u - l) \qquad j = 1, 2, \ldots, n$$

$$x_j = 0 \text{ or } 1, \qquad x_{ij} \geqslant 0, \qquad s_j \geqslant 0, \qquad y_i \geqslant 0, \qquad i, j = 1, 2, \ldots, n.$$

Objective Functions

$$f^1(x) = \sum_{i=1}^{n} \sum_{j=1}^{n} d_{ij} x_{ij}$$

$$f^2(x) = a \sum_{j=1}^{n} x_j + c \sum_{j=1}^{n} s_j$$

$$f^3(x) = \sum_{i=1}^{n} w_i y_i.$$

It is possible to minimize $f^1(x)$, $f^2(x)$, or $f^3(x)$ subject to the constraints, but some compromise is usually required. We will return to this later on in Chapter 4.

The standard location–allocation problem is the Weber problem (see Weber [60]). The assumptions are as follows:

  (i) there are m demand points i for a product, $i = 1, 2, \ldots, m$;
 (ii) the annual demand at point i is s_i;
(iii) there are n possible points j for locating a supply centre, $j = 1, 2, \ldots, n$;
 (iv) the distance from demand point i to supply centre j is d_{ij};
  (v) it is required to locate l supply centres, with at most one centre at each point, and $l \leqslant n$;

(vi) the capacity at a supply centre is unlimited;

(vii) the objective is to minimize the total distance travelled, assuming that the distance travelled from supply point j to demand point i and back is proportional to $s_i d_{ij}$.

The formulation is as follows:

Decisions

Let:

$x_j = 1$ if a supply centre is located at j

$= 0$ otherwise

y_i be the contribution to the product-mileage by demand point i.

Constraints

$$\sum_{j=1}^{n} x_j = l$$

$$y_i \leqslant x_j s_i d_{ij} + (1 - x_j)M, \qquad i = 1, 2, \ldots, m, \qquad j = 1, 2, \ldots, n, \; M \text{ very large}$$

$$x_j = 0 \text{ or } 1, \qquad y \geqslant 0, \qquad i = 1, 2, \ldots, m, \qquad j = 1, 2, \ldots, n.$$

Objective Function

$$f(x, y) = \sum_{i=1}^{m} y_i.$$

$f(x, y)$ is to be maximized subject to the constraints.

Note that the objective in (vii) is to minimize the distance travelled, whereas $f(x, y)$ is to be maximized. The reason for this is that each demand point will be associated with its closest supply point, since capacity is unlimited. The inequalities for $\{y_i\}$ will achieve this providing y_i is effectively the maximum value consistent with these. With $x_j = 0$, no constraint effectively exists. With $x_j = 1$, the constraint is $y_i \leqslant s_i d_{ij}$.

It is possible to reformulate in terms of 0–1 variables, with $x_{ij} = 1$ if i is allocated to j, $x_{ij} = 0$ if not. We leave this to the reader.

Later on we will return to this problem in the form of an analogue problem in section 2.6.

Scheduling jobs on machines to meet specified requirements is also susceptible to mathematical programming. The following example is based on Manne [41] and White [66], and we restrict the problem to a single machine, although the approach is applicable to more than one machine. Our assumptions are as follows:

(i) there is a single machine;

(ii) there are n tasks to be performed;

(iii) task i cannot be performed simultaneously with any task in a specified set S_i;
(iv) task i must be completed before any tasks in a set T_i can be begun;
(v) task i has a due date d_i;
(vi) task i requires t_i time units to complete;
(vii) there is a penalty cost of p_i for task i per unit time after its due date of completion;
(viii) the objective is to schedule the tasks to minimize the total penalty cost.

The formulation is as follows.

Decisions

Let:

x_i be the time at which task i commences
$y_{ij} = 1$ if i and j cannot be performed simultaneously, and task i precedes task j, $i \in S_j \setminus T_j$
$= 0$ if tasks i and j cannot be performed simultaneously and task j precedes task i, $j \in S_i \setminus T_i$.
z_i be the delay in completing task i beyond its due date.

Constraints

$$(M + t_j)y_{ij} + (x_i - x_j) \geq t_j, \qquad i = 1, 2, \ldots, n, \qquad j \in S_i \setminus T_i$$
$$(M + t_i)(1 - y_{ij}) + (x_j - x_i) \geq t_i, \qquad i = 1, 2, \ldots, n, \qquad j \in S_i \setminus T_i$$

(M is a large number).

Note that if $y_{ij} = 1$, the first inequality is automatically satisfied, and the second ensures that j cannot begin before i has finished. Similarly we get the reverse if $y_{ij} = 0$.

$$y_{ij} + y_{ji} = 1, \qquad i = 1, 2, \ldots, n, \qquad j \in S_i \setminus T_i, \qquad i \notin T_j$$
$$t_i + x_i \leq x_j, \qquad i = 1, 2, \ldots, n, \qquad j \in T_i$$
$$z_i \geq t_i + x_i - d_i, \qquad i = 1, 2, \ldots, n$$
$$z_i \geq 0, \qquad x_i \geq 0, \qquad y_{ij} = 0, \text{ or } 1, \qquad i = 1, 2, \ldots, n, \qquad j \in S_i.$$

Objective Function

$$f(x, y, z) = \sum_{i=1}^{n} p_i z_i.$$

The problem is to minimize $f(x, y, z)$ subject to the specified constraints.

Note that z_i will take the value $t_i + x_i - d_i$, if this is non-negative, and value 0 if this is non-positive. It is also to be noted that for m machines a task can be identified with a particular operation on a given machine. An alternative formulation is given in Bowman [6].

2.5.2 Dynamic Programming

When discussing the various problem characterization techniques we have taken the opportunity of showing how dynamic programming may be used to formulate and solve these problems, where sequences of decisions are required over time. The Bellman principle of optimality was stated and used as the principal mechanism by which the models were constructed. It is to be noted that the use of this principle is also credited to Massé [42].

In this, brief, treatment of dynamic programming, we will treat a subset of problems which may be tackled by dynamic programming, in keeping with our modest aims, viz. those in which a sequence of decisions is made over time, and in which the total cost is the sum of the immediate costs of each decision, allowing for discounting if required. For a complete treatment of dynamic programming the readers should consult the texts referred to earlier on.

We begin with a simple framework, making the following assumptions:

(i) a system is operating over K time intervals;
(ii) at the beginning of each time interval it is in one of M states, designated by $y = 1, 2, \ldots, M$, with Y being the set of such states;
(iii) for each state $y \in Y$, a decision set $X_k(y)$ exists, from which the decision must be taken, at the beginning of interval k;
(iv) decisions are made at the beginning of each interval;
(v) if decision x is taken in state y, the state at the beginning of the next interval is z where $z = T_k(x, y)$ depends on y, x, and on the interval k concerned;
(vi) if decision x is taken in state y, there is an immediate cost $q_k(x, y)$;
(vii) there is a discount factor α, $0 \leqslant \alpha \leqslant 1$;
(viii) the objective is to determine which decisions to take to minimize the total discounted cost over K intervals, beginning in state y_K.

Figure 2.8 illustrates the subsequent development of the dynamic programming equation. The minimal discounted cost in the last k intervals, beginning in state y, is $f_k(y)$.

The immediate cost is $q_k(x, y)$, if decision x is chosen.

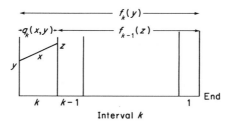

Figure 2.8

The state with $k-1$ periods left is z, and by definition, and using Bellman's principle of optimality, the minimal discounted cost over the last $k-1$ intervals is $f_{k-1}(z)$, which, when discounted back to the beginning of interval k, is $\alpha f_{k-1}(z)$.

For decision x the total discounted cost will be

$$q_k(x, y) + \alpha f_{k-1}(z).$$

Since x may be chosen freely in $X_k(y)$ we obtain:

$K \geqslant k \geqslant 1$

$$f_k(y) = \min_{x \in X_k(y)} [q_k(x, y) + \alpha f_{k-1}(z)]$$

$$z = T_k(x, y).$$

To complete the equation we need the boundary condition:

$$f_0(y) = 0, \quad \text{for all } y.$$

If y_K is the initial condition with k intervals to go, we need to find $f_K(y_K)$. We also need to find the decision rules which give the optimal x for each k, y, i.e. $\theta_k(y)$. To determine the optimal sequence of decisions we find:

$$x_K = \theta_K(y_K), \qquad x_{K-1} = \theta_{K-1}(y_{K-1}), \dots, x_k = \theta_k(y_k), \dots, x_1 = \theta_1(y_1)$$

where

$$y_{K-1} = T_K(x_K, y_K), \dots, y_k = T_{k+1}(x_{k+1}, y_{k+1}), \dots, y_1 = T_2(x_2, y_2).$$

The reader should compare this general formulation with the dynamic programming formulations already given. For the inventory problem with known, but varying, demands we have a slight variation in that the periods are numbered from the beginning rather than from the end, giving the equations (with $\alpha = 1$):

$K \geqslant k \geqslant 1$

$$f_k(y) = \min_{x \in X_k(y)} [q_k(x, y) + f_{k+1}(z)]$$

$$z = T_k(x, y)$$

$$f_{K+1}(y) = 0, \ \forall y.$$

In this case:

x is the amount purchased

y is the inventory level

$X_k(y) = \{x : x \geqslant s_k - y, x \geqslant 0\}$

$T_k(x, y) = y + x - s_k$

$q_k(x, y) = a\tau(x) + cx + h(y + x - \tfrac{1}{2}s_k).$

The simplest form of dynamic programme is the classical optimal route problem in which the problem is to get from some initial state to some prescribed final state, say y_0. For such problems:

$$q_k(x, y) = q(x, y) \geq 0, \quad \text{independent of } k$$
$$X_k(y) = Y \backslash \{y\} \text{ independent of } k$$
$$T_k(x, y) = x, \text{ independent of } k$$
$$\alpha = 1.$$

The equations become

$K \geq k > 1$

$$f_k(y) = \min_{x \neq y}[q(x, y) + f_{k-1}(x)], \quad \forall y$$

$$f_k(y_0) = 0$$
$$f_0(y) = 0 \quad \text{if} \quad y = y_0$$
$$\quad = \infty \quad \text{if} \quad y \neq y_0.$$

$f_k(y)$ has the physical interpretation of being the minimal cost in moving from y to y_0 in at most k moves. If we do not restrict the number of moves, and $f(y)$ is the minimal cost in getting from y to y_0 the equation is as follows:

$$f(y) = \min_{x \neq y}[q(x, y) + f(x)]$$

$$f(y_0) = 0.$$

There are some problems in which the system is described in terms of a single state, to which it returns after various time intervals, and the decisions relate to the choice of time intervals. A special case, to which we will return later on, is the capacity installation problem. (McDowell [44], White [61], Luss [40] and Freidenfolds [19], give a general coverage of capacity expansion problems.) We make the following assumptions:

(i) a company produces a product, the demand for which in year k from now is s_k, and is known, $k = 1, 2, \ldots, K$, s_k increasing in k;
(ii) at the beginning of interval 1, the existing capacity is 0;
(iii) the cost of putting in extra capacity $x > 0$ is $a + cx$, where a is a fixed cost, and c is the cost per unit of capacity put in;
(iv) decisions on installation of extra capacity are taken only at the end of a year in which capacity and demand are equal;
(v) there is a discount factor α, $0 \leq \alpha \leq 1$, for a yearly interval;
(vi) all installations are instantaneous;
(vii) the problem is to determine when, and how much capacity, to install to meet demand at a minimal total discounted cost over K intervals.

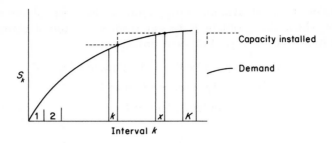

Figure 2.9

Figure 2.9 will serve as a basis to illustrate the development of the equations. In the figure, if demand is treated as continuous, demand and capacity may equalize at times other than the ends of a year; but to keep matters simple we assume this not to be so.

For this problem: the state y is always the same, viz. y_0, the existence of equal capacity and demand; the decision x is, equivalently, the interval up to the end of which the extra capacity installed will last;

$$X_k(y_0) = \{x : k < x \leqslant K\}$$
$$T_k(x, y_0) = y_0$$
$$q_k(x, y_0) = a + c(s_x - s_k).$$

We also note that $k+1$ is replaced by x in the basic equation, and a discount factor of α^{x-k} is needed.

If we replace $f_k(y_0)$ by simply f_k we obtain the following equations.

$K > k \geqslant 1$

$$f_k = \min_{K \geqslant x > k} [a + c(s_x - s_k) + \alpha^{x-k} f_x]$$
$$f_K = 0.$$

It is required to find f_0 and the decision rules to achieve this. The decisions depend only on k, since y is fixed.

This formulation is referred to as the forward formulation, since decisions are made moving forwards. The calculations are made backwards. It is possible to start at the other end and develop a backward formulation as follows. Figure 2.10 illustrates the development of the equation. In this case the decision x is the previous interval at the end of which the last installation, prior to that at the end of interval k, was made. f_k is then the minimal discounted cost, to time 0, up to the end of interval k, given demand and capacity are equal at the end of interval k.

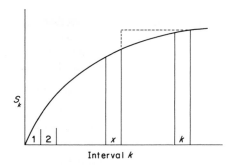

Figure 2.10

We also have:

$$X_k(y_0) = \{x : 0 \leqslant x < k\}$$
$$T_k(x, y_0) = y_0$$
$$q_k(x, y_0) = a + c(s_k - s_x).$$

The discount factor to be applied to the installation at the end of interval x is now α^x. We then have the following equations.

$\underline{0 \leqslant k \leqslant K}$

$$f_k = \min_{0 \leqslant x < k} [\alpha^x(a + c(s_k - s_x)) + f_x]$$

$$f_0 = 0.$$

It is required to find f_K and the decision rules to achieve this.

The calculations proceed forward, viz. $f_0, f_1, f_2, \ldots, f_k, \ldots, f_K$.

For the simple case $s_k = k$, $a = 1$, $c = 1$, $\alpha = 0.7$, $K = 7$ the solution to the backward formulation is as in Table 2.5 (the full calculations are given in Section 2.10 where they are used to illustrate an advantage of dynamic programming). The optimal solution is then $f_7 = 5.42$.

Table 2.5

k	0	1	2	3	4	5	6	7
f_k	0	2	3	3.98	4.47	4.95	5.19	5.42
$\theta_k (= x)$	–	0	0	2	2	4	4	6

$\theta_7 = 6$, $\theta_6 = 4$, $\theta_4 = 2$, $\theta_2 = 0$, i.e. installations cover intervals $(1, 2)$, $(4, 3)$, $(6, 5)$, (7).

We will return to this problem later on, in section 2.10 and in Chapter 3.

So far we have dealt with formulations in which no chance events arise. Let us now look at a formulation where chance vents arise. To do this let us turn back to our first simple equation. We modify this so that:

$q_k(x, y)$ is now the expected cost of the initial decision, given y, k;

z now has a probability $p_k(z; x, y)$, where we keep to discrete problems for simplicity of exposition (for non-discrete problems we replace $p_k(z; x, y)$ by a probability density function);

$T_k(x, y)$ no longer applies, since it is catered for by $p_k(z; x, y)$.

If $f_k(y)$ is now the minimal expected discounted cost over intervals k to K, beginning in state y, we obtain the following equations.

$\underline{K \geqslant k \geqslant 1}$

$$f_k(y) = \min_{x \in X_k(y)} \left[q_k(x, y) + \alpha \sum_z p_k(z; x, y) f_{k-1}(z) \right]$$

$$f_0(y) = 0 \quad \text{for all } y.$$

We require $f_K(y_K)$, as in the simple non-probabilistic case, and the decision rules $\{\theta_k\}$, $1 \leqslant k \leqslant K$.

For probability density functions we replace

$$\sum_z p_k(x; z, y) \quad \text{by} \quad \int_z g_k(z; x, y) \, dz.$$

If z is obtained in terms of x, y, and some random variable s, so that:

$$z = T_k(x, y, s)$$

and s has a probability $g_k(s)$, then we replace

$$p_k(z, x, y) f_{k-1}(z) \quad \text{by} \quad p_k(s) f_{k-1}(T_k(x, y, s))$$

and similarly for the probability density function case.

For the simple probabilistic inventory problem discussed earlier on we have the following identities:

y : inventory level

x : level to which this is raised

$X_k(y) = \{x : x \geqslant y\}$ independent of k

$T_k(x, y, s) = x - s \quad \text{if} \quad s \leqslant x$

$\qquad\qquad\quad = 0 \quad \text{if} \quad s \geqslant x$, independent of k

$g_k(s) = g(s)$, independent of k.

The reader should re-examine the other dynamic programming formulations in terms of the concepts developed here. In the second product defective problem, for example, we may, as with the optimal route problem, dispense with the suffix k, if no restriction is placed on the number of runs allowed.

The probabilistic dynamic programming material comes under the heading of Markov Decision Processes (e.g. see Howard [33]). It is largely restricted to problems where the objective function is the expectation of a sum of costs, or profits, for each interval. As has been indicated in the earlier sections, if we deviate from this (for example to multi-objective problems, to mean-variance analysis) the applicability of dynamic programming becomes rather more questionable although it is possible to handle some such problems (e.g. see White [63–65] and Sobel [53]).

2.6 OPTIMIZATION ANALOGUES

An analogue model is a physical, as distinct from symbolic, model, whose behaviour in certain respects represents the behaviour of the system being studied, although the model and the system may be quite different entities. There are various forms of analogue which are possible, e.g. the use of biological analogues to study organizational behaviour, or the use of entropy analogues in thermodynamics to study disorder in systems. We will, however, confine our attentions largely to optimization analogues, by which we mean physical models, some of whose variables correspond to the variables of the system being studied, and which behave as if they are minimizing some entity which corresponds to the objective function to be minimized in the system being studied. For our limited study this entity will be largely that of potential energy and, as is well known, physical systems under certain conditions will strive to minimize their potential energy. The reader will find the articles by Courant [3] and Woolsey [21] interesting, the former dealing with the solution of optimization problems using soap films, and the latter making a plea for the use of such analogues, including string models.

Let us begin by looking at the transport optimization method of Haley *et al.* [9]. As is well known, the standard balanced transportation problem takes the following form (e.g. see Gass [7]):

$$\text{minimize} \left[f(x) = \sum_{i=1}^{m} \sum_{j=1}^{n} c_{ij} x_{ij} \right]$$

subject to

$$\sum_{j=1}^{n} x_{ij} = a_i, \qquad i = 1, 2, \ldots, m$$

$$\sum_{i=1}^{m} x_{ij} = b_j, \qquad j = 1, 2, \ldots, n$$

$$x_{ij} \geqslant 0 \quad \forall i, j.$$

Now consider a system of $2mn - m - n$ pulleys in a horizontal plane, arranged in rows and columns, with the (i, j)th pulley being in the ith row

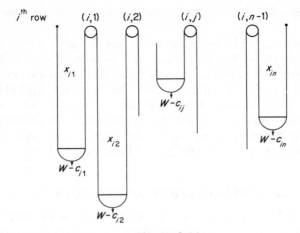

Figure 2.11

and jth column. Figure 2.11 illustrates the ith row. A second (j, i)th pulley (not drawn) will be in the jth column and ith row. If we look at each column, along all the rows we will have a similar configuration with an additional set of pulleys. The strings are fixed at the end. In between the pulleys the strings are attached to weights, the strings being free to move through them, the weight in position (i, j) being $W - c_{ij}$ in suitable units, with $W > c_{ij}$ for all (i, j). The system is left free to find its own resting position which will be a position of minimal potential energy. The potential energy is, in suitable units;

$$\text{P.E.} = \alpha - \beta \sum_{i=1}^{m} \sum_{j=1}^{n} (W - c_{ij}) x_{ij}$$

$$= \alpha - \beta W \sum_{i=1}^{m} \sum_{j=1}^{n} x_{ij} + \beta \sum_{i=1}^{m} \sum_{j=1}^{n} c_{ij} x_{ij}.$$

The total length of each string is fixed, equal to a_i for the ith row, and equal to b_j for the jth column. Hence:

$$\sum_{j=1}^{n} x_{ij} = a_i \qquad i = 1, 2, \ldots, m$$

$$\sum_{i=1}^{m} x_{ij} = b_j \qquad j = 1, 2, \ldots, n$$

$x_{ij} \geq 0$ for all i, j.

Thus the physical analogue minimizes

$$\sum_{i=1}^{m} \sum_{j=1}^{n} c_{ij} x_{ij}$$

and solves the original problem.

In White [19] a fluid analogue is developed which will enable linear programmes, as distinct from simply transportation problems, to be solved, again using potential energy ideas.

Haley [8] also designs an analogue for the classical Weber problem of siting a depot in a plane. Let there be n destination points, $i = 1, 2, \ldots, n$, and let the problem be one of siting a warehouse to minimize the total distance travelled in a year, where each destination i has to be visited c_i times in a year. If x_i is the distance from the warehouse to destination i, the problem becomes one of minimizing

$$f(x) = \sum_{i=1}^{n} c_i x_i.$$

Now consider a smooth horizontal board with holes punched in it to represent the destination points. Take n strings of length L, large, tied together at one end with the other ends threaded through the holes, each destination point having a weight proportional to c_i tied to the string at these ends. Figure 2.12 illustrates the situation. The joining point of the strings representing the depot is located at some point initially (it need only be in the convex hull of the destinations, as established by Hurter *et al.* [10]), and the system is left to find its own resting place.

The potential energy takes the value:

$$\alpha - \beta \sum_{i=1}^{n} c_i (L - x_i) = \alpha - \beta L \sum_{i=1}^{n} c_i + \beta \sum_{i=1}^{n} c_i x_i$$

and again it settles down to its minimal value and solves the Weber problem.

Further analogue models may be found in Fetter *et al.* [5] Friedman [6], Deziel *et al.* [4], Miehle [12] (who uses mechanical and soap film devices, the latter using surface tension properties), Ablow *et al.* [1] (who develop a dynamic portable model, which is an analogue described by differential equations), Rich [15] (a simple plywood model is made to simulate a ship defending itself against an air attack and, although simulation is the term

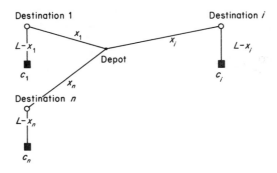

Figure 2.12

used, the model is really an analogue) and Sinden [18] (who describes models involving systems of levers, etc.).

Analogue models do not really find much application in modern Operational Research. Indeed most references are quite old. They are largely of historical interest and do exhibit a different sort of modelling to the conventional symbolic and simulation (in our sense) modelling. However, on occasion they do enable new insights into problems and their solution to be obtained. Thus, in White [19] a study of the dynamics of the analogue suggested a new algorithm for solving linear programmes which avoids having to move solely through vertices. In Rich [15] the analogue model behaviour led to a symbolic (mathematical) description of the problem. In White [19, 20], the analogues led to duality results. In the former case the standard linear programming duality result was obtained where the dual variables were the fluid pressures and the dual objective function was the energy stored up in the fluid, and the constraints were pressure–weight–force balances. In the latter case the dual of the Weber problem turns out to be the following:

$$\text{maximize} \left[\sum_{i=1}^{n} u_i d_i \right]$$

subject to

$$u_i \in \mathbb{R}^2, \qquad i = 1, 2, \ldots, n$$

$$\sum_{i=1}^{n} u_i = 0$$

$$|u_i| \leq c_i, \qquad i = 1, 2, \ldots, n$$

where d_i is the position vector of destination i.

The objective function corresponds to virtual work of the system in moving from one state to the final state and the $\{u_i\}$ correspond to the vector tensions in the strings. The dual problem has been derived earlier by Kuhn [11]. Sinden [18] also looks at duality.

We have concentrated on optimization analogues in the sense that the analogues actually optimize some physical quantity when they settle down to their steady state position. Reference was made to the work of Ablow et al. [11]. Their analogue is not of the same kind as the above and is a forced analogue for solving the general mathematical programming problem specified in section 2.5, viz.

$$\text{maximize} \; [f(x)]$$

subject to

$$g_i(x) \leq b_i, \qquad i = 1, 2, \ldots, p.$$

The analogue of Ablow et al. is an electronic analogue which solves the following differential equations:

$$\frac{\mathrm{d}x_j}{\mathrm{d}t} = -\sum_{i=1}^{p} \lambda_i \frac{\partial g_i(x)}{\partial x_j} + \mu \frac{\partial f(x)}{\partial x_j}, \qquad j = 1, 2, \ldots, p$$

where λ_i is controlled so that

$$\lambda_i > 0 \quad \text{if} \quad g_i(x) > b_i$$
$$\lambda_i = 0 \quad \text{if} \quad g_i(x) \leq b_i$$

and μ is a small positive constant.

When the constraints are satisfied, the analogue will try to increase f by increasing or decreasing x_j as the case may be. As long as the constraints are not satisfied the analogue, in effect, gives priority to satisfying them. When the analogue settles down to its steady state condition it, in effect, solves the Kuhn–Tucker-like optimality conditions (see Shapiro [17]) although it must be stressed that the $\{\lambda_i\}$ are preset equal to 0 in the steady state position and that, although the $\{\lambda_i\}$ look like Lagrange multipliers (see Chapter 4), they are not. The conditions under which the analogue gives an optimal solution to the original problem are not given. It is clear that the analogue will, however, solve linear programming problems where $\partial g_i/\partial x_j$, $\partial f/\partial x_j$ are all constants. Deziel et al. [4] discuss electronic analogues for solving differential equations.

Schwarzschild [16] discusses an algorithm developed by Kirkpatrick, Gelatt, and Veechi for solving large-scale network problems (inclusive of the travelling salesman problem to which we will again turn in Heuristic Programming, section 2.8). The algorithm derives from an analogy with statistical mechanics methods used to find low energy states of condensed matter Hamiltonian functions. It uses the behaviour of a theoretical analogue to produce the algorithm. The algorithm is related to the Las Vegas method we will discuss later on.

Although this author can produce no evidence to support it, with the very large size of some problems (leading to the search for heuristic methods) it may well be that a study of this and other analogues may eventually be useful for the development of algorithms.

2.7 SIMULATION

2.7.1 Introduction

In the previous sections we have studied the mathematical formulations of such dynamic problems as search, queueing, inventory, and product defectives. The problems which we looked at were quite simple and tractable mathematically and computationally. Many real life problems are much more complex, and, although subject to the same mathematical and computational approaches, are not as tractable. These problems are usually tackled by the method of simulation.

Broadly speaking, as indicated in the introduction, simulation models are look-alike models or iconic models. They represent the actual behaviour of a system in real time by a corresponding sequence of decisions, events, state transitions, and rewards or costs, in abstract, but in a much shorter period of time. The framework for dynamic programming can be very helpful here.

We will not study the pros and cons as yet, and will leave this later until we can take a qualitative overview of all the techniques we discuss in this chapter. Nor is this section intended to give more than an elementary introduction to the ideas. For those who wish to study the technique properly, and in more depth, the following references are useful, viz. Fishman [19], Donaldson *et al.* [15], Tocher [42], Mihram [33], Gordon [21], Balintey *et al.* [2], Kleijnen [30], Wagner [45], Zeigler [48], Evans *et al.* [18], Bobillier *et al.* [5], Emshoff *et al.* [17], Schmidt *et al.* [38], Schriber [39], Shannon [40], Watson [46] and Gnugnoli [20]. Malcolm [31] gives a useful, but dated, bibliography on applications. Other useful articles are: Mihram [32], Crookes [14], Shannon [40] and Tocher [41, 43]. Wicks *et al.* [47] give a further elementary introduction.

Perhaps the best way to see how simulation works is to consider some elementary problems, which we will now do.

2.7.2 Some Elementary Applications

Let us consider a simple inventory control problem, given the following data:

(i) a single item is to be controlled over 10 unit time intervals;
(ii) decisions are made at the beginning of each interval;
(iii) the decisions are: if the stock level is less than 2 units, increase the level to 2 units by an appropriate order quantity, otherwise order 0;
(iv) orders are instantaneously supplied;
(v) no backlogs are allowed, i.e. any unsatisfied demand in an interval is left unsatisfied;
(vi) the probability distribution for demand in any one interval is identical and independent from interval to interval and is given by Table 2.6.

Table 2.6

Demand	0	1	2	3	4	5
Probability	0.09	0.23	0.34	0.20	0.11	0.03

To generate the behaviour of the system we have to represent the probability behaviour of demand. We do this by creating a sampling mechanism which generates the demands with the above probabilities.

To do this we consider all the integers 0–99 (100 integers in total). With each demand level we associate a range of these integers in such a manner that, if each such integer can be generated with equal probability 1/100, then the probability that an integer is in a given range is equal to the probability of the associated demand level. We do this as in Table 2.7. The demands are then generated by repeatedly sampling from the numbers 0–99, and associating each such number with its corresponding demand level.

Table 2.7

Range of integer (inclusive)	Probability of range	Associated demand level
0–8	9/100	0
9–31	23/100	1
32–65	34/100	2
66–85	20/100	3
86–96	11/100	4
97–99	3/100	5

In order to sample each number 0–99 with equal probability, we need to generate an appropriate sequence of random numbers. One way of doing this is to use a prepared sequence of random numbers, e.g. Table 2.8

Table 2.8

```
21 47  75 48  59 01  83 72  59 93  76 24  97 08  86 95  23 03  67 44
82 32  55 50  43 10  53 74  35 08  90 61  18 37  44 10  96 22  13 43
94 66  16 03  50 32  40 43  62 23  50 05  10 03  22 11  54 38  08 34
17 58  67 49  51 94  05 17  58 53  78 80  59 01  94 32  42 87  16 95
38 87  26 17  18 99  75 53  08 70  94 25  12 58  41 54  88 21  05 13

11 74  26 93  81 44  33 93  08 72  32 79  73 31  18 22  64 70  68 50
43 36  12 88  59 11  01 64  56 23  93 00  90 04  99 43  64 07  40 36
93 80  62 04  78 38  26 80  44 91  55 75  11 89  32 58  47 55  25 71
49 54  01 31  81 08  42 98  41 87  69 53  82 96  61 77  73 80  95 27
36 76  87 26  33 37  94 82  15 69  41 95  96 86  70 45  27 48  38 80

07 09  25 23  92 24  62 71  26 07  06 55  84 53  44 67  33 84  53 20
43 31  00 10  81 44  86 38  03 07  52 55  51 61  48 89  74 29  46 47
61 57  00 63  60 06  17 36  37 75  63 14  89 51  23 25  01 74  69 93
31 35  28 37  99 10  77 91  89 41  31 57  97 64  48 62  58 48  69 19
57 04  88 65  26 27  79 59  36 82  90 52  95 65  46 35  06 53  22 54

09 24  34 42  00 68  72 10  71 37  30 72  97 57  59 09  29 82  76 50
97 95  53 50  18 40  89 48  83 29  52 23  08 25  21 22  53 26  15 87
93 73  25 95  70 43  78 19  88 85  56 67  16 68  26 95  99 64  45 69
72 62  11 12  25 00  92 26  82 64  35 66  65 94  34 71  68 75  18 67
61 02  07 44  18 45  37 12  07 94  95 91  73 78  66 99  53 21  93 78

97 83  98 54  74 33  05 59  17 18  45 47  35 41  44 22  03 42  30 00
89 16  09 71  92 22  23 29  06 37  35 05  54 54  89 88  43 81  63 61
25 96  68 82  20 62  87 17  92 65  02 82  35 28  62 84  91 95  48 83
81 44  33 17  19 05  04 95  48 06  74 69  00 75  67 65  01 71  65 45
11 32  25 49  31 42  36 23  43 86  08 62  49 76  67 42  24 52  32 45
```

(reproduced, with permission, from Kendall *et al.* [29], for tables, and see Clark [10] for a discussion of such tables). In Table 2.8 a sequence of 4-digit random numbers has been taken and split into two 2-digit numbers. The actual sampling results, plus corresponding system behaviour, is given in Table 2.9, setting the initial stock (before order) equal to 0 at the beginning of the first interval.

Table 2.9

Interval	Random number	Demand	Initial stock	Order	Initial stock plus order	End stock	Shortage
1	21	1	0	2	2	1	0
2	47	2	1	1	2	0	0
3	82	3	0	2	2	0	1
4	32	2	0	2	2	0	0
5	94	4	0	2	2	0	2
6	66	3	0	2	2	0	1
7	17	1	0	2	2	1	0
8	58	2	1	1	2	0	0
9	38	2	0	2	2	0	0
10	87	4	0	2	2	0	2
Average per interval				1.8	2	0.2	0.6

The above results in Table 2.9 are for a specific sample, and hence the performance measurements given are subject to variation dependent on the actual sequence of samples. If we are trying to determine an optimal rule for a 10-interval problem we should repeat the procedure enough times to get a good idea of the probability distribution of the measures of performance given in the last line, and hence of their average values.

For a different sequence of random variables we would get the results shown in Table 2.10. When we have repeated this simulation enough times, we then change the decision rule, and do the same for this.

Table 2.10

Interval	Random number	Demand	Initial stock	Order	Initial stock plus order	End stock	Shortage
1	23	1	0	2	2	1	0
2	5	0	1	1	2	2	0
3	14	1	2	0	2	1	0
4	38	2	1	1	2	0	0
5	97	5	0	2	2	0	3
6	11	1	0	2	2	1	0
7	43	2	1	1	2	0	0
8	93	4	0	2	2	0	2
9	49	2	0	2	2	0	0
10	36	2	0	2	2	0	0
Average per interval				1.5	2	0.5	0.5

A generally accepted procedure for certain problems, to reduce the variation between the performances of different rules, is to use the same sequence of random numbers. This is known as a variance reduction technique, and we will return to this later on in this section as a general principle.

If the decision rule is now changed to 'if the initial stock is less than 3 units, increase the level to 3 units by an appropriate order quantity, otherwise order 0', the results are as given in Tables 2.11 and 2.12, using the same random numbers.

Table 2.11

Interval	Random numbers	Demand	Intial stock	Order	Initial stock plus order	End stock	Shortage
1	21	1	0	3	3	2	0
2	47	2	2	1	3	1	0
3	82	3	1	2	3	0	0
4	32	2	0	3	3	1	0
5	94	4	1	2	3	0	1
6	66	3	0	3	3	0	0
7	17	1	0	3	3	2	0
8	58	2	2	1	3	1	0
9	38	2	1	2	3	1	0
10	87	4	1	2	3	0	1
Average per interval				2.2	3	0.8	0.2

Table 2.12

Interval	Random numbers	Demand	Initial stock	Order	Initial stock plus order	End stock	Shortage
1	23	1	0	3	3	2	0
2	5	0	2	1	3	3	0
3	14	1	3	0	3	2	0
4	38	2	2	1	3	1	0
5	97	5	1	2	3	0	2
6	11	1	0	3	3	2	0
7	43	2	2	1	3	1	0
8	93	4	1	2	3	0	1
9	49	2	0	3	3	1	0
10	36	2	1	2	3	1	0
Average per interval				1.8	3	1.3	0.3

If we accept the result of two simulations for each decision rule as enough for our purposes (and this is not the case in practice) we then have the results given in Table 2.13. These averages are per interval, averaged over two simulations. The final choice might then be made on the basis of this performance, balancing shortages against order quantities and stock levels. In general, the variance in performance will also be important. Ramsay *et al.* [37] and Ehrhardt [16] report on the use of simulation techniques for inventory problems.

Table 2.13

Reorder level	Average order	Average initial stock plus order	Average end stock	Average shortage
2	1.65	2	0.35	0.55
3	2	3	1.05	0.25

Let us now consider a simple queueing problem, given the following data:

(i) a single service facility whose service time is uniformly distributed between $S-1$ and $S+1$ minutes, with S to be chosen by the decision-maker;

(ii) a single arrival stream whose inter-arrival time is uniformly distributed between 1 and 2 minutes;

(iii) the service is first come–first served.

In this problem we have to represent the sequence of arrivals and services by an appropriate sequence of random numbers.

To do this we divide the arrival intervals into ranges of length 0.1, and the service times into ranges of 0.1. We need two sequences of random numbers. If we use the integers 0–99, as before, then we have the correspondence shown in Tables 2.14 and 2.15. Note that we could have used inter-arrival times at the mid-points of the ranges, viz. 1.05, 1.15, etc., but have chosen to simplify the numerical analysis, and, in any case, the errors in doing so will be small. Taking mid-points would give a better match with expectations of course (see Exercise 13).

Again, as for the inter-arrival times, we could have used $S-0.95$, $S-0.85$, etc. but the errors will be small, and calculations simplified.

Table 2.14

Range of integers (inclusive)	Inter-arrival time
0–9	1.1
10–19	1.2
20–29	1.3
30–39	1.4
40–49	1.5
50–59	1.6
60–69	1.7
70–79	1.8
80–89	1.9
90–99	2.0

Table 2.15

Range of integers	Service times
0–4	$S - 0.9$
5–9	$S - 0.8$
10–14	$S - 0.7$
15–19	$S - 0.6$
20–24	$S - 0.5$
25–29	$S - 0.4$
30–34	$S - 0.3$
35–39	$S - 0.2$
40–44	$S - 0.1$
45–49	S
50–54	$S + 0.1$
55–59	$S + 0.2$
60–64	$S + 0.3$
65–69	$S + 0.4$
70–74	$S + 0.5$
75–79	$S + 0.6$
80–84	$S + 0.7$
85–89	$S + 0.8$
90–94	$S + 0.9$
95–99	$S + 1$

Let us first of all draw our random numbers to determine the times of arrival and the service times, and we commence with $S = 2.0$ to give Tables 2.16 and 2.17. We can generate the following time behaviour, given in Table 2.18. Note that the first arrival does not have to wait to commence service, but the second arrival arrives 0.4 minutes before the first arrival has finished his service.

Table 2.16   Arrivals

Random number	Inter-arrival time	Actual arrival time
76	1.8	1.8
90	2.0	3.8
50	1.6	5.4
78	1.8	7.2
94	2.0	9.2
32	1.4	10.6
93	2.0	12.6
55	1.6	14.2
69	1.7	15.9
41	1.5	17.4

Table 2.17   Services

Random number	Service time ($S = 2$)	Service time ($S = 1.8$)
67	2.4	2.2
13	1.3	1.1
08	1.2	1.0
16	1.4	1.2
05	1.2	1.0
68	2.4	2.2
40	1.9	1.7
25	1.6	1.4
55	2.2	2.0
38	1.8	1.6

Table 2.18

Arrival number	Arrival time	Waits to commence service	Leaves	Time in system
1	1.8	0	4.2	2.4
2	3.8	0.4	5.5	1.7
3	5.4	0.1	6.7	1.3
4	7.2	0	8.6	1.4
5	9.2	0	10.4	1.2
6	10.6	0	13.0	2.4
7	12.6	0.4	14.9	2.3
8	14.2	0.7	16.5	2.3
9	15.9	0.6	18.7	2.8
10	17.4	1.3	20.5	3.1
			Average	2.09

Table 2.19

Arrival number	Arrival time	Wait to commence service	Leaves	Time in system
1	1.8	0	4.0	2.2
2	3.8	0.2	5.1	1.3
3	5.4	0	6.4	1.0
4	7.2	0	8.4	1.2
5	9.2	0	10.2	1.0
6	10.6	0	12.8	2.2
7	12.6	0.2	14.5	1.9
8	14.2	0.3	15.9	1.7
9	15.9	0	17.9	2.0
10	17.4	0.5	19.5	2.1
			Average	1.66

If we decide to have $S = 1.8$ we have the results, using the same set of random numbers to reduce the variance between $S = 2$ and $S = 1.8$, given in Table 2.19.

On the basis of these limited simulations, if we change from $S = 2$ to $S = 1.8$, we reduce the average time in the system from 2.09 minutes to 1.66 minutes, and complete the programme in 19.5 minutes instead of 20.5 minutes. However, the faster service will cost more and one must balance the reduced waiting against the increased service costs in making a decision.

More detailed work on the simulation of queues may be found in Page [36], Crane *et al.* [13], Bennett *et al.* [4] and Casson *et al.* [6].

The foregoing examples are simple ones, but the general approach is the same for all problems, although more complicated to operate in general, for example, in the inventory control problem we may have backlogs, the replenishment period (i.e. time to receiving an order) may be uncertain, etc., and, in the queueing problem, arrivals and service may be interdependent in complex ways, service facilities may fail, priority rules may be used, etc. Let us now take a look at the sampling procedures.

2.7.3 Sampling and Random Numbers

The sampling problem (to generate demands, arrivals, services, etc.) may be tackled in the same way, using the cumulative probability function, as follows.

Let r be the random variable being generated, (e.g. demand, time, etc.), and let $F(r) = \{$probability that random variable takes a value $\leq r\}$. $F(r)$ is the cumulative probability function. Then the probability that the random variable lies between $r - \delta r$ and r, excluding $r - \delta r$, is $F(r) - F(r - \delta r)$ (see Figure 2.13).

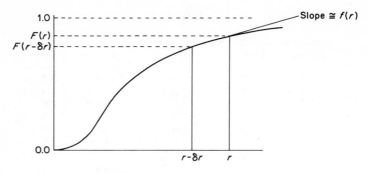

Figure 2.13

If r has a probability density function $f(r)$ (for example, in the queueing example given, $f(r) = \frac{1}{2}$, $S - 1 \leq r \leq S + 1$, $f(r) = 0$ otherwise, $F(r) = 0$, $r \leq S - 1$, $F(r) = 1$, $r \geq S + 1$, and $F(r) = (r + 1 - S)/2$ otherwise (see Figure 2.14)), then, assuming $r \geq 0$, we have:

$$F(r) = \int_{s=0}^{r} f(s)\, ds, \qquad F(r) - F(r - \delta r) \cong f(r)\delta(r) \ (\delta r \text{ small}).$$

If r takes discrete integer values (as in the inventory example) and $p(r)$ is the probability that the random variables takes a value r, then, with $\delta r = 1$, we have:

$$F(r) = \sum_{s=0}^{r} p(r), \qquad F(r) - F(r - 1) = p(r).$$

For the inventory control problem we have Table 2.20.

For the queueing problem arrival distribution we have Table 2.21 where the unit of time is $\delta r = 0.1$.

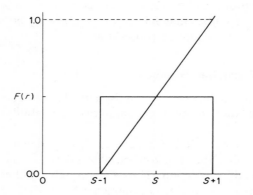

Figure 2.14

Table 2.20

Demand	$F(r)$	$F(r) - F(r-1)$
0	0.09	0.09
1	0.32	0.23
2	0.66	0.34
3	0.86	0.20
4	0.97	0.11
5	1.00	0.03

Table 2.21

Inter-arrival time r	$F(r)$	$F(r) - F(r-0.1)$
1.0	0.00	0.00
1.1	0.10	0.10
1.2	0.20	0.10
1.3	0.30	0.10
1.4	0.40	0.10
1.5	0.50	0.10
1.6	0.60	0.10
1.7	0.70	0.10
1.8	0.80	0.10
1.9	0.90	0.10
2.0	1.00	0.10

For the service distribution we have, for $S = 2$, Table 2.22.

Now when we wish to sample the particular variable r (e.g. stock demand, arrival time), we have to decide which sample values $\{r_1, r_2, \ldots, r_n\}$ will be used. In the discrete case (e.g. inventory control) we may use $r_1 = 0$, $r_2 = 1$, $r_3 = 2$, $r_4 = 3$, $r_5 = 4$, $r_6 = 5$. In the continuous case (e.g. arrival distribution) we may use $r_1 = 1.1$, $r_2 = 1.2, \ldots, r_{10} = 2.0$, in which case any value of r is represented by the r_n in the sequence which is next at, or above, it (see Figure 2.15). Then the random number range associated with r_n is such that the probability that the random number R falls within this range is $F(r_n) - F(r_{n-1})$, providing r_n is chosen to represent the range $r_{n-1} < r \leqslant r_n$. We could choose $\frac{1}{2}(r_n + r_{n-1})$.

Thus for the inventory control problem, the random numbers are $R = 0$ to $R = 99$ and these are broken into groups as indicated previously to ensure that the probability of each range is precisely the required $F(r_n) - F(r_{n-1})$. Similarly for the queueing problem.

It is to be noted that the gaps $\delta r_n = r_{n+1} - r_n$ need not be uniform, although in the examples given this is the case.

Table 2.22

Service time r	$F(r)$	$F(r) - F(r-0.1)$
1.0	0.00	0.00
1.1	0.05	0.05
1.2	0.10	0.05
1.3	0.15	0.05
1.4	0.20	0.05
1.5	0.25	0.05
1.6	0.30	0.05
1.7	0.35	0.05
1.8	0.40	0.05
1.9	0.45	0.05
2.0	0.50	0.05
2.1	0.55	0.05
2.2	0.60	0.05
2.3	0.65	0.05
2.4	0.70	0.05
2.5	0.75	0.05
2.6	0.80	0.05
2.7	0.85	0.05
2.8	0.90	0.05
2.9	0.95	0.05
3.0	1.00	0.05

For some inventory control problems, the demands may be 0, 1, 4, 10, in which case there would be no point in taking uniform intervals. For queueing problems the service time might be from 1 to 2 and from 3 to 4, in which case there would be no point in taking uniform intervals.

Tocher [41] gives sampling procedures for various standard distributions.

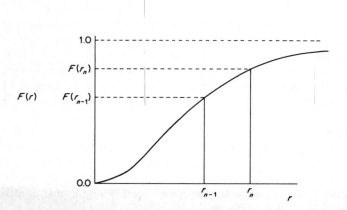

Figure 2.15

2.7.4 Random Number Generation

In order to carry out a simulation, a set of random numbers is needed. These numbers are random in the sense that each number is equi-probable, and that no correlation exists between successive sets. Numbers presented in tables of random numbers are pseudo-random numbers usually, and are generated by specific mathematical expressions. They are deterministic in the sense that they can always be pre-calculated, but, nonetheless, the sequence produced exhibits adequate properties of randomness.

Examples of formulae used are as follows:

Mixed congruential form

$$R_{n+1} = (aR_n + c)\mathrm{mod}(m)$$

Multiplicative congruential form

$$R_{n+1} = aR_n\,\mathrm{mod}(m)$$

Additive contruential form

$$R_{n+1} = (R_n + R_{n-1})\mathrm{mod}(m).$$

The $\mathrm{mod}(m)$ term means that we find the remainder of the term on the left of the $\mathrm{mod}(m)$ expression after dividing throughout by m; for example, if $R_0 = 5$ (called the seed), $a = 17$, $c = 2$, $m = 19$, we have $R_1 = (17 \times 5 + 2)\mathrm{mod}(19) = 87\,\mathrm{mod}(19) = 11$, $R_2 = 18$, $R_3 = 4$, $R_4 = 13$, $R_5 = 14$, $R_6 = 12$, $R_7 = 16$, etc.

Note that we can produce at most m different random numbers. Also, although the above numbers are integers, decimals and fractions can be derived by dividing throughout by m; for example if we take $m = 100$, then if we divide by 100 we obtain decimals of the form $\cdot xy$.

In generating random numbers, care has to be taken in the choice of a, c, m and some advice and experience is available. For detailed consideration of random numbers in simulations see Miller [34], Babington-Smith et al. [1], Greenburger [23], Conveyou [11], Ramsay [37], Heikes et al. [27], Clark [10] and Conveyou et al. [12].

Reference has been made to variance reduction techniques, and to the problem of determining how many simulation runs are needed to get a good enough idea of the differences in performance resulting from different decision rules. There is some literature on the former aspect, but little on the latter, which still presents an open problem. Let us now consider variation reduction via common random numbers and via a companion, antithetic variables.

2.7.5 Variance Reduction

Common Random Numbers

The basic idea behind the use of common random numbers resides in the fact that, if we try to compare the behaviour of a system using simulation,

100

using, for example, two different decisions (e.g. capacity levels) or decision rules (e.g. inventory re-order rules), the difference in performance will be partly due to the different decisions, or rules, which we are trying to evaluate, and partly due to the difference in chance events which arise in each comparison. Therefore, if we ensure that the same chance events occur, the difference in performance will be due to the different rules.

This seems to be sensible, although the proper justification of this can be quite deep. Let us examine this briefly.

Suppose we run a single simulation for n periods to determine an estimate of the expected cost per period, and suppose we do this for two different policies x, x' (see, for example, the inventory problem later on). The difference, Δ, in costs for the policies is

$$C(n) - C'(n).$$

Suppose we consider the average cost per unit time

$$\delta = \Delta/n,$$

and judge x better than x' if and only if $\delta < 0$.
Let:

$$E \text{ be the expected value of } \Delta$$

$$V \text{ be the variance of } \Delta.$$

Then δ has expected value E/n, and variance V/n^2.

We would like to choose x rather than x' if and only if $E/n < 0$, but we only have the observation δ.

Consider two situations, without and with variance reduction using common random numbers. Let $(E/n, V/n^2)$ $(E/n, V^*/n^2)$ be the respective expectations and variances for the two cases, and assume δ, δ^* are approximately normally distributed as in Figures 2.16 and 2.17. Now we suppose we accept policy x if and only if $\delta < 0$ (δ is a random variable).

If $E/n < 0$, we have a much greater chance of accepting x in the second case i.e. when $V^* < V$ or, alternatively, if $\delta^* < 0$, we have much greater confidence that $E/n < 0$.

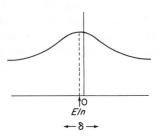

Figure 2.16

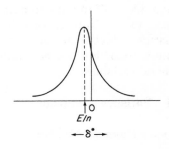

Figure 2.17

This is only a rudimentary explanation and should be tackled rigorously by proper statistical justification. Also we will usually have more than one simulation run but the principles are the same. A similar argument applies to the antithetic variable approach discussed later on.

The alternative to this approach is to have very long simulations, or to run many shorter simulations, as the circumstances may require, and it is in an attempt to help reduce this computational burden that the variance reduction approach of common random numbers has value.

From the point of view of selling analyses it is useful since it is, to some extent, saying that, for a particular sequence of chance events, one decision, or rule, performs better than another. It is rather like saying 'let us see how the decisions, or rules, would have performed for a given series of past chance events which may have happened', and this is meaningful to actual decision makers. This interpretation takes account, however, only of the individual nature of the data, and not of the underlying stochastic structure which generates these events, which form one sample from many.

Nonetheless, with sensible application, the common random number approach can be helpful. Although in practice the method seems to work, as we shall see, it need not always work. In the light of this, perhaps its strongest case for support may well be the one given earlier on.

Let us look at a simple inventory control problem, with the following assumptions, which will illustrate both the general principle and the dangers involved:

(i) demand in each interval is 1 with probability p, or 0 with probability $(1-p)$;
(ii) the cost of a unit order is c;
(iii) the sales value of a unit is s;
(iv) the penalty cost for unit shortage is k;
(v) each interval is considered as independent of other intervals, and any excess stock at the end of an interval is disposed of;
(vi) simulation runs are of length n intervals;
(vii) the order quantity in each interval is $x = 0$ or 1, remaining the same throughout the simulation.

Not Using Common Random Numbers

Let $\{d_i\}$, $\{d_i'\}$ be the two sequences of demands, $i = 1, 2, \ldots, n$, and $C(n)$, $C'(n)$, be the simulated net costs for each run. Then, if x, x' are the respective order quantities, we have:

$$C(n) = ncx + km(1-x) - smx$$
$$C'(n) = ncx' + km'(1-x') - sm'x'$$

where m, m' are the number of times the demand is 1 during each simulation respectively.

Then,

$$\Delta = C(n) - C'(n) = nc(x - x') + m(k(1-x) - sx) - m'(k(1-x') - sx')$$

Using Common Random Numbers

In this case $d_i = d_i'$, $i = 1, 2, \ldots, n$. Hence we have:

$$\Delta^* = C(n) - C'(n) = nc(x - x') + m((x' - x)(k + s)).$$

Let us now look at the expectations and variances of Δ and Δ^*, using E and V for expectation and variance respectively. We have the following, since $E(m) = E(m') = np$:

$$E(\Delta) = nc(x - x') + (x' - x)(k + s)np$$
$$E(\Delta^*) = nc(x - x') + (x' - x)(k + s)np.$$

Hence:

$$E(\Delta) = E(\Delta^*)$$
$$V(\Delta) = np(1-p)((k(1-x) - sx)^2 + (k(1-x') - sx')^2)$$

(since variance (m) = variance $(m') = np(1-p)$)

$$V(\Delta^*) = (k + s)^2(x' - x)^2 np(1-p).$$

For $x = 1$, $x' = 0$ we obtain:

$$V(\Delta) = (k^2 + s^2)np(1-p)$$
$$V(\Delta^*) = (k + s)^2 np(1-p).$$

Hence in this case, the variance is actually increased not decreased.

The reason arises from the negative correlation of the random terms in the costs for each solution. Thus we see that:

$$C(n) = C(n, x) = f(n, x) + r(n, x)$$
$$C'(n) = C(n, x') = f(n, x') + r(n, x')$$

where:

$$f(n, x) = cnx, \qquad f(n, x') = cnx'$$
$$r(n, x) = m(k(1-x) - sx), \qquad r(n, x') = m'(k(1-x') - sx')$$
$$r(n, 1) = -sm, \qquad r(n, 0) = km'.$$

Then:

$$V(\Delta) = V(r(n, 1) - r(n, 0)) = V(-sm - km')$$
$$= (s^2 + k^2)np(1-p).$$

When $m = m'$:

$$V(\Delta^*) = V(r(n, 1) - r(n, 0)) = V(-(s + k)m) = (s + k)^2 np(1-p)$$

and hence

$$V(\Delta^*) > V(\Delta).$$

The reader is referred to Ramsay *et al.* [37] who show that, although the use of common random numbers is likely to reduce the variance, this is not always so.

Although, in this example, the use of common random numbers does not reduce the variance of the differences of the total costs, it is easily shown that it does reduce the variances of the difference between the quantities sold, and it also reduces the variance of the difference between the shortage quantities. In each case the covariance of the difference is $n(x - x')^2 p(1 - p)$. Thus, if we estimated the differences between the component costs we would get better estimates for each, if not for the total cost.

Let us now look at a more general case where $r(n, x)$, $r(n, x')$ are the random parts of general total returns for simulations of length n using decisions x, x' respectively. Then we have the following:

$$V(\Delta) = V(r(n, x) - r(n, x'))$$

given $r(n, x)$, $r(n, x')$ are independent of each other;

$$V(\Delta^*) = V(r(n, x) - r(n, x'))$$

given the same random events.

Then:

$$V(\Delta) = V(r(n, x)) + V(r(n, x'))$$
$$V(\Delta^*) = V(r(n, x)) + V(r(n, x')) - 2\,\text{Covariance}\,(r(n, x), r(n, x')).$$

Note that if a, b are random variables with a joint probability density function $g(a, b)$, then we have:

$$V(a + b) = \int_{a,b} (a + b - E(a) - E(b))^2 g(a, b)\,\mathrm{d}a\,\mathrm{d}b$$

$$= \int_{a,b} ((a - E(a))^2 + (b - E(b))^2 + 2(a - E(a))(b - E(b))g(a, b)\,\mathrm{d}a\,\mathrm{d}b$$

$$= V(a) + V(b) + 2\,\text{Covariance}\,(a, b)$$

$$V(a - b) = V(a) + V(b) - 2\,\text{Covariance}\,(a, b).$$

Hence:

$$V(\Delta) - V(\Delta^*) = 2\,\text{Covariance}\,(r(n, x); r(n, x')).$$

Then, Covariance $(r(n, x), r(n, x')) \geqslant 0 \rightleftarrows V(\Delta) \geqslant V(\Delta^*)$

When $m = m'$ we have:

$$\text{Covariance}\,(r(n, 1), r(n, 0)) = E((-sm + snp)(km - knp))$$
$$= -ksE(m - np)^2 < 0,$$

and hence $V(\Delta) < V(\Delta^*)$.

For the method to work we must have positive correlation between $r(n, x)$ and $r(n, x')$.

In queueing problems, the random events are the arrivals and services, and, if we are considering changes in service rate (our decision x), costs will tend to increase if arrivals increase or if service times (for random arrivals) increase, irrespective of the decision x. Hence there would be positive correlation between the costs for different decisions and one would expect to have

$$V(\Delta^*) < V(\Delta).$$

In order to illustrate why common random numbers are likely to work in queueing problems, consider a discrete approximation to the negative exponential problem of the section 2.1. Let us suppose that, in a small interval of time, δ, the probabilities of an arrival, a service, and no change are, respectively, $\lambda\delta$, $\mu\delta$, $1 - \lambda\delta - \mu\delta$, and suppose we wish to estimate the difference in total waiting time over T small intervals δ for service rates μ, μ' respectively. Assume that changes in the number in the system take place at the end of each interval δ. Then if $\{z_t\}$, $\{z_t'\}$, $t = 1, 2, \ldots, T$, are the events which take place for a simulation of length n using service rates μ, μ' respectively, we get the following results for μ, μ' and the waiting times:

$$w = Tn_1 + (T-1)z_1 + (T-2)z_2 + \ldots + (T-t)z_t + \ldots + z_{T-1}$$
$$w' = Tn_1 + (T-1)z_1' + (T-2)z_2' + \ldots + (T-t)z_t' + \ldots + z_{T-1}'.$$

We assume that we begin with n_1 in the system in each case.

In general it is difficult to evaluate the variance of $w - w'$. However, let us look at the individual component differences $z_t - z_t'$ and let us assume that we have no situations with $n_t = 0$ or $n_t' = 0$. Then we may assume that $\{(z_t - z_t')\}$ form an independently distributed series. Then

$$V(w - w') = \sum_{t=1}^{T} (T-t)^2 V(z_t - z_t')$$

$$= \sum_{t=1}^{T} (T-t)^2 (V(z_t) + V(z_t')) - 2 \sum_{t=1}^{T} (T-t)^2 \text{Cov}(z_t, z_t').$$

A little analysis shows that, if we use common random numbers for the arrivals only, then

$$\text{Cov}(z_t, z_t') = \lambda\delta \text{ plus terms in } \delta^2$$

$$> 0 \text{ if } \delta \text{ is small enough.}$$

The argument given is not a rigorous argument and is only intended to give some support to the use of common random numbers.

A more detailed treatment of variance reduction via common random numbers may be found in Ramsay et al. [37] and Heikes et al. [27]. The former confirms the need to be careful in using common random numbers.

Antithetic Variables

The basic idea behind this approach is that, if we split a simulation run into two parts, we may deliberately select chance variables in the second part to compensate for high or low levels of these variables in the first part, and hence reduce the variation of a given simulation run.

Let us consider a simulation run of length $2n$, in which the random numbers are $R_1, R_2, \ldots, R_n, R'_1, R'_2, \ldots, R'_n$ and the random variables they represent are $r_1, r_2, \ldots, r_n, r'_1, r'_2, \ldots, r'_n$. Let the measure of performance expressed in terms of $R_1, R_2, \ldots, R_n, R'_1, R'_2, \ldots, R'_n$, and $r_1, r_2, \ldots, r_n$, $r'_1, r'_2, \ldots, r'_n$ be, respectively, for a given decision or decision rule,

$$g(R_1, R_2, \ldots, R_n, R'_1, R'_2, \ldots, R'_n)$$
$$f(r_1, r_2, \ldots, r_n, r'_1, r'_2, \ldots, r'_n).$$

Now in some situations an increase (decrease) in r_i, r'_i will increase or decrease (decrease or increase) f, and, if the random numbers are chosen so that the random variables increase or decrease with them, the same will apply to g.

Thus, in queueing, if r_i, r'_i represent inter-arrival times, an increase in these would decrease waiting time.

Now suppose we wish to estimate the expected value, $E(f)$, of f. It would help if the variance $V(f)$, of f, over the simulation, were as small as possible, so that the value of f for the simulation would better approximate $E(f)$.

Let us suppose that our random numbers vary from 0 to 99 with equal probability, and are used to generate the random variables with the specified probability distribution (e.g. see inventory/queueing examples given in section 2.2).

We consider two cases. Note that $f = g$.

Case 1   When $\{R_i\}$, $\{R'_i\}$ are independent, we get an expected value of g equal to $E(g)$, and variance equal to $V(g)$.

Case 2   We may choose $R'_i = 99 - R_i$. This is known as the method of antithetic variables. We obtain $\tilde{E}(g)$, and $\tilde{V}(g)$ as the corresponding expectation and variance. This procedure will maintain the requisite uniform probability distribution for the random numbers.

Since we are assuming that performance, for example, increases with the random numbers, we see that a low value of R_i, is partly compensated for by a high value of R'_i when $R'_i = 99 - R_i$, and a high value of R_i is partly compensated for by a low value of R'_i. Thus one might expect

$$E(g) = \tilde{E}(g)$$
$$V(g) > \tilde{V}(g)$$

because of the negative correlation between the effects of R_i and R'_i.

Consider the simple inventory problem, with the order size $x = 1$ and demands r_i, $r_i' = 0$ or 1. Then, since r_i and r_i' will have the same probability distribution we have:

$$f(r_1, r_2, \ldots, r_n, r_1', r_2', \ldots, r_n') = 2nc - s \sum_{i=1}^{n} (r_i + r_i')$$

$$E(f) = 2nc - 2nps$$

(irrespective of whether we do or do not use the antithetic method)

$$V(f) = ns^2 \text{ (variance } (r) + \text{variance } (r') + 2 \text{ covariance } (r, r'))$$

$$= 2ns^2p(1-p) + 2ns^2 \text{ covariance } (r, r').$$

Hence if the covariance of (r_i, r_i') is negative, we can reduce the variance of f by using the antithetic method.

Now let us return to the sampling of the random numbers $\{R_i, R_i'\}$. We drop the suffix, and use R, R'. For the antithetic method we have the following.

$\underline{r = r' = 1}$ when $0 \leqslant R \leqslant 100p - 1$, $0 \leqslant R' \leqslant 100p - 1$

(where the first $100p$ numbers correspond to $r = 1$ and the remainder correspond to $r = 0$)

i.e. $0 \leqslant R \leqslant 100p - 1$, $0 \leqslant 99 - R \leqslant 100p - 1$

i.e. $100 - 100p \leqslant R \leqslant 100p - 1$ ($200p - 100$ numbers in range).

The probability of this is

$$2p - 1 \quad \text{if} \quad p \geqslant \tfrac{1}{2}$$
$$0 \quad \text{if} \quad p < \tfrac{1}{2}.$$

$\underline{r = r' = 0}$ when $100p \leqslant R \leqslant 99$, $100p \leqslant R' \leqslant 99$

i.e. $100p \leqslant R \leqslant 99$, $100p \leqslant 99 - R \leqslant 99$

i.e. $100p \leqslant R \leqslant 99 - 100p$ ($100 - 200p$ numbers in range).

The probability of this is

$$1 - 2p \quad \text{if} \quad p \leqslant \tfrac{1}{2}$$
$$0 \quad \text{if} \quad p > \tfrac{1}{2}.$$

$\underline{r = 1, r' = 0}$ or $\underline{r = 0, r' = 1}$ The probability of this is

$$1 - (2p - 1) = 2(1 - p) \quad \text{if} \quad p \geqslant \tfrac{1}{2}$$
$$1 - (1 - 2p) = 2p \quad \text{if} \quad p \leqslant \tfrac{1}{2}.$$

Let $p \geqslant \tfrac{1}{2}$.
Then:

Covariance $(r, r') = \text{prob}(r = r' = 1)(1 - p)(1 - p)$
$$+ \text{prob}(r = 1, r' = 0 \text{ or } r = 0, r' = 1)(0 - p)(1 - p)$$
$$= (2p - 1)(1 - p)^2 - 2(1 - p)p(1 - p)$$
$$= -1(1 - p)^2.$$

When $p \leq \frac{1}{2}$:

$$\text{Covariance } (r, r') = \text{prob}(r = r' = 0)(0-p)(0-p)$$
$$+ \text{prob}(r = 1, r' = 0 \text{ or } r = 0, r' = 1)(0-p)(1-p)$$
$$= (1-2p)p^2 - 2pp(1-p) = -p^2.$$

Clearly the reduction in variance obtained by using the antithetic method depends on p, and the maximal value is at $p = \frac{1}{2}$.

We have looked at the covariance between r and r' by using R and R' as the antithetic variables, since R and R' are the actual numbers used. We could do this directly in terms of r and r' by setting $r' = 1 - r$. In this case

$$\text{Covariance } (r, r') = -2p^2(1-p), \text{ for all } p.$$

Mitchell [35] shows that antithetic variables will result in variance reduction of the estimates of waiting time and queue size in some queueing problems.

More details on the antithetic variable method may be found in Hammersley *et al.* [24, 25], Mitchell [35], Cheng [7], Hayya *et al.* [26] and Grant *et al.* [22].

A third method of variance reduction (see Trotter *et al.* [44]), known as the conditional Monte Carlo method, is examined by Ehrhardt [16] in the context of a class of inventory control problems, and performs better than the others.

Casson *et al.* [6] discuss variance reduction for queueing simulations.

2.8 HEURISTIC PROGRAMMING

In section 2.5 on Mathematical and Dynamic Programming we have seen how many problems may be formulated as mathematical programmes, provided the problems have been fully specified in terms of the set of optimal actions, and a clearly specified objective function. There are many algorithms existing in the mathematical programming literature which will enable optimal solutions, or ε-optimal solutions (i.e. those whose objective function value is within an error range of ε from the true optimal value) to be obtained. However, some of these problems, largely those with integer variables, and of a combinatorial nature, will require an enormous amount of computational time, even with the best algorithm known, to obtain such solutions. Stimulated by the pioneering work of Cook [33], Karp [107], and Garey *et al.* [73], a considerable amount of work has been devoted to what is termed complexity theory, the objective of which is to classify problems in terms of the amount of time required to solve them as a function of the size of the problem. Good algorithms are defined as those for which the solution time is bounded above by a polynomial function of the size of the problem. Many common combinatorial type problems have no known good algorithm in this sense. Among these are sub-classes of 0–1 integer programming, travelling salesman, knapsack and job sequencing problems (see Karp

[109]). Until recently, even the standard linear programming problems were conjectured as not being good, since the simplex algorithm is not good. However, recently the Shor-Khachiyan ellipsoid method was developed, and this is a good algorithm in the sense described (see Aspvall [2]).

It must be stressed that the sense of 'good' used above is not necessarily the sense 'important' in the decision as to which algorithm to use, since, for example, the simplex algorithm, on the basis of evidence provided (see Bland *et al.* [19]) considerably out-performs the ellipsoid method. The important point, however, is that, for many problems, the computational time is very large and methods oriented to a reasonable compromise between loss of optimality and computational time need to be used. The choice between one of these methods and an algorithm to obtain optimal or ε-optimal solutions must be based on what evidence we have before us. Such a choice situation is referred to as a secondary problem in White [155], as distinct from primary problems, which relate to the physical problem (e.g. inventory) for which a solution procedure is being designed.

The evidence provided in the complexity theory area is of the worst case kind, and provides upper bounds for the order of the number of calculations, and this is not wholly what is required. Much more satisfactory evidence will come from numerical experimentation, although even this is a little risky unless we know that our particular problem clearly fits within the experiments carried out, and have some explanatory reason as to why the particular approach might be expected to give acceptable results for our particular problem. In the case of the simplex method, its performance in practice is much better than worst case analysis implies, although no satisfactory explanation exists for this.

Let us now turn our attention to the subject matter of this section, viz. heuristic programming. There appears to be no agreed definition of this term. Reitman [136] states: 'One of the more annoying problems facing those who have been concerned with heuristic programming has been the task of making clear just what the term covers'. The essential distinction he tries to draw is one between algorithmic and heuristic programming. He states:

We would suggest that the existence of an algorithm presumes:
(a) an explicitly specifiable class of problems all of which may be solved by
(b) the programme for the algorithm to
(c) some well defined criterion of solution.

In the context of optimization problems, an algorithm has an in-built procedure for testing whether a particular solution is optimal, or ε-optimal, and seeks one or the other type of solution, whereas an heuristic method does not.

Newell *et al.* [127] were, perhaps, the first to emphasize the need for the development of heuristic methods in Operational Research. Their interests in heuristics were much broader than the concern of this section, since they were concerned with heuristics as a means of tackling ill-structured problems in general. An ill-structured problem is a non-well-structured problem, and a well-structured problem is one in which:

(a) the problem can be described in terms of numerical variables, scalar and vector quantities;
(b) the goals to be obtained can be specified in terms of a well-defined objective function;
(c) there exist computational routines (algorithms) that permit the solution to be found and stated in actual numerical terms.

Requirement (b) would exclude more modern multi-objective formulations, but this is merely a matter of the degree to which a problem is well-defined and the intentions are clear enough. The authors do not define heuristic, but, in seeking analogies with the way human beings formulate and solve problems, it is clear that their ideas of heuristics orient around the concepts of intuition, insight and learning. Our own emphasis will, for the purposes of this section, be on the first two concepts. Basically our heuristic methods will be, in lay terms, rule-of-thum methods, backed up by intuition and insight. More formally we will adopt the definition of Nicholson [128], viz.

> a procedure for solving problems by an intuitive approach in which the structure of the problem can be interpreted and exploited intelligently to obtain a reasonable solution.

Beltrami et al. [17], who look specifically at vehicle routing problems, give a parallel definition, viz.

> think of heuristic reasoning as meaning that one brings to bear as much intuition, and as many plausible arguments, as possible on problems which are either computationally intractable, or for which inadequate theory exists.

It is to be noted that the distinction between heuristic and algorithm is not universal. Indeed Müller-Merbach [123] states explicitly that heuristics are algorithms. On the other hand de Werra et al. [57], although they do not explicitly draw this distinction, do so implicitly. Granot [85], for example, uses the combined term 'heuristic algorithms'.

We will consider some simple examples of heuristic programming. It is not intended that these will cover more than a minimal subset of heuristic approaches. It is also significant that we will not cover classical branch-and-bound approaches (see Garfinkel et al. [76] and Bansall [11]) which provides equally competitive approaches to the problems we will treat, and to many others. The reason is that such procedures are not heuristic when fully

110

defined, and are algorithmic, since they aim, in their proper form, to get optimal solutions, or ε-optimal solutions. It is true that the calculations may be terminated in the light of solution behaviour up to a point, and it is also true that the actual sub-procedures for branching and bounding may be selected intuitively, but this is also true of many algorithms, for example, even in the simplex algorithm.

A serious study of heuristic programming will require considerable reading. Streim [148] gives a list of alternative definitions. Müller-Merbach [123], Ball *et al.* [10] and de Werra *et al.* [57] give broad complementary coverage of the many approaches and applications of heuristic programming together with extensive bibliographies. A reference, not on these lists, is Kovaćs [112], which contains a chapter on heuristic methods in integer programming. (See also Côté *et al.* [40], Faaland *et al.* [64], Hockbaum *et al.* [96].)

Hebel *et al.* [92] and Chvatal [29] are texts on heuristic methods. Daellenbach *et al.* [43] have a general chapter on heuristic programming. Newell [126] has a general article on heuristic programming. Evans *et al.* [63], Hillier [94] and Assoch *et al.* [3] have an interesting contribution to the general area. Garey *et al.* [72, 74, 75] give bibliographies on heuristic programming and performance guarantees for combinatorial problems. Bishoff *et al.* [18] contains some general material. Michael [122] gives a useful review. Papoulis [132] discusses some theoretical issues. Dannenbring [45] evaluates some combinatorial heuristics. Johnson [105] discusses heuristics for combinatorial problems.

Let us begin with our first class of problems, viz. the travelling salesman problem. These have already been formulated as mathematical programmes and dynamic programmes (see Exercise (18)) in section 2.5, and the amount of computational time can be quite considerable, as is easily checked. The mathematical programme involves a considerable number of constraints and the dynamic programme involves a considerable number of states for large problems.

Let us consider a numerical example given in the Table 2.23. A common heuristic is the so-called nearest-neighbour heuristic which says 'move to your nearest neighbour which has not already been visited'.

Table 2.23

		To town j				
		1	2	3	4	5
From town i	1	—	10	25	25	20
	2	10	—	10	15	2
	3	8	9	—	20	10
	4	14	10	24	—	15
	5	10	8	25	27	—

t_{ij} is the time to get from town i to town j.

If we start at town 1 we generate two alternative sequences, viz.

(a) $1 \rightarrow 2 \rightarrow 5 \rightarrow 3 \rightarrow 4 \rightarrow 1$ with a total time of 71,
(b) $1 \rightarrow 5 \rightarrow 2 \rightarrow 3 \rightarrow 4 \rightarrow 1$ with a total time of 62.

Sequence (b) is actually an optimal sequence. Had we begun with town 3, we would have generated two sequences, viz.

(c) $3 \rightarrow 1 \rightarrow 2 \rightarrow 5 \rightarrow 4 \rightarrow 3$ with a total time of 71,
(d) $3 \rightarrow 1 \rightarrow 5 \rightarrow 2 \rightarrow 4 \rightarrow 3$ with a total time of 65.

There is no guarantee that even if we begin with all points as starting points, an optimal solution will be obtained among them (see Exercise 9).

The nearest-neighbour heuristic is actually a poor heuristic in the following sense, viz. for problems which satisfy the Euclidean property (i.e. $t_{ij} \leq t_{ik} + t_{kj}, \forall i, j, k$) it is possible to find problems where the ratio of the heuristic solution distance to the optimal time is arbitrarily large. In fact (see Lewis $et\ al.$ [115]) if we have m towns, if $\tilde{f}_m$ is the time obtained for any instance of applying the nearest neighbour heuristic to the travelling salesman problem with m towns, we have

$$\tilde{f}_m \leq ((\log_2(m) + 1)/2) f_m^*$$

where f_m^* is the optimal time, and there exists, for each m, an instance such that

$$\tilde{f}_m > ((\log(m + 1) + 4/3)/3 f_m^*$$

showing just how bad the method can be.

A comprehensive survey of heuristics and their relative performance for the travelling salesman problem is given by Bodin $et\ al.$ [20]. It is to be noted that they also consider the heuristics to be algorithms. Some of the approaches considered are as follows, and are worked out for the numerical example just considered.

The justification for each method should be considered (see Exercise 28). The justification for the nearest-neighbour method is clear, viz. it attempts to minimize the value-added at each stage. It is a greedy heuristic (see Dunstan [58] and Edmunds [60]).

Nearest-Neighbour

Already covered (see Lewis $et\ al.$ [115, 116]).

Cheapest Insertion (via completed sub-tours) (see Lewis $et\ al.$ [115, 116]).

(i) Begin with some point, e.g. $i = 1$.
(ii) Find nearest neighbour, e.g. $j = 2$.

Figure 2.18

(iii) Find $k \neq 1, 2$ to minimize

$$t_{1k} + t_{k2} - t_{12}, \quad \text{or} \quad t_{2k} + t_{k1} - t_{21}$$

$\underline{k = 3}$ $t_{13} + t_{32} - t_{12} = 24$ or $t_{23} + t_{31} - t_{21} = 8$

$\underline{k = 4}$ $t_{14} + t_{42} - t_{12} = 25$ or $t_{24} + t_{41} - t_{21} = 19$

$\underline{k = 5}$ $t_{15} + t_{52} - t_{12} = 8$ or $t_{25} + t_{51} - t_{21} = ②.$

Figure 2.19

(iv) Delete $2 \to 1$. Replace by $2 \to 5 \to 1$. Complete the sub-tour. The minimal added time is 2.

(v) Now find $k \neq 1, 2, 5$ to minimize

$$t_{2k} + t_{k5} - t_{25}$$
$$t_{1k} + t_{k2} - t_{12}$$
$$t_{5k} + t_{k1} - t_{51}$$

$\underline{k = 3}$ $t_{23} + t_{35} - t_{25} = ⑱$

       $t_{13} + t_{32} - t_{12} = 24$

       $t_{53} + t_{31} - t_{51} = 23$

$\underline{k = 4}$ $t_{24} + t_{45} - t_{25} = 28$

       $t_{14} + t_{42} - t_{12} = 25$

       $t_{54} + t_{41} - t_{51} = 31.$

(vi) Delete $2 \to 5$. Replace by $2 \to 3 \to 5$. Complete the sub-tour.

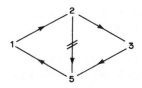

Figure 2.20

(vii) Find $k \neq 1, 2, 3, 5$ to minimize

$$t_{1k} + t_{k2} - t_{12}$$
$$t_{2k} + t_{k3} - t_{23}$$
$$t_{3k} + t_{k5} - t_{35}$$
$$t_{5k} + t_{k1} - t_{51}.$$

$$\underline{k=4} \quad t_{14}+t_{42}-t_{12}=\enclose{circle}{25}$$
$$t_{24}+t_{43}-t_{23}=29$$
$$t_{34}+t_{45}-t_{35}=\enclose{circle}{25}$$
$$t_{54}+t_{41}-t_{51}=31.$$

(viii) Delete $1\rightarrow 2$ or $3\rightarrow 5$, replace by $1\rightarrow 4\rightarrow 2$ or $3\rightarrow 4\rightarrow 5$. Complete the tour.

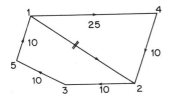

Figure 2.21   Figure 2.22

(iv) Final tour is $1\rightarrow 4\rightarrow 2\rightarrow 3\rightarrow 5\rightarrow 1$(time = 65)

or $1\rightarrow 2\rightarrow 3\rightarrow 5\rightarrow 4\rightarrow 1$(time = 65).

This is not optimal, but for a range of problems the heuristic performs well. The basic idea is to add links by splitting existing links in such a way as to minimize the added time at each stage.

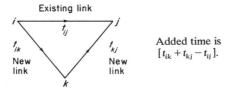

Figure 2.23

Nearest Insertion (see Lewis *et al.* [115, 116]).

As for Cheapest Insertion except that the k chosen to include is nearest to the points already obtained, and then k is inserted to minimize the added time. Thus in step (iii):

$$\underline{k=3} \quad t_{13}=25, \quad t_{32}=9, \quad t_{23}=10, \quad t_{31}=8,$$
$$\underline{k=4} \quad t_{14}=25, \quad t_{42}=10, \quad t_{24}=15, \quad t_{41}=14,$$
$$\underline{k=5} \quad t_{15}=10, \quad t_{52}=8, \quad t_{25}=\enclose{circle}{2}, \quad t_{51}=10.$$

114

Hence take $k = 5$. Continue as before but always choose k for inclusion on the basis of nearest point.

Arbitrary Insertion (see Lewis *et al.* [115, 116]).

As for Cheapest Insertion, but k is chosen on an arbitrary, random, basis.

Furthest Insertion (see Lewis *et al.* [115, 116]).

As for Cheapest Insertion but k is chosen to minimize

$$\underset{i, j}{\text{maximum}}[t_{ik} + t_{kj} - t_{ij}].$$

Convex Hull (see Christofides *et al.* [26]).

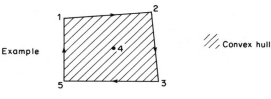

Figure 2.24

For Euclidean problems (i.e. $t_{ij} \leq t_{ik} + t_{kj}$), it is known that the sequence of points in the boundary of the convex hull must be the same in the optimal solution.

Hence we begin with such a tour. We may then apply other heuristics. The initial tour is either $1 \rightarrow 2 \rightarrow 3 \rightarrow 5 \rightarrow 1$ or $1 \rightarrow 5 \rightarrow 3 \rightarrow 2 \rightarrow 1$.

The initial example is not Euclidean e.g.

$$t_{12} + t_{23} = 20 < 25 = t_{13}.$$

Other useful references for the travelling salesman problem are d'Atri [49], Karp [108], Bellmore *et al.* [14], Shapiro [143], Croes [42], Dantzig *et al.* [48], Felts *et al.* [65], Little *et al.* [117] and Lewis *et al.* [115].

Another well-studied problem is the vehicle routing problem, specified as follows:

a depot, P_0, supplying the delivery requirements;
a set of trucks, of capacities $C_1, C_2, \ldots, C_n$;
a set of delivery points $P_1, P_2, \ldots, P_i, \ldots, P_N$;
distances d_{ij} between P_i and P_j (these need not be symmetric);
delivery quantities $s_1, s_2, \ldots, s_i, \ldots s_N$, for points $1, 2, \ldots, i, \ldots, N$.

To find a delivery schedule to minimize total mileage in delivery requirements.

The following method is similar to the cheapest insertion method for the travelling salesman problem (see Clarke *et al.* [30]).

Thus consider any two tours which can be carried out by two vehicles (Figure 2.25). Suppose we now link P_1 and P_3. There are various ways of

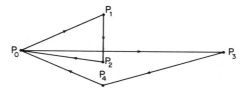

Figure 2.25

doing this. We are only allowed to remove one link containing P_1 or P_3 from each route, but we may reverse the directions if need be (Figure 2.26). The

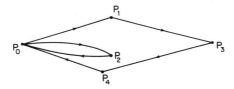

Figure 2.26

difference in distance travelled is calculated, providing each vehicle has the capacity to meet all demands on its route on one run. In the above case this is

$$d_{01}+d_{12}+d_{20}+d_{03}+d_{34}+d_{40}-(d_{01}+d_{13}+d_{34}+d_{40}+d_{02}+d_{20})$$
$$= d_{12}+d_{03}-d_{13}-d_{02}.$$

This is done for all such linking possibilities, and the maximal saving taken over all possible links, and all possible ways of rejoining, subject to feasibility of meeting the required deliveries, determines which changes are made. This is repeated until no extra savings can be made by this method.

Consider the symmetric example shown in Table 2.24 (three vehicles, capacities $C_1 = 8$, $C_2 = 11$, $C_3 = 16$).

Table 2.24

				P_j			
		0	1	2	3	4	Requirement
	0	0	10	12	7	8	—
	1	10	0	8	5	8	10
P_i	2	12	8	0	6	7	5
	3	7	5	6	0	9	11
	4	8	8	7	9	0	6

First iteration

$$\overset{2}{(0 \to 1 \to 0)}, \overset{1}{(0 \to 2 \to 0)}, \overset{2}{(0 \to 3 \to 0)}, \overset{1}{(0 \to 4 \to 0)}. \text{ Distance} = 74.$$

(The numbers at the top indicate which size vehicle; obviously the smallest compatible size is used.)

Second iteration

Note that if P_i and P_j are joined, exactly one link is removed from the routes in the first iteration containing P_i and P_j respectively (i.e. one each) and that, for example, a route $(0 \to 1 \to 0)$ consists of two links.

(i) *Link P_1 and P_2*

The only possibility is $\overset{3}{(0 \to 1 \to 2 \to 0)}, \overset{2}{(0 \to 3 \to 0)}, \overset{1}{(0 \to 4 \to 0)}$ with total distance of 60.

(ii) *Link P_1 and P_3*

This is not possible since a single vehicle cannot carry the total load required.

(iii) *Link P_1 and P_4*

The only possibility is $\overset{3}{(0 \to 1 \to 4 \to 0)}, \overset{1}{(0 \to 2 \to 0)}, \overset{2}{(0 \to 3 \to 0)}$. With a total distance of 74.

(iv) *Link P_2 and P_3*

The only possibility is $\overset{3}{(0 \to 2 \to 3 \to 0)}, \overset{2}{(0 \to 1 \to 0)}, \overset{1}{(0 \to 4 \to 0)}$ with a total distance of 61.

(v) *Link P_2 and P_4*

The only possibility is $\overset{2}{(0 \to 2 \to 4 \to 0)}, \overset{2}{(0 \to 1 \to 0)}, \overset{2}{(0 \to 3 \to 0)}$ with a total distance of 61.

(vi) *Link P_3 and P_4*

This is not possible since a single vehicle cannot carry the total load required.

The link to introduce is therefore $P_1 P_2$, and this gives the routes as shown in Figure 2.27.

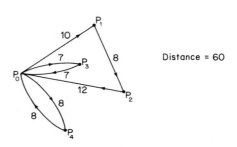

Figure 2.27

Third iteration

(i) *Join* P_1 *and* P_3

This is not possible since a single vehicle cannot carry the total load required.

(ii) *Join* P_1 *and* P_4

The only possibilities are given in Figures 2.28 and 2.29.

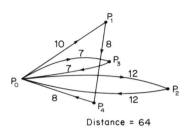

Distance = 64

Figure 2.28

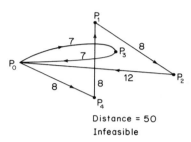

Distance = 50
Infeasible

Figure 2.29

One may now proceed to consider adding links P_2P_3, P_2P_4, P_3P_4 (not feasible because of load requirements), and it will be found that the link to introduce is either P_2P_3 or P_2P_4. Choosing the former, we obtain Figures 2.30 and 2.31. Figure 2.30 is infeasible, and Figure 2.31 was obtained in

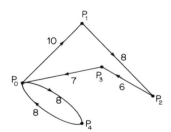

Figure 2.30

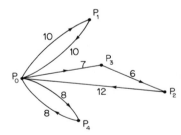

Figure 2.31

iteration 2, step (iv). Choosing P_2P_4 produces similar results. The procedure therefore stops with the solution obtained at the end of iteration 2.

The reader should fill in all the missing steps in the above analysis.

Schultz [140] has a variant of this method which builds up a tour, in one iteration, using the distance saved, as calculated in the Clarke–Wright heuristic to add towns in order of the size of this (also see the heuristic of Benton *et al.* [15]).

These ideas may be extended to removing and adding different numbers of links. (e.g. see Christofides *et al.* [26]). As we increase the number of linking operations allowed we will tend to get better solutions. We might find that if we increase these from three to five, for example, we get little improvement, suggesting that we are already close to optimal. In their paper the authors carry out an empirical evaluation of the relative effectiveness of the method of Clarke *et al.*, of the extension to include the addition of three links, and of a branch-and-bound approach. The authors also indicate that the Clarke *et al.* method can be bad.

Finally, whereas the heuristics suggested for the travelling salesman problem have the form of a greedy heuristic, the heuristics suggested in this section, with the exception of Schultz [140], for the vehicle routing problem have the form of improvement heuristics (see de Werra *et al.* [57]). Other useful references for problems of this kind are Christofides *et al.* [26], Foulds *et al.* [69], Rijckaert *et al.* [137], Fisk *et al.* [67], Foulds *et al.* [70], Gillett *et al.* [81], Hill *et al.* [93] and Oneil *et al.* [130].

A further class of problems which have been extensively studied from an heuristic point of view are location allocation problems, some of which we briefly discussed in section 2.5.

Let us begin with the m supply point, n destination, problem discussed in section 2.5. An intuitive approach is as follows (see White [155]):

(i) choose a suitable initial location for each supply point;
(ii) allocate each destination to its nearest supply point;
(iii) relocate each supply point in a position which is optimal for its destination set given by (ii);
(iv) return to setp (ii), and repeat until no further improvement can be made.

This heuristic is again an improvement heuristic, and will not give optimal solutions in general. It will do so if we cover all starting points of course.

Cooper [36] considers a similar problem, but involving capacity considerations, and allowing the location of the supply points to be continuous variables. His heuristic is an iterative scheme based upon the equations obtained by setting the partial derivatives equal to zero. It is neither greedy nor improvement in form.

Jacobsen *et al.* [102] consider a similar problem, in which however, the problem of determining routes for vehicles is involved, and use the Clarke–Wright procedure as a sub-heuristic.

Geoffrion [77] considers a similar problem to the first one, where the heuristic used is of somewhat of a different nature, and the purpose is somewhat different, the latter point being returned to later on when we discuss sensitivity analysis in Chapter 3. The assumptions are as follows:

(i) a region of m square miles is to be served by x warehouses;
(ii) the demand for the product is uniformly distributed throughout the region with a density of s units of product per year per square mile;
(iii) it costs u to supply a warehouse with one unit of product, irrespective of warehouse location and size;

(iv) it costs v to process one unit of product for delivery to a customer, irrespective of warehouse location or size, or of customer;

(v) it costs c per unit of product per mile distance of the supplying warehouse from any customer it supplies;

(vi) there is a fixed annual cost, a, of putting in a warehouse, irrespective of size and location;

(vii) the objective is to determine how many, x, warehouses and their location, to minimize total annual costs.

The heuristic suggested is to consider each warehouse to be at the centre of an approximately circular region, each one being of the same size and packed into the area m. A warehouse serves customers within its region. The regions are not exactly circular, and the approximation is used only for calculating costs of supplying customers within a region. The annual costs are as follows, where r is the radius of the approximately circular regions:

cost of supplying a warehouse $= (m/x)su$
cost of a warehouse processing $= (m/x)sv$
fixed cost of a warehouse $= a$
cost of supplying customers from a warehouse $=$

$$c \int_{t=0}^{r} t(2\pi t)(s\ \mathrm{d}t) = \tfrac{2}{3}\pi csr^3 = \tfrac{2}{3}\pi cs(m/\pi x)^{3/2}$$

since $\pi r^2 = m/x$.

Hence the total annual cost is:

$$f(x) = x\left\{\frac{m}{x}su + \frac{m}{x}sv + a + \tfrac{2}{3}csm^{3/2}\pi^{-1/2}x^{-3/2}\right\}$$
$$= ms(u+v) + ax + \tfrac{2}{3}\pi^{-1/2}csm^{3/2}x^{-1/2}.$$

Considering, for the moment, x to be continuous, and differentiating with respect to x, we obtain:

$$f'(x) = a - \tfrac{1}{3}\pi^{-1/2}csm^{3/2}x^{-3/2}$$
$$f''(x) = \tfrac{1}{2}\pi^{-1/2}csm^{3/2}x^{-5/2} > 0.$$

Hence the optimal x is given by $f'(x) = 0$, i.e:

$$x^* = m\left(\frac{cs}{a}\right)^{2/3} \Big/ (3\pi^{1/2})^{2/3}$$

and the minimal cost is given by:

$$f^* = ms(u+v) + m(3(sc)^2 a/\pi)^{1/3}.$$

If x^* is not integral, we evaluate $f(\lceil x^* \rceil)$ and $f(\lceil x^* \rceil + 1)$ and take the lowest value, where $\lceil x^* \rceil$ is the integer part of x^*.

This heuristic may be used to give a starting solution, which may then be improved upon by appropriate combinations of contiguous regions. For large

120

initial regions, where x is expected to be large, it seems reasonable that it would give a solution quite close to the optimum, although this would have to be justified rigorously. However, the alternative mathematical programming approach could be quite demanding in computational time.

The heuristic is analytic, and may be considered as an approximation heuristic, or an initial solution heuristic.

A very useful source of material on location–allocation problems may be found in Halpern [90], including many references. Other useful references are Brosch [23], Cooper [36], Jacobsen [101], Wolsey [157], Boffey et al. [21], Cornuejols et al. [38, 39], Gizelis et al. [82], Spielberg [147], Weiss [153], Barker [6], Hamburger et al. [91] and Karp et al. [110].

Perhaps one of the most studied areas from the point of view of heuristic programming is that of machine scheduling, a problem we looked at from a mathematical programming point of view in section 2.5. Let us consider the following problem taken from Smith et al. [146].

Given n jobs and m machines, where each job has to go on each machine in sequence. We assume the job sequence is the same on each machine, and t_{ik} is the time for job i on machine k. The problem is to find the optimal sequence to minimize the time to complete all jobs.

Let us look at a possible situation when job j follows job i follows job s, as shown in Figure 2.32. This shows a mixture of idle times for machines

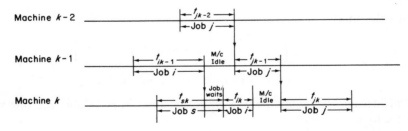

Figure 2.32

and waiting times for jobs. An ideal situation seems to occur when a sequence can be chosen such that, if job j follows job i, then $t_{ik} = t_{jk-1}$, for all such i, j. Thus we pack in the jobs as follows, where we assume the sequences are $1, 2, \ldots, n$, in Figure 2.33. In this case we have no waiting or idleness, but even this may not be optimal, e.g. let $n = m = 2$, $t_{11} = 4$, $t_{12} = 2$, $t_{21} = 2$, $t_{22} = 3$. We then have a sequence with the previous property, but it is not optimal as indicated in Figures 2.34 and 2.35.

The heuristic method uses the packing idea on the assumption that, when Figure 2.33 applies, a good solution will be given by using this sequence. It

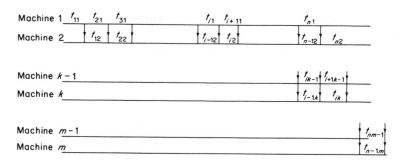

Figure 2.33

Packing method

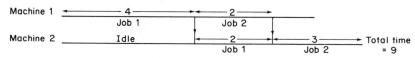

Figure 2.34

Optimum

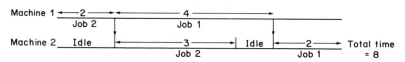

Figure 2.35

defines, therefore, a packing measure as follows:

$$p_{ijk} = t_{ik} - t_{jk-1}, \qquad 2 \leq k \leq m$$

$$p_{ij} = \sum_{k=2}^{m} |p_{ijk}|.$$

Let i_s be the number of the item in the sth position, and $(i_1, i_2, \ldots, i_n)$ be any sequence. The overall packing measure p is defined by:

$$p = \sum_{s=1}^{n-1} p_{i_s i_{s+1}}.$$

When a sequence exists for which

$$t_{i_s k} = t_{i_{s+1} k-1}, \qquad 2 \leq k \leq m,$$

we have $p = 0$. This is true in the example given, but an optimal sequence is not given by the method.

This heuristic is yet again different to the previous heuristics. It is a surrogate objective function heuristic, in that it attempts to construct a more tractable objective function which is positively correlated with the original one.

An alternative approach would be to sequence in terms of the shortest processing time on the first machine, in the hope that this will reduce the idle time on subsequent machines, and the minimization of such idle time will minimize the total time. For the packing method example given previously this gives the optimal solution, and the idle time on the second machine is minimal in the optimal solution. On average, one might expect this heuristic to perform reasonably well. Experimental studies of the effectiveness of various rules have been carried out by Bakru and Rao (see Conway *et al.* [32], Chapter 6).

Baker [7] includes discussions of various heuristic methods for machine scheduling problems. Other useful references are Dannenbring [44, 46, 47], Sisson [144], Gere [79], King [111], Cliffe [31], Beshara *et al.* [16], Day *et al.* [51], Iskander *et al.* [100], Demster *et al.* [55], Enscore *et al.* [62], Hosios *et al.* [97], Potts [134], Campbell *et al.* [25], Forn *et al.* [68], Giglio *et al.* [80], Gupta [86–88], Krone *et al.* [113] and Palmer [131].

A further class of problems which have been extensively studied from the point of view of heuristic programming is the classical knapsack problem. Formulated mathematically this is as follows (see Exercise 29 of Mathematical and Dynamic Programming Exercises):

$$\text{maximize}\left[f(x) = \sum_{j=1}^{n} p_j x_j\right]$$

$$\text{subject to } \sum_{j=1}^{n} a_j x_j \leq b$$

$$x_j \geq 0 \quad \text{and integer}, \qquad j = 1, 2, \ldots, n$$

$$a_j > 0, \qquad j = 1, 2, \ldots, n.$$

The standard heuristic is the so-called greedy heuristic which is as follows. Assume that the numbering is such that:

$$p_1/a_1 \geq p_2/a_2 \ldots \geq p_j/a_j \ldots \geq p_n/a_n.$$

Then set:

$$x_1^* = \lceil b/a_1 \rceil$$

$$x_2^* = \left\lceil \frac{b - a_1 x_1^*}{a_2} \right\rceil$$

$$\vdots$$

$$x_j^* = \left\lceil \frac{b - \sum_{t=1}^{j-1} a_t x_t^*}{a_j} \right\rceil$$

$$x_n^* = \left\lceil \frac{b - \sum_{t=1}^{n-1} a_t x_t^*}{a_n} \right\rceil$$

$\lceil z \rceil$ = integer part of z.

It attempts to maximize the value added at each stage. It can, of course, produce bad results, as can other heuristics. A survey of approaches to this problem is given by de Kluyver et al. [53]. Sahni [139] and Balas et al. [9] consider the special 0–1 knapsack problem.

It may be shown (see Garey et al. [73]) that the greedy knapsack heuristic always gives at least half of the optimal value achievable. In looking at heuristic methods, results of this kind are of fundamental importance in assessing the risks involved in using it. The proof of the above proposition is as follows.

Let f^* be the true optimal attainable level of the objective function and $\bar{x}_1$ be the value of x_1 such that

$$a_1 \bar{x}_1 \leq b < a_1(\bar{x}_1 + 1)$$

and let $\tilde{f}$ be the objective function value attained using the heuristic method. Then

$$\tilde{f} \geq \bar{x}_1 p_1 = (\bar{x}_1 + 1)p_1 - p_1 \geq f^* - p_1$$

and

$$p_1 \leq \tilde{f}$$

if we assume that $\bar{x}_1 \geq 1$ (if not, then x_1 is merely deleted and the analysis repeated with x_2 and so on, and if we delete all such x_j we clearly have $f^* = \tilde{f} = 0$).
Then

$$\tilde{f} \geq \tfrac{1}{2} f^*.$$

It is possible to find examples in which the figure of $\tfrac{1}{2}$ can be approximated as closely as desired (see Exercise 3).

It is to be noted that, for the specific problem,

$$\tilde{f} \geq \bar{x}_1 f^* / (1 + \bar{x}_1).$$

We have mentioned greedy heuristics on various occasions. For some classes of problem these are actually algorithms, in our sense, since they will produce optimal solutions. Hu et al. [98], for example, study conditions under which the knapsack greedy heuristic will give optimal solutions. Dunstan et al. [58] study greedy heuristics for a special class of linear programming problems, using the ideas of matroids, and show that, under matroidal type conditions, optimal solutions will be obtained. Edmunds [60] studies the relationship between matroids and greedy heuristics.

Another area where a greedy heuristic will actually give optimal solutions is in the determination of a minimal weighted spanning tree (see the soap film analogues mentioned earlier on, although the problems discussed there are slightly different since the soap film problem has, in effect, and infinity of possible arcs). In this sort of problem a finite network of points has to be connected by a linking network of arcs with no loops. Each arc has a weighting factor. It is required to find the network that has no loops, connecting all the points, and has a minimal total weight. Kruskal's [114] method is a greedy algorithm which actually gives optimal solutions. This consists of adding arcs in order of increasing weight, excluding any which would form loops, until a spanning tree is found. On the assumption that a spanning tree exists, the solution obtained will be optimal. This is similar to the greedy travelling salesman heuristic, although the latter need not produce an optimal solution.

In the text we discussed an n job, m machine, problem. For such problems, greedy heuristics (such as sequence in order of the shortest processing time on a machine, or, when due dates are given for the jobs, sequence in order of earliest due date) are often suggested. For some problems these can actually give optimal answers (see Exercises 34 and 35).

Finally Exercise 4 on searching, of Chapter 1, illustrates other greedy methods which give optimal solutions for those problems.

The fact that greedy methods will give optimal solutions for some problems supports their use, with judicious care, for related problems.

Other similar classes of problem which have received considerable attention from an heuristic point of view are trim-loss and assortment problems. A simple example of the former problem was considered in section 2.5. More general problems of this kind involve a range of materials, of various sizes, and a range of items to be cut from them. For many problems the combinations to be cut from a particular piece need not fit regularly into the item, and may be cut at different angles in different positions. Hinxman [95] gives a survey of such problems. See also Golden [84], Albano [1], Christofides *et al.* [28], Dyson *et al.* [59], Eisemann [61], Roberts [138], Skalbeck *et al.* [145] and Wang [149, 150].

So far, we have restricted ourselves to static non-probabilistic problems, whereas many problems are dynamic and probabilistic as we have seen earlier on in this chapter. These problems, if tackled in their precise form, can be extremely difficult to handle, and simplified heuristic procedures are used to solve these. We will look at one approach under the heading of infrequent but significant contingencies (see White [154]). The basic idea behind this is that certain events, which are significant enough to be included in the objective function to be optimized, are nontheless infrequent enough in an optimal solution to be ignored in certain parts of the calculations. This is a form of heuristic reasoning and, of course, when a solution is obtained by such means it must be tested to see that, indeed, the assumption is correct. We will use an earlier example to illustrate the approach.

Let us return to the probabilistic inventory problem of section 2.2 and let us change the policy so that now, if the inventory level drops to a level y, we

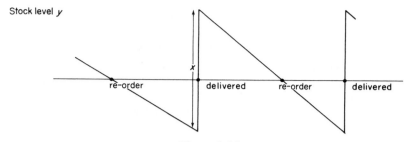

Figure 2.36

order a quantity x. Also let the time for this order to be delivered be one unit of time (we can change the time scale to do this). Otherwise let the problem remain the same. Figure 2.36 describes the situation.

For this problem with $g(s)$ being the probability density function for demand s in unit time (the replenishment time), if we view a cycle between re-order points, the total purchase cost per cycle is $a + cx$.

The stockholding cost in the cycle is better viewed by looking at the time between delivery times. The expected stock level at such times is $\int_{s=0}^{y}(y-s)g(s)\,ds$. However, it is possible that the stock level will drop to zero before the delivery time, and, when calculating the expected stockholding cost for a cycle, one should determine the probability density function for the period U to run out from the delivery time, as we did in section 2.2. Calculating this part is possible, but can add considerable complications to getting the solution. Intuitively, if the penalty cost for shortages is high enough, it is reasonable to assume that, for the purposes of this part of the calculation, the probability of shortage is small. Thus the stockholding cost per unit time is taken to be:

$$h\left(\frac{x}{2} + \int_{s=0}^{y} (y-s)g(s)\,ds\right).$$

The expected shortage cost per cycle is:

$$r\int_{s=y}^{\infty} (s-y)g(s)\,ds.$$

Thus the expected cost per unit time is taken to be:

$$\frac{a + cx + h\left(\frac{x}{2} + \int_{x=0}^{y} (y-s)g(s)\,ds\right)\hat{T} + r\int_{s=y}^{\infty} (s-y)g(s)\,ds}{\hat{T}}$$

where $\hat{T}$ is the expected cycle time.

Now, if we assume that the probability of a shortage is small, we have:

$$\hat{T} = x \Big/ \int_{s=0}^{\infty} sg(s)\,ds = x/\hat{s}.$$

and the expected cost per unit time becomes:

$$f(x, y) = \frac{hx}{2} + \hat{s}\left(a + r\int_{s=y}^{\infty} (s-y)g(s)\,\mathrm{d}s\right)\bigg/ x + h\int_{s=0}^{y} (y-s)g(s)\,\mathrm{d}x + c\hat{s}.$$

The actual expected cycle time is $x/\hat{s}$ plus the expected duration of stock shortage and, although this can also be included, it considerably complicates the derivation of a solution which is rather easier for the $f(x, y)$ function above. For a given value of y, the optimal x is obtained as the usual square-root-type solution and then y can be optimized. When the solution is obtained it must be checked that the errors introduced by assuming that the run-out probability is small are indeed small.

2.9 LAS VEGAS

In any Operational Research study one has to compromise between the cost and time involved in the calculations in the first instance, and the anticipated benefit in obtaining improved solutions in the second instance. Las Vegas is a formalized method for doing this; it is not so much for general use where new alternatives are generated in the light of the best solution to date, but for the situations where the problem is fully structured but where more mathematical means, or even heuristic methods, are not thought to be appropriate. The essential idea is to generate solutions on a controlled random basis and to estimate the probabilities of being able to obtain improved solutions on the basis of performance to date at any point in time, and use these estimates to decide whether to stop and accept the best solution to data, or to sample a further solution.

We take the term Las Vegas from Ackoff [1]. A more modern term is optimal stopping (see Kushmer [5] and Robbins [81]). Part of our development will be similar to that of Radner [7] in the formalization of the stopping rule, since Ackoff does not actually do so. Also see White [10] for a formalization.

Let us briefly sketch the framework for the Las Vegas method.

Let X be our feasible set of actions. This may be specified in many forms. Thus X may be the set of all $x \in \mathbb{R}^n$, satisfying constraints $g_i(x) \leqq b_i$, $i = 1, 2, \ldots, p$. Alternatively X may be the set of all possible decision rules in some dynamic problem, or X may be the set of all possible sequences of jobs, subject possibly to precedence constraints. X is quite general.

Let our objective be a single objective function, $h(x)$, $x \in X$. Again h may be quite general. It could be a linear function on X. It could be some complex function for evaluating the performance of a particular sequence of jobs. All that is required is that we be able to evaluate $h(x)$, or at least some bound in the first instance, for each $x \in X$. We assume h is to be minimized.

We now need to set up a solution sampling procedure. To do this we select a set S containing X. It may be identical with X, but it may not. The reason for this is that it is sometimes difficult to select x, so that it is in

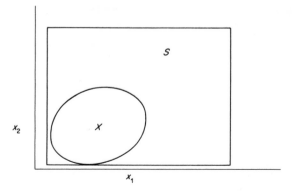

Figure 2.37

X, without considerable effort. Thus if X is a set of integer solutions to an integer linear programme, even finding an initial feasible solution can be difficult. Or if X is a set of decision rules which must satisfy some constraints on dynamic behaviour, such as a constraint on the shortage probability in inventory control, it is usually difficult to ensure that an x can be easily generated to meet this requirement. By making S very simple in structure we can easily select points in S and then all we need to do is to throw away those which are not feasible.

Figure 2.37 illustrates the framework when $X \subseteq \mathbb{R}^2$, i.e. $x = (x_1, x_2)$. The procedure is as follows:

(i) set up a sampling procedure for selecting members of S;
(ii) suppose we have selected a sequence of members of S and, of these, $\{x^1, x^2, \ldots, x^r\}$ have been found to be feasible for X also. All others are discarded, and let

$$z^r = \min_{1 \leqslant s \leqslant r} [h(x^s)]$$

i.e. the best value of the objective function to date;
(iii) stop if the level of z^r is acceptable in the light of further effort needed to improve on this solution, otherwise take a further sample from S, returning to step (ii).

This procedure is used at an intuitive level in any problem-solving process. We may, however, formalize it using a dynamic programming procedure if we are prepared to make certain assumptions as follows:

(i) each solution sample costs an amount c to determine and process (this is not quite correct since, if the sample is infeasible, no further calculations are made with this sample and, to simplify matters, one might find lower bounds on the sample objective function value as a possible elimination step before finding the actual value if need be);

(ii) there is a probability q that a sample solution will be feasible for X;

(iii) the sampling procedure will generate, for the feasible x in X, a probability density function, or discrete probability distribution, for the objective function values h over X (we will use the continuous form, but for such things as sequencing the discrete form is needed) and let ϕ be the random objective function h value with $g(\phi)$ as the probability density function for ϕ;

(iv) the objective is to determine a stopping rule which will minimize the expected total sum of the objective function value and all computational costs up to the time of stopping.

Suppose that we are at some point where the best objective function value to date is z and we now have to decide whether to stop or to seek a further solution. Clearly the expected total sum of future computational costs and the value of the objective function on stopping depends only on z. Let this sum be $f(z)$.

The basic dynamic programming formula is as follows:

$$f(z) = \min \begin{bmatrix} \text{Terminate, accept best value to date: } z \\ \text{Take a further sample: } c + q\int_{\phi<z} f(\phi)g(\phi)\,\mathrm{d}\phi \\ + q\int_{\phi\geqslant z} f(z)g(\phi)\,\mathrm{d}\phi + (1-q)f(z) \end{bmatrix}$$

$$= \min \begin{bmatrix} z \\ \theta(z) \end{bmatrix} \text{say.}$$

We see that, assuming $f(z)$ has a derivative at z;

$$\theta'(z) = qf(z)\phi(z) - qf(z)\phi(z) + qf'(z)\int_{\phi\geqslant z} g(\phi)\,\mathrm{d}\phi + (1-q)f'(z)$$

$$= f'(z)\left(1 - q\int_{\phi<z} g(\phi)\,\mathrm{d}\phi\right) \leqslant f'(z).$$

We do not need to assume $f'(z)$ actually exists, since we could evaluate $\theta(z+\delta z) - \theta(z)$ in terms of $f(z+\delta z) - f(z)$, which would suffice.

It is clear that $f(z)$ is monotonic non-decreasing in z. Hence $\theta(z)$ is monotonic non-decreasing in z, and there will be some point, $z = z^*$, at which $z = \theta(z)$, or we will always have $z < \theta(z)$, or always have $z > \theta(z)$.

Hence there is an optimal decision rule of the form: for some z^*:

terminate if $z < z^*$,

take a further sample if $z \geqslant z^*$,

where z^* may be $\pm\infty$.

Let us now consider such rules and define: $f(z, z^*)$ to be the minimal expected total (sample costs + terminal objective function value) from now onwards, if our best objective function value to date is z, and we use a decision rule with critical value z^*.

Now if $z \geqslant z^*$, we will continue sampling until we reach a $z < z^*$. Thus

$z \geqslant z^*$ is effectively the same as $z = z^*$ and

$z \geqslant z^*$

$$f(z, z^*) = f(z^*, z^*).$$

Alternatively, if $z < z^*$, we stop sampling, and

$z < z^*$

$$f(z, z^*) = z.$$

Then for $z \geqslant z^*$, we have:

$$f(z, z^*) = f(z^*, z^*) = c + q \int_{\phi \geqslant z^*} f(z^*, z^*) g(\phi) \, d\phi$$

$$+ q \int_{\phi < z^*} f(\phi, z^*) g(\phi) \, d\phi + (1-q) f(z^*, z^*)$$

$$= c + q f(z^*, z^*) \int_{\phi \geqslant z^*} g(\phi) \, d\phi + q \int_{\phi < z^*} \phi g(\phi) \, d\phi + (1-q) f(z^*, z^*).$$

Rearranging this we obtain:

$z \geqslant z^*$

$$f(z, z^*) = f(z^*, z^*) = \left(cq^{-1} + \int_{\phi < z^*} \phi g(\phi) \, d\phi \right) \Big/ \int_{\phi < z^*} g(\phi) \, d\phi.$$

Let $f(z^*, z^*) = R(z^*)$, say.
To simplify the analysis let $\min[z] = \underline{z}$, $\max[z] = \bar{z}$ exist, so that:

$$\underline{z} \leqslant z \leqslant \bar{z}.$$

Clearly we may assume that:

$$\underline{z} \leqslant z^* \leqslant \bar{z}$$

since

$$z > \bar{z} \to R(z^*) = R(\bar{z}), \quad z^* < \underline{z} \to R(z^*) = R(\underline{z}).$$

Now let $\hat{z}$ give the minimal value of $R(z^*)$ in the above range and $z^* \neq \hat{z}$.
Let $\hat{z}$ be unique.
The existence of an optimal decision rule of the specified form implies that, for the optimal z^*, $f(z, z^*)$ is optimal for all z.
Since $z^* \neq z$, either we have $z^* < \hat{z}$, in which case:

$$f(\hat{z}, \hat{z}) = R(\hat{z}) < R(z^*) = f(\hat{z}, z^*),$$

i.e. $\hat{z}$ is better than z^*, or we have $\hat{z} < z^*$, in which case:

$$f(z^*, \hat{z}) = R(\hat{z}) < R(z^*) = f(\hat{z}, z^*),$$

i.e. $\hat{z}$ is better than z^*.

Hence, under the specified conditions and uniqueness of $\hat{z}$, the optimal decision rule is to choose $z^* = \hat{z}$.

With more analysis we may remove these conditions to obtain the same result, allowing for the possibility that $z^* = \infty$. A similar analysis may be carried out when we have discrete probabilities, to obtain the same result.

An alternative method of finding the optimal z^* is to note that, at $z = z^*$, it is equally optimal to terminate or continue, in the probability density function case, in which case

$$z^* = R(z^*)(\text{since } f(z^*) = f(z^*, z^*) = z^*)$$

as may easily be checked.

Providing this has a unique solution, this will give us our optimal solution. For non-probability density function cases, z^* must satisfy, for $z = z^*$;

$$z^* \geqslant R(z^*)$$

and we find the smallest value of z^* for which this is true.

Consider the following simple example:

$$g(\phi) = 1/\lambda, \qquad 0 \leqslant \phi \leqslant \lambda \quad (\underline{z} = 0, \bar{z} = \lambda), \qquad 0 \leqslant z^* \leqslant \lambda.$$

Then:

$$R(z^*) = \left(\int_{\phi < z^*} \frac{\phi}{\lambda} \, d\phi + cq^{-1} \right) \Big/ \left(\int_{\phi < z^*} \frac{1}{\lambda} \, d\phi \right)$$

$$= (\lambda cq^{-1} + \tfrac{1}{2} z^{*2})/z^* = \lambda cq^{-1}/z^* + \tfrac{1}{2} z^*.$$

Then:

$$\text{if } \sqrt{(2\lambda cq^{-1})} \leqslant \lambda, \qquad z^* = \sqrt{(2\lambda cq^{-1})}$$
$$\text{if } \sqrt{(2\lambda cq^{-1})} > \lambda, \qquad z^* = \lambda.$$

Further formalizations may be found in Brooks [3, 4] and McQueen *et al.* [6]. The former looks at the probability distribution of the number of samples required to get a solution within a certain neighbourhood of the optimal value (the second reference compares random and non-random methods), and the latter deals with search problems such as looking for a buyer with search costs c.

Central to the Las Vegas method, whether applied using the formal dynamic programming method or subjectively on the basis of observed performance, is the question of determination of the probability density function, $g(\phi)$, or distribution in the discrete case.

For small numbers of sample solutions, the estimation process will be unreliable. Perhaps the only appropriate approach in this case is to use a Bayesian approach, assuming that $g(\phi) = g(\phi, \alpha)$ for some unknown parameter α, which itself has a prior density function $\pi(\alpha)$, say. In this case it is possible to modify the dynamic programming equations to produce an adaptive procedure (see Aoki [2] for a survey of adaptive control studies).

Even without the dynamic programming procedure in adaptive form, one might, as an heuristic, use the updated probability density function at each stage, as if it were the true one, and then use the dynamic programming procedure specified earlier on.

For large numbers of sample solutions one will get a much better estimate of $g(\phi)$. This might be done by simply forming a frequency count. Alternatively one might try to fit suitable standard distributions. A natural one is the Beta-distribution where:

$$g(\phi) = (1/(b-a)^{l+m-1}B(l, m))(\phi-a)^{l-1}(b-\phi)^{m-1}, \qquad a \leqslant \phi \leqslant b$$
$$= 0 \text{ otherwise}$$

and a, b, l, m are unknown parameters.

Figure 2.38 gives the shape of the $g(\phi)$ curve. The true minimal value of ϕ is a, and the maximal vaue b.

$$B(l, m) = \Gamma(l)\Gamma(m)/\Gamma(l+m)$$

where $\Gamma(t) = \int_0^\infty e^{-u}u^{t-1}\,du$ is the gamma function, equal to $(t-1)!$ if t is a positive integer.

If a,b are estimated by suitable smoothing of the data curve, l,m may be estimated from:

$$l = ((\mu-a)/(b-a))((\mu-a)(b-\mu)/\sigma^2 - 1)$$
$$m = ((b-\mu)/(b-a))((\mu-a)(b-\mu)/\sigma^2 - 1)$$

where μ, σ^2 are the expectation and variance of ϕ, estimated from the data.

It is important to make one point about the Las Vegas analysis and the estimation process. Once a has been reliably estimated, this is not enough to be able to terminate the process since we not only need some idea of the value of a but we need to have decisions which will give the appropriate compromise between objective function value and computational costs. Thus, when we terminate, we will have the best objective function value to date, and the decision which will achieve this and, although an additional good estimate of a might be helpful, the decisions which will achieve this will not be known in general.

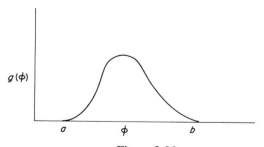

Figure 2.38

It is important to note that Las Vegas is not necessarily just an alternative approach to other methods. For example in dynamic analysis, if x is a decision rule, $\phi(x)$ may need to be evaluated by similation.

Finally, later on, in Chapter 4, we will be discussing multiple-objective interactive programming from particular points of view. One method which will not be discussed is the Las Vegas approach to this in which the candidate solutions are selected randomly rather than by the methods discussed. However, the use of such Las Vegas methods should also be borne in mind (see Törn [9]).

2.10 A QUALITATIVE COMPARISON OF TECHNIQUES

2.10.1 Introduction

We have looked briefly at the following techniques, viz. queueing, inventory, maintenance, defective product, mathematical programming, dynamic programming, optimization analogues, simulation, heuristic programming and Las Vegas, and have demonstrated that, for some problems, we have a choice of which technique to use. Each technique will have points in its favour and points not in its favour, and the operational researcher will need to make some judgement as to which is best for his circumstances. In this section we will give a qualitative discussion of various attributes of the selection of techniques used in this text, and the reader must bear in mind that this is only a sample of available techniques.

In order to set the scene for a general discussion we will make use of the capacity expansion problem discussed in section 2.5 of this chapter. In doing so we will not make use of all the techniques listed but merely concentrate on three, viz. dynamic programming, mathematical programming and simulation. Section 2.5 deals with the dynamic programming formulation of the deterministic problem, Exercise 13 of section 2.5 deals with the mathamatical programming formulation, Exercise 15 of section 2.5 deals with the probabilistic dynamic programming formulation, and Exercise 7 of section 2.7 deals with the simulation of the probabilistic problem, with slightly different conditions to the dynamic programming exercise.

2.10.2 Dynamic Programming, Mathematical Programming and Simulation in Optimal Capacity Installation Problems

The statement of the deterministic problem is given in section 2.5. The forward and backward dynamic programmes were as follows:

$K > k \geqslant 1$

$$f_k = \min_{K \geqslant x > k} [a + c(s_x - s_k) + \alpha^{x-k} f_x]$$

$$f_K = 0$$

$$K \geqslant k \geqslant 1$$

$$f_k = \min_{0 \leqslant x < k} [\alpha^x(a + c(s_k - s_x)) + f_x]$$

$$f_0 = 0.$$

where the definitions of $\{f_k\}$ for forward and backward formulation are given in section 2.5.

In section 2.5 an example was taken in which $s_k = k$, $a = 1$, $c = 1$, $\alpha = 0.7$, $K = 7$.

The solution for the forward and backward problems is then as follows.

Forward Formulation

$f_7 = 0$

$f_6 = 1 + 7 - 6(0.7)^1 f_7 = 2, \qquad x = \theta_6 = 7$

$$f_5 = \min \begin{bmatrix} 1 + 6 - 5 + (0.7)^1 f_6 \\ 1 + 7 - 5 + (0.7)^2 f_7 \end{bmatrix} = \min \begin{bmatrix} 3.4 \\ 3 \end{bmatrix} = 3, \qquad x = \theta_5 = 7$$

$$f_4 = \min \begin{bmatrix} 1 + 5 - 4 + (0.7)^1 f_5 \\ 1 + 6 - 4 + (0.7)^2 f_6 \\ 1 + 7 - 4 + (0.7)^3 f_7 \end{bmatrix} = \min \begin{bmatrix} 4.1 \\ 3.98 \\ 4 \end{bmatrix} = 3.98, \qquad x = \theta_4 = 6$$

$$f_3 = \min \begin{bmatrix} 1 + 4 - 3 + (0.7)^1 f_4 \\ 1 + 5 - 3 + (0.7)^2 f_5 \\ 1 + 6 - 3 + (0.7)^3 f_6 \\ 1 + 7 - 3 + (0.7)^4 f_7 \end{bmatrix} = \min \begin{bmatrix} 4.79 \\ 4.47 \\ 4.69 \\ 5 \end{bmatrix} = 4.47, \quad x = \theta_3 = 5$$

$$f_2 = \min \begin{bmatrix} 1 + 3 - 2 + (0.7)^1 f_3 \\ 1 + 4 - 2 + (0.7)^2 f_4 \\ 1 + 5 - 2 + (0.7)^3 f_5 \\ 1 + 6 - 2 + (0.7)^4 f_6 \\ 1 + 7 - 2 + (0.7)^5 f_7 \end{bmatrix} = \min \begin{bmatrix} 5.13 \\ 4.94 \\ 5.03 \\ 5.48 \\ 6 \end{bmatrix} = 4.94, \qquad x = \theta_2 = 4$$

$$f_1 = \min \begin{bmatrix} 1 + 2 - 1 + (0.7)^1 f_2 \\ 1 + 3 - 1 + (0.7)^2 f_3 \\ 1 + 4 - 1 + (0.7)^3 f_4 \\ 1 + 5 - 1 + (0.7)^4 f_5 \\ 1 + 6 - 1 + (0.7)^5 f_6 \\ 1 + 7 - 1 + (0.7)^6 f_7 \end{bmatrix} = \min \begin{bmatrix} 5.8 \\ 5.19 \\ 5.3 \\ 5.72 \\ 6.34 \\ 7 \end{bmatrix} = 5.19, \qquad x = \theta_1 = 3$$

$$f_0 = \min \begin{bmatrix} 1+1-0+(0.7)^1 f^1 \\ 1+2-0+(0.7)^2 f_2 \\ 1+3-0+(0.7)^3 f_3 \\ 1+4-0+(0.7)^4 f_4 \\ 1+5-0+(0.7)^5 f_5 \\ 1+6-0+(0.7)^6 f_6 \\ 1+7-0+(0.7)^7 f_7 \end{bmatrix} = \min \begin{bmatrix} 5.63 \\ 5.43 \\ 5.53 \\ 5.95 \\ 6.50 \\ 7.24 \\ 8 \end{bmatrix} = 5.43, \qquad x = \theta_0 = 2$$

This is summarized in Table 2.25.

Table 2.25

k	7	6	5	4	3	2	1	0
f_k	0	2	3	3.98	4.47	4.94	5.19	5.43
$\theta_k (= x)$	—	7	7	6	5	4	3	2

For the initial case $K = 7$, the minimal total discounted cost over the seven intervals is $f_0 = 5.43$, and it is optimal to cover years (1, 2) (3, 4), (5, 6) (7) by single installations.

Backward Formulation

$f_0 = 0$

$f_1 = 2, \qquad x = \theta_1 = 0$

$$f_2 = \min \begin{bmatrix} f_0 + (0.7)^0 3 \\ f_1 + (0.7)^1 2 \end{bmatrix} = \min \begin{bmatrix} 3 \\ 3.4 \end{bmatrix} = 3, \qquad x = \theta_2 = 0$$

$$f_3 = \min \begin{bmatrix} f_0 + (0.7)^0 4 \\ f_1 + (0.7)^1 3 \\ f_2 + (0.7)^2 2 \end{bmatrix} = \min \begin{bmatrix} 4 \\ 4.1 \\ 3.98 \end{bmatrix} = 3.98, \qquad x = \theta_3 = 2$$

$$f_4 = \min \begin{bmatrix} f_0 + (0.7)^0 5 \\ f_1 + (0.7)^1 4 \\ f_2 + (0.7)^2 3 \\ f_3 + (0.7)^3 2 \end{bmatrix} = \min \begin{bmatrix} 5 \\ 4.8 \\ 4.47 \\ 4.67 \end{bmatrix} = 4.47, \qquad x = \theta_4 = 2$$

$$f_5 = \min \begin{bmatrix} f_0 + (0.7)^0 6 \\ f_1 + (0.07)^1 5 \\ f_2 + (0.7)^2 4 \\ f_3 + (0.7)^3 3 \\ f_4 + (0.7)^4 2 \end{bmatrix} = \min \begin{bmatrix} 6 \\ 5.48 \\ 4.96 \\ 5.02 \\ 4.94 \end{bmatrix} = 4.94, \qquad x = \theta_5 = 4$$

$$f_6 = \min \begin{bmatrix} f_0 + (0.7)^0 7 \\ f_1 + (0.7)^1 6 \\ f_2 + (0.7)^2 5 \\ f_3 + (0.7)^3 4 \\ f_4 + (0.7)^4 3 \\ f_5 + (0.7)^5 2 \end{bmatrix} = \min \begin{bmatrix} 7 \\ 6.2 \\ 5.45 \\ 5.35 \\ 5.19 \\ 5.29 \end{bmatrix} = 5.19, \qquad x = \theta_6 = 4$$

$$f_7 = \min \begin{bmatrix} f_0 + (0.7)^0 8 \\ f_1 + (0.7)^1 7 \\ f_2 + (0.7)^2 6 \\ f_3 + (0.7)^3 5 \\ f_4 + (0.7)^4 4 \\ f_5 + (0.7)^5 3 \\ f_6 + (0.7)^6 2 \end{bmatrix} = \min \begin{bmatrix} 8 \\ 6.9 \\ 5.94 \\ 5.70 \\ 5.43 \\ 5.45 \\ 5.48 \end{bmatrix} = 5.43, \qquad x = \theta_7 = 6$$

This is summarized in Table 2.26.

Table 2.26

k	0	1	2	3	4	5	6	7
f_k	0	2	3	3.98	4.47	4.94	5.19	5.43
$\theta_k(=x)$	—	0	0	2	2	4	4	6

Tables 2.25 and 2.26 are identical because of the special form of the demand function.

For the initial case $K = 7$, the minimal total discounted cost is $f_7 = 5.43$, and the optimal decisions are as before.

A mathematical programming formulation is as follows where we will assume that installations, if any, are made at discrete multiples of a unit time interval in time, where the unit time interval is subject to choice, in order to maintain comparison with the dynamic programming and simulation formats. A continuous time formulation is clearly possible and may be useful for structural analysis, but any numerical method will, of necessity, need to use discrete multiples of a suitable time interval.

Let there be $r + 1$ installations at points $x_0 (= 0), x_1, \ldots, x_r$ respectively. The problem then becomes one of:

$$\text{minimizing} \left[f(x, r) = \sum_{i=0}^{r} \alpha^{x_i}(a + c(s_{x_{i+1}} - s_{x_i})) \right]$$

136

subject to the constraints

$$0 \leqslant r \leqslant K - 1$$
$$x_0 = 0$$
$$x_{r+1} = K$$
$$x_{i+1} \geqslant x_i + 1, \qquad 0 \leqslant i \leqslant r$$

with

$$x_i \in \{1, 2, \ldots, K - 1\}, \qquad 1 \leqslant i \leqslant r.$$

We will not solve this for the specimen example but will comment on the computational side in due course.

If we were, finally, to use simulation, then we would merely need to evaluate $f(x)$ for all feasible x. Note that, even though this is a deterministic problem, simulation is quite valid.

Let us now look at a few attributes of each technique (see White [8] for related work).

Optimality

Given that the formulation of the problem is correct, both the dynamic programming and mathematical programming procedures will give optimal solutions, where we assume an appropriate algorithm is chosen for the latter, and that the computational time is acceptable (an algorithm which determines a solution to within a specified error ε of the optimal solution value may also be acceptable but we exclude heuristics for our purposes). In principle, simulation would also give the optimal solution but, in practice, the burden of computational work would rule this out *a priori* and, within the context of the formulated problem, would not give optimal solutions or even ε-optimal solutions, in general.

Computational Load

The computational load in getting optimal solutions is likely to be heavy for the dynamic programming approach, very heavy for the simulation approach, and less so for the mathematical programming approach, particularly as the value of K increases. It must be stressed that this is a statement which really needs to be backed up with proper numerical experimentation, and that much may depend upon the algorithm used for the mathematical programming approach, which may depend upon the use of particular structural features of the problem.

The essential feature mitigating against dynamic programming for this deterministic problem is the amount of redundant calculation involved in determining decisions for hypothetical conditions. For example, the condition that demand and capacity are equal at the end of year 1 does not actually arise in the solution for the specified problem, but the solution for this condition is calculated. When the number of possible conditions becomes large, but the number actually realized is small, this can involve much redundant calculation.

The obvious feature mitigating against simulation is the number of possible solutions to be covered. It is easily seen that the number of possible solutions is 2^{K-1}. This is quite acceptable for $K = 7$, but not if K is much larger.

Structural Properties

Dynamic programming and simulation are not unduly hampered by particular structural features of the problem, whereas mathematical programming may be. For example, the particular cost functions involved, or the particular demand functions involved, may make the determination of a suitable algorithm quite difficult in the mathematical programming approach, but no developmental difficulty arises in the other two approaches.

The existence of structural features may be of assistance in the dynamic programming and mathematical programming approaches, and even in the simulation approach, providing an element of mathematical programming is added. Let us look at the backward dynamic programming formulation first of all. If x is close to 0, it might be economic to put in an extra installation between x and k. Hence x need only range from $k-1$ to the smallest value of x for which a single installation for the period x to k is optimal. For a single installation to be optimal from x to k we require:

$$a + c(s_k - s_x) \leqslant a + c(s_l - s_x) + \alpha^{l-x}(a + c(s_k - s_l))$$

for all $l : x < l < k$. If $l(k)$ is the smallest such l, given k, the backward formulation reduces to:

$$\underline{K \geqslant k \geqslant 1}$$

$$f_k = \min_{l(k) \leqslant x < k} [\alpha^x(a + c(s_k - s_x)) + f_x]$$

$$f_0 = 0.$$

Likewise structural analysis may help the mathematical programming approach. The above analysis may enable extra constraints to be added, viz.

$$x_i \geqslant l(x_{i+1}), \qquad 1 \leqslant i \leqslant r.$$

Alternatively, we may obtain a relationship between x_{i-1}, x_i, x_{i+1}, in an optimal solution. The contribution to $f(x,r)$ by the terms $\{x_{i-1}, x_i, x_{i+1}\}$, is:

$$h(x_{i-1}, x_i, x_{i+1}) = c\alpha^{x_{i-1}}s_{x_i} + \alpha^{x_i}(a + c(s_{x_{i+1}} - s_{x_i}))$$

with $x_{i-1} < x_i < x_{i+1}$.

For specified x_{i-1}, x_{i+1} it is possible to find an optimal x_i. We may then

138

express x_{i+1} in terms of x_{i-1}, x_i (this may raise problems, but, for the purposes of this text, we will merely consider the principle). This may then be used to derive the following algorithm:

(i) choose $x_1 > 0$;
(ii) use the above to determine x_2, then x_3 and so on until we get x_{r+1};
(iii) vary x_1 until $x_{r+1} = K$;
(iv) do the above for $r = 1, 2, \ldots, K-1$ and select best solution.

Naturally the above structural analysis may be used in a simulation, but then the procedure becomes a combined procedure, a subject to which we will turn later on, in Chapter 5.

Parametric Analysis

In Chapter 3 we will deal in general with the question of parametric analysis, but it will help pave the way for this to look at the parametric analysis power of the three techniques we have chosen here.

Parametric analysis is concerned with the manner in which optimal solutions and their objective function values vary with changes in model assumptions. Unless simulation attempts to determine optimal solutions, it is not applicable to our problem as it is stated, although, within the chosen subset of solutions simulated, it will be possible to do some (sub-)optimality parametric analysis.

In order to illustrate our argument, let us first of all consider the problem of determining the time horizon K. Usually this will be unknown. It may be possible to treat K as a chance variable (for example, see White [9], who deals with uncertain durations in a different context); but this may not be so. In such a case it is of interest to know how sensitive the first decision is to the value of K. The following is due to White [8]. We begin with dynamic programming.

Using the backward formulation we can find the optimal value of x for each k, i.e. θ_k given in Table 2.26. Beginning with a specific value of K we can work backwards, as in Figure 2.39, to find the period covered by the first installation at $k = 0$. Call this $x(K)$. From this figure we can see how $x(K)$ varies with K. Let us take our specimen example. We then have Table 2.27. In all cases the first installation covers exactly intervals 1 and 2 for $K \geq 2$.

Thus dynamic programming produces a natural way of studying time horizon parametric analysis. For mathematical programming there is no obvious way of handling this issue (although the structural analysis in (iii) may help), other than solving the problem for different K values separately. For simulation this seems certain to be the case.

Another aspect of parametric analysis relates to the question of the number of installations to be used. In the problem, as it has been stated, no constraints have been put on the number of installations. However, the

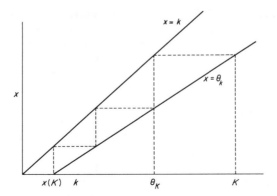

Figure 2.39

Table 2.27

K	7	6	5	4	3	2	1
θ_K	6	4	4	2	2	0	0
θ_{θ_K}	4	2	2	0	0	0	0
θ_{θ_K}	0	0	0	—	—	—	—
$x(K)$	2	2	2	2	2	2	1

number of installations may also be of separate concern in addition to the discounted cost arising from them. A mathematical programming formulation which evaluates the minimal value of $f(x, r)$, over x, in the neighbourhood of the optimal $r = r^*$, say, seems to be the obvious way to do this. If the simulation covers all possible solutions then it is then merely a matter of selecting the optima in the region of $r = r^*$. The dynamic programming approach is not so easily adapted to deal with the parametric analysis in the region of $r = r^*$. It is, of course, possible to modify the formulation by defining, for the backward formulation for example, f_k^{r+1} to be as for f_k but with exactly $r + 1$ installations to be used. The equations then become:

$\underline{K \geqslant k \geqslant r + 1}$

$$f_k^{r+1} = \min_{0 \leqslant x < k} \ [\alpha^x(a + c(s_k - s_x)) + f_x^r]$$

$\underline{r + 1 > k}$

$$f_k^{r+1} = \infty$$
$$f_0^0 = 0.$$

140

If one wished to find optimal solutions for all r, and to treat the problem as a multi-objective one (see Chapter 4) there is an obvious merit in this natural way of tackling the problem. If, however, the number of installations is of secondary importance, as a separate factor, one could not evaluate f_K^r in the region of $r = r^*$ without doing the analysis for all r.

Analytic Form of Analysis

By analytic we will mean some explicit form for the optimal solution to a problem or, in more general terms, an explicit form of the effects of proposed options as a function of the parameters of the problem. The latter form is sometimes quite trivial, as is the case in this problem, but not always so, as we have seen, for example, in queueing problems. We will concentrate here on optimal solutions.

Analytic forms of optimal solutions are very difficult to come by for our problem using mathematical programming and are clearly not possible using simulation. To a limited extent it is possible to obtain an analytic solution using dynamic programming. Let us, for example, consider the case when $s_k = k$. We then have, for the backward formulation;

$$f_0 = 0$$
$$f_1 = a + c$$
$$f_2 = \min[f_0 + a + 2c, f_1 + \alpha(a + c)]$$
$$= \min[a + 2c, (a + c)(1 + \alpha)]$$
$$f_3 = \min[f_0 + a + 3c, f_1 + \alpha(a + 2c), f_2 + \alpha^2(a + c)]$$
$$= \min[a + 2c, a + c + \alpha(a + c), a + 2c + \alpha^2(a + c), (a + c)(1 + \alpha + \alpha^2)]$$

and so on.

In general:

$$f_k = \min_{t=1}^{2^{k-1}} \left[\sum_{s=0}^{k-1} \lambda_{ts} \alpha^s \right]$$

where $\{\lambda_{ts}\}$ may be calculated inductively quite easily, although the number of such is large in general.

The fact that f_k is the minimum of 2^{k-1} terms arises as follows.

$$f_k = \min[f_0 + (a + kc), f_1 + \alpha(a + (k-1)c), \ldots, f_{k-1} + \alpha^{k-1}(a + c)]$$

Let f_k be the minimum of T_k terms. Then:

$$T_k = T_0 + T_1 + \ldots + T_{k-1}$$

with $T_0 = T_1 = 1$, and the requisite result follows. In fact it is easily seen that the expression for f_k is equivalent to install/not install decisions for each interval.

Instead of going directly to the calculation of $\{\lambda_{ts}\}$ a direct step-by-step analysis is possible, although somewhat complicated, which carries out an intermediate parametric analysis which may be useful to eliminate some possibilities and which would be essential in any large problem in order to apply the approach in practice. We carry out a few steps of this analysis.

$$f_2 = a + 2c \qquad \text{if} \quad \alpha \geqslant c/(a+c) = \alpha_1, \quad \text{say,}$$
$$= (a+c)(1+\alpha) \quad \text{if} \quad \alpha \leqslant c/(a+c).$$

For $\alpha \geqq \alpha_1$:

$$f_3 = \min[a + 3c, \, a + c + \alpha(a + 2c), \, a + 2c + \alpha^2(a+c)]$$
$$= a + c + \min[2c, \, \alpha(a+2c), \, c + \alpha^2(a+c)].$$

Now:

$$2c \leqslant \alpha(a+2c) \rightleftarrows \alpha \geqslant 2c/(a+2c) = \alpha_2(>\alpha_1)$$
$$2c \leqslant c + \alpha^2(a+c) \rightleftarrows \alpha \geqslant \sqrt{c/(a+c)} = \alpha_3(= \sqrt{\alpha_1} > \alpha_1)$$
$$\alpha(a+2c) \leqslant c + \alpha^2(a+c) \rightleftarrows (\alpha - 1)(\alpha(a+c) - c) \geqslant 0 \rightleftarrows \alpha \leqslant c/(a+c) = \alpha_1.$$

Hence:

$$f_3 = a + 3c \quad \text{if} \quad \alpha \geqslant \alpha_3$$
$$= a + 2c + \alpha^2(a+c) \quad \text{if} \quad \alpha_1 \leqslant \alpha \leqslant \alpha_3.$$

Now let $\alpha \leqslant \alpha_1$. Then:

$$f_3 = \min[a + 3c, \, a + c + \alpha(a+2c), \, (a+c)(1+\alpha) + \alpha^2(a+c)]$$
$$= a + c + \min[2c, \, \alpha(a+2c), \, (a+c)(\alpha + \alpha^2)].$$

Now:

$$2c \leqslant \alpha(a+2c) \rightleftarrows \alpha \geqslant 2c/(a+2c) = \alpha_2(>\alpha_1).$$

Hence:

$$2c > \alpha(a+2c).$$

Also:

$$2c \leqslant (a+c)(\alpha + \alpha^2) \rightleftarrows (\alpha - \lambda)(\alpha + \mu) \geqslant 0, \quad \text{where} \quad \lambda, \mu > 0.$$

and

$$\lambda = (\sqrt{1 + 8c/(a+c)} - 1)/2 > \alpha_1.$$

Hence:

$$2c > (a+c)(\alpha + \alpha^2).$$

Finally:

$$\alpha(a+2c) \leqslant (a+c)(\alpha + \alpha^2) \rightleftarrows a + 2c \leqslant (a+c)(1+\alpha)$$
$$\rightleftarrows c \leqslant (a+c)\alpha$$
$$\rightleftarrows \alpha \geqslant c/(a+c) = \alpha_1.$$

142

Hence:

$$\alpha(a+2c) \geq (a+c)(\alpha+\alpha^2).$$

Thus, for $\alpha \leqq \alpha_1$:

$$f_3 = (a+c(1+\alpha+\alpha^2)).$$

Hence we have the final results in Table 2.28 for $k \leq 3$, where

$$\alpha_1 = c/(a+c)$$
$$\alpha_3 = \sqrt{\alpha_1}$$

Table 2.28

	Case 1			Case 2			Case 3	
k	$\alpha < \alpha_1$ f_k		θ_k	$\alpha_1 < \alpha < \alpha_3$ f_k		θ_k	$\alpha > \alpha_3$ f_k	θ_k
1	$a+c$		0	$a+c$		0	$a+c$	0
2	$(a+c)(1+\alpha)$		1	$a+2c$		0	$a+2c$	0
3	$(a+c)(1+\alpha+\alpha^2)$		2	$a+2c+\alpha^2(a+c)$		2	$a+3c$	0

For $\alpha = \alpha_1$, or $\alpha = \alpha_3$ there will be a choice of optimal actions.

An analysis of the above kind enables the effects of variations in parameter values to be studied systematically. Clearly, continuing the analysis for larger values of k will be quite demanding, but this has to be balanced against the value of such analysis. For some problems the analysis may be much easier.

Howrey *et al.* [1] discuss simulation vs. analytic solutions in general.

Probabilistic Models

Our present model is deterministic for which there are no uncertain demands. It is quite possible to tackle problems for which the demand exhibits a probabilistic behaviour, as has been suggested in Exercises 15 and 7 of sections 2.5 and 2.7 respectively. Whereas, for the deterministic problem, an optimal sequence of decisions is required, in the probabilistic problem we require an optimal decision rule in order to respond to the events as they eventually unfurl. The dynamic programming approach is a natural one to take. If we consider Exercise 7 of section 2.7 and assume that the demand, y, in any interval $(k+1)$, is actually known at the beginning of that interval, and that the error in demand, ε, for the next interval, has probability $p(\varepsilon)$, we have the following dynamic programming formulation where $f_k(z,y)$ is the minimal expected discounted cost from the end of interval k to the end of interval K when the demand in interval $(k+1)$ is known to be y and the capacity level at the beginning of that interval is z.

The formulation is a forward formulation which is the only one which may be used for probabilistic problems:

$K > k \geq 1$

$$f_k(z, y) = \min_{x \geq y-z} \left[(a + cx)\tau(x) + \alpha \sum_\varepsilon p(\varepsilon)f_{k+1}(x + z, s_{k+2} + \varepsilon) \right]$$

$f_K(z, y) = 0$ for all z, y

$\tau(x) = 1$ if $x > 0$, $\tau(x) = 0$ if $x = 0$.

Although the computations may be heavy they are straightforward.

An alternative mathematical programming approach may be developed in a similar manner to those discussed in the queueing and other sections, but this is equivalent to the above and no advantage is gained. It is difficult to envisage an alternative, computable, mathematical programming form.

A simulation approach would only be able to cover a limited number of decision rules and would be sub-optimal. Let us look at the number of possible decision rules. At the end of interval k, the demand y for interval $(k + 1)$ can take E possible values if ε takes E possible values. The capacity at the end of interval k must be able to cope with the demand in interval k and this can take one of E possible values. The capacity can be much bigger, but clearly will not be bigger than the maximal possible demand over the intervals 1 to K. Hence, if s_k is increasing with k, the capacity will not be greater than $s_K + F$ if F is the number of values of ε which are non-negative. Hence the capacity at the end of interval k can take $s_K - s_k + F + 1$ values. Hence we have $s_K - s_k + F + 1$ possible values. For each state we can put in extra capacity. The extra capacity put in can range between $s_K + F$ and $\max[z, s_{k+1} + \varepsilon]$, since it cannot be greater than the former and must be at least as great as the latter. The number of decision rules, $\phi(k)$, at the end of interval k, is then, if $k \geq 1$;

$$\phi(k) = \prod_\varepsilon \prod_{z \,:\, s_k \leq z \leq s_K} (1 + s_K + F - \max[z, s_{k+1} + \varepsilon]).$$

For $k = 0$, since $z = 0$ at $k = 0$, the number of decision rules is:

$$\phi(0) = \prod_\varepsilon (1 + s_K + F - \max[0, s_1 + \varepsilon]).$$

These expressions merely represent the fact that if, for each state (z, y) the number of allowable decisions is $A(z, y)$, then the number of decision rules is $\prod_{z,y} A(z, y)$.

Let $K = 7$, $s_k = k$, $\varepsilon = 0, 1, -1$. We then have the calculations in Table 2.29.

We can likewise calculate $\{\theta(k)\}$, $k = 3, 4, 5, 6$.

It is seen that the number of decision rules for each k is quite large. In addition to this, the number of composite decision rules which decide what

Table 2.29

	ε	-1	0	1	$\theta(k)$
$k=0$	z				$10.9.8$
	0	10	9	8	
$k=1$	1	9	8	7	$9.8^3.7^5.6^3.5^3.4^3.3^3$
	2	8	8	7	
	3	7	7	7	
	4	6	6	6	
	5	5	5	5	
	6	4	4	4	
	7	3	3	3	
$k=2$	2	8	7	6	$9.7^3.6^5.4^3.3^3$
	3	7	7	6	
	4	6	6	6	
	5	5	5	5	
	6	4	4	4	
	7	3	3	3	

to do at each point in time is

$$\prod_{k=0}^{k=6} \phi(k)$$

and this is very large indeed.

This is actually greater than is required since the states at interval k influence states at interval r, $r \geq k$, and hence not all combinations of states are allowable. Nevertheless the number is very large. However, specific structures of the problems pose no difficulties for simulation, which is its main attribute, It requires little mathematical analysis in its design, although some mathematical analysis will be required in drawing inferences from the results.

If the errors ε are small then it may be possible to use the deterministic analysis, setting the errors equal to zero. In this case the rule given in Table 2.25 may be used to respond to changes in demand and, if the errors are small, the error in cost using this rule will be small. Thus suppose, instead of actual demand being 0, 1, 2, 3, 4, 5, 6, 7, the demands were 0, 1, 2.1, 2.8, 3.7, 5.2, 6.5, 6.9, respectively at the end of each interval (but known at the beginning of each interval). Our decisions would then be as follows, beginning with $\theta_0 = 2$.

At the beginning of interval 2 (end of interval 1) we would know that capacity is not enough for interval 2. We then use $\theta_1 = 3$ (add enough capacity to get us to the end of interval 3, using estimated demand). At the beginning of interval 3 we have enough capacity. At the end of interval 3, $\theta_3 = 5$, and we put in enough capacity to last until the end of interval 5 using the estimated demand. At the end of interval 4 (beginning of interval 5) we

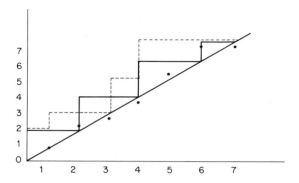

Figure 2.40   Straight line = estimated demand;
dot = actual demand; zigzag broken line = actual
installations and zigzag unbroken line = installations based on estimated demand

find this capacity is not enough for interval 5. Hence we use $\theta_5 = 7$ and put in enough capacity to last until the end of interval 7. From here onwards everything is all right, but we end up with a slight extra capacity at the end of interval 7. Figure 2.40 illustrates the behaviour (see also White [8]).

Norman *et al.* [2] and White [7] discuss the use of expected state transitions in dynamic probabilistic problems.

Thus, if demand variations are not too great, the forward dynamic programming approach will provide a decision rule to respond to demand variations which will be approximately optimal. The other approaches will not do this. We will look more deeply at sensitivity analysis in Chapter 3.

2.10.3   A General Appraisal of the Techniques

In the previous section we have used the capacity installation problem to provide a qualitative comparison of dynamic programming, mathematical programming, and simulation with respect to the characteristics of optimality, computational load, structural properties, parametric analysis, analytic form, and probabilistic models. We have not covered the remaining techniques of queueing, inventory, maintenance, defective product, heuristics, optimization analogues, and Las Vegas. Nor have we covered some of the other characteristics such as faithfulness of representation and insight.

Let us take a look at queueing, a topic to which we will return later on when we consider combined techniques. What we have to say about queueing will apply also to the other techniques of inventory, maintenance, and defective product.

When considering queueing, it is possible to consider closed form (analytic) approaches as we have done in this text, numerical approaches which we have also considered in an optimization context (but which may also be considered in a non-optimization form using similar Markov analysis), and simulation which we have also considered in this text.

Wallace [6], who considers queueing processes within computers, stresses the fact that faithfulness of representation is highest for simulation, lowest for closed form analysis, with numerical methods being in between for many large problems, although for small problems the approaches may be equally faithful. In Chapters 4 and 5, we will briefly look at a problem of setting up an emergency unit in a hospital. Although emergency arrivals are to some extent Poisson in character, the rate will vary from one time of the day to another and even from one day to the next. The service time is certainly not Poisson. Also the manner in which emergencies are handled when the unit is full, involving a combination of early discharges, sending emergencies to other hospitals, or even putting up extra beds, can create problems. A satisfactory faithful representation seems only possible, if at all, by using simulation. In principle a numerical method is also possible but seems to be somewhat more demanding computationally. Wallace's views must be conditional on the amount of computational effort to be used, since the framework sufficient to build any simulation is also sufficient to provide a formal numerical method wilth equal faithfulness.

Although simulation seems to have a (qualified) advantage over numerical methods, it does not provide the insight into the important parameters which a closed form solution would give. A numerical method could be expected to have an insight level somewhere between the two.

In making the comparison between numerical and simulation methods, it must be stressed that this is merely a statement of general belief, although no real comparative study has been made of the two approaches with respect to the faithfulness and insight criteria in terms of computational effort. Although it is much easier to build a simulation model, and operate it, than to build a numerical model and develop an algorithm, there is always the question of understanding enough about the simulation behaviour to be able to obtain the requisite performance estimates with adequate confidence. Vazsonyi [5] refers to the problems involved in making sure that the simulation makes sense and queries the ability to carry out a satisfactory simulation without some supporting theory. Taha [4] indicates how expensive it can be to obtain the requisite information to within the specified degree of accuracy. Siegel et al. [3] discuss a queueing network problem concerning surveillance systems for collecting, correlating, and disseminating information to users, which simply cannot be simulated, and for which a certain amount of faithfulness has to be sacrificed to be able to get any results at all. All this points to the need for approximations, perhaps combined with simulation in some cases, a point to which we will return later on, in Chapter 5.

Some comments on the remaining optimization techniques need to be made, i.e. Las Vegas, heuristics, and optimization analogues. None of these is really capable of easily providing insight into the importance of the various parameters, or of sensitivity analysis; heuristics not being really an optimization technique but seeking good solutions, cannot deal with parametric analysis in principle. Although Las Vegas lacks these features, it is particularly easy to apply once the feasibility testing and objective function calculations have been specified, since it involves none of the difficulties of mathematical programming. In comparison with heuristics, the randomization process avoids, to some extent, the possibility of a particularly poor solution which an heuristic can produce for a specified problem. Optimization analogues are of little use in practical Operational Research since, to be effective, they need to be restricted to relatively simple and very repetitive problems. As has been indicated in the section dealing with this, it is possible that the analogues may lead to alternative algorithms or to duality theories.

Finally, let us refer back to some problem formulational aspects of the stochastic problems we have discussed. It has been pointed out that, if mean-variance analysis is used, then it can be very difficult analytically, or numerically, to handle this for dynamic problems and, in many cases, at a loss from other points of view, simulation may be necessary. A different formulation of the problem using, for example, utility ideas (to be discussed in Chapters 4 and 6) may remove this necessity.

In general, where several objectives are involved for such dynamic problems, if these relate to expectations of the sum of contributions made in each time interval, linear programming approaches may be used, especially for finding efficient solutions—something which is not possible if simulation is used other than on an exhaustive basis. Indeed the general problem of handling multiple objectives, in a guided sense, with simulation, is quite difficult, other than by enumeration of an explicit set of policies. The same applies to heuristics. In addition, both simulation and heuristics have no systematic way of studying constraints. Constraints and multiple objectives will be examined in Chapter 4.

This section is intended to merely provide a qualitative appreciation of the various techniques covered. It is not intended to be definitive but merely to provide a framework within which an examination of the choice of techniques to use may be made for a given problem.

2.11 EXERCISES

Queueing

1. Use the standard formula

$n \geq 1$

$$P_n = (\lambda(0)\lambda(1)\ldots\lambda(n-1)/\mu(1)\mu(2)\ldots\mu(n))P_0$$

to find P_n in the following cases:

  (i) single arrival stream, x identical servers;

 (ii) single arrival stream, single server, arrival does not join system when x or more in the system;

(iii) single arrival stream, x identical servers, arrival does not join the system when all servers occupied (Cox *et al.* [8]);

(iv) m machines, each with probability $\lambda \delta t$ of breaking down in next interval of time δt, and a single server (Cox *et al.* [8]);

 (v) single server, single arrival stream, and any customer in the queue, not being served, has a probability $\alpha \delta t$ of leaving the system (i.e. reneging) in the next interval of time δt (Ancker *et al.* [2]).

2. In case (ii) of Exercise 1 show that the expected waiting time $\hat{w}(J)$ of a customer who joins the system may be obtained either from the formula

$$\hat{w}(J) = (\hat{n}(J) + 1)/\mu$$

or from the formula

$$\hat{w}(J) = \hat{n}/\hat{\lambda}$$

where $\hat{n}$ is the expected number in the system, $\hat{n}(J)$ is the expected number in the system when an arrival joins the system and $\hat{\lambda}$ is the expected arrival rate into the system (i.e. of those who join the system).

Do this

(a) by formal calculation (but it is not necessary to actually evaluate $\hat{n}$, $\hat{n}(J)\hat{\lambda}$ explicitly);

(b) by looking at the general waiting time analysis.

    Note. The same applies to case (iii) of Exercise 1 and the formula $\hat{w}(J) = \hat{n}/\hat{\lambda}$ is valid also for case (v), providing waiting time is taken into account for those who leave the system before service.

3. An airport has a number of runways. For various reasons (e.g. maintenance) at the end of interval t (measured in units of a given length) there will be x_t runways available, $t = 0, 1, 2, \ldots, T-1$. $q_t(k)$ is the probability of k arrivals in the tth time interval. Set down the equations in terms of $\{P_t(n)\}$, the probabilities that there will be n aircraft waiting for service at the end of the tth service interval, if any aircraft arriving in an interval will have their service completed at the end of the next time interval, subject to the constraint that not more than x_t aircraft can be serviced in time interval t (See Galliher *et al.* [13]).

    If there are b runways in total and every one has to be closed once in the next T time intervals, if $c(x_1, x_2, \ldots, x_T)$ is the associated cost of doing so to produce the pattern of availability specified, and if γ is the cost of keeping an aircraft waiting for one time interval, formulate as a mathematical programme the problem of choosing $(x_1, x_2, \ldots, x_T)$ to minimize expected costs.

4. Refer back to the transient equations for the single server, single arrival stream, negative exponential problem. Assume that the service rate $x(n) = \mu(n)$ can be varied, that the service cost per unit time is $c(x)$ for service rate x, and that the cost of an individual waiting per unit time is γ. Formulate the problem of minimizing the expected discounted costs over K small time intervals δ with discount factor α,

 (i) as a mathematical programme
(ii) as a dynamic programme.

Include the time being served in the waiting time.

5. If $\lambda \delta t$ is the probability that an arrival will take place in the next interval of time δt, independently of when the last arrival occurred, show that the inter-arrival time has a probability density function

$$f(t) = \lambda e^{-\lambda t}.$$

6. Consider Cobham's priority system with $L = 2$. Show that the rule which minimizes the expected number in the queue is the one which gives a higher priority to the one with the largest value of μ_l (see Aczel [1] for a more general result).

7. Consider the following modification of parts (i) and (iv) of Exercise 1. There are k machines and x servers. Each machine has the same, independent, probability distribution, $g(t)$, of time t between commencing operation and failure, and each server has the same, independent, probability distribution, $h(s)$, of service time s. $g(t)$ and $h(s)$ are quite general. By using discrete approximations for small intervals of time δ set up the equations to determine the steady state probability distribution of the system states.

8. In Chapter 4 we will consider the mean-variance analysis in a multi-objective framework. In Exercise 1 either find explicitly, or set up equations for the determination of, the mean (i.e. expected) waiting time of an individual, and its variance. Do this also for the cases covered in the text.

9. Suppose that, in the dynamic programming queueing problem of the text, the objective was one of maximizing the expected utility $u(f^1, f^2)$ of the total waiting times $\{f^1, f^2\}$ of the two streams of customers at the end of K intervals. Reformulate the problem as a dynamic programme with two extra state variables. Note that if $K \rightarrow \infty$, f^1, f^2 may be replaced by the expected waiting times per time interval. This reduces the problem to a multi-objective problem which is rather harder to tackle, but for which the linear programming approach may be useful in the context of efficient solutions (see Chapter 4) (see Kallenberg [17] for the use of linear programming in Markov decision processes, to which class of problems our problem belongs).

10. In Exercise 1, (ii) and (v), we introduced the ideas of a limited capacity

queueing situation and the possibility of customers reneging. In the text we also introduced the ideas of transient queues and dynamic programming. The following airline-booking exercise has some of each of these features although, initially, the queue is allowed to exceed capacity.

Airline bookings for a flight with capacity m, due to depart K days from now, are handled on a daily basis. Cancellations take place each day. On day k from the departure date a booking which has already been made, and not yet cancelled, will be cancelled during the day with probability p_k, with no cancellations on the departure date. Also during each day k from the departure date there will be new applications for bookings and $q_k(r)$ is the probability of r such applications. On the day of the flight no new applications of this kind arise but there will be standby passengers, the probability of there being s such passengers being $h(s)$. The net income from a normal booking which is not cancelled is a. No income or cost is incurred from a cancellation. The net income from a standby passenger is b. The airline can, if it wishes, deliberately overbook normal passengers to allow for cancellations. If, however, on the flight date it has more definite bookings (excluding standby) than capacity, it will incur a penalty of c for each booking exceeding capacity.

Formulate as a dynamic programme the problem of finding a decision rule which will maximize the net expected income from the flight. Explain why this is like a queueing problem (see Rothstein [27]).

Inventory

1. For the simple Wilson economic order quantity problem show that, for any $x > 0$,

$$\frac{f(x) - cs}{f(x^*) - cs} = \frac{1}{2}\left(\frac{x}{x^*} + \frac{x^*}{x}\right)$$

(see Donaldson et al. [6]).

We will use this example for sensitivity analysis later on, in Chapter 3.

2. Consider the simple Wilson economic order quantity problem with two commodities, where $\{a_j, h_j, c_j, s_j\}$, $j = 1, 2$ are the corresponding parameters for each item. Assume that $h_j = \alpha c_j$, for some α, and $j = 1, 2$, and that there is an upper limit of b placed upon the average amount of money tied up in inventory. Formulate the problem of minimizing the total annual costs as a mathematical programme and cast into the Lagrange multiplier form (see Donaldson et al. [6]).

We will use this example for constraint analysis later on, in Chapter 4.

3. For the simple Wilson economic order quantity problem show that an optimal solution exists in which the order quantities are always the same. Note that this also applies to Exercise 2.

4. Consider the problem in the text in which the demands in intervals

$k = 1, 2, \ldots, K$, respectively are $s_1, s_2, \ldots, s_K$, and with the specified cost structure. Suppose now that any inventory bought and held before use for l intervals costs a_l per unit to restore to its usable condition, this arising from deterioration of the commodity. Beginning with zero inventory at the beginning of interval 1, formulate the problem of minimizing the total costs over K intervals, in meeting all demands

(i) as a mathematical programme
(ii) as a dynamic programme.

(Nahmias [17] and Raafat [18] deal with deteriorating inventory problems.)

5. Consider the problem in the text for which the re-order period was $T = 1$ and the probability density function for demand was $g(s, T) = g(s)$. Now assume that all unsatisfied demand is backlogged, i.e. can be satisfied from future inventory, and that, instead of a penalty r per unit shortage, there is a penalty w for each unit delayed by one unit of time in being satisfied. What differences would this make to the mathematical programming formulation?

6. Consider the simple Wilson economic order quantity problem in which, now, the costs are subject to discounting, so that the value of £1 after t units of time is $\alpha(t) = e^{-\beta t}$, for some $\beta > 0$. Derive the expression for the infinite horizon discounted cost as a function of order size x. (Buzacott [4] and Aggarwal [1] discuss a similar problem for a finite time horizon, making allowance for inflation, and in which $\{c, h, s\}$ become functions of time. Also see George [9] and Bierman et al. [3].)

7. A central purchasing unit orders n different items j, $j = 1, 2, \ldots, m$. The parameters for item j are $\{a_j, h_j, c_j, s_j\}$, as for the simple Wilson economic quantity model. However, the central unit places an order for items each T time units, and an order for an individual item, and thus block orders, can only be placed at one of these block order points. There is a fixed cost, a, in addition, for each block order. Formulate the problem of deciding when to place block and individual orders to minimize the total annual costs in the long run as a mathematical programme. You may assume that for each item the order sizes are always the same, although differing from item to item (see Naddor et al. [16] and Schweitzer et al. [19]).

8. As has already been mentioned in Chapter 1, inventory problems can be viewed as queueing problems. Suppose that the demand for a product is such that the time between demands for a single unit is negative exponen- tail, with λ being the demand per unit time, and the supply procedure is that the demand is satisfied immediately if a unit of inventory is available, or the demand is not satisfied at all (e.g. a lost sale). Suppose that the inventory storage capacity is L units and that, if a unit is used to supply a demand, an order is placed for a replacement unit, and the time for this order to arrive is negative exponential with supply rate parameter μ. By identifying this problem with one of the problems in Exercise 1 of the Queueing section,

demonstrate how this can be solved as a queueing problem, and find the proportion of demand which is not satisfied in terms of λ,μ. (Karush [11] and Vazsonyi [22] discuss this problem, and Gaver [8] and Serfozo [20] also discuss an inventory problem using queueing theory, the latter also using a mathematical programming formulation.)

9. Solve the standard economic order quantity problem when the unit production cost c takes the form cs^γ ($\gamma = 0$ is the standard case) (see Muth *et al.* [14]). (Muth *et al.* [15] also consider six variants of this problem when the production (purchase) costs depend on the order quantity x.)

10. Later on, in Chapter 4, we will consider mean-variance analysis in a multi-objective framework, in which it may be necessary to evaluate each contribution to performance. In the example given in the text, where x, T have to be determined to find the minimal expected cost per unit time, find, for $T = 1$, and general x, the mean and variances of the amounts ordered, of the stock levels at the end of the cycle (before ordering) and of the shortage in the cycle, for the case of $g(s, 1) = g(s) = 1/S$, $0 \leqslant s \leqslant S$.

11. We have mentioned that inventory problems may be viewed as queueing problems. The converse is also true. Explain how the problem in Exercise 10 of the Queueing section may be viewed as an inventory problem.

Maintenance

1. Consider the simple text model with which we began but with the following modifications:

 (ii) the time taken to carry out routine maintenance is negligible;
 (iii) major repairs exhibit a negative exponential arrival pattern with rate $\lambda(x)$;
 (v) there is a fixed cost c per routine maintenance operation;
 (vi) there is a fixed cost C per major repair operation.

(Hence, in (v), (vi), no time costs arise except loss of revenue arising from major repairs.)

In addition, whereas in the text model a major repair was carried out as soon as it was needed, let us assume we have a single repair facility with negative exponential service rate, and that we have two identical pieces of equipment, so that, if one is undergoing a major repair when the other is also in need of a major repair, the second must wait until the service facility is free.

Reformulate the problem of determining x to maximize the net expected revenue per unit time, $N(x)$. Use the queueing formulae for negative exponential systems, noting that, in order to identify P_n, the arrival rate of major repairs combining both pieces of equipment is $(2 - n)\lambda(x)$ for $0 \leqslant n \leqslant 2$, and 0 for $n > 2$, where n is the number of pieces of equipment in the state of major repair requirements at any time.

2. In Queueing Exercise 1(iv) a problem with k machines, each subject to breakdown, is considered. Suppose now that, in the steady state, it is possible to vary the service rate (i.e. repair rate) dependent on the number of machines waiting for repair or being repaired, with $c(x)$ being the cost per unit time for service rate x, and w being the cost per unit time of a machine waiting. Set down in mathematical programming form the problem of controlling the service rates to minimize the expected cost per unit time.

3. Formulate Exercise 2 as a dynamic programme over an infinite time horizon, using a discount factor α, using small intervals of time δ between decisions.

4. The discounted return from a process over m periods of time is $r(a, b, m)$, inclusive of overhaul cost, where (a, b) are parameters known to the decision maker at the beginning of the m periods. After m periods the process may be overhauled and begins again with new parameters (a,b), which will be known as soon as the overhaul is completed. The parameters (a,b) have known probabilities $p(a,b)$ of arising. Formulate, as an infinite horizon discounted dynamic programming problem, the problem of deciding how long to run the process for a given value of (a,b) before overhauling it. Find an expression to optimize for each value of (a,b) from the dynamic programming formulation. (White [9] considers the same problem using expected returns per period instead of discounted returns. Note that this model may be adapted to cover the case when a maintenance operation can actually make the equipment worse than before the operation.)

5. A piece of equipment costs $c(t)$ to operate in the tth time interval after it is purchased. A new piece of equipment costs p and a piece of equipment of age u has a trade-in value of $s(u)$. Formulate, as a dynamic programme, the problem of finding a replacement policy to minimize the infinite horizon discounted net cost. Examine how the problem may be solved (see White [9]).

6. Consider the simple maintenance example of the text in which the maintenance time and repair times are constants with values $1/m$, $1/\mu$ respectively. Now suppose that the objective is to maximize the interval availability, where interval availability is the proportion of time the equipment is operating within tolerance and, for our purposes, tolerance means that the total time lost in a week is $\leq u$, for a specified u. Formulate, as an optimization problem, the problem of maximizing interval availability over a long time period by an appropriate choice of maintenance frequency.

Defective Product

1. A steel manufacturing company produces steel bars with a required length s_0. The bars are produced from billets whose size, x, may be varied. For each size x the probability density function for bar sizes s is $g(s, x)$. It costs $c(x)$ to process a billet of size x. If the bar is of size $s < s_0$ it is scrapped

154

and has a scrap value $v(s)$, with a new production operation to produce the bar of length s_0 commenced. If the bar is of size $s > s_0$ the excess may be cut off to produce a bar of the required length. The cost of this is $b(s)$ and the excess has a scrap value of $v(z)$ if z is the excess. Formulate, as an optimization problem, the problem of determining the billet size required to minimize the expected net cost of eventually producing the right size of bar. (See Goodeve [4], Passano [5] and Brigham *et al.* [1] for a discussion of this problem). Solve the problem when $s_0 = 1$, $\mu(x)$ $(=$ expected bar size given $x) = x$, $c(x) = 1 + 2x$, $b(s) = 1$, for all s, $v(z) = z$, for all z, and s is normally distributed with expected value x and variance 0.01.

2. A company produces rolls of insulation tape of a specified width w from wider tape of width Kw. It does this by using a set of $(K-1)$ cutters placed at distances w apart. The edge regions of the tape are defective to a depth of s, where s is a random variable with probability density function $g(s)$. It wishes to set the first cutter at a distance within the edge to minimize the expected waste arising from any strip which contains defective material having to be thrown away. Formulate this problem as an optimization problem. You may assume that $g(s) = 0$ if $s > K/2$ so that damaged regions on each edge do not overlap (see Sculli [6] for a discussion of this problem).

3. Consider the production overage problem in which the manufacturer is supplying a different specialist product to each of two customers, and in which the data are $\{Y_i, a_i, c_i, p_i\ (n, s)\}$, $i = 1, 2$, for the two customers C_1 and C_2. In addition assume the following:

 (i) once a customer's requirements have been met no further production takes place for that customer;
 (ii) production runs take place at the same time on different machines for each customer as long as a deficit remains for both customers;
(iii) once one customer's requirement has been met, any surplus may be converted to the product specification of the other customer, the cost of converting one unit of customer C_i's product for the other customer is r_i, $i = 1, 2$, no wastage arises in such operations and conversion is only allowed for a product within the acceptable specification of the customer being cannibalized;
(iv) conversion must take place, if at all, when the first surplus arises.

Follow similar analyses as in the text to determine the minimal expected cost of eventually satisfying both orders:

(a) using specified decision rules;
(b) using dynamic programming;
(c) using mathematical programming.

4. A mail order company supplies orders of various sizes z for an item. It always supplies exactly what is required. Each item has a probability p of being defective. If a customer finds that only m of the items are non-

defective, the company will supply a further $z - m$, and the process continues until the customer's original order is eventually satisfied. Derive a recurrence relation for the expected number of batches which has to be despatched before the customer's order is satisfied (Spencer [8] discusses this problem.)

5. Let us suppose that an item is being produced continually and it is either non-defective or defective. If an item is non-defective the probability that the next item is non-defective is p. If an item is defective the probability that the next item is non-defective is q. Each item may be inspected at a cost c, as it is produced, and its true condition determined. A defective item thus found is not sent to the customer and is scrapped. A non-defective item thus found is sent to the customer. The value of a non-defective item supplied to a customer, to the supplier, is $v_1 > 0$. The value of a defective item supplied to a customer, to the supplier, is $v_2 < 0$, arising from penalty clauses or other actions taken by the customer. Assume that an item has just been inspected and has been found to be defective. Formulate, as a dynamic programme, the problem of determining an inspection policy to maximize the total expected net value to the supplier for a production run of N items. (White [10] discusses a similar problem.)

6. Later on in Chapter 4 we will consider mean-variance analysis in a multi-objective framework in which it may be necessary, for each decision rule, to determine the mean and variance of numbers of set-ups and total quantity produced in the defective product problem of the text. This can be quite difficult to do. Set up recurrence relations to determine the (separate) probability distributions of the number of set-ups, and total quantity produced in meeting an order, for the numerical example given in the text. (Sobel [7] gives a general method for calculating means and variances in discounted probabilistic dynamic problems, which may be adapted to this problem, but it may be better to calculate the probabilities first and then the mean and variance.)

7. In section 2.2 we discussed (a) an inventory control problem in which the inventory level was to be restored to a level x at the end of each cycle of length T, and (b) an inventory problem in which decisions were to be made at the end of each unit time interval, the latter problem being formulated as a dynamic programme. Now suppose that if a quantity z is ordered the probability density function for the amount of good material, u, supplied is $h(z, u)$ (or alternatively use the discrete probability approach), and that u is known when the order is received. Modify both (a) and (b) to take account of this feature.

Mathematical and Dynamic Programming

1. (i) A company has one of each of m types of machine and produces n products. Product j requires t_{ij} units of time per unit on each machine i

before it is finished. The sales value of one unit of product j is v_j. It costs c_i to operate machine i for one unit of time, and machine i has time a_i available. Formulate a linear programme for the problem of choosing the quantities of each product to produce the maximum net revenue.

(ii) Now suppose that the time a_i may be exceeded, but that this results in an extra maintenance cost r_i per unit time used in excess of a_i, and that an upper limit on time available is $\bar{a}_i$. Reformulate (i) as a linear programme.

(iii) Returning to (i), now assume that there is a cost b_j per unit of product j, arising from raw material costs, and that there is an upper limit u_j on the amount of product j which can be sold in a year. Let us suppose that, initially, we have only one of each type of machine i, but that we may hire extra machines of each type i, with a capital cost h_i for the period of optimization concerned.

Reformulate (i) as a partly continuous variable, partly integer variable, linear programme, to determine production quantities and numbers of machines to hire to maximize net revenue.

2. Explain, for the cutting stock problem, why the objective function stated is not equivalent to the total residual material scrapped.

3. During a 40-hour teaching week, m subjects are taught $(i = 1, 2, \ldots, m)$, and exactly b_i periods of each subject i are required. In each period a combination, j, of subjects can be taught, subject to constraints on teacher availability. Teachers can be classified according to the set S_k of subjects they can teach, each teacher belonging to only one set, and $S_k \cap S_{k'} = \phi$, for $k \neq k'$, k, $k' = 1, 2, \ldots, l$. Group k contains t_k teachers. The jth combination of subjects in each period requires r_{kj} teachers from group k. There are r_k teacher hours available, in total, in group k in a week. Assuming that the n combinations to be considered are given in advance, formulate as a linear programme in integer variables the problem of finding combinations of subjects to teach to meet the requirements and constraints.

Note. An example of a combination of subjects taught in a given period is, for $j = 1$ (2 hours mathematics, taught by two different teachers in the period, 1 hour science, 2 hours English, 2 hours history), and groups $k = 1, 2$ might be (mathematics, science), (English, history). Then $r_{11} = 3$, $r_{21} = 4$.

4. (a) Consider a problem of deciding how many buses to put on specific routes in which:

(i) the routes to be considered are $k = 1, 2, \ldots, l$;
(ii) d_{ijk} is the distance between location i and location j on route k, $i, j = 1, 2, \ldots, m$.
(iii) a_{ik} is the frequency with which a given bus on route k visits location i in a day;
(iv) a_i is the minimal frequency with which location i must be visited on a given day, in total;
(v) p_{ij} is the number of passengers who wish to go from location i to location j in a day;

(vi) the number of buses available in a day is g;
(vii) all passengers wishing to go from location i to location j use the same route;
(viii) it is required to minimize the total passenger miles in a day.

Formulate as an integer linear programme, including some $(0, 1)$ variables, the problem of bus and passenger assignment to achieve objective (viii).

(b) Part (a) ignores bus carrying capacity. What other constraint would you add if a bus on route k can cope with q_k passenger miles?

(c) If a bus can carry c passengers at a time, what constraint would you add to part (a) to meet this constraint? Assume passenger demand is uniformly distributed, for each i, j, during the day.

(See Foulkes *et al.* [16] for problems of bus schedules.)

5. A bus company runs an express service which can stop at any one of n bus stops. However, the service is only allowed to stop at g bus stops. There are p_i potential passengers for stop i, who will board at i if the service stops at i, but will walk to a stop j, a distance d_{ij}, if the service does not stop at i, providing j is close enough, i.e. $j \in S_i$, where S_i is a subset of bus stops. Formulate, as a linear programme in $(0, 1)$ variables, the problem of deciding at which stops the service should pick up passengers, to minimize total distance walked by passengers (see Gleason [26]).

6. A set of n activities have to be completed in order to complete a project. Activity i cannot commence until a set of activities U_i have all been completed. Activity i takes time t_i to complete. Formulate as a linear programme the problem of finding the minimal time to complete the project. (See Kelly [35].)

7. (i) A company purchases a mixture of n items, j, $j = 1, 2, \ldots, n$, from among m suppliers. The unit price of item j from supplier i depends on the total number of all items purchased from him. If the total number, z, purchased from supplier i, satisfies $q_{i\alpha} \leq z < q_{i\alpha+1}$, the unit price of item j will be c_{ij}^α, $\alpha = 1, 2, \ldots, l$. The total requirement for item j is d_j, $j = 1, 2, \ldots, n$. Formulate the problem, of determining how many items of each type j to purchase from each supplier in order to minimize the total costs of at least meeting the requirements, as a mathematical programme in integer variables, some of which are $(0, 1)$ (see Tsarouchis [55]). Assume $q_{i1} = 0$.

(ii) What modifications to the above would you make if some $q_{i1} \neq 0$?

8. A company has m machines and n jobs to process. Each job must be processed on the machines in the order $k = 1, 2, \ldots, m$. The sequence of jobs is the same on each machine. The time required for job i on machine k is t_{ik}. Formulate as a mathematical programme in continuous and integer variables, some of which are $(0, 1)$, the problem of finding the optimal sequence of jobs to minimize the total time to complete all jobs (see Day [9]).

9. Consider the following modification of the cutting stock problem in the

text. A company has a demand for various sizes of steel sheet, i, $i = 1, 2, \ldots, m$. It has l possible raw material sizes, r, $r = 1, 2, \ldots, l$, from which it may produce the required orders. The required sizes may be produced in combinations j, $j = 1, 2, \ldots, n$, as in the text. The cost of producing combination j from raw material size r is c_{rj} ($c_{rj} = K$ if j cannot be produced from r, where K is very large). The requirement is for b_i items of size i. There is also a fixed cost a_r if raw material size r is used at all. Formulate as a linear programme in integer variables, some of which are $(0, 1)$, the problem of minimizing the total raw material cost in at least meeting the demands (this is rather like the fixed charge problem of Garfinkel et al. [20], and Steinberg [54]).

10. Consider the following school-bus stop allocation problem, which is similar to Exercise 5. An education authority has to assign pupils from each of m schools to each of n bus stops to provide transport to and from school. The distance between bus stop i and school j is d_{ij}, b_j is the maximal number of pupils allowed to go to school j, p_i is the number of pupils near to bus stop i, and S_i is the set of schools to which students from bus stop i may be sent. Formulate, as a linear programme, the problem of allocating pupils to schools to minimize the total distance travelled. You may allow for students near to a bus stop to go to different schools (see McKeown et al. [45]).

11. Consider Inventory Exercise 2. Suppose that:

 (i) there are m possible machines for producing the products;
 (ii) the cost per unit time of producing product i on machine j in batch size q_k is c_{ijk}, and that the allowable batch sizes are limited to specified values of q_k, $k = 1, 2, \ldots, l$;
 (iii) the proportion of time required to produce all demand for product i on machine j in batch size k is p_{ijk};
 (iv) a product, when produced, must always use the same machine and batch size;
 (v) it is assumed that, providing capacity exists to meet the production plan, it is possible to schedule so that, as in the simple inventory problem, production of product i can be commenced as soon as it has run out.

Formulate, as a linear programme in 0–1 variables, the problem of determining production quantities to minimize the average cost per unit time, and give expressions for $\{c_{ijk}, p_{ijk}\}$ if t_{ij} is the proportion of time taken to set up machine j to produce product i, for each batch, τ_{ij} is the proportion of time taken to produce one unit of product i on machine j, and the various costs (a_i, c_i) now depend on machine j used, i.e. (a_{ij}, c_{ij}) (see Glover et al. [27] for a discussion of the first part).

12. A local authority controls n regions, $i = 1, 2, \ldots, n$, and has to locate fire stations in some of the regions, with at most one in each case. The first station will be located at specific points in each region. Region i is reachable from region j, from a fire station in region j, if the time taken to respond to a

call is small enough. Thus region *i* either is reachable or is not reachable from region *j*. Because of local conditions, regions may have to be reachable from at least one station, from at least two stations, and so on. Formulate, as a mathematical programme in 0–1 variables, the problem of minimizing the number of fire stations subject to meeting specified reachability conditions (see Schreuder [51]).

13. Formulate the capacity installation problem as a mathematical programme (see McDowell [44].)

14. What modifications would you make to the optimal route problem if, for states $y \neq y_0$:

(a) the final state y_0 has to be reached in exactly k moves once only;
(b) the final state y_0 has to be reached in exactly k moves, but you are allowed to visit it at least once in doing so?

15. Consider the capacity installation problem, where demand is now uncertain. If t is the demand in interval k, let us assume that the demand s in interval $k+1$ has a probability density function $g_k(s, t)$, dependent on k. If the initial demand s_1 is known, and the demand in every interval is known at the beginning of the interval, but not before, reformulate as a dynamic programme the problem of determining at the beginning of each interval how much extra capacity to put in to minimize the expected discounted costs over K intervals. You will require two state variables to describe the problem.

16. For the second defective product problem identify the components

$$y, \quad x, \quad f(y), \quad q(x, y), \quad X(y), \quad p(z; x, y).$$

17. Formulate the optimal redundancy problem of Chapter 1 as a dynamic programme (see Bellman [2]). This is slightly different to the standard form given in the text because the objective function is not, initially, additive.

18. Consider the travelling salesman problem studied in section 2.5. Formulate this as a dynamic programme (see Dreyfus *et al.* [10]).

19. Formulate the optimal route problem given in the text as a mathematical programme.

20. Formulate Exercise 6 as a dynamic programme.

21. A company operates a machine whose cost performance deteriorates between major overhauls, and it operates no routine maintenance service. The operating cost per unit time between overhauls is $c(t)$, where t is the time since the last overhaul took place. The cost of an overall is $a(t)$, if the overhaul interval is t. Formulate:

(a) as a dynamic programme
(b) as a mathematical programme

the problem of deciding when to undertake exactly n overhauls over a total time horizon T, beginning with overhauled equipment, to minimize the total cost. Treat time as a continuous variable.

22. Suppose that you have a supply of identical tap cassettes and n pieces of music to be recorded on the cassettes. Piece i of music takes a time t_i, $i = 1, 2, \ldots, n$. Each cassette can record up to a total time T. Each piece of music must be recorded on one cassette. Give two mathematical programming formulations for the problem of minimizing the number of cassettes to record all the music.

23. Consider the following modification of Exercise 6. The activities may now be reduced by allocating extra resources to each activity. Suppose we have a single resource in quantity b and that, if x_i is allocated to activity i, the time of activity i is $t_i = \bar{t}_i - a_i x_i$, but that t_i cannot be reduced below a level $\underline{t}_i$. Now formulate the problem as a linear programming problem to minimize the completion time of the project.

24. Consider the following variant of the inventory control problem discussed as a dynamic programme in section 2.3. The details are the same except that orders are not necessarily satisfied immediately. Each order placed will be supplied in total at times which are multiples of the time unit, but with certain probabilities, so that $q_{tz}(x)$ is the probability that, if an order for x items is placed, z will be delivered at time t. No new order is to be placed as long as any outstanding orders from two or more previous orders remain. Formulate as a dynamic programme the problem of minimizing the expected cost over K time units.

25. Consider Exercise 1 of the Maintenance Exercises where, now, decisions on maintenance frequency are made for each unit time interval at beginning of each time interval k (i.e. x_k is to be the frequency of routine maintenance in this interval). Suppose that λ is now a function of k and of x_k, i.e. $\lambda = \lambda(k; x_k)$. Formulate as a mathematical programme, and as a dynamic programme, the problem of maximizing the net revenue over K time intervals.

26. Consider the following simplified aircraft usage–maintenance problem. Initially there are y aircraft available for flying. On each day t it has to be decided how many aircraft to fly and how many hours each is to fly on each day (each flies the same number). If x is the hours flown by an aircraft, a proportion $\lambda(x)$ require maintenance on day $t + 1$ and a proportion $\mu(x)$ are destroyed. On day t a number of new aircraft n_t are delivered. Formulate, as a mathematical programming problem, the problem of maximizing the total hours flown over the next T days, assuming that the maximal number of aircraft which can be repaired on any day is m and that all aircraft are repaired immediately subject to this constraint.

Now consider a very long period of time and assume that a steady state is eventually reached. What would the problem then reduce to? Assume $n_t = n$, $\forall t$. (Waddington [57] discusses a similar problem.)

27. Consider the following problem which is a hybrid problem from sections 2.3 and 2.4. A rubber tyre manufacturer uses a machine which contains two bladders each one of which simultaneously produces a tyre. If a bladder fails in service a faulty tyre is produced and a cost c_2 incurred. The machine must then be stripped down for replacement, a process resulting in a cost c_3 for labour and a cost c_4 for lost production. A replacement bladder costs c_1. Once a machine has been stripped the cost of replacing the second bladder, if it is replaced, is c_1 alone. A bladder which has successfully produced i tyres will produce a good tyre next time with probability p_i. Formulate as a dynamic programme, and as a mathematical programme, the problem of determining an optimal bladder replacement policy to minimize the expected cost of producing at least N good tyres. (See Sasieni [50] and Dreyfus [11].)

Note that, in keeping with our view on the overlap of techniques, this problem has features of a defective product problem.

In addition note that, whereas Sasieni assumes that an optimal policy has a specific form, Dreyfus, using dyanmic programming, shows otherwise.

28. In section 2.8 a simple warehouse location problem is treated by an heuristic method by locating warehouses at the centres of circles. How would you tackle that problem using mathematical programming?

29. A vehicle has a capacity b. There are n types of item to be loaded, with item j requiring capacity a_j for each unit and having a value p_j. Formulate

(a) as a mathematical programming problem
(b) as a dynamic programming problem

the problem of deciding how many of each type of item to load on to the vehicle to maximize total value. What would the solution be if we did not require an integer number of units?

(This is discussed in section 2.8. See Garfinkel et al. [20] for a treatment.)

30. Consider the redundancy problem of the text (Chapter 1). Suppose that the unit is used for a mission. If the unit fails, it is lost, and the mission must begin again with a new unit. The missions continue until one is successful. Formulate, as an optimization problem, the problem of minimizing the expected cost until the process terminates, with no constraint on the money available for the components. Now suppose that an amount C is available in total. Formulate as a dynamic programme the problem of maximizing the probability of an eventual successful mission.

31. Consider the following generalization of Exercise 4(b) of Chapter 1. A target is known to be in one of n locations i, $i = 1, 2, \ldots, n$. Once the target has been located in one of these, i, it has then to be more specifically located

162

in one of n_i sub-locations j, $j = 1, 2, \ldots, n_i$, of location i. If the target is located to be in location i, then p_{ij} is the probability that it will be in sub-location j of location i. In addition to $1 - q_i$ as in Exercise 4(b), suppose that $1 - r_i$ is the probability that, if location i is checked and the target is not actually there, then the check will indicate that it is not there. We have similar definitions $\{1 - q_{ij}\}$, $\{i - r_{ij}\}$ for sub-locations j of location i when location i is now searched over its sub-locations. Let there be, in addition to the search times $\{t_i\}$, search times $\{t_{ij}\}$ for sub-locations. Formulate the problem of minimizing the expected time to locate the target as a dynamic programme and examine the nature of an optimal policy. Note that this problem derives from a fault detection problem and hence it is also related to maintenance problems, thus emphasizing the overlap between characteristic problem areas.

Optimization Analogues

1. A set of fixed points has to be linked by a connected network of links (i.e. each pair of points is connected by a set of links). Given a framework of any kind dipped in a soap solution, soap films will form connecting all parts of the framework in such a way that the area of the soap film will be minimal. How can you use this to develop an optimization analogue for the first problem? (See Ollerenshaw [14], Miehle [12] and Courant [3].) Note that this is not quite the same problem as the minimal spanning tree problem (see Shapiro [17]) since some of the links may meet at points not in the original set. It should also be pointed out that, in general, the soap film solutions will not be global minima (see Courant) but for simple problems they are likely to be (Miehle).

2. In section 2.5 we discussed the optimal routing problem. Devise a mechanical device for finding the minimal distance between two points when the distance matrix is symmetric (see Minty [13]).

3. An ancient Greek problem is to find the shortest route between two fixed points on the same side of a river bank, which is assumed to form a straight line, and during which journey it is required to fill a container of water from the river. Construct an analogue for solving this problem (see Miehle [12]).

4. A set of points is divided into two subsets, viz. fixed and free. A network of links is to be devised connecting all of the fixed points and a subset of the free points (to be chosen) to minimize the weighted total network length connecting the points, where the weights are integral. Devise a mechanical analogue to solve this problem (see Miehle [12]). Note that this is a minimal spanning tree problem if there are no free points.

5. Design an analogue made up of strings and rods to solve the standard linear programming problem given in Chapter 2 where the coefficients a_{ij} are 0, 1, or -1 (see Sinden [18]).

6. A communications network consisting of an intercommunicating set of stations is given. A communication capacity (transmission rate) of c_k for each pair, k, of stations, and a route i (a route being a connecting sequence of links) may or may not connect a pair k of stations. The present capacities of links $\{j\}$, from which routes are formed, are $\{c_j\}$. Route i may or may not contain link j. It costs f_j to increase the capacity of link j be one unit. It is required to add extra capacities to the links to meet the overall capacity requirements $\{c_k\}$ at a minimal total cost. This will also involve decisions on the assignments of traffic to routes. Design a string and rod analogue to solve this problem (see Sinden [18]).

7. (i) Consider an open electrical network consisting of a set of resistances, $\{r_{ij}\}$, joining points $\{(i, j)\}$ in the network. Suppose that there are two distinguished points $i = 1$, $i = N$ with a current x entering at $i = 1$ and leaving at $i = N$. If $\{x_{ij}\}$ are the currents flowing between $\{(i, j)\}$ pairs, then it is known that $\{x_{ij}\}$ is such as to minimize $\sum_i \sum_j r_{ij} x_{ij}^2$ (see Coulson [2]).

(ii) Consider a closed network which is similar to the above, with no distinguished points, and no inflowing or outgoing current, but with a set of batteries joining $\{(i, j)\}$ with voltages $\{v_{ij}\}$. In this case the currents $\{x_{ij}\}$ minimize $\sum_i \sum_j x_{ij}(r_{ij}x_{ij} - 2v_{ij})$ (see Coulson [2]).

Suggest optimizations of an Operational Research type which will be solved by using electrical analogues of the types given in (i) and (ii).

Simulation

1. A housing maintenance depot is located in a region R, at X, which it serves. Its policy is to wait until it has received a request for x jobs and then send out a maintenance engineer to do all x jobs. The maintenance engineer visits the nearest job location to depot X first of all, and then continues to move to the next nearest job location to the one he has already visited, before finally returning to the depot X. In deciding what the optimal x value should be, it is required to determine the expected total distance for a round (consisting of x jobs, commencing and finishing at depot X), i.e. $a(x)$. Devise an appropriate simulation procedure, and using two simulation runs for each value of $x = 5$, 10, 20, estimate $a(x)$ roughly by visual fit (not by statistical analysis) (see Christofides [8], Bearwood et al. [3], Christofides et al. [9]). Assume that the demands for jobs are uniformly distributed over region R.

2. Consider a single server problem in which the arrivals have an inter-arrival time which is negatively exponentially distributed with arrival rate fiver per hour (so that the cumulative probability function $F(t) = 1 - e^{-5t}$), and in which the services have also a negative exponential distribution with service rate ten per hour (so that the cumulative probability function $F(t) = 1 - e^{-10t}$), with the usual first come–first served rule. Begin with the system empty. Using an appropriate simulation procedure, run one simula-

tion involving ten arrivals, as for the example done in the text, but also recording the number in the system graphically. You may use the following tabulations of $1 - e^{-m}$ (approximate):

$1 - e^{-m}$	1.00	0.95	0.90	0.85	0.80	0.75	0.70	0.65	0.60	0.55	0.50	0.45	0.40
m	∞	3	2.3	1.9	1.6	1.4	1.2	1.05	0.90	0.80	0.70	0.60	0.50

$1 - e^{-m}$	0.35	0.30	0.25	0.20	0.15	0.10	0.05	0.00
m	0.43	0.35	0.28	0.22	0.16	0.11	0.06	0.00

To avoid difficulties arising from t being arbitrarily large ignore all t sample values in the top 5 per cent of the probability interval. Estimate the probability of the system being empty and check with the theoretical result.

3. (a) Prove that each of the congruential pseudo-random number generators will eventually cycle, i.e. produce a series of numbers repeatedly and that, in case of the mixed and multiplicative forms, each number in the series is different.

(b) For such methods to work, m, and the length of the cycle, must be large. Even so the series produced by the first two methods contain no repeated numbers, and hence are not strictly random. However, in many cases it does not matter if a number is, for example, 6 or 7, or even 8. What is important is that basic randomness is preserved in a broad sense. Thus, if we divide the numbers into equal blocks, then the probability of transition between blocks is the same. Consider the multiplicative form with $R_0 = 1$, $a = 7$, $m = 61$, and check that the above property is roughly satisfied by taking blocks 1–15, 16–30, 31–45 and 46–60.

4. Consider the simple inventory control example used to illustrate variance reduction, but with $s = 0$ to simplify the problem. Do the following.

(a) Show that the optimal policy is to order a unit if $c < kp$, and to order nothing if $c > kp$, with either decision being optimal if $c = kp$, when the objective is to minimize expected costs per unit time.

(b) Now suppose two simulation runs, each of length n, are made, and with order sizes 1 and 0 respectively. Let the order size eventually chosen be the one whose simulation gives the smallest cost per unit time. Assume $pk > c$.

Find an expression for the expected loss of optimal cost per unit time which this procedure will give, and show that this expected loss $\to 0$ as $n \to \infty$.

You may assume that if $\{d_i\}$, $i = 1, 2, \ldots, n$ are random variables with values 0,1, and probabilities $1 - p, p$ respectively, independent of each other, then $(\sum_{i=1}^{n} d_i)/n$ is approximately normally distributed with mean p, and variance $p(1 - p)/n$.

5. Design a simulation for the simple production overage problem given in the text and run a simulation of up to five production operations, for each of two decision rules.

6. Design a simulation for the single server, single arrival stream problem given in the text, which is negative exponential, with service rate μ, and arrival rate $\lambda/(n+1)$. Do not use the approach of Exercise 2. Split the total time period into K small intervals of length δt and let all events take place at the end of such intervals.

7. Design a simulation for the capacity installation problem discussed in the dynamic programming section where the demand in interval k is $s_k + r$ where r is a random error normally distributed with zero mean and unit variance.

8. A port has a single berth for incoming ships. There are two streams of ships arriving, requiring use of the berth. The inter-arrival time between ships, taking both streams together, is negative exponential with cumulative probability function $F(t) = 1 - e^{-5t}$. The service times for each stream are negative exponential, one with a cumulative distribution function $F(t) = 1 - e^{-10t}$, and the other with a cumulative distribution function $F(t) = 1 - e^{-20t}$. An arrival is equally likely to be from either stream. A policy is operated by which a ship in the first stream is always allocated the berth when it becomes empty provided such a ship is waiting for the berth. Otherwise the berth is allocated to a ship from the second stream, provided such a ship is waiting for the berth.

Design and run a simulation for 20 arrivals, recording the arrivals, services, waiting times, and numbers of ships in each stream in the system. The approximate tabulations of Exercise 2 will be needed. Ignore any times which arise in the top 5 per cent probability of the cumulative probability function, and use random variables which occur at 5 per cent probability intervals for these functions.

9. A company installs capacity at the beginning of each year to meet the demand in that year, which is always known for definite at the beginning of each year. It is known that the demand in any year is related to the demand in the previous year in a probabilistic manner as follows, where z is treated as a continuous variable.

$$\text{demand in year } (n+1) = \text{demand in year } (n) + z$$

where z has a cumulative probability distribution of the form

$$F(z) = 1 - e^{-z}.$$

At the beginning of year (1) it is known that the demand in year (1) is 1 and the capacity, in equivalent units of demand, is 0.

At the beginning of each year at least enough capacity must be installed so that, together with existing capacity at the beginning of that year, enough capacity exists to at least meet the demand for that year.

It costs 1 unit of fixed cost every time a positive capacity addition is made, and a further cost of 1 unit is incurred for every unit of capacity put in. Capacity can only be increased by unit amounts.

It is required to select a decision rule which determines any additional capacity for a given year in terms of the demand for that year and existing capacity at the beginning of that year.

Design, with explanation, a simulation for this problem, and run it for 10 successive years, recording what you think are the pertinent aspects of the problem, for the following decision rule:

if demand in year (n) exceeds capacity at the beginning of year (n), then increase capacity so that the total capacity exceeds demand by 1 unit, otherwise do not add any extra capacity for that year.

10. In Exercise 6 of the Mathematical and Dynamic Programming Exercises, a problem in which activity times $\{t_i\}$ were deterministic was discussed. Suppose now that each t_i is independently distributed with probabilities given as follows in a specific case.

| Activity i | Precedence Set | \multicolumn{5}{c|}{Activity time t_i} |
	U_i	1	2	3	4	5
1	—	0.3	0.7			
2	—	0.3	0.4	0.3	—	—
3	1	0.1	0.2	0.4	0.3	—
4	2,3	—	0.2	0.2	0.4	0.2
5	3	0.2	0.5	0.3	—	—
6	4,5	0.1	0.2	0.5	0.2	—
7	1	—	—	0.2	0.6	0.2
8	6.7	0.7	0.3	—	—	—

Design and run a simulation, using the antithetic variate method, to determine an estimate of the probability distribution of the project completion time. Use the dynamic programming formulation of Exercise 20 of the Mathematical and Dynamic Programming Exercises to calculate the completion times. (See Hayya *et al.* [26], and Grant [22], who show that the antithetic variate method will reduce the variance of the estimate).

11. A region R has x fire engines located at points reasonably uniformly distributed over R. Calls are uniformly distributed over R. Assuming each fire engine is available when a call arises (i.e. the time between calls is somewhat longer than the service time) each call is served by its nearest fire engine. Design and run a simulation to estimate the average response time

to serve a call, selecting your own data, and estimate the average response time $t(x)$ as a function of x (it may be demonstrated that $t(x) \cong k\sqrt{m/x}$, where m is the area of R and k is a constant, and note that this problem has some similarity to the warehouse location problem discussed in section 2.8). section 2.8).

12. Consider the probabilistic (x, T) problem discussed in section 2.2 and illustrated at the beginning of this section for $T = 1$.

 (i) Choose a simple example to show that the variances of the differences between the total costs for two values of x can be increased by using common random numbers.
(ii) Show that, in general, the variance of the difference of each component cost (i.e. purchase, stockholding, shortage) for two values of x will not increase and will usually decrease.

13. Consider sampling a random variable r and suppose that if r falls into a small interval $[(k-1)\delta, k\delta]$ we either

(a) assign the value $k\delta$ to r, or
(b) assign the value $(k - \frac{1}{2})\delta$ to r.

   Show that, if we have a probability density function $g(r)$ for r, then procedure (b) will give a better approximation to the expected value of r in the interval, providing δ is small enough.

Heuristic Programming

1. Consider the inventory illustration discussed in section 2.2 in which the demands in period k are s_k, $k = 1, 2, \ldots, K$, with the various cost factors, and in which the initial inventory y is 0. Suggest several heuristic programmes for getting a solution and explain the rationale behind each (see Axsäter [4, 5]). Look at the worst case analysis. Comment on the relative advantages and disadvantages of the heuristics as compared with the dynamic programming formulation.

2. For the machine scheduling problem discussed in the text, suggest two further heuristic procedures which might be used, explain their rationale, and test them against the simple example given in the text (see Dannenbring [44] for 11 heuristics).

3. For the simple knapsack problem construct an example for which the greedy heuristic given will give a poor answer.

4. Construct a simple location–allocation problem for which the heuristic suggested in the text will give a poor answer for some starting solutions (see White [155]).

5. (a) Use the Clarke–Wright heuristic for the following problem with two

vehicles of capacities 10 and 35, respectively, beginning with three routes, assigning each destination to one and only one route.

		0	P_j 1	2	3	Demand
	0	0	13	8	9	—
P_i	1	13	0	6	9	6
	2	8	6	0	10	8
	3	9	9	10	0	10

Assume, however, that the matrix entries are times, and that every call at the depot involves a fixed waiting time of 2 units, in addition to the time taken to load the vehicles which is proportional to the load carried, and that there is an additional time for each load depending on the number of destinations it covers as follows:

Number of destinations covered by load	1	2	3
Extra time	0	8	15

(b) What difference would it make to the calculations if company policy did not allow loads of less than 50 per cent of vehicle capacity?

6. Consider the following cassette loading problem.

(i) there are n jobs (pieces of music);
(ii) there are m machines (cassettes), m large enough to ensure a feasible schedule;
(iii) job i takes time t_i on machine k (for the cassette problem this is the length of the piece of music) independent of the machine k;
(iv) each machine can work for T time units (length of tape, in time, on cassette).

The problem is to complete the programme of loading each job on to (any) one machine, using the minimal number of machines.

Suggest heuristic methods for this problem and explain why you think they might work, and determine worst case bounds. (See Fisher [66], Brown [24], George *et al.* [78], Garey *et al.* [71], Johnson [103], [104], Demers *et al.* [54], Rayward-Smith *et al.* [135] on bin-packing.)

Now do the same if the objective is to minimize the time to complete all jobs.

7. A single machine is used to produce n products. The machine is set to give production runs of each product in turn, but not necessarily with the same frequency per year (thus we may run product 1, then product 2, then product 1, then product 3, and so on).

For each product i the following data is given:

s_i: annual demand rate;
p_i: the annual production rate when producing;
a_i: fixed set up cost for production run for product i;
h_i: cost of holding one unit of product i for one year.

All demand must be met, with no shortages or delays, and the capacity of the machine is exactly related to the demand for the products overall

$$\left(\text{i.e. } \sum_{i=1}^{n} \frac{s_i}{p_i} = 1\right).$$

Suggest an heuristic method for minimizing the annual cost, making use of the simple inventory theory given in the text, explaining why you think it might work (see Cook *et al.* [34]). (Schweitzer *et al.* [141] discuss pitfalls in modelling this problem).

8. Consider the simple economic costs quantity inventory problem with n commodities with parameters $\{s_i, h_i\}$, $i = 1, 2, \ldots, n$, as in Exercise 7, but with the possibility of ordering several items at the same time, with a fixed order cost of $a(q)$ for each such group order containing q items, with each item in a group being ordered at the same time. Formulate, as a mathematical programme, the problem of deciding how to group the items, and what the re-order intervals for each group should be in order to minimize the total annual cost. Then suggest an heuristic method for getting a solution.

9. Construct a travelling salesman problem for which the nearest-neighbour heuristic does not give an optimal solution, no matter where we begin. It need not be a symmetric problem but symmetric counter-examples exist.

10. There are n students in a class for whom tutorials have to be arranged. The tutorials take place at one of m times, i, $i = 1, 2, \ldots, m$. The times feasible for student j form a subset, S_j. It is required to find a tutorial assignment which smoothes out the variation between tutorial group sizes. Suggest an heuristic method for this, explaining its rationale.

11. Extend the knapsack problem of the text to the case when we have several constraints

$$\sum_{j=1}^{n} a_{ij}x_j \leqslant b_i, \qquad i = 1, 2, \ldots, m.$$

What heuristic would you now use and determine worst case bounds. (Loulo *et al.* [118], Sahni [139] and Magazine *et al.* [120] discuss the special 0–1 case. Also see Loulou *et al.* [119]).

12. (i) In section 2.5 we discussed a problem of cutting material of a given width to meet requirements for other widths. In that simple problem it was

assumed that it was easy to list all the combinations to consider. Suppose now that the number of possible combinations is large. Suggest an heuristic method to solve the problem (see Coverdale *et al.* [41]).

(ii) Suppose now that the raw material costs c per unit and that, in addition, there is a cost d for changing from one cutting combination to another. Formulate a mathematical programme and suggest an heuristic for solving this problem. (Haessler [89] discusses a similar problem.) Also suggest an heuristic for solving Exercise 9 of the Mathematical Programming Exercises.

13. There are n possible locations in a plane and m facilities have to be located among the n locations (no more than one facility at each location). It is required to locate the facilities in such a way that the maximal number of locations come within a distance R of some facility. Suggest an heuristic for solving this problem (see Watson-Gandy [152] who also discusses applications).

14. In the standard transportation problem (see section 2.6), Vogel's method may be used to find an initial solution (see McMillan [121]). This proceeds by identifying a row or column with a largest difference between the two smallest unit costs, allocating as much as possible to a minimal unit cost position in such a row or column, deleting the saturated row or column containing this smallest unit cost, and then repeating the procedure. This method is an heuristic for getting good starting solutions. Explain why it might work well and that it gives optimal solutions for 2×2 problems, and study the worst case analysis.

15. Consider an inventory control problem for a single interval in which there are n products with demand probability density functions $g_i(s)$, $i = 1, 2, \ldots, n$. There are the usual inventory holding costs, purchase costs and shortage costs. If $\{x_i\}$ are the purchase quantities it is required to determine these to minimize the expected total costs subject to a constraint

$$\sum_{i=1}^{n} v_i x_i \leq V$$

where $\{v_i\}$, V are constants. Formulate the problem as an optimization problem using a Lagrange multiplier (see Chapter 4 for fuller details for this) and suggest an heuristic for solving it (see Nahmias *et al.* [124]). It is worth noting that the use of Lagrange multipliers, in the way they are used in Chapter 4, is an heuristic in itself. Nahmias *et al.* [124] do not use it in the same way, but rather use an heuristic method to solve an exact problem.

16. Develop an algorithm for exactly solving the warehouse location problem, based on the use of the heuristic in this section as a starting point.

17. Develop an heuristic for solving the nursery location problem discussed in section 2.5 (Bovet [22] discusses a related problem).

18. Complete all the calculations for heuristics 3–6 given in this section for the travelling salesman problem.

19. A teaching programme has to be timetabled to meet certain requirements. There is a set S of lectures to be timetabled. There are n students, and each student has to attend a subset S_i of lectures, $i = 1, 2, \ldots, n$. No two lectures in any S_i, $i = 1, 2, \ldots, n$, may be timetabled simultaneously. It is required to minimize the total number of teaching periods to provide a feasible timetable. Develop an heuristic to solve this problem (see Barham *et al.* [12]). The problem is essentially a vertex colouring problem for graphs (see de Werra *et al.* [56] and Johnson [106]). Also see Scott [142] for another timetabling heuristic).

20. Develop an heuristic to solve the school timetabling problem of Exercise 3 of the Mathematical and Dynamic Programming Exercises (de Gans [52] discusses a similar problem).

21. In Chapter 4 we will discuss a Lagrangean relaxation method for solving constrained problems. Use these ideas to construct an heuristic method for solving the vehicle routing problem (see Golden *et al.* [83]).

22. Suggest several heuristic methods for solving the problem of Exercise 23 of the Mathematical and Dynamic Programming Exercises (see Davis *et al.* [50] who study eight methods).

23. Consider the Dynamic Programming Exercise 24 in the Mathematical and Dynamic Programming Exercises. Develop an heuristic method along the lines of the infrequent but significant contingencies approach of the text (see White [154]).

24. In Exercise 7 of the Queueing Exercises a machine repair problem was given. In principle it is possible to determine the steady state probabilities, and hence determine the proportion of time each machine will be in a failed state, and hence not producing a product. Now assume that the optimal answer will involve only a small proportion of such time spent non-operational, and use the infrequent but significant contingencies principle to obtain an expression for the lost time as a function of x, the number of servers (see White [154]).

25. Consider Exercise 1 in which we now have n products and s_{ik} is now the demand for product i in interval k, and in which each unit of product type i takes r_{iu} units of resource type u, $u = 1, 2, \ldots, m_y$ each set up for product type i takes an amount g_{iu} of resource type u, and there are b_{uk} units of resource type u available in interval k. Suggest several heuristics for tackling this problem (see Newson [125]).

26. In section 2.2 we considered a simple problem of a single commodity and a single production point. Now suppose that we have a network of production points $\{i\}$ in which a final product is produced by various

172

operations as it passes through the network in its various pieces and combinations. At each node i of the network the batch quantity is x_i and the various costs are $\{a_i, c_i, h_i\}$, as in section 2.2. The total demand rate of the completed product at the exit node of the network is s, and this is the requisite throughput rate, in appropriate units, at each node. If the output of node i goes to node j, then x_i is an integer multiple of x_j. Suggest several heuristics for finding the $\{x_i\}$ to minimize annual total cost (see Williams [156]).

27. Give justifications for each of the heuristic methods suggested in the text for the travelling salesman problem.

28. Suggest and justify an heuristic for solving the capacity installation problem introduced in section 2.5 and further studied in section 2.10.

29. Suggest and justify a greedy heuristic for solving the plant location–allocation problem discussed in the text. (Hamburger *et al.* [91] discuss a similar problem, and Fisher [66] gives worst case bounds for a greedy heuristic.)

30. In the text reference is made to the fact that Kruskal's heuristic for finding the minimal weighted spanning tree will give optimal solutions (i.e. is an algorithm in our sense). Prove this, assuming that a spanning tree exists. (See Garfinkel *et al.* [76] for an easier proof.)

31. In the text we have mentioned the significant but infrequent contingencies heuristic approach to some stochastic problems. Consider Queueing Exercise 1(iv), where we now have x servers, and each machine has an identical and independently distributed inter-failure time probability density function, $g(t)$, and each server has an identical and independently distributed service time probability density function, $h(s)$. The annual cost of a server is a, and the value of a full year's output for a machine is V. Use the infrequent but significant contingencies heuristic to find a value of x which gives a good approximation to optimal total annual net income of output value less service cost (see White [154]).

32. Exercise 18 of the Mathematical and Dynamic Programming Exercises asked for the formulation of the travelling salesman problem as a dynamic programme (e.g. see Bellman [13]). Suggest an heuristic approach to this formulation and justify it. (Norman [129] discusses various heuristics in dynamic programming, inclusive of stochastic dynamic programming).

33. In the text we discussed a dynamic programming approach to the control of queues which had two different arrival streams. Suggest, and justify, an heuristic approach to this problem where there are more than two arrival streams (again see Norman [129] for ideas).

34. A set of n jobs has to be done in some sequence on a machine. Job i takes time t_i, $i = 1, 2, \ldots, m$. Let T_i be the total time spent in the system by job i for a specific sequence, assuming all the jobs are always ready when

wanted. It is required to find a sequence to minimize $\sum_i T_i$. Show that the following greedy method will actually give an optimal solution, viz, sequence in order of shortest processing times (Baker [7]).

35. For the same set of jobs, each job has a due date d_i. The lateness of job i is defined as $T_i - d_i$. The tardiness of job i is defined as $\max[T_i - d_i, 0]$. Show that the following greedy method will minimize both the maximal job lateness and the maximal tardiness, viz. sequence in order of earliest due dates (Baker [7]).

Las Vegas

1. Consider the machine sequencing problem discussed in section 2.8, with two machines and ten jobs, with the times of each job on each machine given below:

| m/c | \multicolumn{10}{c}{Job} |
	1	2	3	4	5	6	7	8	9	10
1	9	8	7	6	4	8	2	8	6	10
2	5	9	8	6	7	9	8	3	4	10

(i) Explain in principle how you would apply the Las Vegas method to this problem, where the sequence on each machine is the same, and where the objective is to minimize the total time to complete all jobs.
(ii) Find ten random sequences and calculate the total time for two of those sequences, and explain how you took the random sequences.
(iii) Find a time t_1, as high as you can, below which the minimum total time cannot go.
(iv) Now assume that the probability distribution of total completion time is uniform between that in (iii) and the lowest in (ii), that the probability of a feasible sample is 1, and the value of unit time saved is 0.5, and determine what the optimal policy is.
(v) This problem is easy using other methods and, in fact, an optimal sequence is (7, 5, 4, 3, 6, 2, 10, 1, 9, 8), but how good is the optimal solution in (iv) as compared with the optimal solution in (v)?
(iv) What are the dangers in mis-estimating the minimal possible value of the objective function?

2. Consider the linear programme

$$\text{maximize}[h = 10x_1 + 12x_2]$$

subject to

$$3x_1 + 3x_2 \leqslant 40$$
$$2x_1 + 4x_2 \leqslant 50$$
$$x_1 \geqslant 0, \qquad x_2 \geqslant 0.$$

174

(i) Take a sample of 200 points using a suitable region S, as in the text, to allow for infeasible points.
(ii) Use the Beta distribution theory as given in the text to estimate a probability density function for values of h in the feasible region.
(iii) If the cost of a single sample is $c = 1$, use the Las Vegas theory of the text to find the optimal stopping rule on the basis of (ii).

3. Carry out a Las Vegas analysis of the capacity installation problem for the data given in section 2.5, and later studied in section 2.10, for $K = 10$.

2.12 REFERENCES

Queueing

1. Aczel, M. A., The effect of introducing priorities, *Operations Research*, **8**, 730–733, 1960.
2. Ancker, C. J. and Gafarian, A. V., Some queueing problems with balking and reneging, I., *Operations Research*, **11**, 88–93, 1963.
3. Bellman, R., *Dynamic Programming*, Princeton University Press, 1957.
4. Bhat, W. N., Sixty years of queueing theory, *Management Science*, **15**, 280–294, 1969.
5. Bhat, U. N., Shalaby, M., and Fischer, M. J., Approximation techniques in the solution of queueing problems, *Naval Research Logistics Quarterly*, **26**, 311–326, 1979.
6. Brockmeyer, E., Holstrøm, H. L., and Jensen, A., *The Life and Works of A. K. Erlang*, Translation, Transaction of the Danish Academy of Technical Sciences, Vol. 2, Copenhagen, 1960.
7. Cobham, A., Priority assignment in waiting line problems, *Operations Research*, **2**, 70–76, 1954.
8. Cox, D. R. and Smith, W. L., *Queues*, Chapman & Hall, 1974.
9. Donaldson, W. A., Lawrie, N. L., and White, D. J., *Operational Research Techniques*, Vol. 2, Business Books, 1974.
10. Eilon, S., A simpler proof of $L = \lambda W$, *Operations Research*, **17**, 915–917, 1969.
11. Ellis, H. F., Written in a queue, *Operations Research*, **6**, 125–127, 1958.
12. Erikson, W., Management science and gas shortage, *Interfaces*, **4**, 47–51, 1974.
13. Galliher, H. P. and Wheeler, R. C., Loading congestion of aircraft, *Operations Research*, **6**, 264–275, 1958.
14. Heyman, D. P. and Sobel, M., *Stochastic Models in Operations Research*, Vol. I, McGraw-Hill, 1982.
15. Jaiswal, N. K., *Priority Queues*, New York, 1968.
16. Jewell, W. S., A simple proof of: $L = \lambda W$, *Operations Research*, **15**, 1109–1116, 1967.
17. Kallenberg, L. C. M., Linear programming and finite Markovian control problems, *Mathematical Centre Tracts*, **148**, Mathematisch Centrum, Amsterdam, 1983.
18. Kohlas, J., *Stochastic Methods of Operations Research*, Cambridge University Press, 1982.
19. Lee, A., *Applied Queueing Theory*, St. Martin's Press, 1966.
20. Lemoine, A. J., Networks of queues—a survey of equilibrium analysis, *Management science*, **24**, 464–481, 1977.
21. Little, J. D. C., A proof of the queueing formula: $L = \lambda W$, *Operations Research*, **9**, 383–387, 1961.

22. Morse, P. M., *Queues, Inventories and Maintenance*, Wiley, 1958.
23. Neuts, M. F., Matrix analytic methods in queueing theory, *European Journal of Operational Research*, **15**, 2–12, 1983.
24. Ovuwarie, G. C., Multi-channel queues: a survey and bibliography, *International Statistical Review*, **48**, 49–71, 1980.
25. Pegeden, C. D. and Rosenshine, M., Some new results for the M/M/1 queue, *Management Science*, **28**, 821–828, 1982.
26. Prabhu, N. A. and Stidham, S., Optimal control of queueing systems, in *Mathematical Methods in Queueing Theory*, A. B. Clarke (Ed.), Springer, 1974.
27. Rothstein, M., An airline overbooking model, *Transportation science*, **5**, 180–192, 1971.
28. Saaty, T. L., Resumé of useful formulas in queueing theory, *Operations Research*, **5**, 161–200, 1957.
29. Sobel, M. J., Optimal operation of queues, in *Mathematical Methods in Queueing Theory*, A. B. Clarke (Ed.), Springer, 1974.
30. Sobel, M. J., The variance of discounted Markov decision processes, *Journal of Applied Probability*, **19**, 794–802, 1982.
31. Taha, H. A., Queueing theory in practice, *Interfaces*, **11**, 43–49, 1981.
32. White, D. J., Probabilistic constraints and variance in Markov decision processes, *Notes in Decision Theory, No.* 159, Department of Decision Theory, Manchester University, 1984.
33. White, D. J., Dynamic programming and probabilistic constraints, *Operations Research*, **22**, 654–664, 1972.

Inventory

1. Aggarwal, S., Purchase inventory decision models for inflationary conditions, *Interfaces*, **11**, 18–23, 1981.
2. Bellman, R., *Dynamic Programming*, Princeton University Press, 1957.
3. Bierman, H. and Thomas, L. J., Inventory decisions under inflationary conditions, *Decision Sciences*, **8**, 151–155, 1977.
4. Buzacott, J. A., Economic order quantities with inflation, *Operational Research Quarterly*, **26**, 553–558, 1975.
5. Crowe, W., The language of lot size revisited, *Interfaces*, **9**, 138–142, 1979.
6. Donaldson, W. A., Lawrie, N. L., and White, D. J., *Operational Research Techniques*, Vol. 1, Business Books, 1969.
7. Gardner, E. S., Inventory theory and the gods of Olympus, *Interfaces*, **10**, 42–45, 1980.
8. Gaver, D. P., Operating characteristics for a simple production, inventory control model, *Operations Research*, **9**, 635–649, 1961.
9. George, J. A., Discounting a slow moving stock item, *Interfaces*, **12**, 53–56, 1982.
10. Hollier, R. H. and Vrat, P., A proposal for the classification of inventory systems, *Omega*, **16**, 227–279, 1978.
11. Karush, W., A queueing model for an inventory problem, *Operations Research*, **5**, 693–703, 1957.
12. Lockett, A. G. and Muhlemann, A. P., The use of formal inventory control models, a preliminary survey, *Omega*, **6**, 227–230, 1978.
13. Muhlemann, A. P. and Voltis-Spanopoulos, N. P., A variable holding cost rate E.O.Q. model, *European Journal of Operational Research*, **4**, 132–135, 1980.
14. Muth, E. J. and Spreman, K., A class of stationary E.B.Q. problems, *Lecture Notes in Economics and Mathematical Systems*, Vol. 157, pp. 209–221, Springer-Verlag, 1978.

15. Muth, E. J. and Spreman, K., Learning effects in economic lot sizing, *Management Science*, **29**, 264–269, 1983.
16. Naddor, E. and Saltman, S., Optimal re-order periods for an inventory system with variable costs of ordering, *Operations Research*, **6**, 676–685, 1958.
17. Nahmias, S., Perishable inventory theory: a review, *Operations Research*, **30**, 680–708, 1982.
18. Raafat, F., A review of age-independent deterioration inventory models, Department of decision Sciences, Wichita State University, 1983.
19. Schweitzer, P. J. and Silver, E. A., Mathematical pitfalls in the one machine multi-product economic lot scheduling problem, *Operations Research*, **31**, 401–405, 1983.
20. Serfozo, R. F., An inventory model for part-time television equipment, Technical Memorandum 81-59553-10, Bell Laboratories, 1981.
21. Tinarelli, G. U., Inventory control models and problems, *European Journal of Operational Research*, **14**, 1–12, 1983.
22. Vazsonyi, A., Comments on 'A queueing model for an inventory problem', *Operations Research*, **8**, 418–420, 1960.
23. Wilson, R. H., A scientific routine for stock control, *Harvard Business Review*, **13**, 194–201, 1934.
24. Yaspan, A., An inclusive solution to the inventory problem, *Operations Research*, **9**, 371–382, 1961.

Maintenance

1. Barlow, R., Hunter, L. C., and Proschan, F., *Mathematical Theory of Reliability*, Wiley, 1965.
2. Hastings, N. A. J., Equipment replacement and the repair limit method, in *Operational Research in Maintenance*, A. K. S. Jardine (Ed.), Manchester University Press, 1970.
3. Jardine, A. K. S. (Ed.), *Operational Research in Maintenance*, Machester University Press, 1970.
4. McCall, J., Maintenance policies for stochastically failing equipment: a survey, *Management Science*, **12**, 493–524, 1965.
5. Pierskalla, W. P. and Voelker, J. A., A survey of maintenance models: the control and surveillance of deteriorating systems, *Naval Research Logistics Quarterly*, **23**, 353–388, 1976.
6. Rapp, B., *Models for Optimal Investment and Maintenance Decisions*, Wiley, 1974.
7. Sherif, Y. S., Optimal maintenance models for systems subject to failure—a review, *Naval Research Logistics Quarterly*, **28**, 47–74, 1981.
8. Waddington, C. H., *O.R. in World War II*, Elek Science, 1973.
9. White, D. J., Setting maintenance inspection intervals, *Journal of Industrial Engineering*, **18**, 376–381, 1967.
10. White, D. J., *Dynamic Programming*, Oliver & Boyd, 1969.

Defective Product

1. Brigham, G., Stenöien, J. O., An analytical solution to a problem of balancing opposing loss factors, *Operations Research*, **2**, 90–92, 154.
2. Donaldson, W. A., Lawrie, N. L., and White, D. J., *Operational Research Techniques*, Vol. 1, Business Books, 1969.
3. Gollers, R. and Kleibohm, K., Theoretische Analyse und Praktische Anwending

von Modellen der Optimalen, *Ausschussvorgabe Unter Berucksichtiguing des E.D.V.-Einsatzes*, Westdeutscher, 1980.
4. Goodeve, C., Operational research as a science, *Operations Research*, **1**, 166–180, 1953.
5. Passano, R. F., *Year Book of the American Iron and Steel Institute*, No. 192, 1949.
6. Sculli, D., Stochastic cutting stock procedure, *Management Science*, **27**, 946–951, 1981.
7. Sobel, M. J., Mean variance tradeoffs for discounted Markov decision processes, Georgia Institute of Technology, 1981.
8. Spencer, J. E., Probability, defectives and mail ordering, *Journal of the Operational Research Society*, **10**, 899–906, 1981.
9. White, D. J., Dynamic programming and systems of uncertain duration, *Management Science*, **12**, 37–67, 1965.
10. White, D. J., *Dynamic Programming*, Oliver & Boyd, 1969.

Mathematical and Dynamic Programming

1. Baligh, H. H. and Laughlunn, D. J., An economic and linear model of the hospital, *Health Services Research*, 293–303, Winter, 1967.
2. Bellman, R., *Dynamic Programming*, Princeton University Press, 1957.
3. Bellmore, M. and Nemhauser, G. L., The traveling salesman problem: a survey, *Operations Research*, **16**, 525–537, 1968.
4. Benito-Alonso, M. A. and Devaux, P., Location and size of day nurseries—a multiple goal approach, *European Journal of Operational Research*, **6**, 195–198, 1981.
5. Bertelè, U. and Brioschi, F., *Non-Serial Dynamic Programming*, Academic Press, 1972.
6. Bowman, E. H., The schedule sequencing problem, *Operations Research*, **7**, 621–624, 1959.
7. Cullinan-James, C. and Gray, P., Applied optimisation—a survey, *Interfaces*, **6**, 24–41, 1976.
8. Dantzig, G. B., *Linear Programming and Extensions*, Princeton University Press, 1963.
9. Day, J. E. and Hottenstein, M. P., Review of sequencing research, *Naval Research Logistics Quarterly*, **18**, 11–39, 1971.
10. Dreyfus, S. and Law, A. M., *The Art and Theory of Dynamic Programming*, Academic Press, 1977.
11. Dreyfus, S., A note on an industrial replacement problem, *Operational Research Quarterly*, **8**, 190–193, 1957.
12. Eisemann, K., The train problem, *Mangement Science*, **3**, 279–284, 1957.
13. Ellis, C., Lethbridge, D., and Ulph, A., The application of dynamic programming in United Kingdom companies, *Omega*, **2**, 533–541, 1974.
14. Elshafei, A. N., Haley, K. B. and Lee, S. J., Facilities location: some formulations, methods of solution, applications and computational experience, O.R. Report No. 90., Department of Engineering Production, The University of Birmingham, 1974.
15. Fabozzi, F. J. and Volente, J., Mathematical programming in American companies—a sample survey, *Interfaces*, **7**, 93–99, 1976.
16. Foulkes, J. D., Prager, W., and Warner, W. H., On bus schedules, *Management Science*, **1**, 41–48, 1954.
17. Francis, R. L. and Goldstein, J. M., Location theory: a selective bibliography, *Operations Research*, **22**, 400–410, 1974.

178

18. Francis, R. L., McGinnis, L. F., and White, J. A. Locational analysis—invited review, *European Journal of Operational Research*, **14,** 220–252, 1983.
19. Freidenfolds, J., *Capacity Expansion, Analysis of Simple Methods with Applications*, Elsevier, 1981.
20. Garfinkel, R. S. and Nemhauser, G. L., *Integer Programming*, Wiley, 1972.
21. Geoffrion, A. M. (Ed.), *Perspectives on Optimization*, Addison-Wesley, 1972.
22. Geoffrion, A. M., A guided tour of recent practical advances in integer linear programming, *Omega*, **4,** 49–57, 1976.
23. Geoffrion, A. M. and Marston, R. F., Integer programming algorithms: a framework and state of the art survey, *Management Science*, **18,** 465–491, 1972.
24. Gilmore, P. C. and Gomory, R. E., A linear programming approach to the cutting stock problem, *Operations Research*, **9,** 849–859, 1961.
25. Gilmore, P. C. and Gomory, R. E., A linear programming approach to the cutting stock problem—Part II, *Operations Research*, **11,** 863–888, 1963.
26. Gleason, J. M., A set covering approach to bus stop location, *Omega*, **3,** 605–608, 1975.
27. Glover, F., Hultz, J., and Klingman, D., Improved computer based planning techniques, Part II, *Interfaces*, **9,** 12–23, 1979.
28. Golden, B. L. and Magnanti, T. L., Deterministic network optimisation: a bibliography, *Networks*, **7,** 149–183, 1977.
29. Hadley, G., *Linear Programming*, Addison-Wesley, 1973.
30. Halpern, J. (Ed.), Locational decisions, *European Journal of Operational Research*, **6,** 1981.
31. Hammer, P. L. and Rudeanu, S., *Boolean Methods in Operations Research*, Springer–Verlag, 1968.
32. Hinxman, A. J., The trim loss and assortment problems: a survey, *European Journal of Operational Research*, **5,** 8–18, 1980.
33. Howard, R. A., *Dynamic Programming and Markov Processes*, Wiley, 1960.
34. Hu, T. C., *Integer Programming and Network Flows*, Addison-Wesley, 1969.
35. Kelly, J. E., Critical path planning and scheduling: mathematical basis, *Operations Research*, **9,** 296–320, 1961.
36. Kraemer, A. S., Warehouse location and allocation problems solved by mathematical programming methods, pp. 541–549, *Operational Research 6th I.F.O.R.S. Conference*, North-Holland, 1972.
37. Karup, J. and Pruzan, P. M., Selected families of location problems, *Annals of Discrete Mathematics*, Vol. 5, *Discrete Optimisation II*, pp. 327–387, 1979.
38. Lasdon, L. S. and Woren, A. W., Survey of non-linear programming applications, *Operations Research*, **28,** 1029–1073, 1980.
39. Lea, A. C., Location–allocation systems, an annotated bibliography, Discussion Paper No. 13, Department of Geography, University of Toronto, 1973.
40. Luss, H., Operational research and capacity expansion problems—a survey, *Operations Research*, **30,** 904–947, 1982.
41. Manne, A. S., On the job shop scheduling problem, *Operations research*, **8,** 219–223, 1960.
42. Massé, P., Application des probabilités en chaine a l'hydrologie statistique et au jeu des reservoirs, *Com. à la Societé de Statistique*, **21,** 6, 1944.
43. McClure, R. H. and Miller, R. E., The applications of operations research in commercial banking companies, *Interfaces*, **9,** 24–29, 1979.
44. McDowell, I., The economic planning period for engineering works, *Operations Research*, **8,** 533–542, 1960.
45. McKeown, L. P. and Workman, B., A study in using linear programming to assign students to schools, *Interfaces*, **6,** 96–101, 1976.
46. Miller, C., Tucker, A., and Zemlin, R., Integer programming formulation and travelling salesman problems, *The Association of Computing Machinery*, **7,** 326–329, 1960.

47. Morris, W. T., On the art of modelling, *Management Science*, **13,** B707–B717, 1967.
48. Nemhauser, G. L., *Introduction to Dynamic Programming*, Wiley, 1966.
49. Norman, J. M., *Elementary Dynamic Programming*, Edward Arnold, 1975.
50. Sasieni, M. W., A Markov chain process in industrial replacement, *Operational Research Quarterly*, **7,** 148–155, 1956.
51. Schreuder, J. A. M., Application of a location model to fire stations in Rotterdam, *European Journal of Operational Research*, **6,** 212–219, 1981.
52. Shapiro, S. F., *Mathematical Programming*: Structures and Algorithms, Wiley, 1979.
53. Sobel, M. J., The variance of discounted Markov decision processes, *Journal of Applied Probability*, **19,** 794–802, 1982.
54. Steinberg, D., The fixed charge problem, *Naval Research Logistics Quarterly*, **18,** 217–235, 1971.
55. Tsarouchis, N., Mixed zero–one programming with reference to a purchasing problem, Ph.D. thesis, Manchester University, 1975.
56. Vajda, S., *Mathematical Programming*, Addison-Wesley, 1961.
57. Waddington, C. H., *O.R. in World War 2*, Elek Science, 1973.
58. Wagner, H. M., An integer programming model for machine scheduling, *Naval Research Logistics Quarterly*, **6,** 131–140, 1959.
59. Wagner, H., *Principles of Operations Research*, Prentice-Hall, 1969.
60. Weber, A., *Theory of Location of Industries*, University of Chicago Press, 1929.
61. White, D. J., *Dynamic Programming*, Oliver & Boyd, 1969.
62. White, D. J., *Finite Dynamic Programming*, Wiley, 1978.
63. White, D. J., Probabilistic constraints and variance in Markov decision processes, *Notes in Decision Theory*, *No. 159*, Department of Decision Theory, Manchester University, 1984.
64. White, D. J., Dynamic programming and probabilistic constraints, *Operations Research*, **22,** 654–664, 1972.
65. White, D. J., Multi-objective infinite-horizon discounted Markov decision processes, *Journal of Mathematical Analysis and Applications*, **89,** 639–647, 1982.
66. White, W. W., Comment on a paper by Bowman, *Operations Research*, **9,** 274–276, 1961.
67. Williams, H. P., The formulation of mathematical programming models, *Omega*, **3,** 551–555, 1975.
68. Williams, H. P., Four examples of artless modelling, *Omega*, **7,** 163–165, 1979.
69. Williams, H. P., *Model Building in Mathematical Programming*, Wiley, 1979.
70. Znagwill, W. I., *Non-Linear Programming—A Unified Approach*, Prentice-Hall, 1969.

Optimization Analogues

1. Ablow, C. M. and Brigham, G., An analogue solution of a programming problem, *Operations Research*, **3,** 388–394, 1955.
2. Coulson, C. A., *Electricity*, University Mathematical Texts, Oliver & Boyd, 1953.
3. Courant, R., Soap film experiments, *American Mathematical Monthly*, **47,** 167–174, 1940.
4. Deziel, D. P. and Eilon, S., Siting a distribution centre, an analogue computer application, *Management Science*, **21,** B245–B254, 1966.
5. Fetter, R. B. and Goodman, T. P., An equipment investment analogue, *Operations Research*, **5,** 657–669, 1957.
6. Friedman, C. J., *Alfred Weber's Theory of the Location of Industries*, University of Chicago Press, 1929.

180

7. Gass, S., *Linear Programming*, McGraw-Hill, 1958.
8. Haley, K. B., The siting of depots, *International Journal of Production Research*, **2**, 41–45, 1963.
9. Haley, K. B. and Stringer, J., The application of linear programming to a large scale transportation problem, *First International Conference on Operational Research*, North-Holland, 1957.
10. Hurter, A. and Wendell, R., Location theory, dominance and convexity, *Operations Research*, **21**, 314–320, 1973.
11. Kuhn, H. W., On a pair of dual non-linear programs, in *Non-Linear Programming*, J. Abadie (Ed.), North-Holland, 1967.
12. Miehle, W., Link-length minimisation in networks, *Operations Research*, **6**, 232–243, 1958.
13. Minty, C. J., A comment on the shortest route problem, *Operations Research*, **5**, 724, 1957.
14. Ollerenshaw, K., The magic of mathematics, *Bulletin of the Institute of Mathematics and its Applications*, **15**, 1, 2–12, 1979.
15. Rich, R. P., Simulation as an aid in model building, *Operations Research*, **3**, 15–19, 1955.
16. Schwarzschild, B. M., Statistical mechanics algorithm for Monte Carlo optimisation, *Physics Today*, **35**, 17–19, 1982.
17. Shapiro, J. F., *Mathematical Programming: Structures and Algorithms*, Wiley, 1979.
18. Sinden, F. W., Mechanisms for linear programs, *Operations Research*, **7**, 728–739, 1959.
19. White, D. J., A linear programming analogue, a duality theorem and a dynamic algorithm, *Management Science*, **21**, 47–59, 1974.
20. White, D. J., An analogue derivation of the dual of the general fermat problem, *Management Science*, **23**, 92–94, 1976.
21. Woolsey, G., Whatever happened to simple simulation? A question and answer, *Interfaces*, **9**, 9–11, 1979.

Simulation

1. Babington-Smith, B. and Kendall, M. G., Randomness and random sampling numbers, *Journal of the Royal Statistical Society*, **101**, 147–166, 1938.
2. Balintey, J., Burdick, D. S., Chu, K., and Naylor, T. H., *Computer Simulation Techniques*, Wiley, 1966.
3. Bearwood, J., Halton, J. H., and Hammersley, J. M., The shortest path through many points, *Proceedings of the Cambridge Philosophical Society*, **55**, 299, 1959.
4. Bennett, G. H., Schmidt, J. W., and White, J. A., *Analysis of Queueing Systems*, Academic Press, 1975.
5. Bobillier, P. A., Kahan, B., and Probst, A., *Simulation with GPSS and GPSSV*, Prentice-Hall, 1976.
6. Casson, J. S. and Law, A. M., Conservation equations and variance reduction in queueing simulation, *Operations Research*, **28**, 535–546, 1980.
7. Cheng, R. C. H., The use of antithetic variables in computer simulation, *Journal of the Operational Research Society*, **33**, 229–237, 1982.
8. Christofides, N., The expected length of a travelling salesman tour, Internal Report, Imperial College of Science & Technology, London, 1967.
9. Christofides, N. and Eilon, S., Expected distances in distribution problems, *Operational Research Quarterly*, **20**, 437–443, 1969.
10. Clark, C. E., The utility of statistics of random numbers, *Operations Research*, **8**, 185–195, 1960.

181

11. Coveyou, P. R., Serial correlation in the generation of pseudo random numbers, *Journal of the Association of Computing Machinery*, **7,** 72–74, 1960.
12. Conveyou, P. R. and McPherson, R. D., Fourier analysis of uniform random number generators, *Journal of The Association of Computing Machinery*, **14,** 100–119, 1967.
13. Crane, M. A. and Iglehart, D. L., Simulating stable stochastic systems, I: General multi-server queues, *Journal of the Association of Computing Machinery*, **21,** 103–113, 1974.
14. Crookes, J. G., Simulation in 1981, *European Journal of Operational Research*, **9,** 1–7, 1982.
15. Donaldson, W. A., Lawrie, N. L., and White, D. J., *Operational Research Techniques*, Vol. 2, Business Books, 1974.
16. Ehrhardt, R., *Variance Reduction Techniques for an Inventory Simulation*, University of North Carolina, 1977.
17. Emshoff, J. and Sisson, R., *Design and Use of Computer Simulation Models*, Macmillan, 1970.
18. Evans, G. W., Sutherland, G. L., and Wallace, G. F., *Simulation using Digital Computers*, Prentice-Hall, 1967.
19. Fishman, G. S., *Principles of Discrete Event Simulation*, Wiley, 1978.
20. Gnugnoli, G. and Maisel, H., *Simulation of Discrete Stochastic Systems*, Science Research Association, 1972.
21. Gordon, G., *System Simulation*, Prentice-Hall, 1969.
22. Grant, F. H. and Solberg, J., Variance reduction techniques in stochastic shortest route analysis; application procedures and results, *Journal of Mathematics and Computing in Simulation*, **25,** 366–375, 1983.
23. Greenberger, M., An a priori determination of serial correlation in computer generated random numbers, *Mathematics of Computation*, **15,** 1961.
24. Hammersley, J. M. and Morton, K. W., A new Monte Carlo technique: antithetic variables, *Proceedings of the Cambridge Philosophical Society*, **52,** 449–475, 1956.
25. Hammersley, J. M. and Moulden, J. G., General principles of antithetic variables, *Proceedings of the Cambridge Philosophical Society*, **52,** 476–481, 1956.
26. Hayya, J. C., Schail, R., and Sullivan, R. S., Efficiency of the antithetic variable method for simulating stochastic networks, *Management Science*, **5,** 563–572, 1982.
27. Heikes, R. G., Montgomery, D. C. and Rordin, R. L., Using common random numbers in simulation experiments, *Simulation*, **27,** 81–85, 1976.
28. International Business Machines, Random Number Generation and Testing, Reference Manual, C20-811, New York, 1959.
29. Kendall, M. G. and Smith, B. B., Tables of random sampling numbers, *Tracts for Computers*, No. XXIV, Pearson, S. E. (Ed.), Cambridge University Press, 1954.
30. Kleijnen, J. P. C., *Techniques in Simulation*: Part 1, Marcel Dekker, 1974.
31. Malcolm, D. G., Bibliography on the use of simulation management analysis, *Operations Research*, **8,** 169–177, 1960.
32. Mihram, G. A., Some practical aspects of the verification and validation of simulation models, *Operational Research Quarterly*, **23,** 17–29, 1972.
33. Mihram, G. A., *Simulation: Statistical Foundations and Methodology*, Academic Press, 1972.
34. Miller, J. C. P. and Prentice, M. J., Additive congruential pseudo random number generators, *Computing Journal*, **11,** 341–346, 1969.
35. Mitchell, B., Variance reduction by antithetic variables in GI/G/1 queueing simulations, *Operations Research*, **21,** 988–997, 1973.
36. Page, E. C., On Monte Carlo methods in congestion problems: simulation of queueing systems, *Operations Research*, **13,** 300–305, 1965.

37. Ramsay, T. E. and Wright, R. D., On the effectiveness of common random numbers, *Management Science*, **25,** 649–656, 1979.
38. Schmidt, J. W. and Taylor, R. E., *Simulation and Analysis of Industrial Systems*, Irwin, 1970.
39. Schriber, T., *Simulation using GPSS*, Wiley, 1974.
40. Shannon, R. E., *Systems Simulation: The Art and Science*, Prentice-Hall, 1975.
41. Tocher, K. D., Symposium on Monte Carlo methods, *Journal of the Royal Statistical Society, Series B*, **16,** 1956.
42. Tocher, K. D., *The Art of Simulation*, English Universities Press, 1963.
43. Tocher, K. D., Review of simulation languages, *Operational Research Quarterly*, **15,** 189–217, 1965.
44. Trotter, H. F. and Tukey, J. W., Conditional Monte Carlo for normal samples, in *Symposium on Monte Carlo Methods*, H. Meyer (Ed.), Wiley, 1956.
45. Wagner, H. M., *Principles of Operations Research*, Prentice-Hall, 1975.
46. Watson, J. H., *Computer Simulation in Business*, Wiley, 1981.
47. Wicks, C. T. and Yewdall, G. A., *Operational Research*, Pan Piper, 1971.
48. Zeigler, B. P., *Theory of Modelling and Simulation*, Wiley, 1976.

Heuristic Programming

1. Albano, A. and Sapuppo, G., Optimal allocation of two dimensional irregular shapes using heuristic search methods, *Institute of Electrical and Electronic Engineers, Transactions in Systems Management and Cybernetics*, **10,** 242–248, 1980.
2. Aspvall, B. and Stone, R. E., Khachiyan's linear programming algorithm, *Journal of Algorithms*, **1,** 1–13, 1980.
3. Assoch, A., Golden, B., and Wasil E., Alternative methods for comparing heuristic procedures on the basis of accuracy, Working Paper MS/S 83-012, College of Business and Management, University of Maryland, 1983.
4. Axsäter, S. and Case, W., Performance of lot size heuristics, *European Journal of Operational Research*, **9,** 339–343, 1980.
5. Axsäter, S., Economic lot sizes and vehicle scheduling, *European Journal of Operational Research*, **4,** 395–398, 1980.
6. Baker, E. K., Efficient heuristic algorithms for the weighted set covering problem, *Computers and Operations Research*, **8,** 303–310, 1981.
7. Baker, K. R., *Introduction to Sequencing and Scheduling*, Wiley, 1974.
8. Baker, K. R., A comparative study of flow shop algorithms, *Operations Research*, **23,** 62–73, 1975.
9. Balas, E. and Zemal, E., An algorithm for large zero one knapsack problems, *Operations Research*, **28,** 1130–1154, 1980.
10. Ball, M. and Magazine, M., The design and analysis of heuristics, networks, **11,** 215–219, 1981.
11. Bansal, S. P., Single machine scheduling to minimise weighted sum of completion times with secondary criterion—a branch and bound approach, *European Journal of Operational Research*, **5,** 177–181, 1980.
12. Barham, A. M. and Westwood, J. B., A simple heuristic to facilitate course timetabling, *Journal of the Operational Research Society*, **29,** 1055–1040, 1978.
13. Bellman, R., Dynamic programming treatment of the traveling salesman problem, *Journal of the Association of Computing Machinery*, **9,** 61–63, 1962.
14. Bellmore, M. and Malone, J. C., Pathology of traveling salesman subtour elimination procedures, *Operations Research*, **19,** 2, 1971.
15. Benton, W. C. and Shrikar, B., Evaluating an efficient heuristic for the multiple

vehicle scheduling problem, College of Administrative Science, Ohio State University, WPS, 82–74, 1982.

16. Beshara, S., Myopic heuristics for single machine scheduling problems, *International Journal of Production Research*, **19**, 85–95, 1981.

17. Beltrami, E. and Bodin, L., Networks and vehicle routing for municipal waste collection, *Networks*, **4**, 65–94, 1974.

18. Bishoff, W. F., Groner, R., and Groner, M., *Methods of Heuristics*, Lawrence Erlbaum, 1982.

19. Bland, R. G., Goldfarb, D., and Todd, M. J., The ellipsoid method: a survey, *Operations Research*, **29**, 1039–1091, 1981.

20. Bodin, L., Doyle, T., Golden, B., and Stewart, W., Approximate travelling salesman algorithms, *Operations Research*, **28**, 694–709, 1980.

21. Boffey, T. B. and Pursglove, C. J., Heuristic improvement methods: how should starting solutions be chosen? *Mathematical Programming Study*, **13**, 135–142, 1980.

22. Bovet, J., Simple heuristics for the school assignment problem, *Journal of the Operational Research Society*, **33**, 695–704, 1982.

23. Brosch, I. and Hersch, M., A mixed integer programming and heuristic algorithm for a warehouse location problem, *Omega*, **2**, 805–808, 1974.

24. Brown, A. R. *Optimum Packing and Depletion: The Computer in Space and Resource Usage Problems*, American Elsevier, 1971.

25. Campbell, H. G., Dudek, R. A., and Smith, M. L., A heuristic algorithm for the n job m machine sequencing problem, *Management Science*, **16**, B630–B637, 1970.

26. Christofides, N. and Eilon, S., An algorithm for the vehicle dispatching problem, *Operations Research Quarterly*, **20**, 309–318, 1969.

27. Christofides, N., Eilon, S., and Watson-Gandy, C., *Distribution Management*, Griffin, 1971.

28. Christofides, N. and Whitlock, C., An algorithm for two dimensional cutting problems, *Operations Research*, **25**, 30–44, 1977.

29. Chvatal, V., *Lecture Notes on Heuristics*, McGill University, 1978.

30. Clarke, G. and Wright, J. W., Scheduling of vehicles from a central depot to a number of delivery points, *Operations Research*, **11**, 568–581, 1963.

31. Cliffe, R. W., An approach to optimisation with heuristic methods of scheduling, *International Journal of Production Research*, **18**, 479–490, 1980.

32. Conway, R. W., Maxwell, W. L., and Miller, L. W., *Theory of Scheduling*, Addison–Wesley, 1967.

33. Cook, S. A., The complexity of theorem proving procedures, in *Proceedings of 3rd ACM Annual Symposium on the Theory of Computing*, Association of Computing Machinery, pp. 151–158, 1971.

34. Cook, W. D., Saipe, A. L., and Seiford, L. M., Production runs for multiple products: the full capacity heuristic, *Journal of the Operational Research Society*, **31**, 405–412, 1980.

35. Cooper, L., Location–allocation problems, *Operations Research*, **11**, 331–343, 1963.

36. Cooper, L., Heuristic methods for location, allocation problems, *Society for Industrial & Applied Mathematics Review*, **6**, 37–52, 1964.

37. Cornuejols, G., Fisher, M. L., and Nemhauser, G. L., Location of bank accounts to optimise float: an analytic study of exact and approximate algorithms, *Management Science*, **23**, 789–810, 1977.

38. Cornuejols, G., Fisher, M. L., and Nemhauser, G. L., An analysis of heuristics and relaxations for the uncapacitated location problem, *Management Science*, **23**, 789–810, 1977.

39. Cornuejols, G., Nemhauser, G. L., and Wolsey, L. A., Worst case and

184

probabilistic analysis of algorithms for a location problem, *Operations Research*, **28**, 847–858, 1980.
40. Côté, G. and Laughton, M. A., Large scale mixed integer programming: Benders-type heuristics, *European Journal of Operational Research*, **16**, 327–333, 1984.
41. Coverdale, I. L. and Wharton, F., An improved heuristic procedure for a nonlinear cutting stock problem, *Management Science*, **23**, 78–86, 1976.
42. Croes, G. A., A method of solving travelling salesman problems, *Operations Research*, **6**, 791–812.
43. Daellenbach, H. G. and George, J. A., *Introduction to Operational Research Techniques*, Allyn & Bacon, 1978.
44. Dannenbring, D. G., An evaluation of flow shop sequencing heuristics, *Management Science*, **23**, 1174–1182, 1977.
45. Dannenbring, D. G., The evaluation of heuristic solution procedures for large combinatorial problems, Unpublished Ph.D. dissertation, Columbia University, New York, 1973.
46. Dannenbring, D. G., An evaluation of flow shop sequencing heuristics, University of North Carolina, 1974.
47. Dannenbring, D. G., An experimental investigation and comparative evaluation of flow shop sequencing techniques, *Operations Research*, **18**, 541–548, 1970.
48. Dantzig, G., Fulkerson, R., and Johnson, S., Solution of a large scale travelling salesman problem, *Operations Research*, **2**, 393–410, 1954.
49. D'Atri, G., A note on heuristics for the travelling salesman problem, *Mathematical Programming*, **19**, 111–114, 1980.
50. Davis, E. W. and Patterson, J. H., A comparison of heuristic and optimum solutions in resource constrained project scheduling, *Management Science*, **21**, 944–955, 1975.
51. Day, J. E. and Hottenstein, M. P., Review of sequencing research, *Naval Research Logistics Quarterly*, **18**, 11–39, 1979.
52. de Gans, O. B., A computer timetabling system for secondary schools in the Netherlands, *European Journal of Operational Research*, **7**, 175–182, 1981.
53. de Kluyver, C. A. and Salkin, H. M., The knapsack problem: a survey, *Naval Research Logistics Quarterly*, **22**, 127–144, 1975.
54. Demers, A., Garey, M. R., Graham, R. L., Johnson, D. S., and Ullman, J. D., Worst case performance bounds for simple one-dimensional packing algorithms, *Society for Industrial and Applied Mathematics, Journal of Computing*, **3**, 299–325, 1974.
55. Demster, M., Fisher, M., Jansen, L., Lagweg, B., Lenstra, J., and Rinnooy Kan, A., Analysis of heuristics for stochastic programming: results of hierarchical scheduling problems, Mathematical Centrum, Amsterdam, 1983.
56. de Werra, D. and Krarup, J., Chromatic optimisation, *European Journal of Operational Research*, **11**, 1–19, 1982.
57. de Werra, D. Silver, E. A., and Vidal, R. V., A tutorial on heuristic methods, *European Journal of Operational Research*, **5**, 153–162, 1980.
58. Dunstan, F. D. J. and Welsh, D. J. A., A greedy algorithm for solving a certain class of linear programmes, *Mathematical Programming* **5**, 338–353, 1973.
59. Dyson, R. G. and Gregory, A. S., The cutting stock problem in the flat glass industry, *Operational Research Quarterly*, **25**, 41–53, 1974.
60. Edmunds, J., Matroids and the greedy algorithm, *Mathematical Programming*, **1**, 127–136, 1971.
61. Eisemann, K., The trim problem, *Management Science*, **3**, 279–284, 1957.
62. Enscore, E. J., Ham, I. and Zawaz, N., A heuristic algorithm for the m-machine n-job flow shop sequencing problem, *Omega*, **11**, 91–95, 1983.

185

63. Evans, J. R. and Zanakis, S. H., Heuristic optimisation, when and how to use it, *Interfaces*, **11**, 84–91, 1981.
64. Faaland, B. H. and Hillier, F. S., Interior path methods for heuristic integer programming procedures, *Operations Research*, **27**, 1069–1087, 1979.
65. Felts, W., Krolack, P., and Marble, G., A man-machine approach toward solving the travelling salesman problem, *CACM*, **14**, 327–334, 1971.
66. Fisher, M. L., Worst case analysis of heuristic algorithms, *Management Science*, **26**, 1–17, 1980.
67. Fisk, J. C. and Hung, M. S., A heuristic routine for solving large loading problems, *Naval Research Logistics Quarterly*, **26**, 643–650, 1979.
68. Forn, C. K., Lockett, A. G., and Muhlemann, A. P., Job scheduling heuristics and frequency scheduling, *International Journal of Production Research*, **20**, 227–241, 1982.
69. Foulds, L. R., Ghare, P. M., and Turner, W. C., Transportation routing problem—a survey, *American Institute of Electronic and Electrical Engineers, Transactions*, **6**, 288–301, 1974.
70. Foulds, L. R. and Watson-Gandy, C., The vehicle scheduling problem, a survey, *New Zealand Journal of Operational Research*, **9**, 73–92, 1981.
71. Garey, M. R., Graham, R. L., Johnson, D. S., and Yao, A. C.-C., Resource constrained scheduling as generalised bin packing, *Journal of Combinatorial Theory, Series A*, **21**, 257–298, 1976.
72. Garey, M. R. and Johnson, D. S., Approximation algorithms for combinatorial problems: an annotated bibliography, in *Algorithms and Complexity*, J. F. Traub (Ed.), Academic Press, 1976.
73. Garey, M. R. and Johnson, D. S., *Computers and Intractability: A Guide to the Theory of N.P. Completeness*, Freeman, 1979.
74. Garey, M. R. and Johnson, D. S., Performance guarantees for scheduling algorithms, *Operations Research*, **26**, 3–21, 1978.
75. Garey, M. R. and Johnson, D. S., Performance guarantees for heuristic algorithms: an annotated bibliography, Bell Laboratories, Murray Hill, New Jersey, 1975.
76. Garfinkel, R. S. and Nemhauser, G. L., *Integer Programming*, Wiley, 1972.
77. Geoffrion, A. M., Purpose of mathematical programming is insight not numbers, *Interfaces*, **7**, 81–92, 1976.
78. George, J. A. and Robinson, D. F., A heuristic for packing boxes into a container, *Computers & Operations Research*, **7**, 147–156, 1980.
79. Gere, W. S., Heuristics and job shop scheduling, *Management Science*, **13**, 167–190, 1966.
80. Giglio, R. J. and Wagner, H. M., Approximate solutions to the three machine scheduling problem, *Operations Research*, **12**, 305–324, 1964.
81. Gillett, B. E. and Miller, L. R., A heuristic algorithm for the vehicle dispatch problem, *Operations Research*, **22**, 340–349, 1974.
82. Gizelis, A. G. and Samoulidis, J. E., A simplified algorithm for the depot location problem, *Omega*, **8**, 465–472, 1980.
83. Golden, B. L. and Stewart, W. R., A Lagrangean relaxation heuristic for vehicle routing, *European Journal of Operational Research*, **15**, 84–88, 1983.
84. Golden, B., Approaches to the cutting stock problem, *American Institute for Industrial Engineering*, **8**, 265–274, 1976.
85. Granot, F., Efficient heuristic algorithms for the positive 0–1 polynomial programming problems, *Management Science*, **28**, 829–836, 1982.
86. Gupta, J. N. D., Heuristic algorithms for multi-stage flow shop scheduling problem, *American Institute of Industrial Engineers, Transactions*, **4**, 11–18, 1972.

87. Gupta, J. N. D., A functional heuristic algorithm for the flow shop scheduling problem, *Operational Research Quarterly*, **22**, 39–47, 1971.
88. Gupta, J. N. D. and Maykut, A. R., Flow shop scheduling by heuristic decomposition, *International Journal of Production Research*, **11**, 105–111, 1973.
89. Haessler, R. W., Developing an industrial grade heuristic problem solving procedure, *Interfaces*, **13**, 62–71, 1983.
90. Halpern, J. (Ed.), Locational decisions, *European Journal of Operational Research*, **6**, 94–231, 1981.
91. Hamburger, M. J. and Kuehn, A. A., A heuristic program for locating warehouses, *Management Science*, **9**, 643–666, 1963.
92. Hebel, R. and Pfohl, H. C., Bewertung heuristisher Methoden, *Zeitschrift für Operations Research*, **4**, 123–139, 1982.
93. Hill, A. and Whybark, D. C., Comparing exact solution procedures for the multiple vehicle routing problem, Working Paper No. 551, Purdue University, 1976.
94. Hillier, F. S., Heuristics: a gambler's role, *Interfaces*, **13**, 9–12, 1983.
95. Hinxman, A. I., The trim loss and assortment problems: a survey, *European Journal of Operational Research*, **5**, 8–18, 1980.
96. Hockbaum, D., Fast approximation algorithms for some integer programming problems, Graduate School of Industrial Administration, Carnegie-Mellon University, 1980.
97. Hosios, A. J. and Roussedu, J. M., A heuristic scheduling algorithm, *Journal of The Operational Research Society*, **31**, 749–753, 1981.
98. Hu, T. C. and Lenard, M. L., Optimality of a heuristic solution for a class of knapsack problems, *Operations Research*, **24**, 193–196, 1976.
99. Huckert, K., Rodhe, R., and Weber, R., On the interactive solution to a multicriteria scheduling problem, *Zeitschrift für Operations Research*, **24**, 47–60, 1980.
100. Iskander, W. and Panwalker, S. S., A survey of scheduling rules, *Operations Research*, **25**, 45–61, 1977.
101. Jacobsen, S. K., Heuristics for the capacitated plant location model, *European Journal of Operational Research*, **12**, 253–261, 1983.
102. Jacobsen, S. K. and Madsen, V. B. G., A comparative study of heuristics for a two level routing-location problem, *European Journal of Operational Research*, **5**, 378–387, 1980.
103. Johnson, D. S., Near-optimal bin packing algorithms, Doctoral thesis, Massachussetts Institute of Technology, 1973.
104. Johnson, D. S., Fast algorithms for bin packing, *Journal of Computing and Systems Science*, **8**, 272–314, 1974.
105. Johnson, D. S., Approximation algorithms for combinatorial problems, *Journal of Computing and Systems Science*, **9**, 256–278, 1974.
106. Johnson, D. S., Worst case behaviour of graph colouring algorithms, *Proceedings of the 5th S/Eastern Conference on Combinatorics, Graph Theory, and Computing*, Utilitas Mathematica, Winnipeg, 1974.
107. Karp, R. M., Reducibility among combinatorial problems, in *Complexity of Computer Computations*, R. E. Miller and J. W. Thatcher (Eds.), Plenum Press, 1972.
108. Karp, R. M., Probabilistic analysis of partitioning algorithms for the traveling salesman problem in the plane, *Mathematics of Operations Research*, **2**, 209–224, 1977.
109. Karp, R. M., On the computational complexity of combinatorial problems, *Networks*, **5**, 45–68, 1975.
110. Karp, R. M., McKellar, A. C., and Wong, C. K., Near-optimal solutions to a

2-dimensional placement problem, *Society of Industrial and Applied Mathematics, Journal of Computing,* **4,** 271–286, 1975.

111. King, J. R. and Spachis, A., Heuristics for flow shop scheduling, *International Journal of Production Research,* **18,** 345–357, 1980.
112. Kovaćs, B., *Combinational Methods of Discrete Programming,* Vol. 2 *Mathematical Methods of Operations Research,* Akademiai Kiado, Budapest, 1980.
113. Krone, M. J. and Steiglitz, K., Heuristic programming solution of a flow shop scheduling problem, *Operations Research,* **22,** 629–638, 1974.
114. Kruskal, J. B., On the shortest spanning subtree of a graph and the traveling salesman problem, *Proceedings of the American Mathematical Society,* **7,** 48–50, 1956.
115. Lewis, P. M., Rosenkrantz, D., and Stearns, R., Approximate algorithms for the travelling salesperson problem, *Proceedings of 15th Annual I.E.E.E. Symposium on Switching & Automation Theory,* pp. 33–42, 1974.
116. Lewis, P. M., Rosenkrantz, D. J., and Stearns, R. E., An analysis of several heuristics for the traveling salesman problem, *Society for Industrial and Applied Mathematics, Journal of Computing,* **6,** 563–581, 1977.
117. Little, J. D. C., Murty, V. G., Sweeney, D. W., and Karel, C., An algorithm for the traveling salesman problem, *Operations Research,* **11,** 972–989, 1963.
118. Loulo, R. and Michaelides, E., New greedy-like heuristics for the multidimensional 0–1 knapsack problem, Working Paper, McGill University, 1977.
119. Loulou, R. and Machaelides, E., New greedy-like heuristics for the multi-dimensional knapsack problem, *Operations research,* **27,** 1101–1114, 1979.
120. Magazine, M. J. and Oguz, O., A heuristic algorithm for the multidimensional zero–one knapsack problem, *European Journal of Operational Research,* **16,** 319–326, 1984.
121. McMillan, C., *Mathematical Programming,* Wiley, 1975.
122. Michael, G. C., A review of heuristic programming, *Decision Sciences,* **3,** 74–100, 1972.
123. Müller-Merbach, H., Heuristics and their design: a survey, *European Journal of Operational Research,* **8,** 1–23, 1981.
124. Nahmias, S. and Schmidt, C. P., Heuristic methods for space allocation in retail environment, Department of Decision and Information Sciences, University of Santa Clara, 1983.
125. Newson, E. F. P., Multi-item lot scheduling by heuristic, *Management Science,* **21,** 1186–1193, 1975.
126. Newell, A., Heuristic programming—ill structured problems, in *Progress in Operations Research,* Vol. III, J. S. Aronofsky (Ed.), Wiley, 1969.
127. Newell, A. and Simon, H. A., Heuristic problem solving: the next advance in operations research, *Operations Research,* **6,** 1–10, 1958.
128. Nicholson, T., *Optimisation in Industry,* Vol. I, *Optimisation Techniques,* Longman Press, 1971.
129. Norman, J. M., *Heuristic Procedures in Dynamic Programming,* Manchester University Press, 1972.
130. Oneil, B. F. and Whybark, D. C., The multiple-vehicle routing problem, *The Logistics and Transportation Review,* 1976.
131. Palmer, D. S., Sequencing jobs through a multi-stage process in the minimum total time—a quick method of obtaining a near optimum, *Operational Research Quarterly,* **16,** 101–107, 1965.
132. Papoulis, D. B., Heuristics: some theoretical issues, Operational Research Society Conference, 1981.
133. Pearl, J., *Heuristics,* Addison-Wesley, 1984.

134. Potts, C., Analysis of a heuristic for one machine sequencing with release dates and delivery times, *Operations Research*, **28**, 1436–1441, 1980.
135. Rayward-Smith V. J. and Shing, N. T., Bin packing, *Bulletin of the Institute of Mathematics and its applications*, **19**, 142–148, 1983.
136. Reitman, W. R., Heuristic decision procedures, open constraints, and the structure of ill-defined problems, in *Human Judgements and Optimality*, M. Shelley and G. Bryan (Eds.), Wiley, 1964.
137. Rijckaert, M. J. and Van der Cruyssen, P., Heuristic for asymmetric travelling salesman problem, *Journal of the Operational Research Society*, **29**, 697–701, 1978.
138. Roberts, S. A., Application of heuristic techniques to the cutting stock problem for worktops, *Journal of the Operational Research Society*, **35**, 369–378, 1984.
139. Sahni, S., Approximate algorithms for the 0–1 knapsack problem, *Journal of the Association of Computing Machinery*, **22**, 115–124, 1975.
140. Schultz, H. K., A practical method for vehicle scheduling, *Interfaces*, **9**, 13–19, 1979.
141. Schweitzer, P. J. and Silver, E. A., Mathematical pitfalls in the one machine multiproduct economic lot scheduling problem, *Operations Research*, **31**, 401, 1983.
142. Scott, J. L., A heuristic algorithm for examination timetabling, *New Zealand Journal of Operational Research*, **8**, 103–108, 1980.
143. Shapiro, D., Algorithms for the solution of the optimal cost traveling salesman problem, Sub. thesis, Washington University, 1966.
144. Sisson, R. L., Sequencing in job shops, *Operations Research*, 10–29, 1959.
145. Skalbeck, B. A. and Schultz, H. K., Reducing trim waste in panel cutting using integer and linear programming, Proceedings of Western AIDS Conference, American Institute of Decision Sciences, March, 1976.
146. Smith, A. W. and Stinson, J. P., A heuristic programming procedure for sequencing the static flow shop, *International Journal of Production Research*, **20**, 753–764, 1982.
147. Spielberg, K., Algorithms for simple plant-location problem with some side conditions, *Operations Research*, **17**, 85–111, 1969.
148. Streim, H., Heuristische Lösungsverfahren—Versuch Einer Begriffsklarung, *Zeitschrifte für Operations Research*, **19**, 143–162, 1975.
149. Wang, P. Y., Computational techniques for two-dimensional rectangular cutting stock problems, Ph.D. dissertation, University of Wisconsin/Milwaukee, August, 1980.
150. Wang, P. Y., Two algorithms for constrained two-dimensional cutting stock problems, Mathematical Research Report No. 81–3, University of Maryland, Catonsville, 1981.
151. Wang, P. Y., Two algorithms for constrained two-dimensional cutting stock problems, *Operations Research*, **31**, 573–586, 1983.
152. Watson-Gandy, C., Heuristic procedures for the M-partial cover problem on a plane, *European Journal of Operational Research*, **11**, 149–157, 1982.
153. Weiss, H. J., A greedy heuristic for single machine-sequencing with precedence constraints, *Management Science*, **27**, 1209–1216, 1981.
154. White, D. J., Problems involving infrequent but significant contingencies, *Operational Research Quarterly*, **20**, 45–57, 1969.
155. White, D. J., *Decision Methodology*, Wiley, 1975.
156. Williams, J. F., Heuristic techniques for simultaneous scheduling of production and distribution in multi-echelon structures: theory and empirical comparison, *Management Science*, **27**, 336–352, 1981.
157. Wolsey, L., Heuristic analysis, linear programming, and branch and bound, *Mathematical Programming Study*, **13**, 121–134, 1980.

Further Heuristic Programming References

Avis, D., A survey of heuristics for the weighted matching problem, *Networks*, **13**, 4, 475–493, 1983.

Baker, B. S. and Schwarz, J. S., Shelf algorithms for two-dimensional packing problems, *Society of Industrial and Applied Mathematics, Journal of Computing*, **12**, 508–525, 1983.

Barcelo, J. and Casanovas, J., A heuristic Lagrangean algorithm for the capacitated plant location problem, *European Journal of Operational Research*, **15**, 2, 212–226, 1984.

Bartholdi, J. J. and Platzman, L. K., A fast heuristic based on spacefilling curves for minimum-weight matching in the plane, *Information Processing Letters*, **17**, 4, 177–180, 1983.

Bazaraa, M. S. and Kirca, O., A branch and bound based heuristic for solving the quadratic assignment problem, *Naval Research Logistics Quarterly*, **30**, 2, 287–304, 1983.

Bruijs, P. A., On the quality of the heuristic solutions to a 19×19 quadratic assignment problem, *European Journal of Operational Research*, **17**, 21–30, 1984.

Coffman, E. C. and Garey, M. R., Dynamic bin packing, *Society of Industrial and Applied Mathematics, Journal of Computing*, **12**, 2, 227–258, 1983.

Czap, H., A heuristic for lot sizing and scheduling, *Methods of Operational Research (Germany)*, **43**, 181–192, 1981.

Daskin, M. S., A maximum expected covering location model: formulation, properties, and heuristic solution, *Transportation Science*, **17**, 1, 48–70, 1983.

Frieze, A. M. and Clarke, M. R. B., Approximation algorithms for the m-dimensional 0–1 knapsack problem: worst case and probabilistic analysis, *European Journal of Operational Research*, **15**, 1, 100–109, 1984.

Kamei, K., Araki, Y., and Inove, K., A heuristic method for searching for global maximum of multimodel unknown functions, *Transactions of the Society of Instrument and Control Engineers (Japan)*, **6**, 466–471, 1983.

Karni, R. and Roll, Y., A heuristic algorithm for the multi-item lot sizing problem with capacity constraints, *Institute of Industrial Engineers Transactions (U.S.)*, **14**, 4, 249–256, 1982.

Marcotorchino, F. and Michand, P., Heuristic approach of the similarity aggregation problem, *Methods of Operational Research (Germany)*, **43**, 395–404, 1981.

Masuda, T., Ishii, H., and Nishida, T., Some bounds on approximation algorithms for $n/m/I/L_{max}$ and $n/2/F/L_{max}$ scheduling problems, *Journal of the Operational Research Society of Japan*, **26**, 3, 212–224, 1983.

Mazzola, J. B. and Neebe, A. W., A heuristic procedure for allocating tasks in fault-tolerant distributed computer systems, *Naval Research Logistics Quarterly*, **30**, 3, 493–504, 1983.

Müller-Merbach, H., A five facets frame for the design of heuristics, *European Journal of Operational Research*, **17**, 313–316, 1984.

Papoulias, D. B. and Stainton, R. S., Heuristics—the relational approach, *European Journal of Operational Research*, **17**, 16–20, 1984.

Psaraftis, H. N., Analysis of an $0(N^2)$ heuristic for the single vehicle many-to-many Euclidian dial-a-ride problem, *Transportation Research, B*, **17B**, 2, 133–145, 1983.

Roeck, H. and Schmidt, G., Machine aggregation heuristics in shop scheduling, *Methods of Operational Research (Germany)*, **45**, 301–314, 1983.

Stainton, R. S., A five facets frame for the design of heuristics—a rejoinder, *European Journal of Operational Research*, **17**, 317–319, 1984.

Stewart, W. R. and Golden, B. L., A Lagrangean relaxation heuristic for vehicle routing, *European Journal of Operational Research*, **15**, 1, 84–88, 1984.

190

Tsilgirides, T., Heuristic methods applied to orienteering, *Journal of the Operational Research Society*, **35**, 797–809, 1984.

West, D. H., Algorithm 608: approximate solution of the quadratic assignment problem, *Transactions on Mathematical Software*, **9**, 4, 461–466, 1983.

Las Vegas

1. Ackoff, R., Gupta, S. K., and Minas, J. S., *Scientific Method: Optimizing Applied Research Decisions*, Wiley, 1962.
2. Aoki, M., Adaptive control theory: survey and potential applications to decision processes, *Decision Sciences*, **10**, 666–687, 1979.
3. Brooks, S. H., A discussion of random methods of seeking maxima, *Operations Research*, **6**, 244–251, 1958.
4. Brooks, S. H., Comparison of methods for estimating the optimal factor combination, Sc. D. thesis, The Johns Hopkins University, 1955.
5. Kushner, H., *Introduction to Stochastic Control*, Holt, Rinehart & Winston, 1971.
6. McQueen, J. and Miller, R. G., Optimal persistance policies, *Operations Research*, **8**, 362–380, 1960.
7. Radner, R., Mathematical specification of goals for decision problems, in *Human Judgments and Optimality*, M. W. Shelley and G. L. Bryan (Eds.), Wiley, 1964.
8. Robbins, H. E., Optimal stopping, *American Mathematical Monthly*, **77**, 333–343, 1970.
9. Törn, A. A., A sample-search–clustering approach for exploring the feasible/efficient solutions of MCDM problems, *Computers and Operations Research*, **7**, 67–79, 1980.
10. White, D. J., *Decision Methodology*, Wiley, 1975.

A Qualitative Comparison of the Techniques

1. Howrey, P. and Kelejian, H. H., Simulation vs. analytic solutions, in *Design of Computer Simulation Experiments*, T. H. Naylor (Ed.), Duke University Press, 1969.
2. Norman, J. M. and White, D. J., A method for approximate solutions to stochastic dynamic programming problems using expectations, *Operations Research*, **16**, 296–306, 1968.
3. Siegel, S. and Torelli, P., The value of queueing theory: a case study, *Interfaces*, **9**, 148–151, 1979.
4. Taha, H. A., Queueing theory in practice, *Interfaces*, **11**, 43–49, 1981.
5. Vazsonyi, A., To queue or not to queue: a rejoinder, *Interfaces*, **9**, 83–86, 1979.
6. Wallace, V., Faithfulness vs. insight: the economics of computer stochastic models, Paper given to the British Ship Research Association, Wallsend, 1970.
7. White, D. J., Approximating Markov decision processes using expected state transitions, Notes in Decision Theory, No. 101, Department of Decision Theory, University of Manchester, 1981.
8. White, D. J., *Decision Methodology*, Wiley, 1975.
9. White, D. J., Dynamic programming and systems of uncertain duration, *Management Science*, **12**, 37–67, 1965.

CHAPTER 3

Sensitivity, Parametric, and Post-Optimality Analysis

3.1 INTRODUCTION

In each of the models discussed in the earlier chapters it has been assumed that the parameters have been determined. In general they will be determined by some statistical analysis, but estimators will be subject to some degree of error with respect to their true value. It is therefore important to study to what extent the solution, and its effect on eventual performance, depends on the degree of error involved. If the effect is minimal, then the estimate and its solution may be quite acceptable. If the effect is not minimal then this may suggest the need to try to determine a better estimate of the true parameter value.

The general problem tackled in this chapter is parametric post-optimality analysis, in which the problem is to determine the extent to which solutions (in terms of actual decisions and objective function levels) depend upon the parameters of the problem. Ideally one would wish to do this in terms of the whole parametric range and we do look briefly at this. More often, however, we have an estimate of the parameters, then solve the problem for these estimates, and then wish to see how far we can move from these estimates with either no loss or an acceptable loss in using the initial decisions determined. When the parametric variations are small we use the term 'sensitivity analysis to describe this situation in this text. Otherwise general parametric analysis is required.

To begin with, let us look at the simple economic order quantity inventory problem discussed in the previous chapter, where $\{c, a, s, h\}$ are the usual parameters.

The minimal annual variable cost is $f = \sqrt{(2ash)}$ and the optimal order size is $x = \sqrt{(2as/h)}$.

Now suppose that: s is known for definite $= s^0$
h is known for definite $= h^0$
a is uncertain, with an estimate $\hat{a}$ of the true value a^0.

Then the annual variable cost using $\hat{x}$ (i.e. the optimal x given $(\hat{a}, s^0, h^0)$) is:

$$\hat{f}^0 = \tfrac{1}{2}h^0\hat{x} + a^0 s^0/\hat{x}$$
$$= \sqrt{(a^0 s^0 h^0/2)}(\sqrt{(\hat{a}/a_0)} + \sqrt{(a^0/\hat{a})}).$$

Let $\rho = \hat{a}/a^0$. Then:

$$\hat{f}^0 = (f^0/2)(\sqrt{\rho} + 1/\sqrt{\rho}).$$

Then the proportional loss of optimality using $\hat{a}$ when a^0 is true is:

$$\Delta = (f^0(\hat{x}) - f^0(x^0))/f^0 = (\sqrt{\rho} + 1/\sqrt{\rho} - 2)/2.$$

Let $\rho = 1 + \varepsilon$, $\sqrt{\rho} \cong 1 + \frac{1}{2}\varepsilon - \frac{1}{8}\varepsilon^2$, $1/\sqrt{\rho} \cong 1 - \frac{1}{2}\varepsilon + \frac{3}{8}\varepsilon^2$, ε small. Then:

$$\Delta \cong (\tfrac{1}{8})\varepsilon^2.$$

Hence small errors in estimation result in very small losses in optimality.

Although we have used proportional losses, it may be the absolute losses which are really important, but the ε^2 loss still holds.

3.2 GENERAL POST-OPTIMALITY SENSITIVITY ANALYSIS

Let us suppose that we have a feasible set of actions, X, and a value (or utility) function, $v(x, \alpha)$, where α is an unknown parameter in a set $\boldsymbol{\alpha}$, and $v(x, \alpha)$ is to be maximized. Let x be continuously variable in X.

For this section we will assume, for simplicity, that $X \subseteq \mathbb{R}^1$, i.e. X is single-dimensional, although the basic ideas are applicable in a more general sense.

Also we will formally introduce the notion of a value function in section 3.9 later on, and again in Chapters 4 and 6. The reader may, for simplicity, wish to assume that $v(x)$ relates to a single objective function $f(x)$ which we will have occasion to use.

For a given α, let $x(\alpha)$ be the optimal $x \in X$, and let us assume $x(\alpha)$ is unique for each $\alpha \in \boldsymbol{\alpha}$ (this is not necessary, but it complicates the arguments a little to allow for non-uniqueness).

Let us suppose that there is a true α (e.g. a true cost parameter), which might be found by further research, but, if the research is costly in relationship to the economies involved in the problem being solved, we wish to ascertain just how important it is to determine the true parameter. Let the true parameter value be α^0.

The optimal value of $v(x, \alpha^0)$ is then attained at $x^0 = x(\alpha^0)$, and given by:

$$v^0 = v(x(\alpha^0), \alpha^0).$$

Now let $\hat{\alpha}$ be an estimated value of α. If we use $\hat{\alpha}$ to determine x, we get $\hat{x} = x(\hat{\alpha})$ and the actual cost will be:

$$\hat{v}^0 = v(x(\hat{\alpha}), \alpha^0).$$

Note that this is the cost of using $x(\hat{\alpha})$ when α^0 is the true α.

The loss in optimality is then $v^0 - \hat{v}^0 = \Delta$, i.e.

$$\Delta = v(x(\alpha^0), \alpha^0) - v(x(\hat{\alpha}), \alpha^0).$$

In order to determine whether or not $\hat{\alpha}$ is a good enough estimate, for our purposes, we should see how Δ varies, when $\hat{\alpha}$ is the estimate, and α^0 is allowed to vary over $\boldsymbol{\alpha}$.

Now, in many circumstances, we may be confident that $|\hat{\alpha} - \alpha^0|$ is small as α^0 ranges over $\boldsymbol{\alpha}$. Let us now look at Δ when this is the case. We will assume that:

(i) $x(\alpha)$, and $v(x, \alpha)$ have derivatives of all required orders, and $v(x, \alpha)$ is locally concave at $x = x(\alpha^0)$;

(ii) for each $\alpha \in \boldsymbol{\alpha}$, the optimal $x(\alpha)$ is interior to X and is given by

$$\frac{\partial v(x, \alpha)}{\partial x} = 0.$$

For some problems (e.g. linear programming problems) where the optimal x is on the boundary, this is not true and a separate analysis of Δ is needed.

Expanding Δ about $x = x(\alpha^0)$ using $-\Delta$ instead of Δ, we obtain, to a second order approximation:

$$-\Delta = (x(\hat{\alpha}) - x(\alpha^0)) \frac{\partial v}{\partial x}(x, \alpha^0) + \tfrac{1}{2}(x(\hat{\alpha}) - x(\alpha^0))^2 \frac{\partial^2 v(x, \alpha^0)}{\partial^2 x}$$

i.e.

$$\Delta = -(x(\hat{\alpha}) - x(\alpha^0)) \frac{\partial v(x, \alpha^0)}{\partial x} - \tfrac{1}{2}(x(\hat{\alpha}) - x(\alpha^0))^2 \frac{\partial^2 v(x, \alpha^0)}{\partial^2 x}$$

where the partial derivatives are all evaluated at $x = x(\alpha^0)$.

Now we have $(\partial v/\partial x)(x, \alpha^0) = 0$ at $x = x(\alpha^0)$. Hence Δ becomes:

$$\Delta = -\tfrac{1}{2}(x(\hat{\alpha}) - x(\alpha^0))^2 \frac{\partial^2 v(x, \alpha^0)}{\partial^2 x}.$$

Now let us expand $x(\hat{\alpha}) - x(\alpha^0)$. We need only do this to first order terms since when we square it we get second order terms. Then:

$$x(\hat{\alpha}) - x(\alpha^0) \cong (\hat{\alpha} - \alpha^0) \frac{dx(\alpha)}{d\alpha}$$

where $dx(\alpha)/d\alpha$ is evaluated at $\alpha = \alpha^0$.

Combining these we obtain:

$$\Delta = -\tfrac{1}{2}(\alpha - \alpha^0)^2 \frac{\partial^2 v(x, \alpha^0)}{\partial^2 x} \left(\frac{dx(\alpha)}{d\alpha}\right)^2$$

where the derivatives are evaluated at $x = x(\alpha^0)$, $\alpha = \alpha^0$. Note that, for our problem, $\partial^2 v(x, \alpha^0)/\partial^2 x$ is non-positive.

We thus see that the error in optimality is of second order in the error of estimation of α, if the error of estimation in α is first order. Of course it all depends on the size of the deviations, but the general qualitative results still holds.

It is to be noted that:

(i) the error in $x(\alpha)$ is not the only important factor, i.e. it is the effective change in v not in x which is really required;

(ii) the effective change in v is given by Δ and not, for example, by $v(x(\alpha^0), \alpha^0) - v(x(\hat{\alpha}), \hat{\alpha})$, this latter term being meaningless. It may be seen that, to first order terms, if $\tilde{\Delta}$ is the difference,

$$-\tilde{\Delta} = -(v(x(\alpha^0), \alpha^0) - v(x(\hat{\alpha}), \hat{\alpha}))$$

$$= (x(\hat{\alpha}) - x(\alpha^0)) \frac{\partial v(x, \alpha)}{\partial x} + (\hat{\alpha} - \alpha^0) \frac{v(x, \alpha)}{\partial \alpha}$$

where the partial derivatives are evaluated at $x = x(\alpha^0)$, $\alpha = \alpha^0$.

Now $\partial v(x, \alpha)/\partial x = 0$, at $x = x(\alpha^0)$, $\alpha = \alpha^0$, and we are left with the term:

$$\tilde{\Delta} = (\alpha^0 - \hat{\alpha}) \frac{\partial v(x, \alpha)}{\partial \alpha}$$

where the partial derivative is evaluated at $x = x(\alpha^0)$, $\alpha = \alpha^0$.

Thus the term in $\tilde{\Delta}$ is first order in $(\alpha^0 - \hat{\alpha})$. This latter form is valid for constraint sensitivity analysis discussed later on.

An interesting sensitivity study is given in Fowler *et al.* [7] concerning the number of vehicles, x, needed for a university motor pool. The annual cost $f(x)$ takes a similar form to that for the economic order quantity problem, viz. (with $v(x, \alpha) = f(x)$):

$$f(x) = a/x + hx + k$$

where a, h, k are parameters which have to be estimated from past data. A sensitivity analysis validated the results of the general analysis of this section, and, indeed, quite large variations in parametric values produced relatively small losses of optimality.

The general mathematical programming problem takes the form:

$$\text{maximize } [v(x, \alpha)]$$

$$\text{subject to}$$

$$g_i(x, \beta) \leq \gamma_i, \qquad i = 1, 2, \ldots, l,$$

where α, β, γ are given parameters of the problem.

The reader should note that the notation reflecting the use of a utility, or value, function and the three sorts of parametric contribution, is different to that used in Chapters 2 and 4, where $v(x, \alpha)$, $\{g_i(x, \beta)\}$, $\{\gamma_i\}$ take the usual form $f(x)$, $\{g_i(x)\}$, $\{b_i\}$ respectively.

We have examined the effect of errors in the estimation of α on the loss of optimality, in the context of possible true values of $\alpha = \alpha^0$. It is not meaningful to do the same, in this context, for the constraint parameters β, $\{\gamma_i\}$, since, as it stands, the constraints have to be satisfied. However, it is possible that an actual violation of the constraints might take place when any decision is implemented because β, $\{\gamma_i\}$ may be in error, e.g. underestimation of product process times, etc. However, in order to study this it is

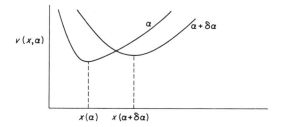

Figure 3.1

important to find some measure of the effects of violation of actual constraints, and these should then become part of the objective (or value) function $v(x, \alpha)$. Thus, for example, $v(x, \alpha)$ might be replaced by:

$$v^1(x, \alpha) = v(x, \alpha) - \sum_{i=1}^{l} \lambda_i \max[g_i(x, \beta) - \gamma_i, 0]$$

where λ_i is some penalty factor, and $\alpha = (\beta, \{\gamma_i\})$.

The analysis may then be carried out as previously given, but considering errors in β, $\{\gamma_i\}$ only from the point of view of $v^1(x, \alpha)$, and viewing $x(\alpha)$, only, as a function of α. This situation is not, of course, the same as the one in which we are free to set the constraint levels, and wish to examine the effect of deliberately departing from these, a situation we will look at later on.

In this section we have assumed that the optimal $x(\alpha)$ is interior to the admissible X set. For example, for the inventory problem, we have $X = \{x : 0 \leqslant x < \infty\}$ and Figure 3.1 shows $x(\alpha)$ to be interior to X, so that we may freely vary x in the locality of $x(\alpha)$ without violating constraints.

Not all situations are like this, and, in mathematical programming, $x(\alpha)$ is typically on the boundary (e.g. in linear programming). In such cases we may not get $(\partial v/\partial x)(x, \alpha) = 0$ at an optimal solution, nor $dx(\alpha)/d\alpha$ exist, nor indeed $x(\alpha)$ continuous, as Figure 3.2 shows. Thus if

$$v(x, \alpha) = \alpha_1 x_1 + \alpha_2 x_2$$
$$v(x, \alpha + \delta\alpha) = (\alpha_1 + \delta\alpha_1)x_1 + (\alpha_2 + \delta\alpha_2)x_2$$

we see that small variations in $\delta\alpha$ can cause large variations in $x(\alpha)$.

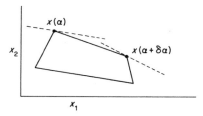

Figure 3.2

196

If it so happens that $x(\alpha^0 + \delta\alpha) = x(\alpha^0)$, then

$$\Delta = v(x(\alpha^0), \alpha^0) - v(x(\alpha^0), \alpha^0) = 0$$

but this is rarely the case, applying essentially for linear constraints.

A study of such sensitivity analysis may be found in Wagner [19], Dantzig [4], Shapiro [17], Saaty [13], Webb [20], Saaty *et al.* [14], and Gal [8].

3.3 VARIATION OF OPTIMAL DECISION IN RESPONSE TO VARIATION IN PARAMETERS

We have already said that, in actual fact, it is the loss of optimality which should be considered when looking at errors in estimating the parameters. In some cases, however, the optimal decision may remain fixed within the range of variation of parameters which is considered admissible.

Thus, if the unknown parameter is a constraint level, it may be that the constraint is not violated by optimal solutions providing small variations of constraint are allowed. When we get to problem formulation we will study constraint analysis in detail.

We will look at a problem where an upper limit γ will be placed on the amount of cash tied up in stock for the simple inventory problem involving a number of items (see Chapter 2, Inventory Exercise 2, and also Chapter 4). We obtain Figure 3.3. In this case the unconstrained solution is optimal for all acceptable variations in γ. Note that γ need not denote a cash limit, it might denote some unknown physical constraint for next year.

When the action space is discrete, e.g. $x = 0$ or 1, then there will usually be a range of variation of parameters for which, for example, $x = 0$ stays optimal (see Exercise 5 on a queueing problem where we have two possible service rates).

In linear programming problems, if, for example, the objective function coefficients do not vary too much, the same solution may remain optimal (see Figure 3.4 and section 4.5). In this problem A will remain optimal for a range of objective function slopes.

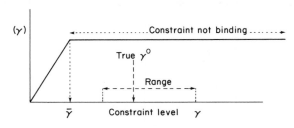

Figure 3.3

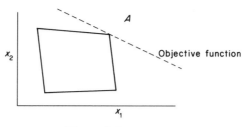

Figure 3.4

There are other cases where, although the optimal decision may not remain fixed for reasonable variations in parameter, nonetheless the variation in the optimal decision may be quite limited, and this may be useful, i.e. larger variations in parameters may have limited variations in optimal decisions. Let us look at the capacity installation problem discussed in section 2.5.

Let us consider the backward formulation as illustrated by Figure 2.39. The calculations for a simple example are given in Table 2.9.

Now, for many problems of this kind, the time horizon will not be known with any degree of certainty. The only decision which has to be taken now is the first one. Adjustments to the rest of the programme may be made later on, in the light of further consideration of the residual time horizon. It is important to know how dependent the first decision is on the time horizon. We may make use of the optimal decision rule, for the initial time horizon, to examine the question. We will assume, for simplicity, that the true time horizon is $K \leqslant 7$.

Figure 3.5 illustrates the procedure, drawn on a continuous time basis to simplify presentation: Beginning with K, we find the previous installation time $\theta(K)$. We then find the previous installation time for $\theta(K)$, i.e. $\theta(\theta(K)) = \theta^2(K)$ and so on until we get down to time 0. This may be obtained from the above figure by reflection in the line $\theta = K$ at each stage.

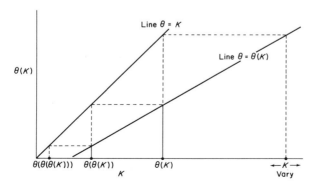

Figure 3.5

For the example given we have Table 3.1.

Table 3.1

K	7	6	5	4	3	2	1
$\theta(K)$	6	4	4	2	2	0	0
$\theta^2(K)$	4	2	2	0	0	0	0
$\theta^3(K)$	2	0	0	—	—	—	—
$\theta^4(K)$	0	—	—	—	—	—	—

In all cases the first installation covers the first two periods irrespective of K if $K \geqslant 2$.

This formulation contains redundant calculations if K is known in advance, since we have to calculate solutions for situations which do not actually arise, i.e. if $K = 7$ is the actual time horizon, we also calculate solutions for $K = 5, 3, 1$ which do not appear in the actual solution to $K = 7$. It is possible to tackle this via mathematical programming (see Exercise 13 of the Mathematical and Dynamic Programming Exercises) but this approach is not as useful for this particular question.

3.4 OPTIMALITY ANALYSIS WITH RESPECT TO CONSTRAINTS AS DIRECTLY CONTROLLABLE PARAMETERS

In some cases we may not be unsure of parameters but the parameters themselves may be subject to decision. Thus, as we shall see in a more general context, in Chapter 4 on Problem Formulation, we should, for soft constraints, study the loss of optimality involved by setting constraints at various levels different from the preset ones, so that, if γ^0 is the preset constraint level, and $\alpha = \alpha^0$ is known for definite, one should evaluate:

$$\tilde{\Delta} = \max_{x \in X(\gamma)} [v(x, \alpha^0)] - \max_{x \in X(\gamma_0)} [v(x, \alpha^0)]$$

where $X(\gamma)$ is the feasible set of actions given γ.

A considerable amount of work has been done on this sort of analysis. The references [4], [8], [13], [14], [19], [20], are useful, largely for linear problems. For more general problems, the duality theory of, for example, Geoffrion [9], is very useful, since the optimal dual variables when unique, give the rates of change of the maximal value of $v(x, \alpha^0)$ with respect to changes in $\{\gamma_i\}$, and give ready-made sensitivity analyses.

It is also worth pointing out that some dynamic programming analyses give important parametric analysis information. Thus Exercise 17 on redundancy, in the Mathematical and Dynamic Programming Exercises, shows how $f_n(y_n)$ varies with y_n.

Consider the following simple illustration which is also considered in Chapter 4 using Lagrange multipliers (in Chapter 4 we take logs but will not do so here):

$$\text{maximize}[f(x) = (1 - 0.2^{x_1})(1 - 0.5^{x_2})]$$

subject to

$$3x_1 + x_2 \leq b$$

x_1, x_2 non-negative integers.

Define $f_n(y_n)$ to be the maximal value of the reliability for the last n components with resource y_n available. Then we have the following:

$$f_2(y_2) = \max[(1 - 0.5^{x_2})f_1(y_2 - x_2)]$$
$$0 \leq x_2 \leq y_2$$
$$x_2 \text{ integer}$$
$$f_1(y_1) = \max[1 - 0.2^{x_1}]$$
$$0 \leq x_1 \leq y_1/3$$
$$x_1 \text{ integer}$$
$$= 1 - 0.2^{\lceil y_1/3 \rceil}$$

where $\lceil \; \rceil$ means integer part.

Using these equations, if b^0 is the initial value of b, we may find $f_2(b)$ in a region of b^0, and thus obtain a sensitivity analysis with respect to the resource level b. Bellman et al. [2] discuss the use of dynamic programming for sensitivity analysis.

3.5 OPTIMALITY ANALYSIS WHEN PARAMETERS CAN BE INDIRECTLY INFLUENCED

Let us consider the simple inventory problem and let the parameters $\{c, a, s, h\}$ be known for definite, but where, if it is thought worthwhile, the cost parameters $\{a, h\}$ can be varied by taking particular actions, for example by changing the ordering procedure, we might make a different. Let us suppose a is some function of some decision, x, viz. $a = a(x)$. Then the optimal variable cost is:

$$f(x) = (\sqrt{2sh})\sqrt{(a(x))}.$$

We can then see how $f(x)$ varies with the available decision x, to see what savings may be made, and to see if the extra costs, if any, involved in changing the ordering procedure, are worthwhile.

If we can associate a cost with decision x, in order to change a, then we can convert the problem into an overall optimization problem as follows.

Suppose x is the rate at which invoices can be processed, and suppose we pay a bonus, bx, to those doing the invoicing (or setting up, if it is a production problem). Then the problem becomes one of choosing x to minimize, with $a(x) = a/x$ say:

$$v(x) = \sqrt{2ash}/\sqrt{x} + bx.$$

The value of x to minimize this is given by:

$$\tfrac{1}{2}\sqrt{2ash}\, x^{-3/2} = b$$

i.e.

$$x = (ash/2b^2)^{1/3}$$
$$v(x) = 3(bash/2)^{1/3}.$$

If one cannot associate a cost with changing x (for example, if it is merely a question of exhorting people to speed up their work), then $f(x)$ will enable the possible financial gains to be obtained, to be offset against any dissatisfaction which the request to speed up might induce.

3.6 SENSITIVITY ANALYSIS FOR COMPUTATIONAL PURPOSES

For some problems the optimal cost, profit, etc. is not very sensitive to the decision actually taken and this is useful for computational purposes. Thus consider Exercise 1 of the Inventory Exercises.

For a single item, the variable cost $f(x)$, as a function of x, satisfies (where we use * to denote optimal quantities for this section):

$$f(x) = f^*(x/x^* + x^*/x).$$

Now let

$$x = x^* + \delta, \qquad |\delta| \le \overline{\delta}.$$

Then:

$$f(x) = \tfrac{1}{2}f^*(1 + \delta/x^* + (1 + \delta/x^*)^{-1})$$
$$\cong \tfrac{1}{2}f^*(2 + (\delta/x^*)^2) = f^* + \tfrac{1}{2}f^*(\delta/x^*)^2.$$

Hence the loss of optimality is approximately $\tfrac{1}{2}(\delta/x^*)^2$ as a proportion of f^*.

If we now assume that δ_i is small, for each i, when we have n items, the objective function then becomes:

$$f(\delta_1, \delta_2, \ldots, \delta_n) = \sum f^{*i} + \tfrac{1}{2}\sum \frac{\delta_i^2 f^{*i}}{(x^{*i})^2}$$

i.e. quadratic in $\{\delta_i\}$.

If we set the cycle time at T, we can set down the equations to make sure demand is satisfied in each cycle for each item. The problem is then a quadratic programming problem. T depends on $\{\delta_i\}$ or vice versa. Hence we have only one degree of freedom.

Clapham [3] discusses a problem of replacing equipment over a long time period so as to minimize the average annual cost. If x is the replacement period, a is the purchase price, and $h(t)$ is the cost of operating equipment of age t per unit time, the annual cost is as follows:

$$f(x) = a/x + \left(\int_{t=0}^{x} h(t)\, dt \right) \Big/ x.$$

He notes that $f(x)$ might be quite close to its optimal value for a range of values of x. This would allow such a choice to be satisfactorily handled in the context of other factors which influence the problem. For example other machines may be competing for replacement finance.

Such sensitivity analysis may sometimes be useful for integer problems, by finding the optimal non-integer solutions, and seeking integer solutions in the locality of the non-integer optimum. Eleithy et al. [6] discuss a problem of determining how many vehicles to have for transporting equipment and materials in oil drilling operations. The annual cost takes the form:

$$f(x) = a/x + hx + c, \qquad x \geqslant \underline{x},\ x \text{ integer},$$

where x is the number of vehicles to use and $\underline{x}$ is a lower limit on the number needed to transport the materials, as distinct from transporting rigs. Costs involved in rig transportation arise partly from loss of time and partly from normal transportation costs.

For this problem an optimal continuous x may be obtained and a search for a local integer solution made. The problem is not restricted to one size of vehicle and, with various sizes available, the problem can be generalized to one in which $f(x)$ is a function of integers $(x_1, x_2, \ldots, x_n)$ and various other constraints operate. Of course a more subtle sensitivity analysis is needed.

3.7 PARAMETRIC ANALYSIS AND ANALYTIC MODELS

Analytic models have at least two uses, viz.

(i) they provide a very ready way of seeing how solutions and optimality vary with parameters;
(ii) they provide a useful method of ascertaining which solutions may be good, and then more realistic formulations may be analysed using these solutions as an indication of the area which might profitably be studied.

Both (i) and (ii) are related to parametric analysis in the ways already discussed. (ii) really provides an initial heuristic, to be used as a basis for final analysis.

The simplest sort of analytic model is the economic order quantity model. The dynamic programming approach can also be used to get analytic solutions which can form the basis of a parametric analysis and are useful for discrete problems where mathematical programming faces difficulties.

In Chapter 2, section 2.10, we discussed the capacity installation problem from the general parametric analysis point of view. In general this can be quite difficult but, in theory, it is possible. If, however, we treat the problem as a sensitivity analysis problem, with small variations in the parameters

202

allowed, then, under certain conditions, we may be able to provide some useful information. For the example used in Chapter 2 the estimates of $\{a, c, \alpha\}$ were respectively $\{1, 1, 0.7\}$, with the demand linear in time and a time horizon of $K = 7$. The solution to this problem was (backward form) given in Table 3.1, where $\theta(k)$ is tabulated, with k variable from 1 to 7. Let us assume that all parameters are known precisely, with the exception of a, which takes the value $a = 1 + \varepsilon$. We might then ask ourselves how big ε has to be before the optimal decision rule changes. From section 2.10, we obtain the following equations:

$$f_0 = 0$$
$$f_1 = 2 + \varepsilon$$
$$f_2 = \min[3 + 2\varepsilon, 3.4 + 2.7\varepsilon] = 3 + 2\varepsilon$$
$$\text{providing } \varepsilon \geq -4/7$$
$$\text{(we henceforth assume that } \varepsilon \geq -4/7)$$
$$f_3 = \min[4 + 3\varepsilon, 4.1 + 2.4\varepsilon, 3.98 + 2.49\varepsilon]$$
$$= 3.98 + 2.49\varepsilon$$
$$\text{providing } -0.04 \leq \varepsilon \leq 1\tfrac{1}{3}.$$

We may now complete the analysis (see Exercise 16) up to $k = 7$ and find the range of ε for which the original decision rules remain optimal.

For this example the analysis was essentially a parametric analysis for the parameter $a = 1 + \varepsilon$. Since, as is seen from section 2.10, the form of f_k is piecewise linear in ε, all we need are linear inequalities in ε, and, in principle, ε need not be small. However, if we wished to examine the effect of variations in the parameter $\alpha = 0.7(1 + \varepsilon)$, then a strict sensitivity analysis might then require us to linearize α^x as $0.7^x + 0.7^x x\varepsilon$, and, for this approximation to be satisfactory, ε must be small enough. Of course we could use higher order approximations but this becomes a tedious exercise, although still possible.

3.8 OPTIMALITY ANALYSIS FOR VARIATIONS IN MODEL STRUCTURE

So far we have been looking at given structural models where the uncertainty lies in the parameter α. There are problems where several structures are possible and we wish to study the optimality features of the problem with respect to structure. The approaches given for parametric analysis follow in a similar way providing we now interpret α as a model structural parameter, although the concept of small deviations in models no longer exists.

Let us consider the problem of locating warehouses, discussed in Chapter

2 in the section 2.8 on Heuristic Programming, where the problem is to determine the optimal number of warehouses. An heuristic method was suggested by which the area was split up into approximate circles covering the region. This approximation would make no sense if it were dependent on the use of circles alone. Why not squares, or triangles? In fact the errors incurred in using one rather than another are quite small. Let $f_t(x)$ be the total annual cost for the models circle ($t = 1$), square ($t = 2$), triangle ($t = 3$) respectively, when x warehouses are used. Then we obtain the following results:

$$f_t(x) = ms(u + v) + ax + \alpha_t csm^{3/2}x^{-1/2}$$

when:

$$\alpha_1 = 2/3\pi^{-1/2}$$
$$\alpha_2 = (\log((\sqrt{2} + 1)/(\sqrt{2} - 1)) + 2\sqrt{2})$$
$$\alpha_3 = \left(\frac{1}{2(3)^{5/4}}\right)(4\sqrt{3} + \log((2 + \sqrt{3})/(2 - \sqrt{3}))).$$

It is easily checked that the difference between the $\{\alpha_t\}$ is such as to make little difference as to which model is used.

A similar problem is referred to in Exercise 6, part (iv), of Chapter 1, in the context of models for the level of damage a depth charge will do to a submarine.

Let us now refer back to some of our earlier work on queueing. The standard assumption there is that arrivals and service are negative exponential, whereas, in practice, this is not so. The question that arises is whether the use of negative exponential distributions, when the true distributions are not negative exponential, will give dangerously misleading results. If not, then there are clear analytical advantages for using the former. We will return to this later on. For the moment it is of interest to refer to Taha [18] who considers a simple negative exponential arrival, problem, with rate λ, with a general service distribution with expected service time of μ^{-1} and variance $\alpha^2\mu^{-2}$. Using the complete negative exponential model, the expected number in the system is, with $\rho = \lambda/\mu$;

$$\hat{n}_M = \rho/(1 - \rho).$$

For the model treating the service time correctly, we obtain:

$$\hat{n}_G = \rho + \rho^2(1 + \alpha^2)/2(1 - \rho).$$

Then:

$$\Delta = (\hat{n}_G - \hat{n}_M)/\hat{n}_G = \rho(\alpha^2 - 1)/(2 + \rho(\alpha^2 - 1)).$$

His analysis indicated that, for certain ranges of the parameters, not much error arises. This does not prove that we can generally use negative exponential distributions, but it does indicate that there is some scope for such considerations. Further study is needed to be definitive on this issue.

204

3.9 PARAMETRIC ANALYSIS AND UTILITY THEORY

So far we have taken a pragmatic view on parametric analysis, and not set this in the context of an appropriate theory of decision making. Let us now do so and take as our paradigm the theory of expected utility either in the form of Morgenstern *et al.* [12] or Savage [16]. We will take up the general issue of errors and measurement in Chapter 6 to which forward reference may be made.

If X is the action space, and a random event, or uncertain parameter $\alpha \in \boldsymbol{\alpha}$ has a probability density function g (discrete cases may likewise be tackled), then if x R y means that x is at least as good as y, the results of these theories are that there is a utility function v on X, and a utility function $v(x, \alpha)$ on $X \times \boldsymbol{\alpha}$ such that:

$$x \text{ R } y \rightleftarrows v(x) \geqslant v(y)$$

where:

$$v(x) = \int_{\alpha} v(x, \alpha) g(\alpha) \, d\alpha$$

and

$$(x, \alpha) \text{ R } (y, \beta) \rightleftarrows v(x, \alpha) \geqslant v(y, \beta).$$

The difference between the theories in [12] and [16] is, essentially, that g is specified in the former, in some objective sense, and is derived in the latter, in some subjective sense (see White [21], [22]).

In the above analysis α plays the role of our unknown parameter a used in the text.

For the remainder of this section we will confine ourselves to the analysis of sections 3.1 and 3.2. Let us return to the simple economic order quantity problem of section 3.1, where α is the parameter a. In that problem $f(x, \alpha)$ is a cash quantity. If the utility of cash is linear in cash level, then we may take $f(x, \alpha)$ as our utility function.

We then obtain, for the variable part to be minimized:

$$v(x) = \int_{a} (as/x + \tfrac{1}{2}hx) g(a) \, da$$

$$= \hat{a}s/x + \tfrac{1}{2}hx$$

where $\hat{a}$ is the expected value of a, and takes the role of our estimated a. If the theory is accepted, then the action to take is the one which optimizes $v(x)$, i.e. $x(\hat{a})$, and, as it stands, no further consideration of parametric analysis is required. However, the question arises as to whether or not research should be undertaken to determine what the actual value of a is, so that x may be chosen as optimal for that a. a plays the role of a^{0}. This depends on the cost, r, of such research, and, given the linearity of the utility function, if $x(a)$ is the optimal x given a, it is optimal to do research if

$$\int_{a} f(x(a), a) g(a) \, da - \int_{a} f(x(\hat{a}), a) g(a) \, da \leqslant -r$$

i.e.

$$\int_a \sqrt{(2ash)}\,g(a)\,\mathrm{d}a - \int_a \left(\frac{as}{\sqrt{(2\hat{a}s/h)}} + \tfrac{1}{2}h\sqrt{(2\hat{a}s/h)}\right)g(a)\,\mathrm{d}a \leqslant -r$$

i.e.

$$\int_a \sqrt{(2ash)}\,g(a)\,\mathrm{d}a \leqslant \sqrt{(2\hat{a}sh)} - r.$$

If the underlying utility function is non-linear this can easily be modified (see White [22]).

Continuing with the above analysis, let $a = (1+\varepsilon)\hat{a}$ (note this is the reverse of $\hat{a} = (1+\varepsilon)a^0$, since $\hat{a}$ is now fixed and a is a random variable). We then have research as being optimal if:

$$\sqrt{2\hat{a}sh}\int_\varepsilon (\sqrt{(1+\varepsilon)} - 1)l(\varepsilon)\,\mathrm{d}\varepsilon \leqslant -r$$

where $l(\varepsilon)$ is the probability density function for $\varepsilon = a/\hat{a} - 1$.

This reduces to, approximately:

$$f(x(\hat{a}),\hat{a})\int_\varepsilon (1 + \tfrac{1}{2}\varepsilon - \tfrac{1}{8}\varepsilon^2 - 1)l(\varepsilon)\,\mathrm{d}\varepsilon \leqslant -r$$

i.e.

$$\frac{r}{f(x(\hat{a}),\hat{a})} \leqslant \tfrac{1}{8}\sigma^2$$

since $\int_\varepsilon l(\varepsilon)\,\mathrm{d}\varepsilon = 0$.

The right-hand side is precisely the expression for Δ given in section 3.1.

A similar analysis can be carried out for the general case of section 3.2, for a linear utility function, to obtain the result that research is optimal if:

$$r \leqslant -\tfrac{1}{2}\frac{\partial^2 f(x,\alpha)}{\partial^2 x}\left(\frac{\mathrm{d}x(\alpha)}{\mathrm{d}\alpha}\right)^2 \sigma^2$$

where derivatives are evaluated at $\alpha = \hat{\alpha}$. Readers should verify this for themselves.

For non-linear utility functions, modifications need to be made. If the outcome is still cash, say $\theta(x,\alpha)$ given x and α, then we would have

$$v(x,\alpha) = u(\theta(x,\alpha))$$

for some utility function u, in which case research will be optimal if

$$\int_\alpha u(\theta(x(\alpha),\alpha) - r)g(\alpha)\,\mathrm{d}\alpha \geqslant \int_\alpha u(\theta(x(\hat{\alpha}),\alpha))g(\alpha)\,\mathrm{d}\alpha$$

for maximization problems.

Thus, in principle, this, or some alternative decision theoretic framework that directly incorporates the research decision, is really needed. In practice, however, difficulties, or straight reluctance on the part of those involved,

206

arise when taking this point of view. The sort of analysis given in section 3.2 is used in a manner which seems appropriate to the individuals concerned.

Let us return to the ratio approach used in section 3.1. In general measurement scales are not unique. Some scales are unique up to certain transformations.

The general utility scale is unique up to positive affine transformations of the form, for any admissible utility functions $v^1(x, \alpha)$, $v(x, \alpha)$:

$$v^1(x, \alpha) = \lambda v(x, \alpha) + \mu, \qquad \lambda > 0.$$

In this case it is clear that the ratio of losses to total utility can be made quite arbitrary by appropriate choices of λ, μ. The general utility scale is an interval scale (see Krantz et al. [10]). Hence this reinforces the real need for a proper decision theoretic base in parametric analysis.

Some scales are ratio scales (see Krantz et al. [10]) and are unique up to positive linear transformations, i.e. $\mu = 0$ in the above. For such problems, the ratios used are independent of λ. Such scales include time, cash, etc. However, even here, the utility argument is still valid.

If absolute losses, rather than ratios, are used, similar difficulties arise. In all cases, in the absence of a utility framework, the individuals concerned have to subjectively interpret the significance of the parametric analysis for other decisions open to them, which may be dependent on this analysis. We will consider these issues again in Chapter 6.

3.10   EXERCISES

1. In a queueing problem (see main text) the average cost per unit time is:

$$c(x, \lambda) = cx + \lambda w/(x - \lambda) \qquad (x > \lambda)$$

where λ is the arrival rate, and x is the service rate.

Carry out a post-optimality sensitivity analysis from first principles where λ is the unknown parameter, with an estimate $\hat{\lambda}$, and x is the decision variable, and $\hat{\lambda} = (1 + \varepsilon)\lambda^0$, where λ^0 is the true parameter value.

2. In a maintenance problem (see main text) the profit per unit time is:

$$f(x, m) = V - (\lambda/\mu)(V + R)/x - ((V + M)/m)x$$

where $\{\lambda, \mu, V, R, M, m\}$ are parameters, and the decision variable is x, the frequency of inspection.

Carry out a post-optimality sensitivity analysis with respect to the unknown parameter m, where the estimate is $\hat{m} = (1 + \varepsilon)m^0$, and m^0 is the true parameter value.

3. Consider the warehouse problem discussed in the text, given the expressions for $\{f_t(x)\}$.

(i) Standardize the formulae in the form

$$f_t(x) = f_0 + a(x + 2k_t^{3/2}x^{-1/2})$$

and find k_t, $t = 1, 2, 3$.
(ii) Carry out a post-optimality sensitivity analysis for each model.
(iii) Carry out a post-optimality analysis between models for the cases $t = 1, 2$.

The sensitivity analyses are only to be carried out on the variable parts of $\{f_t(x)\}$.

4. Consider the warehousing model in Exercise 3 with the general form:

$$f(x, s) = f_0 + a(x + 2k^{3/2}x^{-1/2}), \qquad f_0 = f_0(s), \qquad k = k(s).$$

Now suppose that the parameter s in the original problem depends upon the actual location of the customers, but that s does not vary too greatly over the total region.

Explain how you would use the above model to get a solution to the new problem.

5. As has been indicated in the text, optimal decisions may remain the same for ranges of a parameter. Suppose now that, in Exercise 1, there are two service rates, x_A and x_B being proposed. Find the range of values of λ for which x_A is preferred to x_B.

6. An organization controls a very large number of items. It cannot determine, or operate, an optimal economic order quantity for each item. Its procedure is to sample a subset of the items, calculate the optimal order quantity for each, and use the average of these as the single order size for all items. The probability density function for the optimal order quantities, x^*, is $g(x^*)$, and the sample size is large enough for the mean and variance of x^* to be adequately approximated from the sample. The mean and variance are μ, σ^2 respectively. If σ^2 is small show that the expected proportional loss of optimality is approximately $\sigma^2/(2\mu^2)$. Use Exercise 1 of the Inventory Exercises, Chapter 2, to solve this. It is to be noted that the calculation of absolute losses may be the appropriate things to calculate in practice.

7. In Exercise 6, part (iv), of Chapter 1, the problem of appropriate models for the depth charge problem was raised. Carry out a post-optimality analysis, for models (not parameters), for the case when the probability density function $g(s)$, for submarine depth, is $2s/S^2$ between 0 and S. The models are:

$$M_1: d(z) = k_0 - k_1|z|$$
$$M_2: d(z) = k_0 - k_2 z^2.$$

k_0, k_1, k_2 to be assumed known (for example, best estimates for the models).

8. In a problem of pipe-laying, the annual cost is given by:

$$f(x, \alpha, \beta) = \alpha x^2 + \beta x^{-5}$$

where x is the pipe diameter. Carry out a post-optimality sensitivity analysis for this problem. [Deininger [5] discusses this problem, where α is a cost of piping parameter, and β is an energy factor].

9. Study Exercise 17 of the Mathematical and Dynamic Programming Exercises, Chapter 2, for $n = 2$, in the same way as the capacity installation problem of section 3.7 was studied, to see how the optimal decisions depend upon the component cost and probability parameters.

10. In Exercise 1 for the single server, negative exponential arrival and service problem, carry out a similar sensitivity analysis with respect to λ where, when we begin with an empty system and the cost is now discounted on a continuous basis, i.e. if $\hat{w}(t)$ is the expected waiting contribution per unit time at time t by those in the system at time t, $c(x, \lambda)$ is replaced by:

$$c(x, \lambda) = cx \int_0^\infty e^{-\alpha t} \, dt + w \int_0^\infty \hat{w}(t) e^{-\alpha t} \, dt.$$

Note that:

(i) $\hat{w}(t) = \sum_{n=0}^\infty n P_n(t)$
(ii) $\sum_{n=0}^\infty n P_n(t)$ will need to be derived from the transient equations of the queueing theory section relating $dP_n(t)/dt$ to $P_n(t)$, $P_{n-1}(t)$, $P_{n+1}(t)$
(iii) $\int_0^\infty e^{-\alpha t}(dP_n(t)/dt) \, dt = -P_n(0) + \int_0^\infty e^{-\alpha t} P_n(t) \, dt$
(iv) (iii) may be used to set up a recurrence relationship which may be used to determine (ii) (see Barzily et al. [1] who actually solve the problem using a prior distribution for λ, and Saaty [15] who solves the recurrence problem).

11. Carry out a parametric analysis using the dynamic programming approach in section 3.7 to the redundancy problem, with $b^0 = 13$, in the range $b^0 \pm 3$.

12. In the section 2.2, on Inventory, of Chapter 2 we discussed a dynamic programming approach to an inventory control problem with probabilistic demand. Examine how you would carry out a sensitivity analysis with respect to the parameters for the infinite horizon case (see Levy [11]).

13. In the text reference was made to a transportation problem of Eleithy et al. [6] where the cost takes the following form, for integer $x \geq 0$:

$$f(x) = a/x + hx + c.$$

A similar problem is to be found in Fowler et al. [7].

Examine how you would carry out a sensitivity analysis of the solution with respect to the parameters of the problem.

14. In Chapter 2, sections 2.5 and 2.10, we discussed a capacity installation

problem. This was again mentioned in this chapter as part of sensitivity, or parametric, analysis. Suppose now that, for an estimated set of parametric values, the optimal solution is to put in extra capacity for each year. Set down inequalities in the parametric values, using dynamic programming, for which this solution will be optimal and, using linear approximations for small variations, reduce these to linear inequalities.

15. Complete the parametric analysis example, where $a = 1 + \varepsilon$, begun in section 3.7, and also do the sensitivity analysis, for small ε, for the case $\alpha = 0.7(1 + \varepsilon)$.

3.11 REFERENCES

1. Barzily, Z. and Yadin, M., The effect of prior assumptions on the expected cost of M/M/1 queueing systems with unknown arrival rate, *Naval Research Logistics Quarterly*, **23**, 663–671, 1976.
2. Bellman, R. E. and Dreyfus, S. E., *Applied Dynamic Programming*, Princeton University Press, 1962.
3. Clapham, J. C. R., Economic life of equipment, *Operational Research Quarterly*, **8**, 181–190, 1957.
4. Dantzig, G. B., *Linear Programming and Extensions*, Princeton University Press, 1963.
5. Deninger, R., Letter to the Editor, *Interfaces*, **9**, 118–120, 1979.
6. Eleithy, S. A. and Mortagy, A. M., Optimising transportation service for oil exploration, *Interfaces*, **10**, 13–19, 1980.
7. Fowler, O. S. and Williams, W. H., Minimum cost fleet sizing for a university motor pool, *Interfaces*, **10**, 21–28, 1980.
8. Gal, T., *Postoptimal Analysis Parametric Programming and Related Topics*, McGraw-Hill, 1979.
9. Geoffrion, A., *Perspectives in Optimisation*, Addison-Wesley, 1972.
10. Krantz, D. H., Luce, R. D., Suppes, and P., Tversky, A., *Foundations of Measurement*, Vol. 1, Academic Press, 1971.
11. Levy, J., Further notes on the loss resulting from the use of incorrect data in computing an optimal inventory policy, *Naval Research Logistics Quarterly*, **6**, 25–32, 1959.
12. Morgenstern, O. and von Neuman, J., *Theory of Games and Economic Behaviour*, Princeton University Press, 1947.
13. Saaty, T., Coefficient perturbation of a constrained extremum, *Operations Research*, **7**, 294–302, 1959.
14. Saaty, T. and Webb, K. W., Sensitivity of the scheduling aircraft, *Proceedings of the Second Conference on Operational Research*, English Universities Press, pp. 708–716, 1960.
15. Saaty, T., *Elements of Queueing Theory*, McGraw-Hill, 1961.
16. Savage, L. J., *The Foundations of Statistics*, Wiley, 1954.
17. Shapiro, J. F., *Mathematical Programming, Structures and Algorithms*, Wiley, 1979.
18. Taha, H. A., Queueing theory in practice, *Interfaces*, **11**, 43–49, 1981.
19. Wagner, H., *Principles of Operations Research*, Prentice-Hall, 1969.
20. Webb, K. W., Some aspects of the Saaty linear programming sensitivity equation, *Operations Research*, **10**, 266–267, 1962.
21. White, D. J., *Decision Theory*, Allen & Unwin, 1969.
22. White, D. J., *Fundamentals of Decision Theory*, North-Holland, 1976.

CHAPTER 4

Problem Formulation

4.1 INTRODUCTION

In the previous chapters we have dealt with the historical aspects of Operational Research, and with the nature of various techniques which tend to characterize Operational Research in terms of some of its technical content.

From time to time we have raised questions concerning some aspects of the models we have discussed. For example, the question of objectives has been raised, this constituting one of the more difficult aspects of an Operational Research investigation. We have also raised the question of constraints, again an aspect of an Operational Research study which can pose difficulties.

Both of these factors are components of the general problem formulation phase of Operational Research, which will be the subject of this chapter.

Exactly what constitutes problem formulation depends on the individual's point of view. For example, Dewey, [42], specifies three components of problem solving, viz.

(i) What is the problem?
(ii) What are the alternatives?
(iii) Which alternative is the best?.

We are concerned, in this chapter, with the pre-problem solution phase, and hence exclude component (iii) which we see as a different phase of the process to that of problem formulation. We will also consider that component (ii) is really part of problem formulation. Component (i) begs the question as to what is meant by the problem.

We will try to make precise what we mean by this under the heading of problem formulation, since it is only by achieving some precision that any scientific examination of such a concept in the context of Operational Research may proceed. Of course there will be lay uses of such terms. Thus, for example, if an operational researcher asks a decision maker what his problem is, he is likely to answer that, for example, costs are high, absenteeism is high, breakdowns are high, in many cases. This is only one aspect of the problem as we will use the term. It merely reflects the fact that some perceived objectives are being unsatisfactorily achieved. Of course, an answer to the original question might be that the decision maker has a

210

choice to make, and needs some help. This is, again, only one aspect of the problem as we will define it.

The following definition will be based on Ackoff [2]. A problem will be said to be well defined if the following criteria are met, and to be, in effect, defined by these criteria, viz.

(i) the decision makers are specified;
(ii) the actions (options, alternatives) are specified;
(iii) the objectives (effects, outcomes, consequences) are specified in numerical terms, as functions of (ii);
(iv) a value function (super-objective) which gives a total measure of value (worth) in terms of the objectives, is specified as a numerical function of (iii).

The following notation will be used, viz.

D denotes the set of decision makers;
X denotes the options being considered;
x is the general member of X;
$\{f^i(x)\}$, $i = 1, 2, \ldots, m$ are the objectives, where we allow for uncertainty to be incorporated in an appropriate form, as functions of $x \in X$;
$v(x) = u(f^1(x), f^2(x), \ldots, f^m(x)) = u(f(x))$, is the overall measure of value as a function of $x \in X$, derived from the measure of value u as a function of components $\{f^i\}$ (we turn to this in Chapter 6).

Newell et al. [118] define well-structured problems in an analogous way, but without actually defining a problem, concentrating on (iii) and (iv), and also including well defined computational routines for actually solving the problem. We would envisage a problem as being capable of being well structured even though the solution method had yet to be devised.

Reitman [132] devises a framework for viewing problems from the point of view of what is given about the problem and what is required to be found. The format has three types of component, viz. $\{A, B, \rightarrow\}$. A is the known part of the problem, B is the desired (or target) result, and $\rightarrow$ is the manner in which B is to be reached from A.

Problems cannot always be expressed as a single $\{A, B, \rightarrow\}$ arrangement and the representation is dynamic and changes with time.

We will look at some of the examples. In doing so it will be noted that the format covers both primary and secondary problems, where a primary problem relates to the decisions for which the analysis is being carried out (e.g. inventory decisions), and a secondary problem relates to the decisions concerning the models to be used, data to be collected, etc. The primary problem formulation phase is defined by (i)–(iv) above, and each of these may be represented by an A, B or $\rightarrow$, depending on the specification of the problem situation. This phase does not include (iii) in Dewey's format, and relates, not to the formulation of the problem, but to its solution. This would, however, be included in Reitman's format.

Let the set of alternative actions, $X = A = \{x^1, x^2, \ldots, x^k, \ldots, x^K\}$ be given, and let it be required to find B, the final choice from A (or final choices, if we cannot reduce B to a single member). In order to find B, we have to determine how B is to be determined from A, i.e. we have to find $\rightarrow$. If A is already specified in terms of cash payments, then finding $\rightarrow$ may be equivalent to finding the value function v. Thus suppose we know, initially, that $x^k = \{r_1^k, r_2^k, \ldots, r_t^k, \ldots\}$, where r_t^k is cash payment at time t if we take action k. Then finding $\rightarrow$ might be equivalent to finding a measure of worth, $v(x^k)$ such that x^k is at least as good as $x^{k'} \rightleftarrows v(x^k) \geqslant v(x^{k'})$.

Possibilities for v are as follows:

Present Worth. For some discount factor, α:

$$v(x^k) = \sum_{t=1}^{\infty} \alpha^{t-1} r_t^k.$$

This is discussed in Chapter 6.

Payback Period. For action x^k, the payback period, T^k, is the smallest value of T for which

$$\sum_{t=1}^{T-1} r_t^k < 0 \leqslant \sum_{t=1}^{T} r_t^k.$$

It is the first point in time at which the net cost flow becomes non-negative. Then:

$$v(x^k) = -T^k.$$

The present worth, or discounted cash flow, formulation was used in various places in Chapter 2 for dynamic problems and we gave a mixed presentation using both average cost, or profit, cases (the case $\alpha = 1$, but averaged over a long time period), and the discounted case. In all these problems, the proper formulation must be determined. Reformulations for example, in terms of payback periods, may be more acceptable to the decision maker and the objectives may be to minimize the payback period, or expected payback period, making the problems rather less tractable.

There is considerable literature on different sorts of evaluation of time series of cash flows (e.g. see Koopmans [93] and White [169]). The important thing is that for a problem of the above form, $\{A, B, \rightarrow\}$, where A is given in appropriate form, and B is to be found, $\rightarrow$ also has to be found somehow if a closed form analysis is to be achieved, or at least some partially closed form (e.g. efficient solutions). We will look at open, closed, and partially closed forms later on in this chapter.

If A_1 is, initially, a physical set of alternative actions, it may be that part of the problem is to determine the cash flows, $\{r_t^k\}$. We then have:

$$A_1 \rightarrow_{12} A_2 \rightarrow_{23} A_3 (= B)$$

where: $A_2 = A_1$ in cash flow form above; $\rightarrow_{23} = \rightarrow$ above; $A_3 = B$ above; $A_1 =$ initial set of physical alternatives, given; $\rightarrow_{12}$, which calculates the cash flows, is to be found. Hence A_1 is given and the rest have to be found.

Rudermann [137] studies the problem of diseases and their economic effects. This problem, slightly expanded, may take the following form:

$$A_1 \rightarrow_{12} A_2 \rightarrow_{23} A_3 \rightarrow_{34} A_4$$
$$\searrow_{25} A_5$$

A_1: available ways of reducing diseases D
A_2: ways to be studied
A_3: reduction in diseases D
A_4: changes in economic benefits E
A_5: final choices in A_2
$\rightarrow_{12}$: method of reducing A_1 to A_2
$\rightarrow_{23}$: relating A_2 to A_3
$\rightarrow_{34}$: relating A_3 to A_4
$\rightarrow_{25}$: method of final choices from A_2.

In this problem, only A_3, A_4 are given, i.e. the problem starts by recognizing that a reduction in disease level will influence economic benefits. The rest are recognized as the problem develops and are all unknown initially. It may be that the problem does not evolve as far as $\rightarrow_{25}$ and A_5, and that the open form of analysis is to be used.

A little later on in this chapter we will consider the problem of selecting which type of option one ought to consider when improving service to customers. This problem, slightly expanded, may take the following form:

$$\nearrow^{A_4}_{24}$$
$$A_1 \rightarrow_{12} A_2 \rightarrow_{23} A_3$$

A_1: methods of scheduling, increased capacity, bonus scheme, production techniques
A_2: subset of A_1 to be studied in detail
A_3: service levels
A_4: final choices from A_2
$\rightarrow_{12}$: method of reducing A_1 to A_2
$\rightarrow_{23}$: relating A_2 to A_3
$\rightarrow_{24}$: method for finding final choices from A_2.

In this problem, A_1 and A_3 are given, and the rest have to be found.

A further illustration is given by the interaction of inventory and production activities which we discuss later on in the chapter. The dynamics of evolution of the problem are illustrated here.

Initially we have the problem in the form:

$A_1 \rightarrow_{12} A_2$

A_1: set of inventory control rules, based on specific production, demand, and supply data

A_2: final choices from A_1

$\rightarrow_{12}$: relating A_2 to A_1

A_1 is given, and A_2, $\rightarrow_{12}$ are to be found.

After further consideration of the production interaction, the problem takes the form:

$A_1^* \rightarrow_{12}^* A_2^*$

A_1^*: set of combined inventory and production control rules based on demand and supply data

A_2^*: final choices from A_1^*

$\rightarrow_{12}^*$: relating A_1^* to A_2^*

A_1^* is given, and A_2^*, $\rightarrow_{12}$ are to be found.

Finally, we may also consider the case when all the components (i)–(iv) of our problem formulation format may be involved. This may be formulated thus, although somewhat incomplete:

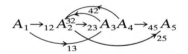

A_1: set of decision makers involved

A_2: types of decision to be considered

A_3: implicit or explicit alternatives

A_4: consequences to be considered

A_5: final choices;

$\rightarrow_{12}$: how to determine A_2 from A_1

$\rightarrow_{23}$: how to determine A_3 from A_2

$\rightarrow_{13}$: how to determine A_3 from A_1

$\rightarrow_{32}$: how to determine A_2 from A_3

$\rightarrow_{42}$: how to determine A_2 from A_4

$\rightarrow_{25}$: how to determine A_5 from A_2

$\rightarrow_{45}$: how to convert A_4 to A_5—this is the value function step (iv).

This picture is somewhat incomplete, and is merely put down to illustrate some possible components and links relating to the problem formulation process. Sometimes several links are needed to identify specific components. The knowns and unknowns will vary from problem situation to problem situation, and will evolve with time.

We will now look in more detail at each of the components (i)–(iv), to examine their significance for the Operational Research investigation. For more general studies on problem formulation, the reader should consult: White [168]; Pidd *et al.* [124, 125], who give a literature survey and look at different ways of viewing this phase; Eden *et al.* [53], who discuss their cognitive mapping approach to problem formulation; Graham [66, 67], who has something specific to say on the use of a computer model for formulating problems; Anderson *et al.* [6], who look at some special methods of managerial problem cause analysis; and Müller-Merbach [114], who provides a framework for problem elicitation.

4.2 PROBLEM FORMULATION PHASES

4.2.1 The Decision Makers

When any decisions are finally made, they will be made in the context of some preference or value structure. Such structures relate, in the final analysis, to the decision makers, whoever they might be.

To begin with, let us consider the queueing Exercise 1 of Chapter 3, the background to which is given in Chapter 2. The problem is one in which we have a single service facility, with negative exponential services, with rate x, negative exponential arrivals, with rate λ, and a cost cx per unit time for service rate x. The objectives of interest are the costs and waiting time in the system for individuals who arrive in a unit time interval, viz.

$$f^1(x) = cx$$
$$f^2(x) = \lambda/(x-\lambda), \qquad x > \lambda.$$

Figure 4.1 shows how f^1 and f^2 vary with each other. The curve is given by the equation:

$$f^2 = c\lambda/(f^1 - c\lambda).$$

Now, if, as given in the queueing exercise 1 of Chapter 3, we can combine f^1 and f^2 by using some weighting factor, w, for f^2, the problem reduces to

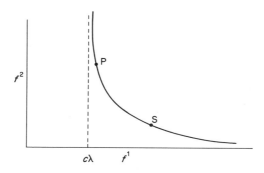

Figure 4.1

finding x to maximize (to be consistent with our definition of a value function)

$$v(x) = -cx - \lambda w/(x - \lambda).$$

However, let us now suppose that we have two potential decision makers, say the production manager and the sales manager. The production manager will be operating close to the immediate cost centres, and the service cost will influence him more than it will influence the sales manager. The reverse situation will arise from the service point of view, where the sales manager will be more influenced by this than will be the production manager.

Given a free choice, the production manager might select point P, and the sales manager might select point S. If, for example, it were possible to find a weighting factor w^P for the production manager, and w^S for the sales manager, their optimal choices would be:

$$x^P = \lambda + \sqrt{(\lambda w^P/c)}$$
$$x^S = \lambda + \sqrt{(\lambda w^S/c)}$$

respectively, with $w^S > w^P$ and $x^S > x^P$.

Beyond this analysis, there is very little to say as to how they might resolve this difference if they have to come to some agreement. For this problem, it is possible to see that, for every $x < x^P$, there is an $x > x^P$ with the same $v(x)$ value, with $w = w^P$, and for $x > x^S$, there is an $x < x^S$ with the same $v(x)$ value, with $w = w^S$. Thus it seems reasonable that some compromise between x^P and x^S should be reached.

If the actual decision is to be made by the managing director the situation may be somewhat different, but his final decision may be dependent on the views of the production and sales managers as expressed in the previous analysis.

Ideally, of course, one would wish to see if one could determine the economic impact of waiting time. This is not always possible. The reader may find the paper by Jones *et al.* [87] interesting in this respect, where a questionnaire was used. Without such a framework only a limited help can be provided. For the problem discussed, all the individuals are working, in principle, in the best interests of the organization, as a team. The paper of Marschak [107] is one of the earliest efforts to develop such a theory.

The example given also indicates that there are other decision makers at work whose objectives are not necessarily compatible with the objectives of the organization, in this case the customers. They may take decisions themselves as, for example, to whether they want to continue to place their custom with the organization. For example, in the queueing example, the net effect of such actions may be that the arrival rate λ will, in the steady state, become a function of the waiting time, e.g.

$$\lambda = g(1/(x - \lambda))$$

from which λ may be found for a given x.

In such a case, since λ represents the ultimate profit source to the company, the company's objective may become:

$$v(x) = p\lambda - cx$$

where λ is a function of x determined by g.

If this were to be the case, then the weighting factor approach may not be a good representation of the actual net profit situation (see Exercise 37).

A similar situation arises in inventory control where cutomer response depends on the frequency of inventory shortages (see Caine *et al.* [30], and Schwartz [145, 146], for development of models for this situation, and also see Exercise 30). A potentially similar situation arises in mail ordering where the defectives content will influence future orders (see Spencer [149]); and also see Chapter 2, on problems involving defective production, Exercise 5 of the Defective Product Exercises, where such models may also be modified to cater for customer reactions.

The above situations do not, overtly, represent the other parties as decision makers, although they could do so. Even in a given company the personal interests of individuals must be taken account of, since they are always in a position to make decisions with adverse effects on the company.

Let us consider the simple economic quantity inventory problem of Chapter 2. The annual cost as a function of batch size is:

$$f(x) = cs + as/x + \tfrac{1}{2}hx = -v(x).$$

The optimum is given by:

$$x^* = \sqrt{(2as/h)}$$

and Figure 4.2 illustrates the situation.

Now the above model assumes, in particular, that x has no influence on the efficient operation of the system. However, if x is too small, or too large, this might mean more physical work for the operators, and hence they may

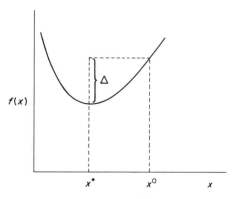

Figure 4.2

be reluctant to move from the present position with $x = x^0$, without some inducement.

If the cost factors remain the same, the gains to the company by moving from x^0 to x^* are given by:

$$\Delta = f(x^0) - f(x^*)$$

and this saving may be used as a basis for negotiation by offering extra payments to the operators for such changes.

Alternatively, the management may recognize that, without such negotiations, the operators will react in certain ways to changes in x. One way in which this may take place is for the costs c, a, h, to become dependent on x, arising from go-slows, etc. If Z represents the set of actions which the operators can take, the operators may have an objective function $g(x, z)$ of their own, taking into account the effects on their earnings. The problem then reduces to the following form.

For a given x, z is chosen to:

$$\underset{z \in Z}{\text{maximize}}[g(x, z)].$$

This gives $z = z(x)$.

The coefficients $\{c, a, h\}$ become a function of z, say $\{c(z), a(z), h(z)\}$, and then the managerial problem is as follows:

$$\text{minimise}_{x \geqslant 0}[f(x) = c(z(x)) + a(z(x))/x + \tfrac{1}{2}h(z(x))x].$$

This is merely illustrative of the situation. Whichever way the problem is resolved, the basic conflicts are still there, and, since g will usually be in conflict with f, they have to be recognized and resolved.

Similar problems arise in any situation in which a member of an organization operates under specified conditions and proceeds to maximize his income subject to these conditions. Sometimes this will be compatible with the organizational objectives, i.e. increasing his income will increase that of the organization. This arises from bonus scheme situations, or profit-sharing situations (see e.g. Pasternak [122] where potential for conflict of objectives does arise and the study aimed at ensuring that the employees' decisions were profitable for the company, and safeguarded the employees' earnings).

In the above problem, the problem is one in which one decision maker acts, first choosing x, and a second decison maker acts afterwards, choosing z. In many situations both x and z have to be chosen simultaneously. For example, in Chapter 1, we referred to the problems of search. In such cases the searcher and the target may have to make simultaneous decisions in the light of their circumstances. Deemer et al. [39] discuss the problem of a submarine which has to traverse a channel, but can only submerge for a limited amount of time, and enemy aircraft traverse the channel from time to time, looking for submarines. Each has to decide on its strategy without knowing what the other's strategy is. Haywood [73] discusses similar situations, one of which relates to the convoy routing decisions of the Japanese, in the South Pacific, and the American deployment of reconnaissance aircraft, and another to the problem of deployment of forces in the Avanches Gap situation in France.

In each case the Operational Research study endeavours to identify the effects, on each decision maker, of the outcomes of actions by each, and then to rationalize the final decisions to be taken.

For such problems, there are various ways of tackling the problem. One comes under the heading of game theory which attempts to provide a framework within which the final decision of one decision maker (in the above cases, the American forces) can be rationalized, whilst taking into account the possible rationalizations of the other decision makers (in this case, the Japanese, or Germans). It is important that it be recognized that the framework is developed for use by a particular decision maker, or decision makers.

There are many arguments for and against the value of using game-theoretic approaches. I will not dwell on these. The interested reader may consult Deemer's paper and such texts as those of Rapoport [130], Davis [38], Harsanyi [72], Luce *et al.* [100], and Howard [81]. A related approach may be found in Radford [129].

The paper by Deemer is also useful for its discussion of operational gaming, a procedure involving pseudo-decision makers as if they were actually taking decisions, but in a short space of time, in a manner similar to that of simulation. As a method of helping formulate problems this has value, since it helps identify not only any final solution, but options and objectives as the process takes place. It has its disadvantages (e.g. limited number of plays possible) and Deemer's view is that a suitable combination of game theory and operational gaming is needed.

Finally, in many situations active decision makers act on behalf of other groups of people. Thus, in Exercise 4 of the Mathematical and Dynamic Programming Exercises of Chapter 2, the problem of utilization of a bus fleet is given. The actual decisions are taken by the transport department executive, but they are taken on behalf of the population. The constraints placed on frequencies are those chosen by the executive, and not necessarily those which would be chosen by the population, although it may be thought that the views might be similar. The executive sets its constraints, and then sets out to meet its own stated objectives (e.g. miles travelled) in the best manner it can. However, had the population been consulted, for example, by seeking their preferences for levels of service combined with appropriate fares, a different answer may be achieved. This particular problem is bedevilled by the fact that, even in the population, different preferences may be made, and raises the question of how such preferences may be aggregated. There is no agreed answer to this problem. The reader may consult the first work aimed at answering this problem, viz. Arrow [7], or Luce *et al.* [100], for more information on this problem.

A similar situation, again in transport, arises over the replacement of buses. For a simple model, the replacement interval, x, might be chosen to:

$$\text{minimize}_{x \geq 0}[f(x) = (p + c(x))/x]$$

where p is the purchase price of a new bus, and $c(x)$ is the total net cost of a bus over its life x.

However, the solution to this may be a value of x so large that the population using the buses might feel that having modern, aesthetically appealing, buses is to be preferred, even if the effect of this is to have increased fares. The point is: whose decision should it be?

It might, in this case, be argued that if we could ascertain the number, $n(x)$, of passengers who would use the buses each year, for policy x, then the executive should:

$$\text{maximize}[f(x) = (n(x)r - p - c(x))/x]$$

where r is the passenger revenue per year.

But why should this be the case? The term $n(x)$ might not reflect the real preferences of the users in terms of possible ages, x, and fares needed to maintain this.

No answer is given to this. Decisions are likely to be taken by the executive on the basis of $f(x)$ of the above types, with some personal view on service factors.

4.2.2 The Actions

4.2.2.1 Types of Action

Let us return to the depth charge problem of Chapter 1. For the quadratic damage function, the maximal expected damage is given by:

$$f^{1*} = f(x^*) = k_0 - k\sigma^2$$

where σ^2 is the variance of the submarine depth.

The type of action considered here, in the first instance, was the depth charge setting, $x = x_1$. This naturally leads to the consideration of two other sorts of actions (see Exercise 6 of Chapter 1) viz.

x_2: the explosive filler for the depth charges

x_3: the level of σ^2 which might be achieved, even to the extent of being able to know exactly where the submarine is.

Assuming that x_1 has been chosen to be optimal, we may write the optimal expected damage as a function of x_2, x_3, viz.

$$f^1(x_2, x_3) = k_0(x_2) - k(x_2)\sigma^2(x_3).$$

We then have the problem of deciding which, if any, of the actions x_2, x_3

might usefully be investigated. This decision is a secondary decision as already mentioned in Chapter 1. On what basis might this be made?

For each action pair (x_2, x_3) there will be an associated cost of experimentation, development and operation, say:

$$f^2(x_2, x_3).$$

Both f^1 and f^2 must be evaluated in the context of the total encounters and costs anticipated. There is then the question of the trade-off between f^1 and f^2. If it so happened that this could be expressed in weighting factor form, say:

$$v(x_2, x_3) = \lambda_1 f^1(x_2, x_3) - \lambda_2 f^2(x_2, x_3)$$

then, in order to make the secondary decision, we must form some prior judgement as to the relative magnitudes of λ_1 and λ_2, and as to the relative magnitudes of the effects of x_2 and x_3.

Thus we have to recognize that we do face a choice as to which areas of investigation we should, initially, undertake, and that considerations of the above kind are essential to this. In the above instance, because of the relative novelty of the situation, such judgements are likely to be quite subjective. For some problems some evidence might be available to help us. Thus let us consider our earlier problem involving service, f^2, as measured by waiting time in the system, and the cost, f^1, of achieving this, and let us suppose that, using Reitman's format, the problem begins with the knowledge that some solution giving an appropriate compromise between costs and service is required. This might be expressed in the form:

$$A \rightarrow' A' \rightarrow'' A'' \rightarrow B$$

where:

A: the set of actions open to us to study
A': the set we finally settle on
A'': the set of combinations of cost and service
B: the final choice in A' to be made
$\rightarrow, \rightarrow', \rightarrow''$ are the appropriate transformations.

The question which faces us is: what should A' be? A might consist of the following possibilities, viz.

x_1: service rate
x_2: scheduling
x_3: bonus scheme
x_4: machine capacity
x_5: technological design.

We could express service f^2 in terms of $(x_1, x_2, x_3, x_4, x_5) = x$, and similarly for cost f^1.

In deciding which of the $\{x_j\}$ might, in the first instance, be usefully studied, the same considerations as given for the depth charge problem arise and, again, the resolution may involve some subjectivity. However, problems involving actions of the above kind are not quite so novel as in the depth charge problem case, and evidence may exist which at least gives some idea of the magnitude of effects of $\{x_i\}$ on f^1 and f^2 which, supplemented by any knowledge specific to the organization itself, may be helpful. Thus, for example, there may already exist excess machine capacity, and it may be felt that a bonus scheme would add little because the operators were already working as efficiently as seems possible.

External evidence might arise from the fact that, in some instances, it is very difficult to improve scheduling operations in terms of the performance achieved by experience over many years.

It is also important to realize that the nature of the actions being considered will influence the decision as to which type to study, for example difficulties involved in studying particular actions, frequency of such actions, timespan of such actions, and so on (see White [168]).

Let us consider a maintenance problem discussed in Chapter 2. In this problem the initial approach was for a study of maintenance frequency x, when the replacement period y was taken to be y^0. If $r(x, t)$ is the return in year t, since purchase, when the maintenance frequency is x, x was to be chosen to maximize the annual revenue (excluding net replacement costs, assumed fixed):

$$f(x, y^0) = \left(\sum_{t=1}^{y^0} r(x, t) \right) \Big/ y^0.$$

Now the optimal frequency, $x^*(y^0)$ given y^0, might not be far removed from the present frequency, x^0, leaving little possibility of gains. Hence the possibility of changing y^0 has to be considered, and $f(x, y^0)$ replaced by:

$$f(x, y) = \left(\sum_{t=1}^{y} r(x, t) \right) \Big/ y + (p - s(y))/y$$

where p is the purchase price and $s(y)$ is trade-in value at age y.

If $x^*(y)$ is the optimal x for a given y, the picture is as shown in Figure 4.3.

Let us look at a potential queueing problem which arose in a hospital. Initially the request was for a study of the redevelopment of beds for emergency use, and of the improved scheduling which might have been possible if emergencies were separated from the main patient wards. However, the best solution to the original problem might be too poor to accept, and the possibility of purchasing new beds and facilities for the emergency unit might have to be considered (see Figure 4.4). $f^1(x)$ may be evaluated using Exercise 1(iii) of the Queueing Exercises of Chapter 2. $f^2(x)$ is, initially, judgemental.

In each of the examples given there is a hierarchy of types of action listed. Ornea et al. [121] rank actions in terms of operational, technological, and investment. In principle, one can consider the combinations of all such

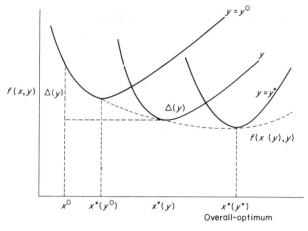

Figure 4.3

possibilities as one grand action and, indeed, this is the ideal Operational Research study. In practice however, this is very difficult to do, although limited attempts do exist to consider such combinations (e.g. see Ornea *et al.* [121] who consider a catalytic reforming operation).

As has been seen in the case of the depth charge problem, a study of one action (depth charge setting) leads naturally to the consideration of other actions (depth charge filler, submarine location). It is not necessary, in this case, that the latter decisions be considered, although it might be desirable. For some problems, however, it can be positively dangerous not to consider related areas of action. Consider the following very simplified inventory

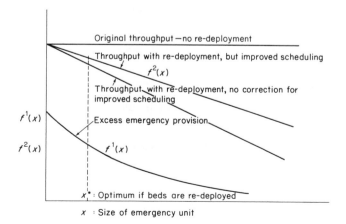

Figure 4.4

problem, the purpose of which is to illustrate the dangers. It adds another dimension to the inventory/production problems we have already considered. It also illustrates the need to know who the decision makers are, and is touched upon when discussing Reitman's format.

The initial request for a study came from the inventory control section, who based their decisions on what they knew of production requirements, together with knowledge of statistical changes in those requirements, and on replenishment patterns of the supplies. The production control based their decisions on what they knew about their requirements, existing inventory, and statistical changes in inventory. The two control sections were highly inter-related, but their decisions were not coordinated, and this can be dangerous.

Let us consider the following simple model of how decisions might be taken over a period of time, where: decisions are made at the beginning of each period t; D_t is the demand in period t; P_t is the production in period t; d_t is the new demand in period t (D_t allows for backlogs); and I_t is the inventory available in period t. Let us assume that:

(i) the production controller knows I_t at the beginning of period t, as well as D_t, and meets the demand requirement exactly if he can, and otherwise as much as he can, and hence we have:

$$P_t = \min[D_t, I_t]$$

where the production decision for period t is made at the beginning of period t;

(ii) the inventory controller does not know P_{t+1} in period $t+1$, and is always one step behind, and estimates P_{t+1} as being equal to the previous P_t, setting out to ensure that I_{t+1} matches P_t, subject to any known carry over from period t, and using the rule:

$$I_{t+1} = \max[P_t, I_t - P_t].$$

Thus the inventory controller has to plan ahead one period.

The demand equation is:

$$D_{t+1} = d_{t+1} + D_t - P_t.$$

Let us examine the possible behaviour of such rules.

Let us suppose we begin with $d_t = 0$ or 1.

(a) If $I_1 = 0$ then $P_1 = 0$; $I_2 = 0$ and so on, and $I_t = P_t = 0$ $\forall t$; D_t increases indefinitely if enough d_ts equal 1.

(b) If $I_1 = 1$. Assume $I_t = 1$. Then $P_t \leqslant 1$, $I_{t+1} = 1$. Hence $I_t = 1$ for all t. Then we have:

$$P_t = \min[D_t, 1]$$
$$D_{t+1} = d_{t+1} + D_t - P_t.$$

Combining these we have:

$$D_{t+1} = d_{t+1} + D_t - \min[D_t, 1]$$
$$= d_{t+1} + D_t - 1, \quad \text{if} \quad D_t \geqslant 1$$
$$= d_{t+1}, \quad \text{if} \quad D_t \leqslant 1.$$

We have $D_1 = d_1 \leqslant 1$. Assume $D_t = d_t \leqslant 1$. Then $D_{t+1} = d_{t+1} \leqslant 1$. Hence $D_t = d_t \leqslant 1$ for all t, and $P_t = D_t = d_t \leqslant 1$ for all t, and $I_t = 1$ for all t. Hence we keep a stock of 1 unit all the time, even though the demands may be 0 most of the time, which may be far from economic.

This example merely shows the potential errors if decision making is not integrated enough.

There are some problems in which, after investigation, the original type of action might be virtually removed from consideration. This can occur, for example, in some routing problems. The actual routing problem can, as we have seen in Chapter 2, be quite complex to solve, and anything which can ease this problem is to be valued. The complexity of solution depends upon the pattern of demand to be met by the vehicle fleet providing the service. If the pattern of demand can be suitably influenced, the routing problem may become easier. Thus, for a company delivering and picking up items for particular customers, a pricing system, which would influence the timing of requirements and nature of requirements, might result in very cost effective routes being possible. In a hospital appointments system, collaboration between those making appointments and the ambulance schedulers might result in routes being possible which are both cost effective and provide acceptable service. These examples are similar to the one involving production and inventory decisions.

4.2.2.2 Formal Specification of Feasible Actions

Explicit and implicit forms

The two basic forms of specification are the explicit and implicit forms.

The explicit form involves a straight enumeration of the actions open to the decision maker. Thus, for example: in queueing problems, the feasible set might be: $X = \{$one server or two servers$\}$, $X = \{$one of two specified service rates$\}$; in warehouse location problems, the feasible set might be $X = \{$locate a warehouse in one of two regions$\}$, $X = \{$one of two warehouse sizes$\}$.

The implicit form involves a statement of the boundaries of the options open to the decision maker in algebraic form. Thus, for example: in queueing problems, the number of servers may be quite open to analysis but subject to constraints on service cost and on waiting time such as:

$$0 \leqslant x \leqslant \bar{x}, \qquad x \text{ integer}$$
$$\hat{w}(x) \leqslant \bar{w}$$

where x is the number of servers, and $\hat{w}(x)$ is the expected waiting time of a customer in the system.

Of course, in the simple explicit queueing example, the statement that $x = 1$ or $x = 2$ can be put in the implicit form. The essential difference is that the implicit form does not involve, or may not even permit, an explicit enumeration of options. Thus, in linear programming, constraints take the form:

$$\sum_{j=1}^{n} a_{ij}x \leq b_i, \qquad i = 1, 2, \ldots, p, \qquad x_j \geq 0, \qquad j = 1, 2, \ldots, n.$$

In this case we cannot enumerate the members of X, and the decision maker perceives his problem options simply in terms of the $\{b_i\}$.

There is, of course, the question of generating the actions to be considered; but we will not discuss this in this text. Later on, we will discuss the cyclical nature of problem formulation and the generation of actions is part of this. Abel *et al.* [1], Graham [66], consider specifically the problem of identifying problems and, in particular, generating the actions to be considered.

Hard and soft constraints

Constraints take one of two forms. They are either hard or soft.

A hard constraint is one which cannot physically be broken. Thus, for example, in the salvo problem of Chapter 1, the constraints;

$$\sum_{s=-\infty}^{\infty} x_{ts} = 1, \qquad \forall t$$

where $\{x_{ts}\}$ are probabilities, must be logically satisfied. This applies to many other problems such as the traveling salesman problem, warehouse location problems, etc., which involve logically necessary constraints when particular mathematical programming forms are used.

There are other hard constraints which are not logically necessary, but which follow from the physical impossibility of violating them. Thus (see Chapter 2, section 2.5, on Mathematical and Dynamic Programming) the resources available for the problem on hand may not be subject to variation within the time span of the problem concerned, e.g. manpower, number of machines, etc. For production scheduling there may be precedence constraints which physically prevent one activity being carried out before a second one has been completed.

A soft constraint, on the other hand, is one that represents a value judgement that it would lead to an unacceptable decision if it were broken. It can be physically violated, but the decision maker requires that it should not be. The queueing constraint:

$$\hat{w}(x) \leq \bar{w}$$

falls into this category, and merely implies that it is undesirable to break it.

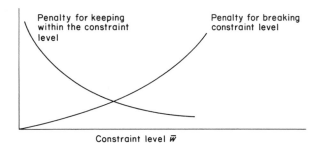

Figure 4.5

However, without some analysis of the penalties for breaking and not breaking this constraint, such a constraint might not be appropriate, and some form of constraint analysis is really required, such as given by Figure 4.5.

If, of course, the penalty for violating constraint levels were explicitly representable in some form, the constraints would really disappear. Thus, if we knew what the cost of each level of $w(x)$ was in terms of its impact on customers, we would merely incorporate $\hat{w}(x)$ into the objective function. Soft constraints are really objectives stated in another form (e.g. see Duesing [46]). However, for some problems, it is not easy to get explicit relationships between degree of violation of constraints and the external effects. All we may be able to do is to examine the effect of such constraints on loss of performance in terms of those objectives which are so expressible in terms of constraint levels. Kendall [90] discusses, for example, hard and soft constraints in linear programming.

Let us now turn our attention to constraint analysis. In doing so we refer to section 3.7 of Chapter 3 on parametric analysis as well, where this aspect has been mentioned in that context. In this section we do not restrict ourselves to small variations of constraint levels.

Constraint analysis

We begin with two problems which we have already studied. The first is the maintenance problem of Chapter 2, now set in the context of constraints. The second is the Inventory Exercise 2 of Chapter 2.

For the maintenance problem, we examine the effect of a constraint on the total work load, W, which the maintenance crew are prepared to accept. Such a constraint may be imposed in the initial formulation of the problem. It is clearly a soft constraint.

If x is the maintenance frequency, m^{-1} is the mean time to carry out a routine maintenance activity, μ^{-1} is the mean time to carry out a repair on failure, and $\lambda(x)$ is the arrival rate of failures, given x, then the total work

228

load on the maintenance/repair team is:

$$W(x) = \frac{x}{m} + \frac{\lambda(x)}{\mu}.$$

The workforce may insist that, if W_0 is the present work load, $W(x) \leq W_0$. This reduces to:

$$\frac{x}{m} + \frac{\lambda(x)}{\mu} \leq W_0.$$

The total profit (see Chapter 2, section 2.3) is:

$$f(x) = \left(1 - \frac{\lambda(x)}{\mu} - \frac{x}{m}\right)V - \frac{\lambda(x)}{\mu}R - \frac{x}{m}M.$$

For the special case $\lambda(x) = \lambda/x$, we obtain:

$$\frac{x}{m} + \frac{\lambda}{x\mu} \leq W_0$$

$$f(x) = V - \left(\frac{\lambda}{\mu}\right)(V+R)/x - \frac{(V+M)}{m}x.$$

Figure 4.6 illustrates the analysis.

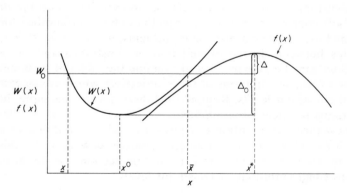

Figure 4.6

x^0 is optimal for the work force; x^* is optimal for profit $\underline{x}$, $\bar{x}$ are the limits of x which satisfy the constraints.
From Chapter 2, section 2.3:

$$x^* = \sqrt{(m\rho(V+R)/(V+M))}, \qquad (\rho = \lambda/\mu)$$
$$f(x^*) = V - 2\sqrt{(\rho(V+R)(V+M)/m)}.$$

Converting the constraints into a quadratic inequality, we have:

$$x^2 - W_0 mx + \rho m \leq 0.$$

The values of $\underline{x}$, $\bar{x}$ are given by equality in the above, and we assume the roots are real, i.e. $m^2 W_0^2 \geqslant 4\rho m$, to obtain:

$$x^0 = \sqrt{(\rho m)}, \qquad \bar{x} = (m W_0 + \sqrt{(m^2 W_0^2 - 4m\rho)})/2,$$
$$\underline{x} = (m W_0 - \sqrt{(m^2 W_0^2 - 4m\rho)})/2.$$

At $x = x^*$:

$$W^* = (\rho/m)\left(\sqrt{\left(\frac{V+R}{V+M}\right)} + \sqrt{\left(\frac{V+M}{V+R}\right)}\right).$$

If $W^* \leqslant W_0$, the constraint is not binding.

Alternatively we can check if $\underline{x} \leqslant x^* \leqslant \bar{x}$.

The loss in optimality, $f(x^*) - f(x)$, may be calculated at $\underline{x}$, x^0, $\bar{x}$. If we calculate it at x^0, we obtain:

$$\begin{aligned}
\Delta_0 &= V - 2\sqrt{(\rho(V+R)(V+M)/m)} \\
&\quad - (V - \rho(V+R)/\sqrt{(\rho m)} - (V+M)\sqrt{(\rho m)}/m) \\
&= \sqrt{(\rho/m)}((V+R) + (V+M) - 2\sqrt{((V+R)(V+M))}) \\
&= \sqrt{(\rho/m)}(\sqrt{(V+R)} - \sqrt{(V+M)})^2.
\end{aligned}$$

Note that, if $R = M$, then $x^0 = x^*$, and $\Delta_0 = 0$.

Δ_0 is useful for negotiation purposes if resistance to movement from x^0 is encountered. Otherwise if anything between $\underline{x}$ and $\bar{x}$ is acceptable, we have to calculate $\Delta = f(x^*) - f(\bar{x})$ if x^* does not lie between $\underline{x}$ and $\bar{x}$.

Now consider the simple stock-control problem of Inventory Exercise 2, Chapter 2, where we now have n items, where: c_j is the unit purchase cost of the jth item; a_j is the fixed cost for the jth item; h_j is the unit holding cost per unit time of the jth item; and s_j is the annual demand for the jth item; for all j, $h_j = \alpha c_j$, where α is constant; the company places a limit b on the average total cash value of all items held at any time. Let us see how the significance of b may be obtained.

In the following we take a simple direct approach to the problem. However, for those who wish to do so, it is possible to use a straight inequality Lagrange multiplier approach to derive the results (e.g. see Donaldson *et al.* [43]).

We will first of all ignore the constraint. This is a useful dodge in some cases since, if the unconstrained optimum satisfies the constraints, it is optimal for the constrained problem.

Unconstrained problem

From standard theory, if $\{f_j^*, x_j^*\}$ are the minimal annual variable costs, and optimal order quantities, respectively, for the jth item, we have, if s_j is the annual demand:

$$f_j^* = \sqrt{(2\alpha a_j s_j c_j)}$$
$$x_j^* = \sqrt{(2a_j s_j/\alpha c_j)}.$$

The total variable annual cost is then:

$$f^* = \sum_{j=1}^{n} f_j^* = \sqrt{(2\alpha)} \sum_{j=1}^{n} \sqrt{(a_j s_j c_j)}.$$

For the optimal solution given by the above, the average total stock value is:

$$b^0 = \sum_{j=1}^{n} c_j \tfrac{1}{2} x_j^* = (1/\sqrt{(2\alpha)}) \sum_{j=1}^{n} \sqrt{(a_j s_j c_j)}$$

and, from this we, have:

$$f^* = 2\alpha b^0.$$

Constrained problem

Now b^0 is the smallest value of the constraint level b for which $\{x_j^*\}$ will solve the constrained problem, i.e. no effective constraints on $\{x_j\}$ exist. The reasons are as follows.

Let $b \geqslant b^0$, and our constraint be $\sum_{j=1}^{n} c_j \tfrac{1}{2} x_j \leqslant b$. Then, since

$$\sum_{j=1}^{n} c_j \tfrac{1}{2} x_j^* = b^0 \leqslant b,$$

we may choose $\{x_j\} = \{x_j^*\}$ to satisfy the constraint, and hence this is the optimal solution. We cannot do better than using the individual unconstrained optima.

Let $b < b^0$, and our constraint be

$$\sum_{j=1}^{n} c_j \tfrac{1}{2} x_j \leqslant b.$$

Then, for any constrained optimal solution, $\{x_j\}$ we have:

$$\sum_{j=1}^{n} c_j \tfrac{1}{2} x_j \leqslant b < b^0 = \sum_{j=1}^{n} c_j \tfrac{1}{2} x_j^*.$$

Hence we must have some $x_j < x_j^*$, and $\{x_j^*\}$ cannot be optimal.

We also see that, if $b < b^0$ and $\{x_j\}$ is optimal, we must have:

$$\sum_{j=1}^{n} c_j \tfrac{1}{2} x_j = b.$$

This follows since, if we have a strict inequality in the constraint, we must have $x_j < x_j^*$ for some j. We could increase x_j, for this j, still keeping within the constraint

$$\sum_{j=1}^{n} c_j \tfrac{1}{2} x_j \leqslant b,$$

and decreasing the contributing cost of x_j, and hence decreasing the total cost.

Hence, when $b < b^0$, the constrained problem becomes one of:

$$\text{minimizing}\left[f(x) = \sum_{j=1}^{n} (\alpha c_j \tfrac{1}{2}x_j + a_j s_j / x_j) \right]$$

subject to the equality constraint above (the non-negativity conditions should be added, but our solutions are non-negative in any case).

To solve this, we introduce a Lagrange multiplier, λ, to give a Lagrangean as follows, where, $x = (x_1, x_2, \ldots, x_n)$:

$$l(x, \lambda) = f(x) + \tfrac{1}{2}\lambda \sum_{j=1}^{n} c_j x_j = \sum_{j=1}^{n} (\tfrac{1}{2}x_j(\alpha + \lambda)c_j + a_j s_j / x_j).$$

We have chosen not to incorporate the constraint level b into the Lagrangean since it merely adds a constant, $-b$, to the Lagrangean and may be ignored when optimizing.

We minimize $l(x, \lambda)$ over x to give a solution for x as a function of λ, and then substitute in the constraint to obtain λ, and then use this to find x. We assume $\alpha + \lambda > 0$, which is required to ensure that $l(x, \lambda)$ has a finite minimum. Putting $\partial l / \partial x_j = 0$ we obtain:

$$x_j^{**} = \sqrt{(2 a_j s_j / c_j(\alpha + \lambda))}.$$

Substituting $\{x_j^{**}\}$ in the constraint we obtain:

$$b = (1/\sqrt{(\alpha + \lambda)}) \sum_{j=1}^{n} \sqrt{(a_j s_j c_j / 2)}.$$

From this we obtain:

$$b = \sqrt{(\alpha/(\alpha + \lambda))}\, b^0.$$

Substituting $\{x_j^{**}\}$ into $f(x)$ we obtain, using the above:

$$f^* = (\alpha/\sqrt{(\alpha + \lambda)}) \sum_{j=1}^{n} \sqrt{(a_j s_j c_j / 2)} + \sqrt{(\alpha + \lambda)} \sum_{j=1}^{n} \sqrt{(a_j s_j c_j / 2)}$$

$$= \alpha b + \sqrt{(\alpha(\alpha + \lambda))}\, b^0$$

$$= \alpha b + \alpha b^{02}/b,$$

Combining the results we have, if f^* is the solution to our initial problem, we have:

$$f^* \doteq 2\alpha b^0 \qquad \text{if} \quad b \geqslant b^0$$

$$= \alpha b + \alpha b^{02}/b \quad \text{if} \quad b \leqslant b^0.$$

This is given in Figure 4.7. It enables us to see what the loss in optimality is for variations in b.

On the basis of this analysis it is possible to re-examine the validity of any original constraint placed upon cash tied up in stock, for whatever reason this might have been originally imposed. If the constraint is placed merely because this causes a loss of interest, or increases overdraft payments, it

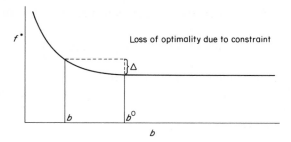

Figure 4.7

should be possible to incorporate this directly into the objective function f. If it is merely that the company wishes to remain fluid enough to meet contingencies, and it is difficult to incorporate this directly into f, the previous analysis at least sets this in a proper context.

The analysis in the last problem is particularly simple. Not all problems are analysable in such precise analytic terms. However, the Lagrange multiplier method used is of general importance in such analysis.

We first of all note that the method is not foolproof, i.e. it is not always true that, for a given constraint level, a Lagrange multiplier will exist which will give us the required level exactly satisfied in the solution. This may arise because no feasible solution exists at this constraint level. However, even if such a feasible solution existed, the constraint may not be satisfied exactly by the solution obtained. For the inventory problem, if $\lambda \geqslant 0$, we must have $b \leqslant b_0$ for it to work. If we allow $-\infty < \lambda < \infty$, we may allow b to range over all possible values although the penalty interpretation of λ may disappear with $\lambda < 0$. For some problems there may exist no λ, whether positive, zero or negative, which enables particular constraint levels to be exactly met (e.g. see Donaldson *et al.* [43]). We refer the reader to, for example, Whittle [173], for a rigorous analysis of such problems.

However, even though there may be gaps in the constraint levels which are amenable to such an approach, we do have two very useful results of Everett [57], which are also studied in Donaldson *et al.* [43]. Let us restate our general mathematical programming problem of section 2.5 of Chapter 2:

$$P: \text{maximize}[f(x)]$$

$$\text{subject to}$$

$$g_i(x) \leqslant b_i, \qquad i = 1, 2, \ldots, p.$$

The inequalities may include non-negativity constraints and, in addition, x may contain integer components. If so, then Y as defined below is also so restricted.

Also similar analysis applies for minimization problems.

Let us now consider a constraint analysis of the constraints $k + 1$, $k + 2, \ldots, p$, by introducing non-negative Lagrange multipliers λ_{k+1},

$\lambda_{k+2}, \ldots, \lambda_p$. The Lagrangean is:

$$l(x, \lambda) = f(x) - \sum_{i=k+1}^{p} \lambda_i g_i(x)$$

and the new feasible region for x is:

$$Y = \{x : g_i(x) \leqslant b_i, \quad i = 1, 2, \ldots, k\}.$$

Everett's result is as follows.

Let $x(\lambda)$ maximize $l(x, \lambda)$ subject to $x \in Y$, and $b_i(\lambda) = g_i(x(\lambda))$, $i = k+1$, $k+2, \ldots, p$. Then $x(\lambda)$ is optimal for the following problem, $I(\lambda)$:

$I(\lambda)$: maximize$[f(x)]$

subject to

$x \in Y$

$g_i(x) \leqslant b_i(\lambda), \quad i = k+1, k+2, \ldots, p.$

The proof is as follows.

$x(\lambda)$ is clearly feasible for the latter problem. Let y also be feasible for this problem. Then, with $x = x(\lambda)$,

$$f(x) - f(y) = l(x, \lambda) - l(y, \lambda) + \sum_{i=k+1}^{p} \lambda_i(g_i(x) - g_i(y))$$
$$\geqslant l(x, \lambda) - l(y, \lambda) \geqslant 0$$

after noting that $y \in Y$ implies the right-hand inequality.

It is easy to see from this, or by direct analysis, that the following is also true, where $\{\lambda_i\}$ are unsigned.

Let $x(\lambda)$ maximize $l(x, \lambda)$ subject to $x \in Y$, and $b_i(\lambda) = g_i(x(\lambda))$, $i = k+1$, $k+2, \ldots, p$. Then $x(\lambda)$ is optimal for the following problem, $E(\lambda)$:

$E(\lambda)$: maximize$[f(x)]$

subject to

$x \in Y$

$g_i(x) = b_i(\lambda), \quad i = k+1, k+2, \ldots, p.$

The inequalities defining Y could equally well be equalities. Also we can mix problems $E(\lambda)$ and $I(\lambda)$, allowing some equalities and some in-equalities.

If we return to the original problem, P, for a given $\{b_i\}$, and if $\{\lambda_i\}$ are such that $b_i(\lambda) \leqslant b_i$, (i.e. $x(\lambda)$ is feasible for b), $i = k+1, k+2, \ldots, p$, then, for $I(\lambda)$, it is easy to derive the following inequalities, for any optimal solution x to P, viz.

$$f(x(\lambda)) \leqslant f(x) \leqslant f(x(\lambda)) + \sum_{i=k+1}^{p} \lambda_i(b_i - b_i(\lambda)).$$

The proof is as follows.

Since $x(\lambda)$ is feasible for b, then, if x is optimal for b, we must have $f(x(\lambda)) \leq f(x)$.

Since $x(\lambda)$ is optimal for the Lagrangean we must have: $l(x(\lambda), \lambda) \geq l(x, \lambda)$, i.e.

$$f(x(\lambda)) - \sum_{i=k+1}^{p} \lambda_i g_i(x(\lambda)) \geq f(x) - \sum_{i=1}^{p} \lambda_i g_i(x)$$

Thus:

$$f(x) \leq f(x(\lambda)) + \sum_{i=1}^{p} \lambda_i (g_i(x) - g_i(x(\lambda)))$$

$$= f(x(\lambda)) + \sum_{i=1}^{p} \lambda_i (g_i(x) - b_i(\lambda))$$

$$\leq f(x(\lambda)) + \sum_{i=1}^{p} \lambda_i (b_i - b_i(\lambda)).$$

These results allow us to study the effects of variations in $\{b_i\}$.

In order to illustrate this, let us look at the Redundancy Problem of Chapter 1, also discussed in the text of Chapter 3, for the case when $n = 2$, $c(1) = 3$, $c(2) = 1$, $q(1) = 0.8$, $q(2) = 0.5$. The problem becomes the following, in inequality form:

maximize$[f(x) = (1 - 0.2^{x_1})(1 - 0.5^{x_2})]$

subject to

$3x_1 + x_2 \leq b$

$x \geq 0$, and integer.

We set $Y = \{x : x \geq 0,$ and integer$\}$, and bring the other constraint into the Lagrangean, to give the following, by taking logarithms of $f(x)$:

$$l(x, \lambda) = \log(1 - 0.2^{x_1}) + \log(1 - 0.5^{x_2}) - 3\lambda x_1 - \lambda x_2.$$

The following results are obtained (taken from Donaldson *et al.* [43]), given in Table 4.1, where, for simplicity we have assumed that $x_1 \leq 4$, $x_2 \leq 4$.

Table 4.1

λ	0–0.0021	0.0021–0.011	0.011–0.061	0.061–0.069	0.069–0.153	0.153–0.408	0.408–∞
$x_1(\lambda)$	4	3	2	1	1	1	1
$x_2(\lambda)$	4	4	4	4	3	2	1
$b(\lambda)$	16	13	10	7	6	5	4

Thus, if the original problem had $b = 15$, not covered by the above analysis, using the solution $x = (3, 4)$ would give a maximal error of $2(0.0021) = 0.0042$.

Note that, at the jump points of λ, either $x(\lambda)$ solution for the adjacent ranges will apply.

Everett's results are particularly useful for large combinatorial and dynamic problems. Thus, for example, if we wished to consider any of the dynamic probabilistic optimization problems, discussed in Chapter 2, sections 2.1–2.4, as multi-objective problems, then the Lagrange multiplier results, without necessarily producing all the requisite solutions, may produce acceptable solutions.

It is to be noted that the use of the Lagrange multiplier method is purely a computational device, and it is not intended that they be interpreted as weighting factors for constraints seen as objectives. In some special cases, when duality theory applies, (e.g. see Whittle [173]), λ_i is equal to the rate of change of the optimal value of f with respect to b_i at the point $b = b(\lambda)$. This applies particularly in the case of linear programming.

Further aspects of constraints

For some problems, constraints are deliberately introduced to serve special purposes in the absence of knowledge about certain effects, or deliberately to cut down the number of options which have to be finally considered.

Let us consider these.

Constraints as surrogates for uncertainty

Let us consider the depth charge problem of Chapter 1, and suppose that we are unsure about the actual damage that an explosion at a distance z between the U-boat and the depth charge would cause. We know that the damage depends on z, and, in order to put some control on this, we might stipulate that the depth x is to be such that, for some $\alpha > 0$, $p > 0$:

$$\text{probability}(|z| \leqslant \alpha) \geqslant p.$$

This may be done in the belief that small z values give high damage levels, without knowing exactly what damage may be caused. Of course, for specific parameters, such a formulation may have no feasible solution.

Another common constraint of this form arises in inventory control, relating to inventory shortages. If z is the shortage in any specified period, a constraint may be imposed of the form, for some $\alpha > 0$, $p > 0$:

$$\text{probability}(z \leqslant \alpha) \geqslant p.$$

Again this is set in the belief that large shortages are undesirable, without knowing exactly what the effects of shortages are on future performance.

The reader should look back through the previous material in the text, including exercises, to try to identify situations in which this ploy is likely to have to be used. In such circumstances the need to do some constraint analysis assumes a significant level.

Constraints as a means of reducing problem size

As we impose more constraints the size of the feasible region will reduce, at least for effective constraints. For general mathematical programming problems, this procedure actually makes the calculations much harder to do. Thus, the more constraints we have in linear programming, the higher the computational demand becomes.

However, there are certain classes of combinatorial problem, which we have already discussed, which do require some prior imposition of constraints in some form to make the problem manageable.

A typical problem is that of selecting bus routes, as described in Exercise 4 of the Mathematical and Dynamic Programming Exercises of Chapter 2. This problem is discussed in more detail in Lampkin *et al.* [95] and Bel *et al.* [14].

The first task is to identify a set of good routes from which the final set of routes may be chosen, for example by the integer linear programming method suggested in the Exercise 4 mentioned above. The total number of routes can be very large, and it is therefore necessary to reduce these to a sensible subset in the first instance. This is accomplished by imposing constraints which rule out routes which are thought not to be good (although actual goodness may depend on how they fit in with other routes).

Some properties required of good routes are as follows:

 (i) they should be reasonably direct and not meander excessively;
 (ii) they should facilitate changing as part of the collection of routes;
(iii) most routes for which a reasonably large potential passenger demand exists should be included.

Similar situations exist for other combinatorial type problems. Thus the cutting stock problem of the Mathematical and Dynamic Programming section (2.5) of Chapter 2, and mentioned in the Heuristic Programming section (2.8) of Chapter 2, can give rise to many possibilities when generalized to problems where various different shapes and sizes have to be cut from raw material. Harrison *et al.* [71] deal with the problem of cutting pieces of wood from raw material pieces for a furniture manufacturer. There is the question of which combinations should be included in the initial set, and good combinations are required to meet upper limit constraints on waste and complexity, for example. Similarly, the timetabling example of Exercise 3 of the Mathematical and Dynamic Programming Exercises raises similar issues.

It should also be added that the restriction of decision rules to take particular forms (e.g. see the Inventory Section (2.2) of Chapter 2) is also a form of constrained analysis, which has the purpose of making the analysis more tractable, although, in some cases, such restrictions may still give solutions optimal within a broader class of policies.

4.2.3 The Objectives

When considering actions designed to control his object system, the decision maker (the subject system) will have certain behavioural aspects of the object system in mind as determinants of the final decision he will take. For example, in an inventory control situation, as we have seen, the behaviour of the system being controlled may be described in terms of identifiable cash payments, the levels of inventory held, the extent of shortages, and so on. These are the so called consequences, outcomes, events, or, broadly speaking, objectives related to the contemplated actions. Without some identification of such objectives, there can be no basis for rationalizing decisions as to which action to take.

A glance at the literature will, even in the context of a single problem situation, show that the number of such objectives which may have a bearing on the decision can be quite large. Cyert *et al.* [36] mention five groups of objectives, viz. profit, production, inventory, sales, and market share. Birkin *et al.* [21] list 51 individual objectives, all in the context of a single problem, viz. the control of defective production, which we discussed in Chapter 2, section 2.4, including such things as success in meeting schedules, productivity per operator, production errors, administrative errors, inspection errors, and so on.

One of the obvious questions which arises is: why do we need so many objectives? Should we not be able to reduce these objectives to a common denominator? Let us take a brief look at this question.

Reducibility to a Common Denominator

If one were concerned with government policies, the obvious objective which springs to mind is quality of life, and it is tempting to try to reduce everything, whether in the defence area, employment area, or educational area, to such terms. Needless to say, even if this were possible in principle, the requisite effort to achieve this reduction would be prohibitively large. Even the task of defining what is meant by quality of life can be demanding. House [80] discusses certain aspects of this problem, and gives related references.

Klahr [92] goes even further, and says that it is more meaningful to treat objectives as separate objectives, rather than to seek a common denominator. He gives two examples. The first one is an example taken from a business context, where profit and volume of business are cited. The second is a military example concerning the design of an aircraft, where range, cruising speed, and spurt speed are cited.

The profit and volume objectives cited are only two of the many appearing in the references given so far, but let us look at these. Is it not credible that the real business objective is some measure of profit, i.e. net income after all expenses have been deducted, for a specified time period? It is true the business volume is important, but is it really only important because it influences profit? For some situations this may be true, but, in some instances, this may not be so. Thus the owner of a business might be quite prepared to operate at a level of business for which his profits are not maximal because he values the contribution his business gives to society, in terms of the addition to quality of life it gives. In such cases it does not seem meaningful to go any further, and the problem may be treated as a multi-objective problem to which we will turn later on. Even in the case where we might see profit as the objective, and business volume influencing it, it may be difficult to find, objectively, exactly what this influence is, and the decision maker may be left to exert his own judgement on this influence, thus, effectively, leaving the problem in a multi-objective form.

The second problem mentioned may be seen in terms of the probability of a kill in an aerial duel, and the factors mentioned would influence this. If such an objective were the real one, in principle one might reduce the factors to this one objective, but the effort involved may again be prohibitive, and again a multi-objective form may be the only real possibility.

Thus the answer to the question of reducibility is partly one of principle, and partly one of economic expedience, and will depend on the circumstances.

This discussion does raise the question of whether, for a particular objective, it should be expressed in terms of its effect on other objectives, and we will now discuss this.

Surrogate Objectives

In order to illustrate this, let us turn to the fire station Exercise 12 of the Mathematical and Dynamic Programming Exercises of Chapter 2. A central objective, in such a situation, is the time taken to get to an emergency if one arises. Now the time itself is not of central interest, and it is the effects of the fire which are important, viz. loss of life, injury, damage to property, and so on. However, the problem is stated in terms of time. Such an objective is a surrogate objective. It is easy to handle, and it is difficult to evaluate how it influences the main objectives.

Similar cases occur in control of blood banks (e.g. see Kendall et al. [91]), which includes among the objectives, blood shortages, and ageing of blood, each of which is a surrogate objective for the impact of blood policy on loss of life, disability, and so on. Mole [110] also discusses this problem. Such problems are nice instances of inventory problems which are not reducible to cash terms as those so far treated in this text have been. Even in standard cash-oriented inventory problems, such things as shortages may be used as surrogate objectives, in a multi-objective form, when the effect of such shortages would be too difficult to determine (see Carlson et al. [32]). The same applies to waiting time in queueing situations, equipment failure in maintenance problems, and so on.

Even when the general nature of the objectives has been determined, there is the question of the relevance of the objectives to the problem on hand. Let us turn to this.

Relevance of Objectives

Let us begin with queueing problems, discussed in Chapter 2, section 2.1. Saaty [138] and Feller [58], consider some objectives which might be relevant in queueing situations. These are as follows:

  (i) the probability that a unit joining a queue will not have to wait;
 (ii) the probability of a unit waiting in the queue greater than a specified time;
(iii) the average number of units in the system, both waiting and in service;
 (iv) the average number of units waiting in the queue;
  (v) the average waiting time in the system;
 (vi) the ratio of the average arrival rate to average service rate;
(vii) the ratio of the number of units in the queue to the number of servers;
(viii) the ratio of the average number of idle servers to the total number of servers.

In a given context, which of these, if any, are the relevant ones? If we are concerned with the effect of queue behaviour on customer behaviour, then one needs to determine what really influences the customers' behaviour. Psychologically, the very fact that one cannot be served straight away, in some cases, might be very important. Thus objective (i) might be relevant. On the other hand, if it is a matter of satisfying a customer's order, the time to do this may be important, and hence objective (v) might be important. Objective (iii) might not be relevant to the customer, but it might be relevant to the servicing operation since this might have financial consequences. Objective (viii) is a measure of utilization of facilities. In a hospital context this might be a measure of bed occupancy. But is this a real objective? This might be increased by asking all prospective patients to queue up until a bed becomes available, and this is nonsense. The real objective is patient care, and utilization need not represent this properly. Thus objective (viii) might very well be irrelevant. A similar situation arises on a factory floor, where machine utilization can be maximized by having large in-process stocks.

Of course, in some situations throughput rate might be a surrogate for patient service, in the hospital problem, or income, in the industrial problem, in which case, provided it is seen in the context of the point made, it would be relevant. In the case of deciding on the size of an emergency unit, it is not very relevant since, in order to give a high probability of a bed being available for an emergency, the occupancy of the unit is likely to be very small.

Hitch [76], discussing defence vs. offence, also stresses, in the context of the convoy problem of Chapter 1, the dangers of accepting plausible objectives without proper thought.

In Chapter 1 we discussed the redundancy problem, and in Chapter 2, section 2.3, we discussed maintenance problems, each of which involve considerations of equipment performance. Hosford [75] discusses these under the general heading of dependability measures. The objectives he gives are as follows:

(i) pointwise availability (operational readiness): the probability that the system will be able to operate within tolerance at a given instance in time;
(ii) reliability: the probability that the system will be able to operate without failure for a given interval of time;
(iii) interval availability (efficiency): the expected fraction of a given interval of time that the system will be able to operate within tolerances.

He illustrates these with an industrial and a military example.

In the industrial case: (i) is important at the beginning and end of day (no repairs required then); (ii) is important if it is important to have a machine available wholly for a given period; (iii) is important if the proportion of time available in a given week is important, even though (ii) may be low, because repairs might be quite quick.

In the military case, involving a radar tracking station: (iii) is important when the probability of the equipment working when it is needed is important; (ii) is important only when the radar must be working for the whole interval for it to be of any value.

One of the arguable issues in the area of objectives is the question of which costs (cash) are relevant in a given context. Stainton [151] discusses the question of storage costs in a production inventory problem, and points out that if the storage and staffing facilities are fixed, then it costs nothing to use them. White [168] raises the issue of overhead costs. These only become relevant to certain operational decisions when decisions are made to reduce or increase capacity.

Even in the standard simple economic order quantity inventory problem, where monetary cost is specified as an objective, it can be difficult to identify the exact monetary items to include. Thus we have assumed that $\{c, a, s, h\}$ are given in this problem, but exactly how should these be determined? Raw material may be bought at one price and the final product sold at another price, and the precise identification of the consequential cash flow is a little more complicated than the simple model suggests (e.g. see White [168]). Gardner [63] discusses some of the difficulties involved in finding the various parameters $\{c, a, s, h\}$ for the standard problem, for example the order cost is difficult to identify since order costs, as such, are very often spread across many items, and it is difficult to attribute such a cost to an individual item. The values used are really surrogates. A multi-objective approach to the problem may be the sensible thing to adopt. The standard value function:

$$v(x) = as/x + cs + \tfrac{1}{2}hx$$

may be justifiable on intuitive grounds, but the parameters $\{a, h\}$ might be subjectively derived somehow.

In the discussion on Reitman's format for problem formulation, the question was raised as to which of two objectives, viz. present worth (discounted cash flow) or payback period, should be used if a single objective is sought. Naturally one might think in terms of a multi-objective problem if it is not possible to reduce the analysis to a single one. It is a question of which are the relevant ones.

If the real objective is total cash generated over a period of time, then the present worth approach could be justified on the grounds of the cash generation power of cash. Thus, if money can be invested at a rate i per unit interval, then the income r_t, invested at the beginning of interval t, will accumulate to $r_t(1+i)^{n-t+1}$ at the end of interval n. Thus the total cash position for income stream $(r_1, r_2, \ldots, r_n)$ will be:

$$\sum_{t=1}^{n} r_t(1+i)^{n-t+1} = (1+i)^n \sum_{t=1}^{n} \alpha^{t-1} r_t$$

where $\alpha = (1+i)^{-1}$.

Thus, in the deterministic case, one might argue that this is the only objective, and that the payback period is irrelevant. Unfortunately, this is not always so simple, particularly where uncertainty arises in the value of i, and it is the desire to break even within the foreseeable future which makes the payback period attractive, although this can be dangerous for a situation where high losses occur after an early break-even point. If cash were the only objective, one could argue for the use of a utility approach to the problem. With other accompanying irreducible objectives, even if surrogate, this is not possible, and the relevance of the objectives must be examined in the context of the problem on hand. They are not the only possibilities (see, for example, Adelson [3]). Spronk [150] discusses a multi-objective approach to the problem. White [167] justifies the use of the discount approach for certain classes of problem involving uncertainty. Koopmans [93] justifies it for certain classes of deterministic problem. It should be noted that discounting may also have a psychological interpretation, representing the lower degree of concern with events further away in time.

In addition to the relevance of objectives there is also the question of form of statement of objectives, which we will now discuss.

Form of Statement of Objectives

Bennett [20] raises the question of whether objectives should be stated in terms of expected levels or probabilities of various levels being achieved. He discusses an inventory problem in which the possibilities of shortages are stated either in terms of expected shortages, or probabilities of shortages. In our inventory models we used expected shortages, on the assumption that the cash penalty was proportional to shortage, and we are dealing with a reasonably long time interval. If these circumstances do not hold, then the statement of objectives in terms of probability may be relevant in some circumstances, e.g. if the penalty for a shortage in a given interval is almost independent of the size of the shortage. If it is not, then the probability of these shortages becomes important. If the shortages have non-linear effects on penalties, expected shortage level is not important, e.g. see the discussion earlier on, on the impact of shortages on future demand. Thus, in the final analysis, the form of objectives we use may be a surrogate for the real objective, but some model is needed in principle to justify the form used.

This applies to all of our probabilistic models and, in particular, to the material of the previous section.

Let us now look at the context of the objectives.

Context of Objectives

Consider the queueing problem considered earlier on in section 4.2.1 of this chapter in which two objectives were discussed, viz. cost (monetary) and service. It was suggested that the decision maker might make a judgement as to the relative values (e.g. weighting factors) of each of these. However, the queueing situation is a small part of the total company operations, and the money required to achieve the service level sought might detract from money available for use in other areas of operation of the company. Hence the judgement of the value of service, in relationship to cost, should reflect the opportunities for use of cash elsewhere in the company.

Indeed, this applies whenever a particular objective requires resources which are not fixed and may detract from, or add to, other company operations which might make use of these resources. In principle, one might attempt a comprehensive model of all company operations, but this can be quite a difficult and costly exercise.

Hoag [78] discusses this sort of problem. For fixed resource inputs he says one can only try to find better ways of using these resources. He discusses this in the context of a problem in which resources are planes and fissile material, which can be used in various ways to attack two targets. He then enquires about the externalities involved if different combinations of planes and fissile material might be used as inputs. These resources will obviously detract from, or add to, other military operations.

His main point relates to the use of monetary value of the resources being considered. If one converted planes and fissile material to cash terms, this is, in itself, inadequate in reality, since the cash implications for other military operations are really only felt in terms of its influence on other resources such as manpower and equipment, and the effects of the same amounts of cash being available, or reduced, in different areas may be different.

This sort of analysis leads us to seek a common denominator, a topic already discussed. Baylis [13] attempts a reduction of all aspects of the armament of a ship to the common denominator of manpower. This is arguable. For example there is the question of the relative values of different types of manpower. However, the problem it was intended to help resolve still remains.

4.2.4 The Value Function

Given a set of feasible actions X, if $x, y \in X$:

$x \, \mathrm{R} \, y$ means x is at least as good as y,

$x \, \mathrm{P} \, y$ means x is preferred to y,

$x \, \mathrm{I} \, y$ means x is indifferent to y.

A value function is a real valued function v on X (see White [169]) such that:

$$x \, \mathrm{R} \, y \rightleftarrows v(x) \geqslant v(y)$$
$$x \, \mathrm{P} \, y \rightleftarrows v(x) > v(y)$$
$$x \, \mathrm{I} \, y \rightleftarrows v(x) = v(y).$$

It is, in effect, a single objective function on X and, in the section on objectives, if the objectives are reducible to a single one, this would be a value function.

We will not consider the various conditions for such a value function to exist. The reader can find these in White [166, 169], and Fishburn [59], and we return to this in Chapter 6.

Let us first of all consider the role such a function can play in Operational Research. For small problems it is not necessary to determine one. Thus, in the investment problem discussed in the context of Reitman's framework, it is conceivable that, for a few options, we could just present the time series of net cash flows and let the decision maker choose. The value function is merely an equivalent representation of the choice situation and adds nothing to such problems unless, of course, it is required that the choice be rationalized, a point to which we will return. For large problems, however, the situation is somewhat different, and a value function enables such problems to be formally evaluated. Thus, for example, consider the difficulties which would be involved in solving a linear programming problem without an explicit representation of preferences in the form of a single objective function which is a value function. A glance at the Mathematical and Dynamic Programming section (2.5) of Chapter 2 will give emphasis to this, as will a glance at the problems discussed in the context of heuristics in Chapter 2. Aumann et al. [10], for example, discuss the absolute necessity of such a value function in a very large assignment problem involving assigning a range of equipment to a range of positions on a ship. This is not to say that there are no problems in finding such value functions, an aspect treated later on in this chapter, in multi-objective interactive programming, but merely to emphasize the positive role it can play.

Let us now look at the problem from the point of view of multiple objectives, where we have m objectives, $\{f^i\}$ $i = 1, 2, \ldots, m$, each being a function on X, and for the moment, let us assume that no chance factors are explicit in the problem. A value function on X may be derived from a value function u on $f(X)$ (all the objective function vectors obtainable by taking some $x \in X$) by setting:

$$v(x) = u(f(x)).$$

Note that $f(x)$ is the vector $(f^1(x), f^2(x), \ldots, f^m(x))$.

The methods of finding v, or u, are implicit in the foundations of decision theory (e.g. see White [166, 169] and Fishburn [59]), and there are (a) the descriptive point of view, which attempts to derive v, u, on the basis of observing choice, and (b) the normative or prescriptive point of view, which attempts to derive v, u, on the basis of how choices ought to be made. We will not discuss these, but they are important issues. Whatever the case, if one believes that decision makers do, or can be led to, have preferences between sets of objective levels, one must have some preference model, which may be a value function, which can then be used in the sense described. If no such preference elicitation is accepted, then there is no point in doing any Operational Research.

The common value function takes the form:

$$u(f) = \sum_{i=1}^{m} \lambda_i f^i, \qquad \sum_{i=1}^{m} \lambda_i = 1, \qquad \lambda_i \geqslant 0, \quad \forall i.$$

This has, of course, to be justified in the context of the particular problem on hand. More general forms are given in Keeney *et al.* [89] for special value functions, called utility functions, to which we will return later on and in Chapter 6.

The value functions are, of course, merely equivalent to some order relations $\{R, P, I\}$ as defined, and it is possible to carry out the analysis in the latter form, although the value function form has certain advantages (e.g. if differentiable we may use calculus). Klahr [92] discusses a potential preference structure which is by no means as simple as the linear case. The two objectives are:

$$f^1 = \text{profit}, \qquad f^2 = \text{volume}.$$

The $\{(f^1, f^2)\}$ space is partitioned into four regions for which $\{\lambda_1, \lambda_2, \alpha, \underline{f}^1, \underline{f}^2\}$ are specified scalar parameters. The regions are as given below:

$$F_1 = \{f : f^1 > \underline{f}^1, f^2 > \underline{f}^2, f^1 < \alpha f^2\}$$
$$F_2 = \{f : f^1 > \underline{f}^1, f^2 > \underline{f}^2, f^1 > \alpha f^2\}$$
$$F_3 = \{f : f^1 < \underline{f}^1, f^2 > \underline{f}^2\}$$
$$F_4 = \{f : f^2 < \underline{f}^2\}.$$

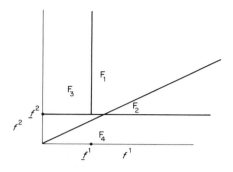

Figure 4.8

Figure 4.8 illustrates this situation. This example is used, not as one which reflects a likely situation, but merely to show that, even in some rather unusual cases, it is still possible to model the situation in terms of value functions, up to a point, i.e. excluding the boundary lines between the regions. The reader may find it useful to consider whether the preference structure of Figure 4.8 is a reasonable one, and, if not, why not. It is as important to study the reasonableness of a decision maker's preferences as it is to model them for further analysis.

The regions F_1–F_4 have highest preferences in this order, and in each of the regions the regional value functions are as follows:

$$\text{in } F_1: \ u_1(f) = f^1,$$
$$\text{in } F_2: \ u_2(f) = \lambda_1 f^1 + \lambda_2 f^2,$$
$$\text{in } F_3: \ u_3(f) = f^1,$$
$$\text{in } F_4: \ u_4(f) = f^2.$$

The model does not specify what the preferences are on the boundaries of the regions and to do so would introduce inconsistencies, or discontinuities (e.g. on the F_3/F_4 boundary). Nonetheless it is a preference structure and it has a value function. In fact define $\delta_i(f) = 1$ if $f \in F_i$, $\delta_i(f) = 0$ otherwise, and then, if $\lambda_1, \lambda_2 > 0$:

$$u(f) = \sum_{i=1}^{4} \delta_i(f)\phi_i(u_i(f)), \qquad \phi_i(\omega) = 4 - i - e^{-\omega}, \qquad i = 1, 2, 3, 4, \quad \forall \omega \in \mathbb{R}^1$$

is a value function, except on the boundary lines.

As has been mentioned, the proper determination of value functions does raise some issues, such as the descriptive/prescriptive issue. To leave it merely to a process of description opens up the possibilities of poor subjective assessments in some sense. The normative aspects of utility theory (e.g. Morgensten and von Neumann), attempts one way of doing this. Other approaches attempt it by a quasi-rationalization process. For example Epstein [56], dealing with engineering design problems, and seeking a way for valuing a design, requires that the ratio $u(f)/u(g)$, for any two objective function vectors $\{f, g\}$, should remain invariant under specific transformations of scale of $\{f\}$ (see Chapter 6 on ratio scales). This requirement is certainly not made in the usual value theory (see White [166, 169], Fishburn [59]). It is helpful in sensitivity analysis (see Chapters 3 and 6) where proportional errors might be of concern, for then, if f^* is an optimal vector; we have:

$$\Delta = (u(f^*) - u(f))/u(f^*)$$

is independent of the specific scale transformations. However, as will be indicated in Chapters 3 and 6, proper sensitivity analysis requires a proper decision theoretic foundation.

A further attempt to rationalize value functions is given by Eilon [54]. For the simple case of a single item, the problem is to determine the optimal batch size x. Three objectives are stated, viz.

f^1: −(cost per unit produced)
f^2:   total profit from the batch
f^3: −(time to complete the batch).

Negative signs are used so that higher values of $\{f^i\}$ are preferred.

Four possible value functions are given, viz.

$u_1(f) = f^1$
$u_2(f) = f^2$
$u_3(f) = -f^2/xf^1 = f^2/\alpha f^3 f^1$ (defined as the return, and where, for simplicity, we assume that $x = -\alpha f^3$)
$u_4(f) = -f^2/xf^1(-f^3) = -f^2/\alpha(f^3)^2 f^1$.

The value function settled for is u_4, part of the argument being that, in particular, u_1 and u_2 do not reflect all the factors which should influence the decision in the light of resources, profits, and time, and their impact on other activities at the time of the decision and in future. It is obvious that it is preferable to increase each of the $\{f^i\}$, given that the others are fixed, but there are many value functions which will permit this. The value functions have to be derived from other considerations, although such a framework might help.

Such considerations lead on to a consideration of the use of ratios as value functions. Hitch [76, 77] stresses the dangers of using ratio value functions. The example he cites is the convoy–U-boat one discussed in Chapter 1, where he says that maximizing the ratio:

$$f^1(= \text{number of U-boats sunk})/f^2(= \text{number of convoy ships sunk})$$

is not necessarily compatible with maximizing the probability of winning the war.

Decisions of the kind we have discussed are temporal, or short-term, in the sense that they are to be followed by other decisions. Such decisions, and their value functions, must be compatible with the optimization of some long-term value function. Again Hitch stresses the need to ensure that low level value functions are compatible with high level value functions, of which the short-term–long-term issue is one realization. Other realizations exist in the context of hierarchical objectives (the study of surrogate objectives relates to this).

The ratio approach may, in certain circumstances, be correct. Let us turn to Eilon's problem and let us suppose that we have some initial resource, y, and that deciding on x is equivalent to using an amount rx of this resource. Let us suppose that the long-term objective is to maximize profit, and that the time horizon is t units of time. Once decision x has been taken, further decisions will be taken once the batch has been produced. We may now make use of our dynamic programming framework of Chapter 2 conceptually. If $v(y, t)$ is the maximal total profit over the next t time units beginning with resource level y we obtain:

$$v(y, t) = \max_{x \geqslant 0}[f^2(x) + v(y - rx, t + f^3(x))].$$

Note that $f^3 \leqslant 0$.

Now suppose we can differentiate v, and that $rx \ll y$, $-f^3(x) \ll t$. Then, approximating, we obtain:

$$v(y, t) = \max_{x \geqslant 0}\left[f^2(x) + v(y, t) - rx\frac{\partial v}{\partial y} + f^3(x)\frac{\partial v}{\partial t}\right]$$

where $\partial v/\partial y$, $\partial v/\partial t$ are evaluated at the current point (y, t).

Using the asumption that $f^3(x) = -x/\alpha$, and rearranging (a matter of technicality) we obtain:

$$r\frac{\partial v}{\partial y} + 1/\alpha\frac{\partial v}{\partial t} = \max_{x \geqslant 0}[f^2(x)/x] = \max_{x \geqslant 0}[-f^2(x)/\alpha f^3(x)].$$

This approach is given by Bellman ([16] p. 93, Ex (18)).

Thus, on the basis of the assumptions made, an appropriate short-term value function is

$$u(f) = -f^2/\alpha f^3.$$

The assumptions may not be correct, but the point about rationalizing $u(f)$ from other considerations is important. Brady et al. [25], who discuss the effectiveness of various cargoes transported between terminals, use a value function which is equivalent to the above, viz. profit from cargo/costs of transportation. Schaible [143] gives a survey of applications of fractional programming, which is precisely the ratio problem, each of which would need to be examined from the point of view of its rationalization, unless they are merely descriptive of how actual choices are made.

So far, we have discussed value functions in the context of situations in which no uncertainty explicitly arises in the problem formulation. The standard references to value functions in the probabilistic area are those of Morgenstern et al. [111], Savage [141], and Keeney et al. [89].

The first deals with situations in which probabilities are specified in advance for the decision maker. The second deals with subjective probabilities to be elicited from the decision maker. They are both normative theories, giving axioms which it is felt decision makers should observe. The result of these theories is a special kind of value function, commonly called a utility function, such that, if $g(f, x)$ is a probability density function (the theory is, of course, applicable to other probability structures) of the vector outcome $f = (f^1, f^2, \ldots, f^m)$ given action x, the value function takes the form:

$$v(x) = \int_{f^1 f^2, \ldots, f^m} u(f^1, f^2, \ldots, f^m) g(f^1, f^2, \ldots, f^m, x) \, d(f^1, f^2, \ldots, f^m)$$

$$= \int_f u(f) g(f, x) \, df$$

The third reference deals with conditions under which $u(f)$ takes a specific form, e.g. linear in f. The axioms used are not normative.

For discrete problems, if $p(f_z, x) = p^z(x)$, $u(f_z) = \lambda_z$ then v may be written in the form:

$$v(x) = \sum_{z=1}^{Z} \lambda_z p^z(x)$$

and this is really a multi-objective problem of a weighted factor kind in which the objectives are:

$$p^z, \qquad z = 1, 2, \ldots, Z.$$

For $m = 1$, f_z is single-dimensional, and it is to be noted that $v(x)$ is not equal to the expected level of f_z in general, the latter being given by:

$$E(x) = \sum_{z=1}^{Z} f_z p^z(x).$$

This raises questions about the use of $E(x)$. Let us, for example, return to our depth charge problem in which we evaluated our expected damage in the form (returning to the notation of Chapter 1):

$$f(x) = \sum_{s=0}^{\infty} p(s) \, d(x - s) = \sum_{z=-\infty}^{x} d(z) p(x - z)$$

where $p(x - z) = p^z(x)$, $d(z) = f_z$.

Now the important thing is not, directly, the damage, $d(z)$, but the impact this damage has on winning the war, and, strictly speaking, $d(z)$ should be replaced by $u(d(z))$ for a suitable u. d is, in the sense described in the section on objectives, merely a surrogate for u.

Similar issues arise in the context of previous examples studied in Chapter 1, and in subsequent material (e.g. product defective problems, inventory control, queueing, etc.) where chance effects arise.

As with the discussions on value functions with no explicit uncertainty, which is a special case of the uncertainty case, there is the question of validating the eventual function used. Reference has been made to normative axiomatics, and it is for the decision maker to examine whether he wishes to accept the coherence requirements surrounding these axioms. There is also the question of possible rationalization of, for example, short-term value functions in terms of long-term value functions, as in the non-explicit-uncertainty case. For example, returning to the present worth discussion for the investment problem discussed in the context of Reitman's format, given certain assumptions about the long-term problem, involving assumptions about the arrival pattern of investment opportunities, it can be shown that the present worth value function would be correct, and the discount factor α is given by the solution to the following equation (see White [167]):

$$1 = \alpha \sum_S \left\{ \max_{r \in S} \left[\max \left[(1+i), \sum_{t=1}^{\infty} \alpha^{(t-1)} r_t \right] \right] \right\} p(S)$$

where S is a set of investment opportunities, $p(S)$ is the probability of S, and, in this problem, we allow the retention of any cash, but at a current rate of interest i, as an option to taking up investments in S. If S is empty for all S, we obtain $\alpha = (1+i)^{-1}$ as indicated in section 2.3.

4.2.5 Mean-Variance Analysis

Although the value, or utility, form of analysis is the most ideal form of analysis (a point to which we will return later on) it is not always appropriate to try this form of analysis. As has been indicated, where probabilistic problems arise, one way of tackling them is to introduce objectives in the form of probabilities, for example, of queue sizes being below a certain level, or of running out of stock, and so on, where the use of expected levels (which will in this section be referred to as 'means') is unacceptable. An alternative approach, which is equivalent in special cases, is to look at the mean and variance of the appropriate effect, to which we will also return later on in the context of efficient solutions, e.g. for a portfolio problem. We may thus treat mean and variance as two objective functions to be evaluated for each of the options open to the decision maker.

As a simple example let us look at the simple single server, negative exponential service, negative exponential inter-arrival, problem introduced in Chapter 2, section 2.1, and used later on in Chapter 3 and at the beginning of this chapter. If λ is the arrival rate and if x is the service rate, we suggested two objectives, viz.

$$f^1(x) = cx$$
$$f^2(x) = \lambda/(x-\lambda)$$

the first being the service cost and the second being the mean waiting time for customers as a whole. In order to keep the analysis simple we will replace $f^2(x)$ by the individual mean waiting time for a customer, viz.

$$f^2(x) = 1/(x - \lambda).$$

This may be important to the company decision maker since it is a factor influencing the customer.

In addition, the customer may be interested in the variance of the waiting time, viz.

$$f^3(x) = ((x - \lambda)^2 + \lambda^2)/(x(x - \lambda)^3)$$

(see Exercise 8 of the Queueing Exercises of Chapter 2).

It is, of course, up to the company decision maker to judge the impact of f^2, f^3 on the customer, but certainly f^3 may influence the customer since it may not only be the fact that he will have to wait, but the fact that the waiting time may exceed certain levels, or be below certain levels, may be important in the context of his other activities.

The mean-variance issue is relevant in all the probabilistic problems we have discussed. In some simple cases they are calculable, but in others, although calculations may exist in practice, with present capabilities one may have to resort to simulation. We refer the reader back to Chapter 2, sections 2.5 and 2.10, where the classical approach of stochastic dynamic programming (see Howard [82]) faces difficulties in handling such cases.

As has been indicated, one may try to use, for example, utility analysis. In this context Markowitz [106] has shown how, for example, mean-variance analysis relates to utilities. Under certain conditions, if a decision maker makes his decisions only on the basis of the first m moments about the origin of his outcome variable, r, then he shows that there exists a utility function of the form:

$$u(r) = \sum_{i=1}^{m} \lambda_i r^i$$

and hence, if $f^i(x)$ is the ith moment of the return about the origin, we have a utility function v, for x, given by:

$$v(x) = \sum_{i=1}^{m} \lambda_i f^i(x).$$

The problem becomes a multiple objective problem.

For the mean-variance problem:

$$v(x) = \lambda_1 f^1(x) + \lambda_2(\sigma^2(x) + (f^1(x))^2)$$

(where $\sigma^2(x)$ is the variance)

$$= \lambda_1 f^1(x) + \lambda_2(f^1(x))^2 + \lambda_2\sigma^2(x).$$

We will return to this in Chapter 6.

4.2.6 Interaction and Cycling in the Problem Formulation Phases

As will be clear from the foregoing sections, there can be a great deal of interaction and cycling between the four components of the problem formulation paradigm. Figure 4.9 illustrates the interactions. It is to be stressed that this paradigm is for the use of a specific decision maker being advised by the operational researcher, and the various components are intended to reflect other decision makers who may be relevant, and their objectives, actions, and value functions.

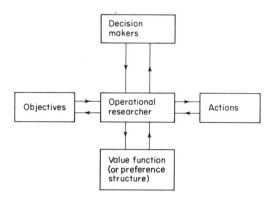

Figure 4.9

Let us look back at some of the examples we have discussed. In section 2.1, we looked at a problem involving two objectives, $f^1 = $ cost, and $f^2 = $ service, and the decision maker on behalf of whom the analysis is being carried out. The initial value function was taken to be a weighted average of cost and service. Then the recognition that the customers could make decisions and influence the arrival rate resulted in a modified formulation of the problem. The two problem formulations are as below, where P_i is the ith formulation.

P₁

Decision makers D_1:	manufacturing company
Actions	service rate x
Objectives	$f^1 = \text{cost} = cx$
	$f^2 = \text{service} = \lambda/(x - \lambda)$
Value function	$v^1(x) = cx + w\lambda/(x - \lambda)$

Recognition that λ depends on decisions of customers.

↓

P₂

Decision makers D_1:	manufacturing company
D_2:	customers

Actions	D_1: x
	D_2: λ
Objectives	D_1: $f^3 = \text{profit} = p\lambda - cx$
	D_2: $g^1 = \text{service} = \lambda/(x - \lambda)$
Value functions	D_1: $v^1(x) = f^3(x)$
	D_2: $v^2(x) = g^1(x)$.

The inventory example of section 2.2 might evolve as follows:

P_1

Decision makers D_1:	inventory controllers
Action	inventory control policy, x
Objectives	f^1: inventory levels
	f^2: run-out probabilities for production
Value function	$v^1(x) = \lambda_1 f^1(x) + \lambda_2 f^2(x)$.

$\downarrow$

Recognition of production controllers responding to inventory behaviour.

$\downarrow$

P_2

Decision makers D_1:	inventory controllers
D_2:	production controllers
Actions D_1:	inventory control policy, x
D_2:	production control policy, y
Objectives D_1:	f^1: inventory levels
	f^2: run-out probabilities for production
D_2:	g^1: service to customers
Value function D_1:	$v^1(x) = \lambda_1 f^1(x, y) + \lambda_2 f^2(x, y)$
D_2:	$v^2(x) = f^2(x, y)$.

The reader will find it useful to look at the other illustrations to see how problems can evolve.

One of the most elusive components in the above paradigm is that of objectives. Brill *et al.* [29] and McGarity *et al.* [108] discuss the manner in which the Operational Research analysis can be designed to elicit objectives which might not be explicit in the initial formulation of the problem, and it is emphasized that the actions themselves, and not just the consequential objective levels, should also be made explicit to the decision maker, since the actions may trigger off a recognition of other objectives which the initial objectives themselves would not. This occurs, for example, in the simple economic batch quantity problem of section 2.2, where the size of x may eventually trigger off a recognition of work load factors.

An example given by McGarity *et al.* [108] relates to the location of emergency ambulance facilities. The initial objectives are:

f^1: coverage of daytime population

f^2: coverage of evening population.

The objectives are different since the movement of population from offices to homes is significant.

Five efficient solutions (see section 4.3, later, for a definition) were obtained. Three of these had (f^1, f^2) values which were close. The need to discriminate between these led to a recognition of further objectives, viz.

f^3: site accessibility

f^4: neighbourhood resistance.

It is possible that this recognition could result in a reformulation of the problem so that these new objectives would then be examined for the other options as well.

The paper by Brill *et al.* [29] stresses a different point, viz. a selection of sufficiently different options, from the initial set, must be retained for the decision maker, since this may also trigger off recognition of objectives which are more easily recognized for some options and not for others. Thus, in the example cited, the recognition of neighbourhood resistance might not arise unless sufficiently different areas were involved in solutions to trigger this off. With the economic quantity problem the same point arises, viz. the recognition of the work load effects of different batch sizes might not arise unless the decision maker was presented with such options, at least in the final presentation of the results of the study.

The classic example of interaction between actions and objectives is given in Blackett [22]. It is reported that, during the Second World War, the question of gun armaments (actions) arose. On querying the purpose (objective) of the enquiry, this was given as sinking of enemy ships, by blowing holes in them. The suggestion was then made that it might be possible to spray the water around the ships with some chemical (new actions) which would alter the properties of the water and achieve the same objective. This did not materialize, but the importance of the interaction between components of problem formulation is nonetheless illustrated.

An interesting illustration of what might be involved in formulating even the simplest problem is given by Leibowitz [97]. He begins by asking 'why do I go fishing?', and ends up with a consideration of many of the aspects discussed in this chapter, and the conclusion that, if a proper formulation requires a complete understanding of the universe, some surrogate problem must be accepted. The reader may care to read this.

Graham [67] discusses the manner in which one may be able to work back from the solutions which decision makers propose, to identify the problem which they were intended to solve. This, of course, gives impetus to the cyclical nature of the problem formulation process.

Finally, referring back to our earlier discussion on techniques in Chapter 1, let us emphasize that the more we can identify, understand, and characterize particular classes of problem, then the more able we will be to obtain acceptable formulations of our problems which will reduce the need to continually reformulate our problems, at least those we would expect to find in an organizational context.

4.3 OPEN AND CLOSED FORMS OF ANALYSIS

In Chapter 1 we introduced the concepts of subject and object system, and of open and closed forms of analysis. Let us now look at the latter concepts and, to set the framework, let us assume that our feasible action space is X, and that we have m objective function, $\{f^i\}$, $i = 1, 2, \ldots, m$, $\{f^i\}$ being functions of $x \in X$. To fix our ideas let us consider the example of nursery location discussed in the Mathematical and Dynamic Programming section (2.5) of Chapter 2, where $m = 3$, and:

$f^1(x)$ = total distance associated with a specific location–allocation plan x;

$f^2(x)$ = the total cost associated with a specific location–allocation plan x;

$f^3(x)$ = the total weighted deficit of all children for whom a place is not available associated with a specific location–allocation plan.

Closed Form of Analysis

If we have a value function u on f, and

$$v(x) = u(f(x)) = u(f^1(x), f^2(x), f^3(x)),$$

then the problem reduces to the following one:

$$\text{maximize}[v(x)]$$
$$\text{subject to}$$
$$x \in X.$$

A special case arises when:

$$u(f) = -\{\lambda_1 f^1 + \lambda_2 f^2 + \lambda_3 f^3\}, \qquad \lambda_i > 0, \qquad i = 1, 2, 3,$$

and if, as is the case for the above example,

$$f^i(x) = \sum_j p_{ij} x_j$$

and X is defined by the constraints:

$$\sum_j a_{ij} x_j \leq b_i, \qquad i = 1, 2, \ldots, p$$

we have a linear programming problem, with the exception that some of the variables are integer.

In the closed form the maximal use of existing optimization procedures is possible, and allows us to handle problems where X contains a very large number of actions.

The above closed form is not the only one. We may wish to constrain, for example, f^2, and the problem may take the form:

$$\text{maximize}[v(x)]$$

subject to

$$x \in X \quad \text{and} \quad f^2(x) \leqslant \bar{f}^2$$

where $\bar{f}^2$ is a prescribed upper bound on f^2.

The following extreme forms are also a closed form:
find some $x \in X$

or

find some $x \in X : f^1(x) \leqslant \overline{f^1}, f^2(x) \leqslant \overline{f^2}, f^3(x) \leqslant \overline{f^3}$.

In such cases, at least in the initial instance, any feasible x will do, although it may turn out later on that this is not the case.

Related to this sort of formulation is the goal programming formulation (e.g. see references [35], [44], [48], [84], [86], [94], [96], and [128]). In this case $\{\overline{f^1}, \overline{f^2}, \overline{f^3}\}$ will be target (goal) levels. The constraints may be put in the form (and this is not the only way of doing it):

$$f^1(x) + d_1^+ - d_1^- = \overline{f^1}$$
$$f^2(x) + d_2^+ - d_2^- = \overline{f^2}$$
$$f^3(x) + d_3^+ - d_3^- = \overline{f^3}$$
$$d_i^+ \geqslant 0, \quad d_i^- \geqslant 0, \quad \forall i.$$

The value function may take the form:

$$v(x, d^+, d^-) = -\sum_{i=1}^{3} \lambda_i d_i^-.$$

However, it is to be noted that the weighting factors $\{\lambda_i\}$ need careful consideration, and the approach may be invalid in the context of a proper value function based on preferences. Thus if a true $v(x)$ taking the form:

$$v(x) = -\sum_{i=1}^{3} \lambda_i f^i(x)$$

exists, then, using these weighting factors in the goal programming formulation need not give an optimal solution.

Open Form of Analysis

This merely informs the decision maker as to the levels of $\{f^i(x)\}$, $i = 1, 2, \ldots, m$, for each $x \in X$.

It does not involve the difficult problem of determining the value function, $u(f)$, but it does limit the number of alternatives which can sensibly be given to the decision maker on this basis. As we have already seen in dynamic problems, and in combinatorial problems, in particular, the number of possibilities is very large, as indeed it is for simple linear programmes. Lock [99] stresses the very great difficulties he had in getting decision makers even to rank the alternative actions.

The closed and open forms of analysis are, in reality, two extremes of a range of forms of analysis which are neither fully closed nor fully open. Let us look at these.

Partially Open–Partially Closed Forms of Analysis

In such cases we combine some knowledge of the decision maker's preferences with computational procedures, which then reduce the initial set X to a smaller set $Y \subset X$, which may then be used for a final open form of analysis. The most common form this takes is in the form of determining efficient sets.

Let us assume that a value function u, on f, exists which is monotone-non-decreasing in $\{f^i\}$, i.e.

$$\text{if} \quad f^i(x) \geqslant f^i(y), \qquad i = 1, 2, \ldots, m \quad \text{then} \quad u(f(x)) \geqslant u(f(y)).$$

We need not know u, and we merely require preferences to be non-decreasing in $\{f^i\}$.

The efficient set of X with respect to f, designated by $\mathscr{E}$, is defined as follows:

$$\mathscr{E} = \{x \in X : \nexists y \in X \text{ with } f^i(y) \geqslant f^i(x), i = 1, 2, \ldots, m, f(x) \neq f(y)\}$$

i.e. all the points $x \in X$ for which no other point $y \in X$ exists with at least as good objective levels in all components, and with at least one component $f^i(x)$ strictly preferred to $f^i(y)$.

It is obvious that, if u is strictly monotonic increasing in $\{f^i\}$ (i.e. if $f^i(x) \geqslant f^i(y)$, $i = 1, 2, \ldots, m$, $f^i(x) > f^i(y)$ some i, then $u(f(x)) > u(f(y))$), then if x maximizes $u(f(x))$ over X, we must have $x \in \mathscr{E}$. Otherwise $\exists y \in X$ with $f^i(y) \geqslant f^i(x)$, $i = 1, 2, \ldots, m$, $f^i(y) > f^i(x)$ some i, and then $u(f(y)) > u(f(x))$ contrary to hypothesis.

We actually have a stronger result from White [172], viz. 'if f is continuous on X, u is continuous in f, and X is closed and bounded, then $u(f)$ will attain its maximal value in $\mathscr{E}$' (there may also be points not in $\mathscr{E}$ with the same maximal value).

The above analysis indicates that, in the given circumstances, when seeking optimal solutions, and assuming that the decision maker can always compare two alternatives $x, y \in X$, we lose nothing by first of all finding $\mathscr{E}$, and then presenting $\mathscr{E}$ to the decision maker for his final choice. Of course $\mathscr{E}$ may still contain many members, and a subset of $\mathscr{E}$ may have to be taken.

The classical case of efficient solution analysis is in the portfolio area (see Markowitz [106]). Given n possible investment avenues, j, $j = 1, 2, \ldots, n$, with expected returns per unit invested, $\{\mu_j\}$, $j = 1, 2, \ldots, n$, and with corresponding covariances of return $\{\sigma_{ij}\}$, i, $j = 1, 2, \ldots, n$, if $\{x_j\}$ is the amount invested in avenues $\{j\}$, subject to an availability b of cash, the two objectives are expectation and variance of total return, viz.

$$f^1(x) = \sum_{j=1}^{n} \mu_j x_j$$

$$f^2(x) = -\sum_{i=1}^{n} \sum_{j=1}^{n} \sigma_{ij} x_i x_j.$$

The above results are obtained as follows. If R_j is the return for one unit invested in avenue j, then if $\{x_j\}$ are as above, the return is:

$$R(x) = \sum_{i=1}^{n} x_i R_j.$$

Then:

$$f^1(x) = \exp[R(x)] = \sum_{j=1}^{n} x_j \exp(R_j) = \sum_{j=1}^{n} \mu_j x_j$$

$$f^2(x) = -\exp[R(x) - \exp[R(x)]]^2$$

$$= -\exp\left[\sum_{j=1}^{n} x_j R_j - \sum_{j}^{n} \mu_j x_j\right]^2$$

$$= -\exp\left[\sum_{j=1}^{n} x_j(R_j - \mu_j)\right]^2 = -\sum_{i=1}^{n} \sum_{j=1}^{n} x_i x_j \exp[(R_i - \mu_i)(R_j - \mu_j)]$$

$$= -\sum_{j=1}^{n} \sum_{j=1}^{n} \sigma_{ij} x_i x_j.$$

If smaller variances (for a given expected return) and larger expectations (for a given variance) are preferred, the problem reduces to:

$$\text{find } \mathcal{E} \text{ given } \{X, f\}$$

where

$$X = \left\{x : x \geq 0, \sum_{j=1}^{n} x_j = b\right\}.$$

The efficient set is as indicated in Figure 4.10, where we have used $-f^2$ instead of f^2. The shaded figures gives all the possible f levels obtainable, and the boundary $\overline{A\,B}$ gives $\mathcal{E}$ in terms of objective functions.

One may get even stronger results if more is known about the decision maker's preferences. Thus, if it is known that he has a value function of the form:

$$\lambda_1 f^1 + \lambda_2 f^2, \qquad \text{with } \underline{r} \leq \lambda_1/\lambda_2 \leq \bar{r}$$

where $\bar{r}, \underline{r}$ are bounds on the ratios of λ_1 and λ_2, then we can reduce the final open form to the region $\overline{A^1 B^1}$, since it is clear that all maximizers of the value function lies on this line for the specified range of λ_1, λ_2 values.

258

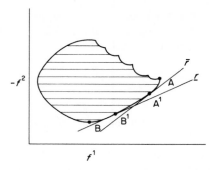

Figure 4.10

Extensions such as this, taking us beyond the standard concept of efficient sets, may be found in Yu [174], White [171].

For classical completely linear, polyhedral, problems, Figure 4.11 illustrates the situation. The efficient set is the boundary region $\overline{A\,B\,C}$, in terms of objective functions (we need to work back to get the decisions).

Earlier on we have mentioned the possibility of linearly weighted value functions of the form:

$$v(x) = \sum_{i=1}^{m} \lambda_i f^i(x).$$

It is clear that if $\lambda_i > 0$ for all i, then any optimal solution is efficient, for otherwise there exists a $y \in X$ with $f^i(y) \geqslant f^i(x)$, for all i, with at least one strict inequality. In this case:

$$\sum_{i=1}^{m} \lambda_i f^i(y) > \sum_{i=1}^{m} \lambda_i f^i(x)$$

and x does not maximize $v(x)$.

We also have a converse result for some problems, viz. if $u(f)$ is monotone non-decreasing in $\{f^i\}$, X is convex, and $\{f^i(x)\}$ are all concave, then, for each efficient solution, x, there exists a set of $\{\lambda_i\}$, $\sum_{i=1}^{m} \lambda_i = 1$, $\lambda_i \geqslant 0$

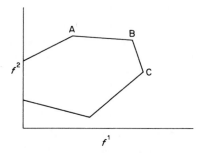

Figure 4.11

for all i, such that x maximizes

$$v(x) = \sum_{i=1}^{m} \lambda_i f^i(x)$$

over X. This value function $v(x)$ is, of course, only a surrogate value function for getting an efficient solution, and may not reflect any true value function. A glance at Figures 4.10, and 4.11, illustrates this result.

Earlier on, we mentioned goal programming. For the formulation given, where preferences are monotone non-increasing in $\{f^i\}$, if the $\{\lambda_i\}$ are positive, then it is easily seen that any solution optimal for the goal programming formulation is also efficient (note that, for non-increasing preferences, the efficiency definition has to be reversed).

We have already mentioned the inter-relation between constraints and objectives. This relationship also leads to a relationship between efficient solutions and constrained objectives problems which we will not, however, explore here (but see Lin [98]).

For a coverage of methods for dealing with linear multi-objective programming the reader should consult Zeleny [175]. For a detailed study of the general problem of the manner in which searches can be reduced using similar ideas to efficiency see White [171].

The use of efficient sets arises in other contexts, for various reasons. Let us look again at the constrained multi-item inventory control problem which we tackled earlier on in this chapter. One real difficulty in practice is, not only determining the values of the parameters $\{c_j, h_j, a_j\}$, but also justifying the validity of the models. In particular the set-up cost parameter, a_j, may be questionable, since different items may be grouped together (e.g. see Inventory Exercise 7 of Chapter 2 where block orders may be placed). Similarly the $\{c_j, h_j\}$ parameters may cause difficulties. Dannenbring *et al.* [37] avoid this problem, by finding the efficient solution with respect to the objective functions:

$f^1 = $ shortage
$f^2 = $ numbers of orders placed
$f^3 = $ stock level.

They do this for a probabilistic problem, but the principle is the same. As indicated earlier on, if we use positive weighting factors $\{\lambda_i\}$, $i = 1, 2, 3$, we can find efficient solutions. For this example, because of the strict convexity of the objective functions, this will find all the efficient solutions. The approach is related to the Lagrange multiplier method we discussed earlier on.

Exercise 10 of the Queueing Exercises of Chapter 2 also illustrates the multi-objective aspect. It is assumed that a known penalty for overbooking is given. However, this may be difficult to determine, and the problem may need to be studied in terms of two objectives, viz.

f^1: expected net income from passengers
f^2: expected number of passengers overbooked.

Another example occurs in our earlier redundancy problem. Let $f^1(x)$ be the specified reliability function $(f(x))$, and $f^2(x) = -c(x)$, where $c(x)$ is the cost of solution x. It is easily seen that the solutions given in Table 4.1 are efficient solutions, as indeed they must be from our weighting factor–efficiency result. For this problem, we face few computational problems. However, real life redundancy problems are much more complicated, and may involve, not only reliability and cost objectives, but also weight and volume factors, either as objectives or as constraints. Bray *et al.* [27] discuss such problems, and provide a method for finding efficient solutions as a precursor to finding optimal solutions, since, clearly, the efficient set will contain optimal solutions, as we have already indicated. Thus, in this case, the use of efficient solutions is a computational aid.

From the foregoing we see that there can be various forms of primary problem statement, let us now look at these.

4.4 FORMS OF PRIMARY PROBLEM STATEMENT

The first form of primary problem statement is:

'find a feasible solution'.

Thus we may merely be required to find some $x \in X$ which satisfies some other constraints and, indeed, X may be redefined to incorporate these constraints. For the location–allocation problem X might be defined as:

$$X = \{x : f^1(x) \leqslant \bar{f}^1, f^2(x) \leqslant \bar{f}^2, f^3(x) \leqslant \bar{f}^3\}.$$

The second form is

'maximize some function of the objectives, subject to constraints on the objectives'.

Thus we may wish to maximize $-f^3(x)$ subject to $f^1(x) \leqslant \bar{f}^1$, $f^2(x) \leqslant \bar{f}^2$. This is the constrained optimization form.

The final form is:

'maximize some function of the objectives'.

Thus we may wish to maximize $-(\lambda_1 f^1(x) + \lambda_2 f^2(x) + \lambda_3 f^3(x))$ subject to no further constraints than those which logically define X (e.g. $x_j = 0$ or 1, $\sum_{j=1}^n x_j = 1$, etc.) This is the unconstrained optimization form.

This form may be derived in various ways. If, for example, each $\{f^i(x)\}$ can be reduced to a common objective, such as cash, then the function given will be a total cash function. Thus if f^1 and f^3 can be expressed in terms of costs which these factors actually generate, in addition to the costs catered for by $f^2(x)$, (for example $f^3(x)$ might be reduced to the costs of meeting such deficits in other ways, or costs to the community arising from not supplying the necessary education), the reduced form would be applicable. On the other hand it may not be possible, or practicable, or economic, to try to obtain this reduction. In such cases the $\{\lambda_i\}$ factors may represent subjective weighting factors of the decision makers and we have a non-reduced form.

It is, of course, possible to have a mixed reduced and non-reduced form of problem statement. Further examples may be found in White [168].

Let us now look at a combination of open and closed forms of analysis under the heading of multi-objective interactive programming.

4.5 MULTI-OBJECTIVE INTERACTIVE PROGRAMMING

As we have seen the whole Operational Research process involves a series of interactions with decision makers in one form or another. One special aspect of this arises in the determination of the overall value function, or criterion function, as we have called it in section 2.4. Once this has been determined, we have a closed form of analysis (see section 4.3 and Chapter 1). The determination of this function may be quite difficult and quite unnecessary in solving the specific problem on hand. Recent years have seen a considerable development of what are termed multi-objective interactive programming methods, which allow the analyst to learn little by little something about the decision maker's preferences, using intermediate results to guide the search for suitable actions, and then using further knowledge of the decision maker's preferences to continue the process. This latter interactive phase is an open form of analysis (see section 4.3 and Chapter 1).

To begin with we will look in detail at two methods, viz. those of Dyer *et al.* [52], who pioneered such work, and White [170], before we look at the general structure of such methods. We begin with some general assumptions.

Let X be the feasible action space, and let there be m objectives (outcomes or consequences) $(f^1(x), f^2(x), \ldots, f^m(x)) = f(x)$, say. Let us suppose that there is a value (worth) function on f, i.e. $u(f^1, f^2, \ldots, f^m)$, and let us assume that u is monotonic increasing in the components of f, i.e. if $f^i \geqslant f^{i\prime}$ then $u(f^1, f^2, \ldots, f^{i-1}, f^i, f^{i+1}, \ldots, f^m) \geqslant (f^{1\prime}, f^{2\prime}, \ldots, f^{i-1\prime}, f^{i\prime}, f^{i+1\prime}, \ldots, f^m)$, e.g. $f^1(x) = -p(x)$, $f^2(x) = -q(x)$, $f^3(x) = -c(x)$, in an inventory problem where $p(x)$, $q(x)$, $c(x)$ are, respectively, expected shortage, stockholding, and purchase costs.

If u is known in advance, then we have the problem:

$$\max_{x \in X}[u(f(x))] = \max_{x \in X}[v(x)].$$

However, as has been indicated, it might be difficult to determine u in advance. Since we do not need to know u, but merely enough to determine the optimum in X, it is possible to use an interactive approach which will either find an optimal solution, or a satisfactory one. Let us deal with a few possibilities.

When the Tangent Planes to the Indifference Surfaces Can Be Determined When Required

Dyer *et al.* [50] suggest the following when $\{X, u, f\}$ satisfy certain conditions (v concave on X, u differentiable on $f(X)$, X compact and convex, f differentiable on X).

(i) Choose an initial solution $x^1 \in X$.

(ii) Find $\{\partial u/\partial f^i\}$ at x^1 (using indifference methods, or weighting factor approaches, since $\partial u/\partial f^i$ is the local weight given to f^i at $x = x^1$) (open form of analysis).

(iii) Find a feasible $y^1 \in X$ such that $\sum_i \sum_j ((\partial u/\partial f^i)(\partial f^i/\partial x_j))x_j$ is maximal (equivalent to a linear objective function on X) (closed form of analysis).

(iv) Find a most preferred point, x^2, of the form

$$x = tx^1 + (1-t)y^1, \qquad x \in X, \qquad 0 \le t \le 1,$$

by asking the decision maker to make his choice (open form of analysis).

(v) Repeat the process at (ii), replacing x^1 by x^2, and continue until $\{x^n\}$ has converged enough (in some cases this will converge in a finite number of moves).

The procedure will either give an optimal, or near-optimal, solution, providing a sufficient number of iterations are used.

One of the properties of the method, related to step (iii), is that any point better than x^n for u must be better for the linear objective function as well.

Figure 4.12, drawn in the x plane, illustrates the procedure. If $x^{n+1} = x^n$ at any stage, x^n is optimal.

In this example, some optima in (iv) are interior to the feasible region, and hence the tangent plane at x^n to v is the line (x^{n-1}, y^{n-1}). However, this need not be the case, for example if $x^2 = y^1$ we have Figure 4.13. This also applies for x^3 in Figure 4.12 where $x^3 = y^2$.

Let us consider an example. Let

$$m = 2, \qquad u(f^1, f^2) = f^1 + f^2$$
$$f^1(x) = 20x_1 - (x_1)^2$$
$$f^2(x) = 30x_2 - (x_2)^2$$

and the feasible region X be given by

$$x_1 + x_2 \le 12$$
$$x_1 + 2x_2 \le 18$$
$$5x_1 + 2x_2 \le 50$$
$$x_1 + x_2 \ge 6$$
$$x_1 \ge 0, \qquad x_2 \ge 0.$$

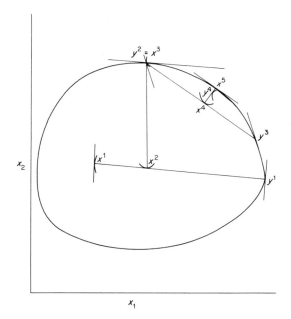

Figure 4.12

Note that a squared term is written, for example, as $(x_1)^2$, whereas x_1^2 means the first component of the point x^2.

The feasible region in the (x_1, x_2) space (not in the (f^1, f^2) space) is given in Figure 4.14. We have

$$\frac{\partial v}{\partial x_1} = \frac{\partial u}{\partial f^1} \frac{\partial f^1}{\partial x_1} + \frac{\partial u}{\partial f^2} \frac{\partial f^2}{\partial x_1} = 1 \times (20 - 2x_1) + 1 \times 0 = 20 - 2x_1$$

$$\frac{\partial v}{\partial x_2} = \frac{\partial u}{\partial f^1} \frac{\partial f^1}{\partial x_2} + \frac{\partial u}{\partial f^2} \frac{\partial f^2}{\partial x_2} = 1 \times 0 + 1 \times (30 - 2x_2) = 30 - 2x_2.$$

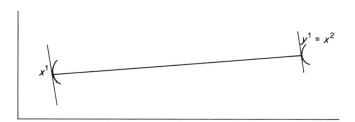

Figure 4.13

264

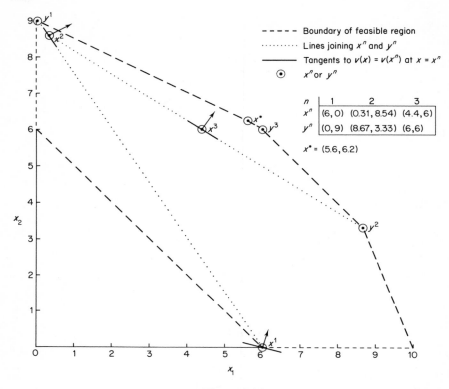

Figure 4.14

Hence, at any point x^n, we treat the objective function as if it were:

$$\left(\frac{\partial v}{\partial x_1}\right)_{x=x^n} x_1 + \left(\frac{\partial v}{\partial x_2}\right)_{x=x^n} x_2 = (20 - 2x_1^n)x_1 + (30 - 2x_2^n)x_2 \quad \text{(closed form)}.$$

We begin at, say, $x^1 = (6, 0)$.

Iteration 1

Step (iii) (*Closed form*)

$$\max[(20 - 2x_1^1)x_1 + (30 - 2x_2^1)x_2] = \max[8x_1 + 30x_2]$$

over feasible region. This is at $y^1 = (0, 9)$.

Step (iv) (*Open form*)

Ask decision maker for a most preferred point on line $\overline{(x^1, y^1)}$. With his (unknown to OR worker) objective function of:

$$20x_1 - (x_1)^2 + 30x_2 - (x_2)^2,$$

with

$$(x_1, x_2) = t(x_1^1, x_2^1) + (1-t)(y_1^1, y_2^1)$$
$$= t(6, 0) + (1-t)(0, 9) = (6t, 9(1-t))$$

we get:

$$w(t) = u(f_1, f_2) = 120t - 36t^2 + 270(1-t) - 81(1-t)^2 \qquad (0 \le t \le 1)$$
$$= 189 + 12t - 117t^2$$
$$w'(t) = 12 - 234t = 0 \quad \text{if} \quad t = 2/39$$
$$w''(t) \le 0,$$

hence $t = 2/39$ is a maximizing value.

Hence

$$x^2 = (6t, 9(1-t)) = (4/13, 111/13).$$

Iteration 2

Step (iii) (Closed form)

$$\max[(20 - 2x_1^2)x_1 + (30 - 2x_2^2)x_2] = \frac{252}{13} x_1 + \frac{168}{13} x_2$$

over the feasible region. This is at $y^2 = (26/3, 10/3)$.

Step (iv) (Open form)

Ask the decision maker for most preferred point on line $\overline{(x^2, y^2)}$. With his (unknown to the OR worker) objective function of:

$$20x_1 - (x_1)^2 + 30x_2 - (x_2)^2,$$

with

$$(x_1, x_2) = t(x_1^2, x_2^2) + (1-t)(y_1^2, y_2^2) = t(4/13, 111/13) + (1-t)(26/3, 10/3)$$
$$= (26/3 - 326/39t, 10/3 + 203/39t).$$

we get:

$$w(t) = u(f_1, f_2) = \frac{520}{3} - \frac{6520}{39} t - \left(\frac{26}{3} - \frac{326}{39} t\right)^2$$
$$+ 100 + \frac{2030}{13} t - \left(\frac{10}{3} + \frac{203}{39} t\right)^2$$
$$w'(t) = -\frac{6520}{39} + 2\left(\frac{326}{39}\right)\left(\frac{26}{3} - \frac{326}{39} t\right) + \frac{2030}{13}$$
$$- 2\left(\frac{203}{39}\right)\left(\frac{10}{3} + \frac{203}{39} t\right) = 0 \quad \text{if} \quad t = 0.515$$
$$w''(t) \le 0,$$

hence $t = 0.515$ is a maximizing value.

266

This then gives:

$$x^3 = 0.515\left(\frac{4}{13}, \frac{111}{13}\right) + 0.485\left(\frac{26}{3}, \frac{10}{3}\right)$$

$$= (4.4, 6.0).$$

Iteration 3

Step (iii) (Closed form)

$$\max[(20 - 2x_1^3)x_1 + (30 - 2x_2^3)x_2] = 11.2x_1 + 18x_2$$

over the feasible region. This is at $y^3 = (6, 6)$.

The steps are then continued until x^n has been narrowed down enough. Eventually we will get very close to the true optimum, $x^* = (28/5, 31/5)$.

In the execution of the above method, it is required to determine $\partial u/\partial f^i$ by interaction with the decision maker. Since the choices given to the decision maker, to determine these, are local, the derivations will be subject to some error. Dyer [51] studies the error problem but, as pointed out in Chapters 3 and 6 the interpretation of utility (or value) differences needs to be thought about very carefully.

When u is Linear with Unknown Weights

Suppose

$$u(f) = \sum_{i=1}^m \lambda_i^* f^i, \qquad \lambda_i^* \geq 0 \quad \forall i, \sum_{i=1}^m \lambda_i^* = 1.$$

Written in scalar product form, $u(f) = \lambda^* f$.

λ^* is the true weighting factor vector but the OR worker does not know λ^*.

We begin with $x^1 \in X$ and $S^1 = \{x^1\}$.

Let us suppose we have found a finite set of points, $S^n \subseteq X$, and that we know the preference over S^n. This will then restrict λ to a set Λ^n. Thus if $x, y \in S^n$, and x is at least as good as y, then:

$$\lambda f(x) \geq \lambda f(y), \qquad \text{i.e.} \quad \lambda(f(x) - f(y)) \geq 0.$$

Inequalities of this form are linear inequalities, and Λ^n takes the form:

$$\Lambda^n = \left\{ \lambda = \sum_k \mu_k \lambda^{nk}, \mu_k \geq 0, \sum_k \mu_k = 1 \right\}$$

where $\{\lambda^{nk}\}$ are, possibly dependent, generators of Λ^n, $k = 1, 2, \ldots, K_n$.

Note that $\lambda^* \in \Lambda^n$.

Suppose we have $S^4 = \{x^1, x^2, x^3, x^4\}$, $x^4 R x^3 R x^2 R x^1$, $x R y$ means that x at least as good as y. The inequalities for λ are as follows:

$$\lambda(f(x^4) - f(x^3)) \geqslant 0, \quad \text{i.e.} \quad \lambda a \geqslant 0, \, a = f(x^4) - f(x_3)$$
$$\lambda(f(x^3) - f(x^2)) \geqslant 0, \quad \text{i.e.} \quad \lambda b \leqslant 0, \, b = f(x^2) - f(x^3)$$
$$\lambda(f(x^2) - f(x^1)) \geqslant 0, \quad \text{i.e.} \quad \lambda c \leqslant 0, \, c = f(x^1) - f(x^2).$$

The inequalities are chosen in this form merely to illustrate the method. In addition let us assume that:

$$a_1 > 0, \quad a_2 < 0$$
$$b_1 > 0, \quad b_2 < 0$$
$$c_1 > 0, \quad c_2 < 0.$$

We then have Figure 4.15.

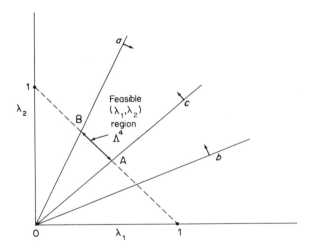

Figure 4.15

Every $\lambda \in \Lambda^4$ takes the form, with $\lambda^1 \equiv A$, $\lambda^2 \equiv B$:

$$\lambda = \mu_1 \lambda^1 + \mu_2 \lambda^2, \quad \mu_1, \mu_2 \geqslant 0, \quad \mu_1 + \mu_2 = 1.$$

We may now carry out the following analysis. Suppose z^n is the best point in S^n, obtained by asking the decision maker (open form of analysis). Now the true λ^* is in Λ^n, by virtue of the way Λ^n is obtained. Then either z^n is an optimum for λ^*, or there is an $x \in X \backslash S^n$ such that:

$$\lambda^{nk} f(x) > \lambda^{nk} f(z^n) \quad \text{for some } k.$$

The reason is as follows (see Figure 4.16 for illustration of case $m = 2$). If

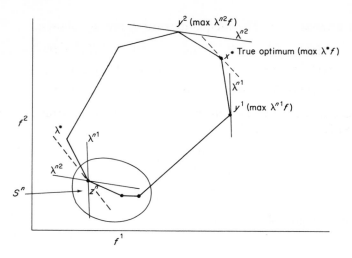

Figure 4.16

$\lambda^{nk}f(x) \leqslant \lambda^{nk}f(z^n)$ for all k, $\forall x \in X\backslash S^n$, we have:

$$\sum_k \mu_k \lambda^{nk}f(x) \leqslant \sum_k \mu_k \lambda^{nk}f(z^n), \quad \forall x \in X\backslash S^n, \quad \mu_k \geqslant 0, \quad \forall k, \sum_k \mu_k = 1.$$

Then:

$$\lambda f(x) \leqslant \lambda f(z^n), \quad \forall \lambda \in \Lambda^n, \quad x \in X\backslash S^n.$$

Hence $\lambda^*f(x) \leqslant \lambda^*f(z^n)$, in particular, $\forall x \in X\backslash S^n$, and z^n is optimal for λ^*f over all $x \in X\backslash S^n$. Clearly z^n is optimal over S^n for λ^*f.

Then $\lambda^*f(z^n) \geqslant \lambda^*f(x)$, $\forall x \in X$, and the result follows.

We then have the following method.

(i) Choose $S^1 = \{x^1\} \subseteq X$.
(ii) Let $\Lambda^1 = \{\lambda \in \mathbb{R}^m$ which maintain the preferences over S^1 with $\lambda \geqslant 0$, and $\sum_{i=1}^m \lambda_i = 1\}$ (in this case $\Lambda^1 = \{\lambda \in \mathbb{R}^m: \lambda \geqslant 0, \sum_{i=1}^m \lambda_i = 1)\}$, $z^1 = x^1 =$ a most preferred member of S^1) (open form).
(iii) Find generators of Λ^1 (in this case $\lambda^{11} = (1, 0, 0, \ldots, 0)$ $\lambda^{12} = (0, 1, 0, 0, \ldots)$, etc.).
(iv) For each k find $y^k \in X$ to maximize $\lambda^{1k}f(x)$ over X (closed form).
(v) If $\lambda^{1k}f(y^k) \leqslant \lambda^{1k}f(z^1)$, $\forall k$, then z^1 is optimal.
(vi) If $\lambda^{1k}f(y^k) > \lambda^{1k}f(z^1)$, some k, choose some such y^k and let $S^2 = \{x^1, y^k\} = \{x^1, x^2\}$, $x^2 = y^k$.
(vii) Go back to (ii), setting $n = 2$, and repeat the process, generating $\{S^n, \Lambda^n\}$ at the nth iteration in general.

It is to be noted that at step (vi) we must have $y^k \notin S^1$, for any such k.

Under certain circumstances this method will lead to an exact, or approximate, optimal solution. When X is a polytope and f is linear, then an exact optimal solution will be obtained in a finite number of steps.

Let us consider the following example. Let $m = 2$, $f^1(x) = x_1$, $f^2(x) = x_2$, $\lambda^* = (9/20, 11/20)$, and the feasible region X be given by:

$$x_1 + 2x_2 \leqslant 12$$
$$2x_1 + 3x_2 \leqslant 20$$
$$x_1 + x_2 \leqslant 9$$
$$x_1, x_2 \geqslant 0.$$

The true optimum is at B, $x_1 = 7$, $x_2 = 2$ (see Figure 4.17). Note that λ^* is not known to the OR worker but he learns about it from the decision maker.

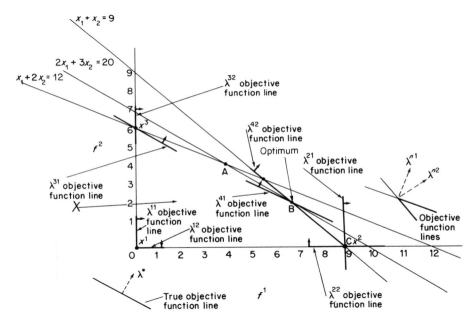

Figure 4.17

Iteration 1

Step (i)
$$S^1 = \{x^1\} = (0, 0).$$

Step (ii)
$$\Lambda^1 = \{\lambda : \lambda_1 \geqslant 0, \lambda_2 \geqslant 0, \lambda_1 + \lambda_2 = 1\}, \quad z^1 = x^1.$$

Step (iii)
$$\lambda^{11} = (1, 0), \quad \lambda^{12} = (0, 1).$$

270

Step (iv)/(v)

(1, 0)x is maximized at $x_1 = 9$, $x_2 = 0$, with value $9 > \lambda^{11} z^1$.
(0, 1)x is maximized at $x_1 = 0$, $x_2 = 6$, with value $6 > \lambda^{12} z^1$.

Step (vi)

Bring in $x^2 = (9, 0)$.

Iteration 2

Step (i)

$S^2 = \{x^1, x^2\}$, $x^2 = (9, 0)$, $x^1 = (0, 0)$.

Step (ii)

x^2 is at least as good as x^1 (from λ^*), and $z^2 = x^2$,

$$\Lambda^2 = \{\lambda : 9\lambda_1 \geq 0, \lambda_2 \geq 0, \lambda_1 + \lambda_2 = 1\} = \Lambda^1.$$

Step (iii)

$\lambda^{21} = (1, 0)$, $\lambda^{22} = (0, 1)$.

Step (iv)/(v)

$\lambda^{21} x$ is maximized at $x_1 = 9$, $x_2 = 0$, with value $9 = \lambda^{21} z^2$.
$\lambda^{22} x$ is maximized at $x_1 = 0$, $x_2 = 6$, with values $6 > \lambda^{22} z^2$.

Step (vi)

Bring in $x^3 = (0, 6)$.

Iteration 3

Step (i)

$S^3 = \{x^1, x^2, x^3\}$ where $x^3 = (0, 6)$, $x^2 = (9, 0)$, $x^1 = (0, 0)$.

Step (ii)

From λ^*, x^2 is at least as good as x^3 is at least as good as x^1, and $z^3 = x^2$,

$$\Lambda^3 = \{\lambda : \lambda \geq 0, 9\lambda_1 + 6\lambda_2 \geq 0, \lambda_1 + \lambda_2 = 1\}$$

i.e. $\lambda_1 \geq \frac{2}{3}\lambda_2$, (see Figure 4.18).

Step (iii)

$\lambda^{31} = (2/5, 3/5)$, $\lambda^{32} = (1, 0)$.

Step (iv)/(v)

$\lambda^{31} x$ is maximized at any point on $\overline{A\,B}$, with value $4 > \lambda^{31} z^3$
$\lambda^{32} x$ is maximized at $C = z^3$.

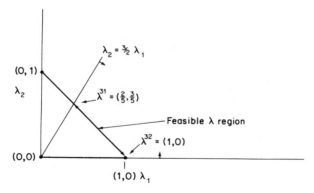

Figure 4.18

Step (vi)

Hence we introduce some point on $\overline{A\,B}$, say, $B = (7, 2) = x^4$.

Iteration 4

Step (i)

$S^4 = \{x^1, x^2, x^3, x^4\}$, $x^4 = (7, 2)$, $x^2 = (9, 0)$, $x^3 = (0, 6)$, $x^1 = (0, 0)$.

Step (ii)

From λ^*, x^4 is at least as good as x^2, x^2 at least as good as x^3, x^3 at least as good as x^1, $z^4 = x^4$,

$$\Lambda^4 = \{\lambda : 7\lambda_1 + 2\lambda_2 \geqslant 9\lambda_1 \geqslant 6\lambda_2 \geqslant 0, \lambda_1 + \lambda_2 = 1\}$$

i.e. $\lambda_2 \geqslant \lambda_1 \geqslant \frac{2}{3}\lambda_2$ (see Figure 4.19).

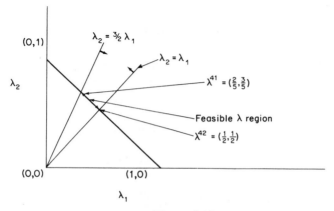

Figure 4.19

272

Step (iii)

$\lambda^{41} = (2/5, 3/5), \ \lambda^{42} = (1/2, 1/2).$

Step (iv)/(v)

$\lambda^{41}x$ is maximized at any point on $\overline{A\,B}$, with value $4 = \lambda^{41}z^4$.
$\lambda^{42}x$ is maximized at any point on $\overline{B\,C}$, with value $9/2 = \lambda^{42}z^4$.
Hence z^4 is optimal.

We may obtain some information about the uniqueness of z^4 as an optimal solution, or about the location of λ^*.

Suppose now that z^4 is not uniquely optimal for the true λ^*, and let x^* be some other optimum. Then $\lambda^* = \sum_k \mu_k \lambda^{4k}$ for some $\{\mu_k\} \geqslant 0$, $k = 1, 2$, and $\mu_1 + \mu_2 = 1$.

If $\lambda^* z^4 = \lambda^* x^*$, then $\lambda^*(z^4 - x^*) = 0$ and $\sum_k \lambda^{4k}(z^4 - x^*) = 0$.

Now, since z^4 is optimal for λ^{41} and λ^{42}, we obtain:

$$\lambda^{4k}(z^4 - x^*) = 0, \qquad k = 1, 2.$$

Hence:

$$\mu_k \lambda^{4k}(z^4 - x^*) = 0, \qquad k = 1, 2.$$

Now z^4 is the only point which maximizes both $\lambda^{41}x$ and $\lambda^{42}x$. Hence either $\lambda^{41}(z^4 - x^*) > 0$ or $\lambda^{42}(z^4 - x^*) > 0$ (if we had equalities in both cases, x^* would also maximize $\lambda^{41}x$ and $\lambda^{42}x$).

Hence either $\mu_1 = 0$ or $\mu_2 = 0$, and we deduce that either $\lambda^* = \lambda^{41}$ or $\lambda^* = \lambda^{42}$. Note that we do not know λ^*. However, in the answers by the decision maker, to the preferences between x^1, x^2, x^3 and $x^4(=z^4)$, it is found that x^4 is preferred to x^2, x^2 is preferred to x^3, x^3 is preferred to x^1. Hence it can be deduced that $\lambda^* \neq \lambda^{41}$, $\lambda^* \neq \lambda^{42}$. Hence we deduce that, from this contradiction, z^4 is a unique optimum, merely on the basis of the stated preferences, and without knowing λ^*.

For the general problem, if we end up with some optimum z^n, then we have as above, if z^n is not uniquely optimal for λ^*, for some $x^* \neq z^n$:

$$\sum_k \mu_k \lambda^{nk}(f(z^n) - f(x^*)) = 0.$$

Then if, by chance, z^n uniquely optimizes $\lambda^{nk}f(x)$ for all k, we have $\lambda^{nk}(f(z^n) - f(x^*)) > 0$ for all k, and hence $\mu_k = 0$ for all k. This is not possible since $\mu_k \geqslant 0$ for all k, and $\sum_k \mu_k = 1$. Hence z^n must be a unique optimum.

In general we can only get some information about the location of λ^*, not necessarily identifying λ^* exactly.

Instead of continuing until an optimal solution is obtained, it may be preferable to stop at step n and accept z^n. The question arises as to how close z^n is to an optimal solution, in a value sense. We can do this as follows, but the reader should be cautioned about interpreting this, a matter which was discussed in Chapter 3 and will again be discussed in Chapter 6.

Let us define:

$$\Delta_n = \max_k \max_{x \in X} [\lambda^{nk}(f(x) - f(z^n))].$$

This is, in effect, our test quantity to determine if z^n is optimal. Thus, if $\Delta_n = 0$, then z^n is optimal. Thus the size of Δ_n might be expected to measure the closeness to optimality. In fact we have the following:

$$\Delta_n = \max_k \max_{x \in X} [\lambda^{nk}(f(x) - f(z^n))]$$

$$= \max_{x \in X} \max_k [\lambda^{nk}(f(x) - f(z^n))]$$

$$= \max_{x \in X} \max_{\lambda \in \Lambda^n} [\lambda(f(x) - f(z^n))]$$

(the latter part is clearly true, since, if $\lambda = \sum_k \mu_k \lambda^{nk}$, then

$$\max_\mu \left[\sum_k \mu_k \lambda^{nk}(f(x) - f(z^n)) \right] = \max_k [\lambda^{nk}(f(x) - f(z^n))])$$

$$\geq \max_{x \in X} [\lambda^*(f(x) - f(z^n))]$$

(since $\lambda^* \in \Lambda^n$).

Hence:

$$\lambda^* f(z^n) \leq \lambda^* f(x^*) \leq \lambda^* f(z^n) + \Delta_n$$

since the inequalities apply to all x, and hence to x^* in particular, and the first inequality is clearly true.

Thus Δ_n gives a bound on the loss of optimality if we stop at z^n, measured on the specified value scale. Of course we do not know λ^*. If we wish to consider a lower bound on $\lambda^* f(z^n)$, we can compare Δ_n with $\min_{\lambda \in \Lambda^n} [\lambda f(z^n)]$.

Let us take another look at the efficiency ideas, already introduced in section 4.3, in the context of this method.

If $u(f)$ is strictly monotonic increasing in $\{f^1, f^2, \ldots, f^m\}$, then the optima of u must be in the efficient set, as we have shown. Hence we may restrict our searches to the efficient set with no loss.

Let us now consider the portfolio problem of section 4.3 in which we assume that we already have the efficient set in terms of $\mu = f^1$, $-\sigma^2 = f^2$. Following the previous procedure, beginning with x^1, we have the following (see Figure 4.20). Note that we plot f^1 against $-f^2$.

Iteration 1

Step (i)/(ii)

$S^1 = \{x^1\} = \{A\}$, $\Lambda^1 = \{\lambda : \lambda_1 \geq 0, \lambda_2 \geq 0, \lambda_1 + \lambda_2 = 1\}$, $z^1 = x^1$.

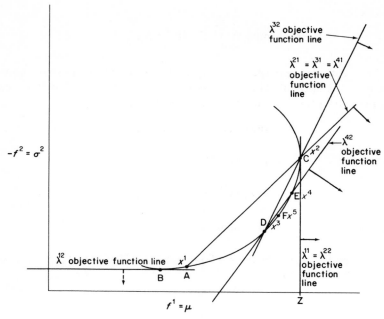

Figure 4.20

Step (*iii*)

$\lambda^{11} = (1, 0)$, $\lambda^{12} = (0, 1)$.

Step (*iv*)/(*v*)

$\lambda^{11}(\mu, -\sigma^2)$ is maximized at C, with value $>\lambda^{11}(\mu_A, -\sigma_A^2)$.
$\lambda^{12}(\mu, -\sigma^2)$ is maximized at B, with value $>\lambda^{12}(\mu_A, -\sigma_A^2)$.

Step (*vi*)

Bring in (e.g.) C. Suppose C is at least as good as A.

Iteration 2

Step (*i*)/(*ii*)

$S^2 = \{x^2, x^1\} = \{C, A\}$, $z^2 = x^2$.

$\Lambda^2 = \{\lambda : \lambda_1 \mu_C - \lambda_2 \sigma_C^2 \geqslant \lambda_1 \mu_A - \lambda_2 \sigma_A^2, \lambda_1, \lambda_2 \geqslant 0, \lambda_1 + \lambda_2 = 1\}$,

This corresponds to any line between CA and CZ.

Step (*iii*)

Hence λ^{21} corresponds to CA
$\qquad \lambda^{22}$ corresponds to CZ.

Step (iv)/(v)

$\lambda^{21}(\mu, -\sigma^2)$ is maximized at D, with value $> \lambda^{21}(\mu_C, -\mu_C^2)$.

$\lambda^{22}(\mu, -\sigma^2)$ is maximized at C, with value $= \lambda^{22}(\mu_C, -\mu_C^2)$.

Step (vi)

Bring in D.
Suppose D is at least as good as C and C is at least as good as A.

Iteration 3

Step (i)/(ii)

$S^3 = \{x^3, x^2, x^1\} = \{D, C, A\}$, $z^3 = x^3$,

$\Lambda^3 = \{\lambda: \lambda_1\mu_D - \lambda_2\sigma_D^2 \geqslant \lambda_1\mu_C - \lambda_2\sigma_C^2 \geqslant \lambda_1\mu_A - \lambda_2\sigma_A^2,$
$\lambda_1, \lambda_2 \geqslant 0, \lambda_1 + \lambda_2 = 1\}$.

Λ^3 corresponds to any line between CA and CD.

Step (iii)

λ^{31} corresponds to CA.
λ^{32} corresponds to CD.

Step (iv)/(v)

$\lambda^{31}(\mu, -\sigma^2)$ is maximal at D, with value $= \lambda^{31}(\mu_D, -\sigma_D^2)$.
$\lambda^{32}(\mu, -\sigma^2)$ is maximal at E, with value $> \lambda^{32}(\mu_D, -\sigma_D^2)$.

Step (vi)

Bring in E.
Suppose D is at least as good as E, E is at least as good as C and C is at least as good as A.

Iteration 4

Step (i)/(ii)

$S^4 = \{x^4, x^3, x^2, x^1\} = \{D, E, C, A\}$, $z^4 = x^4$. In this case
$$\Lambda^4 = \{\lambda: \lambda_1\mu_D - \lambda_2\sigma_D^2 \geqslant \lambda_1\mu_E - \lambda_2\sigma_E^2$$
$$\geqslant \lambda_1\mu_C - \lambda_2\sigma_C^2 \geqslant \lambda_1\mu_A - \lambda_2\sigma_A^2, \lambda_1, \lambda_2 \geqslant 0, \lambda_1 + \lambda_2 = 1\}.$$

Step (iii)

λ^{41} corresponds to CA
λ^{42} corresponds to ED.

Applying the approach again leads to F being included, and so on.

Let us now look at a general framework for interactive procedure. A general procedure may be described as follows.

(i) Choose an initial set $S^1 \subseteq X$.
(ii) Let us assume that, by following the procedure, that we arrive at a set $S^n \subseteq X$.
(iii) Find the preference order over S^n, and let U^n be the set of value functions consistent with this order (in the linear case U^n corresponds to Λ^n).
(iv) Using U^n, extend S^n to S^{n+1}, or stop if S^n, and the best in S^n, is acceptable (note the best in S^n is best for all $u \in U^n$).
(v) Repeat at (iii).

The essential problem is to be able to choose S^{n+1} given U^n. In the linear case, a method is given which is guaranteed to give an optimal, or near optimal, solution. Other methods may be used, for example select members $V^n \subseteq U^n$ randomly and, for each $u \in V^n$, find $x^n(u) \in X$ to maximize $u(f(x))$; if each such $x^n(u) \in S^n$, stop at (iv). Otherwise add any $x^n(u) \notin S^n$ to S^n to get S^{n+1} and go to (iii).

It is to be noted that, analogously to the linear case of U, if the optimal x^n in S^n, $\forall u \in U^n$, is not optimal over X for the true $u^* \in U^n$, then, for some u (e.g. $u = u^0) \in U^n$, $\exists x \notin S^n$ such that $u^0(f(x)) > u^0(f(x^n))$.

The previous analysis assumes that the decision maker does have definite preferences over $\{f\}$ but that it is difficult and unnecessary to determine these fully over $\{f\}$. We do enough merely to get an optimal, or near-optimal, solution. Since $U^{n+1} \subseteq U^n$ we get some convergence properties which are needed. However, in practice, a decision maker wish to change his preferences as he goes along. In this case we may not have $U^{n+1} \subseteq U^n$ or $U^n \subseteq U^{n+1}$. However, providing a reasonable amount of stability exists in the preferences, the method will still work.

For many methods, specific structural assumptions are made about the nature of the underlying preference structure and these have to be verified somehow. For example, the concavity assumption of Dyer et al. If we accept the expected utility theory of Morgenstern et al. [111], if X is convex, and if $x, y \in X$, $x\,p\,y$ means x with probability p, y with probability $(1-p)$, then v is concave on $X \rightleftarrows (px + (1-p)y)\,R\,(x\,p\,y)$, $\forall\ 0 \leqslant p \leqslant 1$, where R means at least as good as.

This follows since v is concave on

$$X \rightleftarrows v(px + (1-p)y) \geqslant pv(x) + (1-p)v(y), \quad \forall p : 0 \leqslant p \leqslant 1$$
$$\rightleftarrows v(px + (1-p)y) \geqslant v(x\,p\,y), \quad \forall p : 0 \leqslant p \leqslant 1$$
$$\rightleftarrows (px + (1-p)y)\,R\,(x\,p\,y), \quad \forall p : 0 \leqslant p \leqslant 1.$$

Other tests must be used to validate any structural assumptions made.

Törn [157] includes a discussion of random sampling methods in multi-objective problems, which is an extension of the ideas discussed in the section on the Las Vegas method in Chapter 2, but it is not formalized, and no explicit objective function is given.

A number of other references are given, largely covering multi-objective interactive programming, but with a small number of supporting references. Out of these, perhaps the ones which exhibit an essential difference to the others are those of Yu [174], who allows for partial choice, and Stewart [155], who allows for probabilistic choice.

4.6 EXERCISES

1. In section 4.2.3 we mentioned the possibility of expressing the resources required to perform certain activities solely in terms of manhours (see Baylis [13]). Consider the following problem. There is a finite set of machines $I = \{i\}$, $i = 1, 2, \ldots, m$, and a finite set of materials $U = \{u\}$, $u = 1, 2, \ldots, n$, such that every member of I requires only members of I and/or U to make it, and every member of U similarly requires only members of I to obtain it. Let: M_i be the direct manhours needed to make one machine of type i; x_{ij} be the number (not necessarily a whole number) of machine lives of type j to make machine type i (thus if machine j has life l_j and is required to operate for one year to produce i, then $x_{ij} = 1/l_j$); y_{ui} be the amount of material type u required to make one machine of type i; m_u be the direct number of manhours to obtain one unit of material u; z_{ui} be the number of machine lives type i to obtain one unit of material type u. Set down the equations for E_i (the total cumulative number of manhours required to produce one machine of type i), R_u (the total cumulative number of manhours required to produce one unit of material u). Defining appropriate costs, set down the corresponding cost equations. Under what conditions would the two sets of equations have equivalent solutions?

2. In the Mathematical and Dynamic Programming Exercise 4, on the bus services, certain objectives were mentioned. Discuss these, and any others you might feel as being relevant, and the quetion of surrogate and reducible objectives (see Lampkin et al. [95] and Bel et al. [14]).

3. Kendall et al. [91] list the following objectives in the context of blood supplies:

(1) blood shortages in general
(2) blood shortages for special cases
(3) inventory levels
(4) age of blood inventory—out-dating
(5) average size of blood inventory
(6) operating (running) costs.

Examine these as to their relevance to the problem, and in the context of the issues raised in section 4.2.3.

4. In Chapter 2, section 2.8 on Heuristic Programming, the Clarke–Wright heuristic for vehicle scheduling was discussed, based on time or distance. Other measures have been suggested for this type of problem, e.g. ton-mileage. What do you think the objectives of such a problem ought to be and what do you think is the relevance of the three objectives given above, either in their own right or as surrogates for other objectives? Give examples when you think they fail as surrogates (see Webb [163]).

5. Macon *et al.* [103] discuss the objectives of a government agency in providing audits for energy consumption for customers. The objectives they give are as follows:

(1) average waiting time per customer
(2) maximal waiting time per customer
(3) size of backlog
(4) utilization of auditors.

Discuss the relevance of these objectives, and other aspects as discussed in section 4.2.3.

6. Olcott [120] discusses the flow of traffic on highways. If v is the volume of traffic per hour, s is the speed of traffic in miles per hour, and ρ is the traffic density (cars per mile), empirical evidence gives:

$$s = 42.1 - 0.324\rho.$$

The situation can be influenced by highway design or speed restrictions. What do you think the relevant objectives ought to be, and examine these in the context of the discussion of section 2.3 (see also Newell [117] and Haight [68]).

7. Machol [102] discusses the problem of optimizing the thickness of a coin and feels that it is not really a sensible question to look at. What do you think the relevant objectives for such a problem should be and examine them in the context of the issues discussed in section 4.2.3.

8. Gazis *et al.* [64] discuss the behaviour of a driver approaching a traffic light confronted with a change to an amber light. What do you think the relevant objectives might be and examine them in the context of the discussion in section 4.2.3.

9. In section 4.2.3 we listed some objectives in queueing situations given by Saaty [138]. Give an example for each of a situation in which you think these are relevant, explaining why. Also return to the queueing material in section 1.1 of Chapter 1, and give examples of where you think $\hat{w}$, w^*, $\hat{w}(J)$ might be relevant. Also discuss the relevance of the objectives time in the queue and time in the system.

10. Presutti *et al.* [127] discuss the different situations one may have in inventory problems. The following objectives are mentioned:

(1) fixed order cost
(2) inventory holding cost
(3) occurrence of a shortage
(4) level of the shortage
(5) duration of the shortage.

Give an example of each objective where you think it is relevant and irrelevant and discuss their reducibility.

11. In the section 2.4 of Chapter 2 on Defective Product (Exercise 1) we raised the question of producing steel bars (see Brigham *et al.* [28]). The objective in that paper was to minimize expected loss, whereas the objective we chose was different. Examine both as to their relevance and appropriateness of form.

12. In section 4.2.3 we mentioned quality of life. How would you interpret this; and examine this in the context of the issues raised in the text.

13. In section 2.5 of Chapter 2 on Mathematical and Dynamic Programming a cutting stock problem is mentioned. Harrison *et al.* [71] discuss a complex cutting stock problem in which the objectives are as follows, and when the shapes to be cut are non-uniform:

(1) material loss
(2) complexity of patterns cut
(3) number of different patterns cut.

Explain why these are relevant and examine whether the objectives are reducible.

14. In section 2.5 of Chapter 2 on Mathematical and Dynamic Programming we discussed a hospital problem involving costs, types of patient, and paying and non-paying patients. Discuss the relevance of these objectives and whether they are reducible.

15. In sections 2.5 and 2.8 of Chapter 2 on Mathematical and Dynamic Programming and Heuristic Programming we discussed the problem of sequencing jobs. Sisson [147] lists six objectives which might be considered:

(1) total tardiness $(T = \sum_{i=1}^{n} \max[x_i + t_i - d_i, 0])$
(2) maximal tardiness of all jobs $(T_{\max} = \max_i[\max[x_i + t_i - d_i, 0])$
(3) in-process inventory
(4) machine utilization
(5) total penalty costs for being late
(6) time taken to complete all jobs.

In addition French [60] and Rinnooy Kan [133], discuss some of these plus:

(7) total lateness $(L = \sum_{i=1}^{n} (x_i + t_i - d_i))$

(8) maximal lateness of all jobs $(L_{max} = \max_i [x_i + t_i - d_i])$.

Dudik *et al.* [45] suggest that the following objective is widely applicable:

(9) weighted time and tardiness in completing all jobs

$$\left(M = \sum_{i=1}^{n} (\alpha_i (x_i + t_i) + \beta_i \max[x_i + t_i - d_i, 0]) \right).$$

For each objective give an example where you think this is relevant and irrelevant, and discuss the reducibility of each objective.

16. Haywood [73] discusses the problem of a dual between a fighter and a bomber where the objective of the fighter is to kill the bomber. Examine this objective in the context of the issues of section 4.2.3.

17. In Chapter 1 we specified two possible forms for the damage objective in setting depth charges. Examine these forms as to their relevance. Also in Exercise 6 of Chapter 1 we discussed the higher order decisions relating to the torpedo explosive filler or the submarine detection capabilities. Examine the contextual issues as discussed in section 4.2.3.

18. In section 4.2.3 we mentioned the problems which arise when material purchase and product selling costs are different in the simple inventory batch quantity problem. If p is the selling price of a unit of product and the objective is to minimize the annual cost of operating the inventory system, derive a modified formula to determine economic batch quantities, assuming the other costs are as for the standard problem (see White [168]).

19. In Chapter 1 we discussed the convoy size problem in terms of the objective of proportion of convoy losses. We also mentioned, in Exercise 7 of Chapter 1, the transportation aspects of convoys. Discuss the relevance of these and other objectives and examine their contextual aspects as discussed in section 4.2.3.

20. Imagine that you are required to justify why you go fishing, and begin to examine this in the context of problem cyclical evolution in section 4.2.5 (this is mentioned in that section).

21. Lock [99] lists 12 objectives which might arise in a given study in shoe manufacturing. These are:

  contribution and its configuration through time
  investment requirements (including working capital)
  market share/pairage
  speed of erosion of pairage and rate of recovery
  Bally image—the brand and its survival
  feasibility of manufacture of Bally shoes in the proposed way

impact on the retail business and its possible expansion
impact on the wholesale business
impact on the Swiss parent
ability to present a full range of men's shoes
Bally (UK) corporate objectives
demands made on management resources and skills.

Examine these as to their reducibility in principle (see section 4.2.3).

22. Explore the possibilities of problem cyclical evolution for the problems discussed in this chapter (see section 4.2.6).

23. The following papers make use of ratios as objectives: Ashton *et al.* [8], Chambers [33], Charnes *et al.* [35] and Geoffrion [65]. Examine the validity of the ratios used for decision making in those papers.

24. In the earlier material in Chapter 2, on Queues, Inventory, Maintenance and Defective Product, expected cost was used as the objective function. Examine the validity of this.

25. Consider a problem in which you have n independent queues, $\{j\}$, with arrival rates and service rates $\{\lambda_j, \mu_j\}$ respectively, arrival and service being negative exponential.

Let us assume that there are weighting factors for waiting in each queue, and cost factors for service rate, so that the total objective function is:

$$f(x) = \sum_{j=1}^{n} \alpha/(x_j - \lambda_j) + \sum_{j=1}^{n} \beta_j x_j.$$

Let it be assumed that there is a constraint of the form

$$\sum_j \beta_j x_j \leq L.$$

Analyse this problem in the same way as the inventory problem of section 4.2.2.2, where the decision variables are the service rates $\{x_j\}$, and $x_j > \lambda_j$ in all cases to ensure queues do not build up indefinitely.

26. Consider the following two-decision-makers situation, referred to in section 4.2.1, in which one decision maker is the managing director who has to choose a bonus parameter b, and the second decision maker is the machine operator who can decide what the throughput rate, x, will be, and where x also influences the quality q. The bonus paid takes the form:

$$f(x, q) = b(x - \bar{x})q \quad \text{if } x \geq \bar{x}$$
$$= 0 \quad \text{if } x \leq \bar{x}$$

where $\bar{x}$ is some datum output level which is fixed in advance. The quality q, as a function of x, takes the form $q = 1 - \alpha(x - \bar{x})$ in suitable units and we will assume $q = 1$ if $x \leq \bar{x}$. The normal wage paid, exclusive of bonus, is λ per unit produced, irrespective of quality. For a given b assume that the operator chooses his value of x to maximize his income (bonus + normal wage). Determine how b should be set to maximize the company total income, if the sales value of quantity x at quality q is sqx and if the maximal possible production rate is $k\bar{x}$, $k \geqslant 1$. The problem is to be analysed in terms of its parametric values $\{\bar{x}, \lambda, s, k, \alpha\}$. It may be assumed that $1 - \alpha(k-1)\bar{x} \geqslant 0$ so that $q \geqslant 0$ for all feasible x.

27. In Exercise 5 of Chapter 1 a simple search problem was given in which a fixed time T was given for searching. Use the Lagrange multiplier approach theoretically, or by using particular numbers, for $p = 0.4$, $q = 0.6$, $k = 0.1$, to examine the variation of the solution as a function of $T \leqslant 10$ (see section 4.2.2.2 for similar analysis for a redundancy problem, and assume time available is in discrete units). Assume that no more than 5 units of time may be assigned to each region. Use parametric values for λ equal to 0.01, 0.03, 0.05, and interpret your results.

28. In section 4.2.2.2 a Lagrangean analysis was used to study the effect of resource level on the solution of a redundancy problem. In Exercise 17 of the Mathematical and Dynamic Programming Exercises, this problem is formulated as a dynamic programme. Use the dynamic programming form to study the effect of resource levels on the solution.

29. In the Inventory section (2.2) of Chapter 2, an inventory problem is considered in which there is a penalty r for each unit shortage. Now suppose that the demand is either 2, 1, or 0, with probability p^2, $2(1-p)p$, $(1-p)^2$ respectively, and that the penalty cost for a shortage is not incorporated, but that the probability p now depends upon the probability of shortage, so that $p = p_0(1-q)$ where q is the probability of shortage, and the problem is to maximize the expected profit per unit time, with $T = 1$, and r being the sales value of a unit. Take the average inventory in an interval to be $\frac{1}{2}$ (initial + final) inventory. Reformulate and determine the expected profit for $x = 2$, 1, 0, respectively. Note that q depends upon x and that, since the problem is discrete, a set-up only arises if a positive order is placed and $x > 0$. It is also best to set the model up from scratch rather than use the continuous model as given.

30. In the Inventory section (2.2) of Chapter 2, we introduced the concept of a penalty cost r for each unit shortage. Equally well, in the case of backlogs, we could have a penalty costs per unit shortage per unit time delay in satisfying this. Discuss the reality of such penalties. An alternative is to avoid specifying such penalty costs and put a constraint on the probability of shortages, or shortages for more than a certain length of time as mentioned in sections 4.2.2.2 and 4.2.3. Discuss the validity of this approach.

31. Baligh *et al.* [11] discuss the allocation of resources in a hospital, as described in section 2.5 of Chapter 2, on Mathematical and Dynamic Programming. Discuss the choice of constraints and objectives as given in this problem.

32. In a study of a hospital layout the objective to be minimized was taken to be the weighted sum of the annual distances travelled, within the hospital complex, by various categories of staff (e.g. nurses, surgeons, etc.), in the course of their duties. Discuss the validity of this objective.

33. In sections 4.2.2.1 and 4.2.3 the question of bed occupancy and customer service was introduced. What sort of model could you build to rationalize the calling in of waiting list patients?

34. Ellis [55] reproduces an amusing piece from *Punch* about London Transport Board's attempt to apply queueing theory to congestion of buses and in buses. Buses arrive late, bunch (i.e. several arrive together), and tend to be overcrowded on some, as a result, and less so on others. Some options considered were to allow buses to miss stops or for buses to overtake. Discuss the problem formulational aspects of this problem as you see them in the context of the material of this chapter.

35. The following objectives have been listed as being important in the control of inventory, viz.

frequency of ordering
inventory levels
shortage levels
duration of shortages
condition of inventory.

Consider the three cases:

(a) when the inventory is blood in a blood bank;
(b) when the inventory is material required for a production process;
(c) when the inventory is an item sold by a mail order firm.

Discuss the following factors, to be found in section 4.2.3, for each case:

(i) reducibility of objectives to a common denominator;
(ii) surrogate nature of the objectives;
(iii) relevance of the objectives.

36. You will soon be leaving university and hope to take up a job. Using the framework of this text examine the prolem formulation aspects of job selection as you see them. How does this match up to what you actually did?

37. In section 4.2.1 an example was given where the steady state arrival rate will be some function of the service in terms of waiting time. Suppose that the steady state arrival rate is $\lambda = k/\hat{w}$, where $\hat{w}$ is the expected waiting time of an individual. Solve the problem of determining the service rate to maximize the profit per unit time when x must range between 0 and $\bar{x}$. Compare the result with the weighting factor approach discussed in sections 4.2.1, 4.2.3, 4.2.4, and 4.2.5, and discuss the significance of this.

38. Duncan *et al.* [47] incorporate constraints on inventory levels in the health services. Examine this in the context of hard and soft constraints.

39. Rework the Lagrange multiplier calculations for the redundancy problem in section 4.2.3 using the constraint $2x_1 + x_2 \leqslant b$.

40. In section 4.3 it is suggested that a goal programming approach may not give optimal solutions where value functions exist in principle. Construct an example to illustrate this.

41. Carry out a Lagrangean relaxation analysis for the constrained inventory control problem in section 4.2.2.2, when x_j, $j = 1, 2$, must be integer, and with the following data:

j	1	2
c_j	5	10
s_j	100	60
a_j	20	5
α	0.1	

$$0 \leqslant x_j \leqslant 5, \qquad j = 1, 2.$$

42. Examine the preference structure associated with Figure 4.8 as to its reasonableness.

43. In sections 4.1 and 4.2.3 we have said that decision makers may prefer to use the payback period rather than average profit, or cost, or present worth (discounted cash flow). Consider the first example in the Maintenance section (2.3) of Chapter 2. Assume that there is an initial cost $c(z)$ associated with putting in maintenance units of size z and that the parameters are a function of z also. Examine the formulation of the problem to optimize over z, as well as inspection frequency, in the context of profit per unit time, discounted profit, and in terms of minimal payback period.

44. In the Queueing section (2.1) of Chapter 2 we discussed a linear programming approach to decision making in queues, which has little value for the objective function used there. However, now suppose that we want to find the efficient set with respect to the expected total waiting times of each arrival stream over K intervals. How would you use linear programming ideas to tackle this problem?

Examine the other stochastic problems of Chapter 2, where linear programming approaches have been suggested, from the same point of view.

45. In Section 4.3 we referred to the efficient solution approach of Dannenbring et al. [37] to inventory control problems, when the parameters, or even the model, are difficult to determine. Examine the simple maintenance problem discussed in the Maintenance section (2.3) of Chapter 2, in the same way.

46. In section 4.2.3 the relevance of certain objectives is considered. In some problems two central objectives of a general kind arise, viz. efficiency

of utilization of resources, and effectiveness of the utilization of resources. In addition to this, services provided can be inequitable (see Exercise 8 of Chapter 6 involving the measurement of fairness). In the public services we have refuse collection, public transport, police, educational, and health services. Examine what you might mean by the terms efficiency, effectiveness, and equity of service in each case, and give examples to show that services can have any one of the attributes without having any of the other two. Examine whether such a problem should be treated, therefore, as a multiple objective problem (see Savas [142]).

47. In the text it is noted that Exercise 10 of the Queueing Exercises might need to be formulated as a multi-objective problem, because it may not be easy to find penalties for overbooking. How would you tackle this problem as a multi-objective problem?

48. In the text it is suggested that variance, as well as expectation, of costs might be important as a determinant of choice. Find recurrence relations, for a given decision rule, for calculating the expectation and variance of the cost of eventually satisfying an order for Y items for the problem discussed in the Defective Product section (2.4) of Chapter 2.

4.7 REFERENCES

1. Abel, A. and Tong, R. M., On the generation of alternatives in decision analysis problems, *Journal of the Operational Research Society*, **33,** 377–388, 1982.
2. Ackoff, R., Gupta, S. K., and Minas, J. S., *Scientific Method: Optimizing Applied Research Decisions*, Wiley, 1962.
3. Adelson, R. M., Capital investment criteria, *Operational Research Quarterly*, **16,** 19–50, 1965.
4. Aggarwal, S. K., Optimising techniques for the interactive design of transportation networks under multiple objectives, Ph.D. thesis, Northwestern University, Evanston, 1973.
5. Akashi, H., Inagoki, T., and Inone, K., Interactive optimization of systems reliability under multiple objectives, *Institute of Electronic and Electrical Engineers, Transactions on Reliability*, **R-27,** No. 4, 1978.
6. Anderson, J. C. and Janson, M. A., Methods for managerial cause analysis, *Interfaces*, **9,** 121–128, 1979.
7. Arrow, K. J., *Social Choice and Individual Values*, Wiley, 1966.
8. Ashton, D. J. and Atkins, R. D., Multi-criteria programming for financial planning, *Journal of the Operational Research Society*, **30,** 259–270, 1979.
9. Atkins, D. R. and Chou, E. U., An interactive algorithm for multi-criteria programming, *Computers & Operations Research*, **1,** 81–87, 1977.
10. Aumann, R. J. and Kruskal, J. B., Assigning quantitative values to qualitative factors in the naval electronic problem, *Naval Research Logistics Quarterly*, **6,** 1–16, 1959.
11. Baligh, H. H. and Laughlunn, D. J., An economic and linear model of the hospital, *Health Services Research*, 293–303, Winter, 1969.
12. Baum, S., Carlson, R. C., and Shukla, P. R., Interactive solution of discrete multi-criterion problems: an algorithm for computational results for the binary

286

variable base, Technical Report, 79–82 Department of Industrial Engineering and Engineering Management, Stanford, 1979.

13. Baylis, R., A contribution to the application of systems analysis to manpower planning with a naive model, Department of Econometrics Southampton University, 1970.

14. Bel, G., Dubois, D., and Llibre, M., A set of methods in transportation network synthesis and analysis, *Journal of the Operational Research Society*, **30,** 797–808, 1979.

15. Belenson, S. and Kapur, K., An algorithm for solving multi-criterion linear programming problems with examples, *Operational Research Quarterly*, **24,** 65–77, 1973.

16. Bellman, R., *Dynamic Programming*, Princeton University Press, 1957.

17. Benayoun, R., Larichev, O., de Montgolfier, J., and Tergny, J., Linear programming with multiple objective functions, stem method, *Mathematical Programming*, **1,** 366–375, 1971.

18. Benajoun, R. and Tergny, S., Mathematical programming with multiple objective functions: a solution by P.O.P., *Revue Metra*, **9,** 279–299, 1970.

19. Benito, F., Markov decision processes and linear aggregation: a dialogue algorithm, *European Operational Research Conference*, 1980.

20. Bennett, W. S., Allocation of acceptable risk instead of expected value, *Operations Research*, **9,** 163–168, 1961.

21. Birkin, S. J. and Ford, J. S., The quantity/quality dilemma: the impact of a zero defects program, in *Multiple Criteria Decision Making*, J. L. Cochrane, M. Zeleny (Eds.), University of South Carolina Press, 1973.

22. Blackett, P. S., *Studies of War*, Oliver & Boyd, 1962.

23. Bowman, J., On the relationship of the Tchebychef norm and the efficient frontier in multiple criteria objectives, in *Multiple Criteria Decision Making*, H. Thiriez and S. Zionts (Eds.), Springer, 1976.

24. Boyd, W., Interactive preference assessment for decisions with multiple attribute outcomes, *4th Research Conference on Subjective Utility and Decision Making*, Rome, 1973.

25. Brady, R. P. and Walsh, J. E., Efficiency criteria for comparing cargo aircraft in deliveries between two terminals, *Operations Research*, **8,** 350–361, 1960.

26. Braggard, L., A critical analysis of stem like solutions to multi-objective programming problems, in *Multi-Objective Decision Making*, S. French, R. Hartley, L. C. Thomas, and D. J. White (Eds.), Academic Press, 1983.

27. Bray, T. A. and Proschan, F., Optimum redundancy under multiple constraints, *Operations Research*, **13,** 800–814, 1965.

28. Brigham, G. and Stenoien, J. O., An analytical solution to the problem of balancing opposing loss facors, *Operations Research*, **2,** 90–92, 1954.

29. Brill, E. D., Chang, S. Y., and Hopkins, L. D., Modelling to generate alternatives: the HSJ approach and an illustration using a problem in land use planning, *Management Science*, **28,** 211–235, 1982.

30. Caine, C. J. and Plant, R. H., Optimal inventory policy when stockouts alter demand, *Naval Research Logistics Quarterly*, **23,** 1–13, 1976.

31. Carlson, R. C. and Shukla, P. R., Analysis and solution of discrete multi-criterion problems with ranged trade-offs, Technical Report, 9–84, Department of Industrial Engineering and Engineering Management, Stanford University, 1979.

32. Carlson, R. and Thorp, H. H., A multicriterion approach to strategic planning: an application in inventory control, *Omega*, **5,** 57–65, 1977.

33. Chambers, D., Programming the allocation of funds subject to restriction reported results, *Operational Research Quarterly*, **10,** 407–431, 1967.

34. Chankong, V. and Haimes, Y. Y., Optimisation-based methods for multi-objective decision-making: an overview, *Large Scale System*, **5,** 1–33, 1983.

35. Charnes, A. and Cooper, W. W., Goal programming and multiple objective optimisation—Part 1, *European Journal of Operational Research*, **1**, 39–54, 1977.
36. Cyert, R. and March, J., *Behavioural Theory of the Firm*, Prentice-Hall, 1963.
37. Dannenbring, D. G. and Gardner, E. S., Using optimal policy surfaces to analyse aggregate inventory trade-offs, *Management Science*, **25**, 709–720, 1979.
38. Davis, M. D., *Game Theory*, Basic Books, 1970.
39. Deemer, W. L. and Thomas, C., The role of operational gaming in operations research, *Operations Research*, **5**, 1–27, 1957.
40. Dendrou, B. A., Dendrou, S., and Houstis, E., Multi-objective decision analysis for engineering systems, *Computers and Operations Research*, **7**, 301–312, 1980.
41. Depraetere, P., Muller, H., and de Sambonckx, S., Critical considerations concerning the multi-criteria analysis by the method of Zionts and Wallenius, *CORS/ORSA/TIMS Conference*, Toronto, 1981.
42. Dewey, T., *How Do We Think?*, Heath & Co., 1910.
43. Donaldson, W. A., Lawrie, N. L., and White, D. J., *Operational Research Techniques*, Vol. 2, Business Books, 1974.
44. Duckstein, L., Monarchi, D., and Weber, J., An interactive multiple objective decision making aid using non-linear goal programming, in *Multiple Criteria Decision Making*, M. Zeleny (Ed.), Springer, 1976.
45. Dudik, R. A., Panwalker, S. S., and Smith, M. L., Sequencing research and the industrial problem, in S.E., Elmaghraby (Ed.), *Symposium on Theory of Scheduling, Its Applications*, Springer, New York, 1973.
46. Duesing, E. C., Analysing soft constraints in L.P. problems, Report 8110, School of Management, University of Scranton, Pa. 18510, 1982.
47. Duncan, I. B. and Norwich, H. S., Opportunity costs and elementary inventory theory in the hospital service, *Operational Research Quarterly*, **24**, 27–34, 1973.
48. Dyer, J. S., Interactive goal programming, *Management Science*, **19**, 62–70 1972.
49. Dyer, J. S., A time sharing computer program for the solution of the multiple criteria problem, *Management Science*, **19**, 1379–1383, 1973.
50. Dyer, J. S., An empirical investigation of a man–machine interactive approach to the solution of the multiple criterion problem, in *Multi-Criteria Decision Making*, M. Zeleny and J. L. Cochrane (Eds.), University of South Carolina Press, 1973.
51. Dyer, J. S., The effects of errors in the estimations of the gradient on the Wolfe-Franke algorithm with implications for interactive programming, *Operations Research*, **22**, 160–174, 1974.
52. Dyer, J. S., Feinberg, A., and Geoffrion, A. M., An interactive approach for multi-criterion optimisation, with an application to the operation of an academic department, *Management Science*, **19**, 357–368, 1972.
53. Eden, C. and Sims, D., Subjectivity in problem identification, *Interfaces*, **11**, 68–74, 1981.
54. Eilon, S., Economic batch size determination for multi-product scheduling, *Operational Research Quarterly*, **10**, 217–227, 1959.
55. Ellis, H. P., Written in a queue, *Operations Research*, **6**, 125–127, 1958.
56. Epstein, L. I., A proposed measure for determining the value of a design, *Operations Research*, **5**, 297–299, 1957.
57. Everett, H., Generalised Lagrange multiplier method for solving problems of optimum allocation of resources, *Operations Research*, **11**, 399–417, 1963.
58. Feller, W., An *Introduction to Probability Theory and its Applications*, Vol. 1, Wiley, 1957.
59. Fishburn, P. C., *Utility Theory for Decision Making*, Wiley, 1970.

60. French, S., *Sequencing and Scheduling*, Ellis Horwood, 1982.
61. Gabbani, D. and Magazine, M. J., An interactive heuristic approach for multi-objective integer programming problems, Working Paper 148, Department of Management Science, University of Waterloo, Ontario, 1981.
62. Gaft, M. G. and Ozernoi, V. M., Multi-criterion decision problems, in *Conflicting Objectives in Decisions*, D. E. Bell, R. L. Keeney, and H. Raiffa (Eds.), Wiley, 1977.
63. Gardner, E. S., Inventory theory and the gods of Olympus, *Interfaces*, **10**, 42–45, 1980.
64. Gazis, D., Herman, R., and Maralaudin, A., The problem of the amber signal light in traffic flow, *Operations Research*, **8**, 112–132, 1960.
65. Geoffrion, A. M., Vector maximal decomposition programming, Working Paper No. 164, Western Management Science Institute, University of California, 1971.
66. Graham, R. J., Problem and opportunity identification in management science, *Interfaces*, **6**, 79–82, 1976.
67. Graham, R. J., The use of solutions for problem identification, *Interfaces*, **7**, 63–65, 1976.
68. Haight, F., The volume–density relationship in the theory of road traffic, *Operations Research*, **8**, 57–73, 1960.
69. Haines, J. J. and Hall, W. A., The surrogate worth trade-off method with multiple decision makers, in M. Zeleny (Ed.), *Multiple Criteria Decision Making*, Springer, 1976.
70. Harris, F. and Steuer, R., Intra set point generation and filtering in decision and criteria space, *Computers and Operations Research*, **7**, 41–53, 1980.
71. Harrison, P. and Smithies, T., The third dimension of two-dimensional cutting, *Omega*, **10**, 81–87, 1982.
72. Harsanyi, J. C., *Rational Behaviour and Bargaining Equilibrium in Games and Social Situations*, Cambridge University Press, 1977.
73. Haywood, O. G., Military decision and game theory, *Operations Research*, **2**, 365–385, 1954.
74. Hemming, T., A new method for interactive multi objective optimisation: a boundary point ranking method, in H. Thiriez and S. Zionts (Eds.), *Multiple Criteria Decision Making*, Springer, 1976.
75. Hosford, J. E., Measures of dependability, *Operations Research*, **8**, 53–64, 1960.
76. Hitch, C., Suboptimisation in operations research problems, *Operations Research*, **1**, 87–99, 1953.
77. Hitch, C. and Koopman, B. O., Comments on 'Fallacies in operations research', *Operations Research*, **4**, 422–426, 1956.
78. Hoag, H. W., The relevance of costs in operations research, *Operations Research*, **4**, 448–459, 1956.
79. Hopkins, D. S. P., Massey, M. W. F., and Wehrung, D., Interactive preference optimisation for university administrators, *Management Science*, **24**, 599–611, 1978.
80. House, P. G., How do you know where you are going, in *Multiple Criteria Decision Making*, J. L. Cochrane and M. Zeleny (Eds.), University of South Carolina Press, 1973.
81. Howard, N., *Paradoxes of Rationality*, Massachussetts Institute of Technology Press, 1971.
82. Howard, R. A., *Dynamic Programming and Markov Processes*, Wiley, 1960.
83. Huckert, K., Rhode, R., Roglin, O., and Weber, R., On the interactive solution to a multi-criteria scheduling problem, *Operations Research*, **24**, 47–60, 1980.
84. Hwang, C. L. and Masud, A. S., Interactive sequential goal programming, *Journal of the Operational Research Society*, **32**, 391–400, 1981.

85. Hwang, C. L., Masud, A. S., Pliady, S. R., and Yoon, K., *Multiple Objective Decision Making, Methods and Applications*, Springer, 1979.
86. Ignizio, J. P., A review of goal programming; a tool for multiobjective analysis, *Journal of the Operational Research, Society*, **29,** 1109–1119, 1978.
87. Jones, M. T., O'Berski, A. M., and Tom, G., Quickening the queue in a grocery store, *Interfaces*, **10,** 90–92, 1980.
88. Karwa, M. H., Vilarreal, B., and Zionts, S., An interactive branch and bound procedure for multi-criterion integer linear programming, *Joint National Meeting of TIMS/ORS*, Washington, 1980.
89. Keeney, R. and Raiffa, H., *Decisions with Multiple Objectives*, Wiley, 1976.
90. Kendall, J. W., Hard and soft constraints in linear programming, *Omega*, **3,** 709–715, 1975.
91. Kendall, K. E. and Lee, S. M., Formulating blood rotation policies with multiple objectives, *Management Science*, **26,** 1145–1157, 1980.
92. Klahr, C. N., Multiple objectives in mathematical programming, *Operations Research*, **6,** 849–855, 1958.
93. Koopmans, T., Stationary ordinal utility and impatience, *Econometrica*, **28,** 287–309, 1960.
94. Kornbluth, J. S. M., A survey of goal programming, *Omega*, **1,** 193–205, 1973.
95. Lampkin, W. and Saalmans, P. D., The design of routes, services, frequencies and schedules for a municipal bus undertaking, a case study, *Operational Research Quarterly*, **18,** 375–398, 1967.
96. Lee, S. M., *Goal Programming for Decision Analysis*, Huerbach, Philadelphia, 1972.
97. Leibowitz, M. L., Metaphysical considerations involved in choosing a measure of effectiveness, *Operations Research*, **6,** 127–130, 1958.
98. Lin, J. G., Proper inequality constraints and maximisation of index vectors, *Journal of Optimisation Theory and Applications*, **21,** 505–522, 1977.
99. Lock, A. R., A strategic business decision with multiple criteria, the Bally men's shoe problem, *Journal of the Operational Research Society*, **33,** 327–332, 1982.
100. Luce, R. D. and Raiffa, H., *Games and Decisions*, Wiley, 1964.
101. Lukka, M., An algorithm for solving the multiple criteria optimal problem, *Journal of Optimisation Theory and Applications*, **28,** 435–438, 1979.
102. Machol, R., The optimum optimorum, *Interfaces*, **4,** 52–53, 1974.
103. Macon, M. R. and Turban, E., Energy audit program simulation, *Interfaces*, **11,** 13–18, 1981.
104. Marcotte, O. and Soland, R. M., An interactive branch and bound algorithm for multiple criteria optimisation, Report T442, School of Engineering and Applied Science, George Washington University, 1981.
105. Marcotte, O. and Soland, R. M., Branch and bound algorithms for multiple criteria optimisation, Universities of Cornell and George Washington, 1980.
106. Markowitz, H., *Portfolio Selections*, Wiley, 1959.
107. Marschak, J., Elements for a theory of teams, in *Economic Information Decision and Prediction, Selected Essays*, Vol. II, J. Marschak (Ed.), D. Reidel, 1974.
108. McGarity, A., Revelle, C., and Schilling, D. A., Hidden attributes and the display of information in multiobjective analysis, *Management Science*, **28,** 236–242, 1982.
109. Michaelowski, W. and Piotrowski, A., Solving multi objective production planning problems by an interactive procedure, in *Multi-Objective Decision Making*, S. French, R. Hartley, L. C. Thomas, and D. J. White (Eds.), *Academic Press*, 1983.
110. Mole, R. H., Inventory control in hospital blood banks, *Omega*, **3,** 461–474, 1975.

111. Morgenstern, O. and Von Neuman, J., *The Theory of Games and Economic Behaviour*, Princeton University Press, 1947.
112. Morris, P. and Oren, S., Multi attribute decision making for sequential resource allocation, *Operations Research*, **28**, 233–252, 1980.
113. Morse, J. N., Reducing the size of the non-dominated set: pruning by clustering, *Computers and Operations Research*, **7**, 55–66, 1980.
114. Müller-Merbach, Morphological techniques for O.R.-approaches, in *Operational Research*, **75**, K. B. Haley (Ed.), North Holland.
115. Musselman, K. and Talavage, J., A trade-off cut approach to multiple objective optimisation, *Operations Research*, **28**, 1424–1435, 1980.
116. Nakayama, H., Sawaragi, Y., and Tanino, T., An interactive optimisation method in multi criteria decision making, *Institute of Electronic and Electrical Engineers, Transactions on Systems Management and Cybernetics*, **10**, 163–169, 1980.
117. Newell, G. F., Mathematical models for freely flowing highway traffic, *Operations Research*, **3**, 176–186, 1955.
118. Newell, A. and Simon, H. A., Heuristic problem solving: the next advance in operations research, *Operations Research*, 1–10, 1958.
119. Oppenheimer, K. R., A proxy approach to multi-attribute decision making, *Management Science*, **24**, 675–689, 1978.
120. Olcott, E. S., Vehicular speed-spacing, *Operations Research*, **3**, 147–167, 1955.
121. Ornea, J. C. and Stillson, P., On the optimum solution in operations research, *Operations Research*, **8**, 616–629, 1960.
122. Pasternak, B. A., Filling out the doughnut: a single period inventory model in corporate policy, *Interfaces*, **10**, 96–100, 1980.
123. Pearman, A., A weighted maximin and maximax approach to multiple criteria decision making, *Operational Research Quarterly*, **28**, 584–587, 1977.
124. Pidd, M. and Woolley, R. N., Four views on problem structuring, *Interfaces*, **10**, 51–54, 1980.
125. Pidd, M. and Woolley, R. N., Problem structuring, *Journal of the Operational Research Society*, **32**, 197–206, 1981.
126. Pollatscheck, M. A., Personnel assignment by multi-objective programming, *Zeitschrift für Operations Research*, **20**, 161–170, 1976.
127. Presutti, V. and Trapp, R. C., More ado about economic order quantities, *Naval Research Logistics Quarterly*, **7**, 243–251, 1970.
128. Price, W. L., An interactive objective function generator for goal programming, in *Multiple Criteria Decision Making*, H. Thiriez and S. Zionts (Eds.), Springer-Verlag, 1976.
129. Radford, K. J., *Strategic Planning: An Analytical Approach*, Reston Publishing Co., 1980.
130. Rapaport, A., *Game Theory as a Theory of Conflict Resolution*, D. Reidel, 1974.
131. Ravindran, A. and Sadagopan, S., Multi-criteria mathematical programming—a unified interactive approach, Research Memorandum 80-3, School of Industrial Engineering, West Lafayette, 1980.
132. Reitman, W. R., Heuristic decision procedures, open constraints and the structure of ill defined problems, in *Human Judgements and Optimality*, M. Shelley and G. Bryan (Eds.), Wiley 1964.
133. Rinnooy Kan, A. H. G., *Machine Scheduling Problems: Classification Complexity and Computations*, Martins Nijhoff, The Hague, 1976.
134. Rivett, P., Policy selection by structural mapping, *Proceedings of the Royal Society, Series A*, **354**, 407–423, 1977.
135. Rosinger, E. E., Interactive algorithm for multi objective optimisation, in *Multiple Criteria Decision Making*, C. Fandel and T. Gal (Eds.), Springer, 1980.

136. Ross, G. T. and Soland, R. M., A multi criteria approach to the location of public facilities, *European Journal of Operational Research*, **4**, 307–321, 1980.
137. Rudermann, A. P., Lessons from Latin American experience, in *Economic Benefits from Public Health Services*, US Department of Health Education and Welfare, 1967.
138. Saaty, T., Resumé of useful formulas in queueing theory, *Operations Research*, **5**, 161–200, 1957.
139. Sarin, R. K., Interactive evaluation and bound procedures for eliciting multi attributed alternatives, in *Multiple Critera Decision Making*, M. K. Starr and M. Zeleny (Eds.), North-Holland, 1977.
140. Sawaka, M., Interactive multi objective decision making by the sequential proxy optimisation technique: spot, *European Journal of Operational Research*, **6**, 386–392, 1982.
141. Savage, L. J., *The Foundations of Statistics*, Wiley, 1954.
142. Savas, E. V., On equity in providing public services, *Management Science*, **24**, 800–808, 1978.
143. Schaible, S., Fractional programming: applications and algorithms, *European Journal of Operational Research*, **3**, 111–122, 1981.
144. Schuler, A. T. and Steuer, R. E., An interactive multiple objective linear programming approach to a problem in forest management, *Operations Research*, **26**, 254–269, 1978.
145. Schwartz, B. L. A new approach to stockout penalties, *Management Science*, B538–B544, 1966.
146. Schwartz, B. L., Optimal inventory policies in perturbed demand models, *Management Science*, **16**, B509–B518, 1970.
147. Sisson, R. L., Methods of sequencing in job shops—a review, *Operations Research*, **7**, 10–29, 1959.
148. Sokawa, M. and Soo, F., A methodology for environmental systems management: dynamic application of the Lagrange multiplier method, *Institute of Electronic and Electrical Engineers, Transactions in Systems Management and Cybernetics*, 794–505, 1979.
149. Spencer, J. E., Probability, defectives and mail ordering, *Journal of the Operational Research Society*, **10**, 899–906, 1981.
150. Spronk, J., Capital Budgeting and Financial Planning with Multiple Goals, in *Multiple Criteria Analysis*, P. Nijkamp and J. Spronk (Eds.), Gower Press, 1981.
151. Stainton,, R. S., Production scheduling with multiple criteria objectives, *Operational Research Quarterly*, **28**, 285–292, 1977.
152. Steuer, R. E., A five phase procedure for implementing a vector maximum algorithm for multiple objective linear programming problems, in *Multiple Criteria Decision Making*, H. Thiriez and S. Zionts (Eds.), Springer-Verlag, 1976.
153. Steuer, R. E., Linear multiple objective programming with interval criterion weights, *Management Science*, **23**, 305–316, 1976.
154. Steuer, R. E., An interactive multiple objective linear programming procedure, *TIMS Studies in the Management Sciences*, **6**, K. Starr and M. Zeleny (Eds.), North-Holland, 1977.
155. Stewart, T. J., An interactive approach to multiple criteria decision making based on statistical inference, Technical Report TWISK204, National Research Institute for Mathematical Sciences, Pretoria, South Africa, 1981.
156. Thanassoulis, E., Paseb, A solution procedure for multi objective linear programming problems, in *Multi-Objective Decision Making*, S. French, R. Hartley, L. C. Thomas, and D. J. White (Eds.), Academic Press, 1983.
157. Törn, A. A., A sample search clustering approach for exploring the

feasible/efficient solutions on MC DM problems, *Computers and Operations Research*, **7**, 67–79, 1980.

158. Walker, J., An interactive method as an aid in solving bicriterion mathematical programming problems, *Operational Research Quarterly*, **29**, 915–922, 1978.

159. Wallenius, J., Comparative evaluation of some interactive approaches to multi criterion optimisation, *Management Science*, **21**, 1387–1396, 1975.

160. Wallenius, J. and Zionts, S., An interactive programming method for solving the multiple criteria problem, *Management Science*, **22**, 652–663, 1976.

161. Wallenius, J. and Zionts, S., A research project on multi-criterion decision making, in D. Bell, R. Keeney, and H. Raiffa (Eds.), *Conflicting Objectives in Decision*, Wiley, 1977.

162. Wallenius, J. and Zionts, S., An interactive multiple objective linear programming method for a class of underlying non linear utility functions, Working Paper No. 451, School of Management, University of Buffalo, 1981.

163. Webb, M. H. J., Cost functions in the location of depots for multiple-delivery journeys, *Operational Research Quarterly*, **19**, 311–320, 1968.

164. Wehrung, D. A., Interactive identification and optimisation using a binary preference relation, *Operations Research*, **26**, 322–332, 1978.

165. Wehrung, D. A., Multidimensional line search using a binary preference relation, *Operations Research*, **27**, 356–363, 1979.

166. White, D. J., *Decision Theory*, Allen & Unwin, 1969.

167. White, D. J., *Dynamic Programming*, Oliver & Boyd, 1969.

168. White, D. J., *Decision Methodology*, Wiley, 1975.

169. White, D. J., *Fundamentals of Decision Theory*, North-Holland, 1976.

170. White, D. J., Multi-objective interactive programming, *Journal of the Operational Research Society*, **31**, 517–523, 1980.

171. White, D. J., Multi-objective interactive programming for efficient sets, in *Multi-Objective Decision Making*, S. French, R. Hartley, L. C. Thomas, and D. J. White (Eds.), Academic Press, 1983.

172. White, D. J., *Optimality and Efficiency*, Wiley, 1982.

173. Whittle, P., *Optimisation under Constraints*, Wiley, 1971.

174. Yu, P. L., Introduction to domination structures in multi criteria decision problems, in *Multiple Criteria Decision Making*, J. L. Cochrane and M. Zeleny (Eds.), University of South Carolina Press, 1973.

175. Zeleny, M., *Linear Multi-Objective Programming*, Springer, 1974.

176. Zionts, S., Multiple criteria decision making for discrete alternatives with ordinal criteria, Working Paper No. 299, State University of New York at Buffalo, School of Management, 1977.

177. Zionts, S., Integer linear programming with multiple objectives in formal methods, in *Policy Formulation*, D. W. Bunn and H. Thomas (Eds.), Birkhauser, 1978.

178. Zionts, S., A survey of multi-criteria integer programming methods, *Annals of Discrete Mathematics*, **5**, 389–398, 1979.

179. Zionts, S., A multiple criteria method for choosing among discrete alternatives, *European Journal of Operational Research*, **5**, 143–147, 1981.

CHAPTER 5

Combined Use of Techniques

5.1 INTRODUCTION

In Chapter 2 we discussed a selection of techniques, each of which was seen in its own right. In addition, we discussed some of the qualitative advantages and disadvantages of the techniques on their own. In recent years there has been a movement towards the use of combinations of techniques in order to make use of their combined advantages. In this chapter we will briefly discuss a few examples of such combinations. In doing this it is to be noted that, in a way, the combination of techniques has an overall heuristic quality, and that much more empirical and mathematical investigation is needed to provide a proper foundation for the ideas which will be discussed.

Before commencing it is worth noting that, taking a broad view on the term techniques, the multi-objective interactive programming procedures of Chapter 4 are examples of combined techniques, as indeed is the overall Operational Research process. It is of course quite possible, for example, to make use of the Las Vegas technique here also. However, we will confine ourselves to the techniques of Chapter 2, with the exception that we will make use of the Lagrange multiplier ideas of Chapter 4 which were originally introduced in Chapter 1.

5.2 QUEUEING THEORY WITH SIMULATION

The first example we will use will concern the combined use of queueing theory and simulation. In recent years queueing theory has been somewhat controversial and we will eventually make use of some material appearing in this controversy. The reader may wish to consult the following references in this context, which is quite illuminating with respect to the role of queueing theory, in particular, in Operational Research, viz. Byrd [5], Kolesar [16], Vazsonyi [29], Cosmetatos [8], and Siegel et al. [24].

To return to our example, this is the emergency unit size problem introduced in Chapter 4, section 4.2, (see Figure 4.4). The size of the emergency unit, x, has to be determined. One important factor to be determined is the extent of emergency provision, viz.

$$f^1(x) = \lambda \text{ (probability that all } x \text{ beds are occupied)}$$

where λ is the arrival rate of emergencies.

It is of course quite possible to build a simulation model which would be

293

subject to the disadvantages discussed in Chapter 2, section 2.10. In operating such a model, it would certainly be of some help to have some idea of the order of magnitude of x to be used in the simulation, and analytic models can help here in the first instance. In constructing such models certain difficulties arise for this particular problem, viz.

(a) although we may assume that emergencies can occur continuously throughout the day, and a negative exponential distribution is not an unreasonable fit (although varying throughout the day and from day to day), discharges may take place at fixed times during a day, and on fixed days, and any assumption of negative exponential service times is at best an approximation;
(b) if an emergency arrives and there is no bed available, one of several things may take place, viz.
  (i) a patient occupying an emergency bed may be discharged early from the emergency unit into another ward, which may be undesirable, but may be thought to be appropriate under the circumstances;
  (ii) the emergency patient may be sent to some other hospital, being undesirable and wasting time;
  (iii) an emergency bed may be set up somewhere else in less than ideal conditions.

In case (iii) we may treat the problem as a queueing problem with unlimited service capacity providing the overflow is small. From Chapter 2, section 2.1, for the negative exponential case, we obtain:

$$P_n = \frac{\rho^n}{n!} e^{-\rho}, \qquad n \geq 0$$

$$f^1(x) = \lambda \left(\sum_{n=x}^{\infty} \frac{\rho^n}{n!} \right) e^{-\rho}$$

$\rho = \lambda/\mu$, μ^{-1} being the average duration of stay.

In case (ii) we may treat the problem as a queueing problem in which the bed capacity is fixed at x. From Chapter 2, Queueing Exercise 1, for the negative exponential case, we have:

$$P_n = \frac{\rho^n}{n!} \bigg/ \left(\sum_{l=0}^{x} \frac{\rho^l}{l!} \right), \qquad 0 \leq n \leq x$$

$$f^1(x) = \frac{\lambda \rho^x}{x!} \bigg/ \left(\sum_{n=0}^{x} \frac{\rho^n}{n!} \right).$$

We tackle case (i) from scratch using the general formula from Chapter 2, section 2.1, for P_n.

We have:

$\underline{0 \leq n \leq x-1} \quad \lambda(n) = \lambda$

$\underline{n \geq x} \quad \lambda(n) = 0$

(the case $n = x$ gives a net flow rate $\lambda(x) = 0$)

$$\mu(n) = n \quad \text{for all } n.$$

Then:

$$P_n = \frac{\rho^n}{n!} \Big/ \Big(\sum_{l=0}^{x} \frac{\rho^l}{l!} \Big), \qquad 0 \le n \le x$$

$$f^1(x) = \frac{\lambda \rho^x}{x!} \Big/ \Big(\sum_{n=0}^{x} \frac{\rho^n}{n!} \Big).$$

It is to be noted that $f^1(x)$ is the same for cases (i) and (ii), because arriving patients are really no different to discharged patients with respect to residual stay distributions in the negative exponential case.

We need still to calculate the reduction in duration of stay using the policy in (i). To do this we use the waiting time results of Chapter 2, section 2.1. We have:

$$w^* = \hat{w} = \hat{n}/\lambda = \Big(\sum_{n=0}^{x-1} \frac{\rho^n}{n!} \Big/ \sum_{n=0}^{x} \frac{\rho^n}{n!} \Big) \mu^{-1}.$$

Then:

$$\Delta(\mu^{-1})(x) = \text{reduction in duration of stay, given } x,$$
$$= \mu^{-1} - w^*$$
$$= \Big(\frac{\rho^x}{x!} \Big/ \sum_{n=0}^{x} \frac{\rho^n}{n!} \Big) \mu^{-1}.$$

The total reduction in duration of stay is:

$$\lambda \Delta(\mu^{-1})(x) = \Big(\lambda \frac{\rho^x}{x!} \Big/ \Big(\sum_{n=0}^{x} \frac{\rho^n}{n!} \Big) \Big) \mu^{-1}.$$

Each of these models may be used as a starting point to determine the range of x values to simulate, depending on the conditions (i)–(iii) which are to be accepted as valid. Sometimes, a mixture of these conditions may apply, and all three models may be needed with some judgement on the extent to which each would be applied. It is to be noted that $f^1(x)$ may not differ greatly in the cases (i)–(iii).

As a check on the validity of the approximations, the analytic queueing results should be compared with the simulation results. If large differences arise then the analytic results must be discarded or modified.

Cosmetatos [8] discusses the problem of determining the number of trucks to provide internal transport services for a company. The number in use was three, and the question was whether or not a fourth truck was profitable. The inter-arrival time distribution was approximately negatively exponential, but the service time distribution was skewed unimodal. For this problem, it is quite feasible to simulate the behaviour, although this was not done. The problem was modelled in two ways, viz.

(a) negative exponential inter-arrival time, negative exponential service time, N servers;

(b) negative exponential inter-arrival time, constant service time, N servers.

The expected waiting times of (a) and (b) were taken to be, respectively, upper and lower bounds on the true expected waiting times. For the case $N = 3$ the actual expected waiting time was found to lie nicely between the two limits, which were not too far apart. This was then used as a justification for estimating the true expected waiting time for the case $N = 4$. The ideas may be equally well used for larger problems to determine a suitable range of values of N to simulate.

The development of approximate queueing theory results, which may be used without any further study, or which may be used to get some idea of range of policies to be simulated in the first instance, are further illustrated by Taha [27], Page [20], Sakasawaga [21], and Bissinger et al. [2].

Taha illustrates his approximation ideas with reference to problems in which we have a single server, negative exponential inter-arrival time, and in which:

(a) the service time is negative exponential, or
(b) the service time is general.

Analytic results are known for both cases, although we have not covered case (b) in this text. If $\hat{n}_a$, $\hat{n}_b$, are the expected numbers in the system for cases (a), (b), respectively, we have:

$$\hat{n}_a = \rho/(1-\rho) \text{ (see Chapter 2, section 2.1)}$$

$$\hat{n}_b = \rho + \rho^2(1+\alpha^2)/2(1-\rho)$$

where $\alpha^2 =$ (variance of service time) μ^2 (see, for example, Cox et al. [9]).

The proportional error incurred by using $\hat{n}_a$ instead of $\hat{n}_b$ is:

$$e = \rho(\alpha^2 - 1)/(2 + \rho(\alpha^2 - 1)).$$

This may take quite small values for certain parametric values.

For this problem we do not, of course, need the approximation, and the real question is one of knowing, for more complex cases, where tractable analytic solutions do not yet exist, whether the approximations used will be adequate. A general study comparing the approximations with simulated results would help.

Page suggests an approximation scheme for waiting times as follows:

$$\hat{w}(\alpha_a, \alpha_s, u) = \hat{w}(1, 0, u)\alpha_a(1-\alpha_s) + \hat{w}(0, 1, u)\alpha_s(1-\alpha_a)$$

$$+ \hat{w}(1, 1, u)\alpha_a\alpha_s$$

where: $\hat{w}$ are all evaluated in units of service time;

u is the utilization level of the service facility;

$\hat{w}(1, 0, u)$ is the expected waiting time for deterministic inter-arrival times and negative exponential service times;

$\hat{w}(0, 1, u)$ is the expected waiting time for deterministic service times and negative exponential inter-arrival times;

$\hat{w}(1, 1, u)$ is the expected waiting time for negative exponential inter-arrival and service times;

α_a, α_s, are as for Taha's model for inter-arrival times and service times respectively;

each $\hat{w}$ is evaluated for the general case of N servers.

Page tabulates $\hat{w}(1, 0, u)$, $\hat{w}(0, 1, u)$, $\hat{w}(1, 1, u)$ for a range of values of u and N.

The empirical simulation work needed to support these approximations has yet to be done, but they can always be used as a starting point for a simulation for a given Operational Research study.

Sakasawaga [21] produces similar tables for a restricted class of problems.

Another way in which queueing theory may be used in conjunction with simulation is via the use of inequalities for the key parameters of the problem. Marshall [17] gives some useful results.

Chelst et al. [6] discuss a problem of supplying a power station with coal, and the consequential queueing problems. A single unloader is available which is subject to breakdown. The initial question is one of whether another unloader would be profitable. The times to failure and repair of the unloaders are approximately negative exponential but the unloading times and cycle times (times for trains to return to coalfield and then to power station) are not. The model used assumed that all times were negative exponential and was a Markovian model, similar to the dynamic programming and mathematical programming models developed in the Queueing section (2.1) of Chapter 2, but with no actual optimization taking place, and with the state (n_1, n_2) now being as follows:

n_1: number of broken unloaders
n_2: number of trains waiting to be unloaded or being unloaded.

The approximation was tested against a simulation and produced close results. Although the original problem was to determine whether a second unloader was profitable, the real value of the study, once the approximations had been validated, was to be able to use the analytic results to explore other possible changes in the system, such as effects of speeding up repairs, and so on. Eventually further simulations would be needed to support any final decision based on the analytic model.

Ingall et al. [13] deal with the combined use of simulation and queueing theory making use of the priority queueing theory of Cobham [7], discussed in Chapter 2, but for several servers, in a problem involving priority rules for a fleet of police patrol cars. The servers are the police cars and the customers are the calls for help, categorized into different types. The problem is to determine the number, x, of patrol cars to have. The argument is that it is very expensive to have to simulate for each value of x in each set of circumstances, and simulation was used to validate approximations and to produce useful formulae for determining x in terms of the data of the problem.

Finally, there is another sense in which techniques such as simulation and queueing theory may be combined, and that is in the verification that the simulation is behaving properly. Thus, if we specialize the input data into the simulation so that it represents a standard queueing problem, for which the behaviour is known, the simulation may then be run and checked against the known results.

5.3 DYNAMIC PROGRAMMING WITH SIMULATION

In Chapter 2, sections 2.1–2.4, we discussed some dynamic programming models of queueing, inventory, maintenance, and defective product situations. Each of these models is quite tractable providing, for example, we put a limit on the number of states allowable in the problems. In many real life situations, the number of states can, however, be very large, in fact so large as to defeat present computational capabilities. The only realistic approach is to use simulation. However, as has been indicated in Chapter 2, section 2.10, if we are dealing with the determination of decision rules, we may have an enormous number of possibilities, and, without some guidance on the choice of these, it is difficult to know how to select the decision rules to be simulated.

Buzacott *et al.* [4] deal with just such a problem. The full details are given in that paper and we will deal briefly with the problem here. The basic problem concerns the determination of decision rules for loading steel ingots into soaking pits which serve primary rolling mills. The purpose of a soaking pit is to raise the temperature of the ingot so that it is ready for rolling by the primary mill. At certain points in time, pits will become empty, and a choice will exist as to whether they should be loaded with ingots, hot and cold, available for loading into the pits, or to wait for hotter ingots which will be due later on. The objective is to maximize the utilization of the primary mills.

The problem may be described in terms of the state of the system at any point in time. This state has several components, viz.

n_1: the amount of steel (in pit units) awaiting stripping (before becoming available for loading into the pits)
n_2: the amount of hot steel (in pit units) waiting to be loaded into the pits
n_3: the number of empty pits
n_4: the number of pits holding cold steel
n_5: the number of pits holding hot steel
n_6: the number of pits with steel ready for rolling by the primary mill
n_7: whether or not the primary mill is waiting for steel.

The decisions available are:

$x = 1$: load pit with hot steel
$x = 2$: load pit with cold steel
$x = 3$; wait for hot steel (from stripper).

In order to make the model tractable, Buzacott *et al.* [4] make certain assumptions. For example, assumptions of a negative exponential nature are made about the transition times for steel in the soaking pit to move from a cold to a hot state. In addition the decisions take place, for example, when pits become available for loading. In order to keep matters at a simple level compatible with our simple dynamic programming models, we will assume that we take decisions after each unit time interval. Then let:

$i = (n_1, n_2, n_3, n_4, n_5, n_6, n_7)$ be the state of the system
$x = 1, 2, 3$ be the three possible actions

p_{ij}^x be the probability of transition from state i to state j given action x
r_i^x be the expected amount of steel rolled at the primary mill in the next unit time interval if we begin in state i and take action x
$f_k(i)$ be the expected total amount of steel rolled at the primary mill over the next k unit time intervals, using an optimal decision rule.

Then, as with the development of our previous dynamic programming equations, we have the following:

$K \geqslant k \geqslant 1$

$$f_k(i) = \max_x \left[r_i^x + \sum_j p_{ij}^x f_{k-1}(j) \right], \quad \text{for all } i.$$

$k = 0$

$$f_0(i) = 0, \quad \text{for all } i.$$

We may calculate, as before, $f_0, f_1, \ldots, f_k$ recursively and the decision rules giving x, i.e. $x = \theta_k(i)$ for each k and i.

Buzacott *et al.* [4] actually solve the problem for infinite K, and use an equivalent linear programming model, which equates with our mathematical programming models in Chapter 2, sections 2.1–2.4, although we have used discount factors.

Now let us return to our main point. The model used is very much a simplification of the actual situation with which programming methods, as they stand, would not be able to cope. On the other hand, the simulation of the actual situation requires some guidance as to the decision rules to be simulated. Buzacott *et al.* [4] used their model to give just such guidance. The decision rule they arrived at was as follows:
(a) if $n_2 > 0$, then $x = 1$
(b) if $n_2 = 0$, $n_1 = 2$, then $x = 3$

(c) if $n_2 = 0$, $n_1 = 1$, $n_3 = 0$ or ($n_3 = 1$, $n_1 = 0$, $n_4 > 0$) then $x = 3$.
(d) if $n_2 = 0$, ($n_3 = n_1 = 0$) or ($n_3 = 0$, $n_1 = 1$, $n_4 > 0$) then $x = 3$.
(e) if not (a)–(d) then $x = 2$.

This decision rule was then used as a guide as to which decision rules to use in the simulations. As a safeguard, one can always supplement the set of rules simulated by other suitable rules, for example by including the rule used in practice and suitable deviations from this.

5.4 SIMULATION WITH OTHER TECHNIQUES

In addition to providing simulation guidance, as in the previous section, mathematical models, combined with simulation, may allow a greater understanding of the effects of design parameters on performance than the use of simulation on its own. Consider the following trawler design problem. For a single trawler let:

T	be the time available for fishing in a year, plus port leave
λ	be the catch rate of the trawler when fishing
x	be the trawler speed to and from the fishing grounds
y	be the fish-holding capacity of the trawler
d	be the distance from the port to the fishing ground
$g(x, y)$	be the fuel cost per unit time when travelling between port and fishing ground
$c(x, y)$	be the capital cost per year
$l(x, y)$	be the labour costs per year
s	be the sales value per unit catch
$m(x, y)$	be the maintenance costs per year.

Trawlers have to return to port within a period t of completing fishing and spend 1 day in port for every 10 days away.

The objective is to choose x, y to maximize the profit per year. The analysis is as follows.

The number of cycles (trips) per year is:

$$T/(1.1(y/\lambda + 2d/x)).$$

The total annual sales value is:

$$syT/(1.1(y/\lambda + 2d/x)).$$

Then the annual profit is:

$$f(x, y) = (T/(1.1(y/\lambda + 2d/x)))(sy - 2(d/x)g(x, y)$$
$$- l(x, y)(y/\lambda + 2d/x) - m(x, y)).$$

This gives a mathematical expression for the annual profit which may be studied to determine the optimal value subject to the constraints:

$$x \geqslant d/t, \qquad y \geqslant 0.$$

Now this is a very much simplified model. It ignores the effects of weather variations, the randomness of catches, the possible movements from one fishing ground to another, and so on. A satisfactory approach, for a given design, would clearly be a simulation model, but guidance is required as to which designs should be simulated. The mathematical model may help here and, once the simulations have been carried out, the expression for total cost might be modified, analysed, and the process repeated.

A much more realistic problem is tackled by Nickerson et al. [18], who evaluate twenty possible trawler designs, and also include decision rules for the trawler skipper to use in the light of such things as bad weather, and so on. The simulations were not aided by any analytic model but this would have been possible, and possibly necessary if any optimization over all feasible designs was to be considered.

In Chapter 2, sections 2.5 and 2.8, we discussed various facility location problems. In Exercise 12 of the Mathematical and Dynamic Programming Exercises, in particular, we looked at the problem of locating fire stations in which, once the locations were specified, we could determine which regions were reachable by which fire stations. The problem may, however, have been somewhat different if we had actually looked at the dynamics of allocation of vehicles as the demands arose, and if, for example, the expected distances or response times were to be optimized. Swoveland et al. [26] discuss a similar problem involving ambulances rather than fire stations. An ambulance depot has to be located in each of n regions. Within each region a set of possible locations is given. The decision x is a specification of the set of locations to be used, $N(x)$. Requests for an ambulance will arise at any such location i, but may actually be served by some other ambulance depot, which may be the same depot, the closest depot, the next-closest depot, and in general by the qth-closest depot. For a given $\{i, x\}$, $l_x(i, q)$ is the qth-closest depot location to i. If d_{ij} is the distance between locations i and j and if $w(i, q)$ is the proportion of requests at location i which are served by the qth closest location to i, the objective function to be minimized is:

$$f(x) = \sum_{i \in N(x)} \sum_{q=1}^{n} w(i, q) d_{i, l_x(i, q)}.$$

The essential problem is one of determining $w(i, q)$, and, in their paper, Swoveland et al. [26] use simulation to estimate this quantity, and then use the mathematical programming formulation, and then use branch and bound procedures (which we have not covered, but see Shapiro [23] for background) to obtain the appropriate x. Alternative procedures, such as the Las Vegas approach discussed in this text, may be used.

A similar situation may arise in the maintenance problem discussed in Exercise 1 of the Simulation section (2.7) of Chapter 2. If, with an appropriate objective function, an optimization problem, relating either to the location of the depot and/or to the determination of the number, x, of jobs to handle in each cycle, had been proposed, then the expected distance per job would be required. This could be obtained by simulation, and then the problem could be reduced to an optimization problem. Even if we use the approximating theoretical result (viz. $a/\sqrt{x}$), the value of a still has to be estimated.

A related problem is discussed by Ignall *et al.* [13] (see also Exercise 11 of the Simulation Exercises of Chapter 2) in which x units are located either uniformly or randomly in a given region, and each call for service is met by the nearest unit at the time. The analytic result for the expected distance travelled to a call is $k\sqrt{(m/x)}$ where m is the area being served (see Blum *et al.* [3]). Simulations were used to validate approximations to determine the parameter k, and then the results used for decision making. For example, given b units and n regions, if the problem is to determine how many units, x_i, to assign to region i to minimize the total distance travelled, the problem reduces to one very similar to the constrained inventory problem discussed in Chapter 4 using Lagrange multipliers, viz.

$$\text{minimize} \left[f(x) = k \sum_{i=1}^{n} \sqrt{(m_i/x_i)} \right]$$

subject to

$$\sum_{i=1}^{n} x_i = b$$

$x_i \geq 0$ and integer for all i. m_i is the area of region i.

To solve this we might use heuristic methods such as the appropriate ones in Chapter 2, section 2.8.

Note that, in relationship to the earlier maintenance example, $a = k\sqrt{(m)}$.

Sargent *et al.* [22] provide useful information on the use of simulation and other techniques.

Finally, the Las Vegas technique itself may be used, for example, for determining approximately optimal decision rules in our queueing, inventory, and other problems. In order to determine the values of $\phi(x)$, where x is now a decision rule, ϕ may need to be determined by a simulation process.

5.5 LAGRANGE MULTIPLIERS WITH OTHER TECHNIQUES

In Chapter 4, it was shown that, if $x(\lambda)$ optimizes $l(x, \lambda)$ over the remaining constraints not included in $l(x, \lambda)$, and if $g_i(x(\lambda)) = b_i(\lambda) \leq b_i$, for the constraints included in $l(x, \lambda)$, then, if x is an optimal solution to the initial problem with constraint levels $\{b_i\}$, $i = k+1, \ldots, p$, we have

$$f(x(\lambda)) \leq f(x) \leq f(x(\lambda)) + \sum_{i=k+1}^{p} \lambda_i (b_i - b_i(\lambda)).$$

Now, in practice, we may not be able, within an acceptable computational cost, to determine $x(\lambda)$, and may only derive a sub-optimum $\hat{x}(\lambda)$ for $l(x, \lambda)$. In this case, the above expression must be modified. The analysis is as follows:

$$l(x, \lambda) = f(x) - \sum_{i=k+1}^{p} \lambda_i (g_i(x) - b_i)$$

$$l(\hat{x}(\lambda), \lambda) = f(\hat{x}(\lambda)) - \sum_{i=k+1}^{p} \lambda_i (g_i(\hat{x}(\lambda)) - b_i).$$

Then, with $l(x(\lambda), \lambda) - l(\hat{x}(\lambda), \lambda) = \varepsilon$, we have

$$l(x(\lambda), \lambda) - l(x, \lambda) - \varepsilon = f(\hat{x}(\lambda)) - f(x) + \sum_{i=k+1}^{p} \lambda_i (g_i(x) - g_i(\hat{x}(\lambda)))$$

$$= \ \leqslant f(\hat{x}(\lambda)) - f(x) + \sum_{i=k+1}^{p} \lambda_i (b_i - \hat{b}_i(\lambda))$$

where $g_i(\hat{x}(\lambda)) = \hat{b}_i(\lambda) \leqslant b_i$ and x is feasible for b_i, $i = 1, 2, \ldots, p$.

Then, since $l(x(\lambda), \lambda) - l(x, \lambda) \geqslant 0$, we have, noting that $\hat{x}(\lambda)$ is also feasible for $\{b_i\}$, if x is optimal for the given $\{b_i\}$,

$$f(\hat{x}(\lambda)) \leqslant f(x) \leqslant f(\hat{x}(\lambda)) + \sum_{i=k+1}^{p} \lambda_i (b_i - \hat{b}_i(\lambda)) + \varepsilon.$$

This reduces to the original result when $\varepsilon = 0$ and $x(\lambda) = \hat{x}(\lambda)$.

Thus, the use of this method will depend upon how good an approximation $\hat{x}(\lambda)$ is to $x(\lambda)$. Various methods are available for obtaining $\hat{x}(\lambda)$, such as the Las Vegas and Heuristic Programming methods discussed in Chapter 2, sections 2.9 and 2.8, of this text, which depend upon the form of the problem. Thus, if the problem is a constrained scheduling problem (see the Heuristic Programming section (2.8) of Chapter 2), an appropriate heuristic method may be used.

When using the Lagrangean method, obviously a judicious choice of which constraints to incorporate into the Lagrangean, and which to leave out, is important. In Exercise 3 of the Mathematical and Dynamic Programming Exercises we discussed the problem of determining a timetable for teaching a programme of subjects which involves constraints for which the Lagrangean method may be used. Tipathy et al. [28] discuss an extension of a problem of Barham et al. [1] where the latter use a special heuristic method, and the former use a Lagrangean method, still heuristic in nature, as the Lagrangean method really is, since it does not guarantee optimal or even approximately optimal solutions. In this paper the problem is as follows. There are m optional subjects, i, to be taught, $i = 1, 2, \ldots, m$, a maximal number N of lecture periods, a total number of times b_i on which subject i has to be taught, $i = 1, 2, \ldots, m$, and a limit d_j on the number of parallel sessions available in period $j, j = 1, 2, \ldots, N$. The objective is to schedule the teaching programme to maximize $\sum_i \sum_j c_{ij} x_{ij}$, where $x_{ij} = 1$ if option i is assigned to period j, and $x_{ij} = 0$ otherwise (if we wish to minimize the total number of periods used, then a modification is possible).

The constraints for the problem are as follows:

$$\sum_{j=1}^{N} x_{ij} = b_i, \qquad i = 1, 2, \ldots, m$$

$$\sum_{i \in S_k} x_{ij} \leqslant 1, \qquad k = 1, 2, \ldots, M, \qquad j = 1, 2, \ldots, N$$

$$\sum_{i=1}^{m} x_{ij} \leqslant d_j, \qquad j = 1, 2, \ldots, N$$

where $\{S_k\}$ are the sets of optional subjects which may be timetabled simultaneously because no student requires more than one option in any set S_k.

The first two sets of constraints have what is referred to as the unimodular property (for example, see Hu [12]) for which special solution procedures exist, and hence the third set of constraints was chosen for inclusion in the Lagrangean, and a branch and bound method used to solve the Lagrangean problem. If the branch and bound method is used to obtain an exact optimum for the Lagrangean, then we will have $\varepsilon = 0$.

5.6 MATHEMATICAL PROGRAMMING WITH HEURISTIC PROGRAMMING

The most obvious way in which mathematical programming and heuristic programming come together is when the original problem has been formulated as a complete mathematical programming problem and then some heuristic technique is used to get good solutions to this. A glance at the Mathematical Programming section (2.5) of Chapter 2 will indicate how difficult it can be to solve some of those problems (for example, see the mathematical programming formulations of the travelling salesman problem) exactly by mathematical programming optimization techniques, and some heuristic method may be needed. Thus, for example, one might relax the integer requirements and find the continuous optimum and then find the integer optimum in a suitable neighbourhood of this.

In Chapter 4, section 4.2.2.1, we mentioned the operational/technological/investment hierarchies of decision making (Ornea *et al.* [19]). They discuss an oil refinery problem with three classes of decision, viz.

x: selection of feedstock type and throughput (operational)
y: selections of feeds to be reformed and conditions of reformation (technological)
z; location and size of refineries (investment).

In principle, it is possible to formulate as a mathematical programming problem, although far too large to solve using standard mathematical programming techniques. For specified values of $\{y, z\}$, the problem reduces to a linear programming problem. If $f(x, y, z)$ is the objective function and $X(y, z)$ is the feasible set of actions x given (y, z), it is possible to evaluate:

$$g(y, z) = \max[f(x, y, z)]$$
$$x \in X(y, z)$$

and then to use some heuristic (or other) procedure for optimizing $g(y, z)$. For example, one heuristic which might be used is to fix z, maximize over y, then maximize over z and so on in a similar manner to the supply point–destination problem discussed in the Heuristic Programming section (2.8) of Chapter 2.

Another manner in which the two approaches may be used, is one in which the main method is an heuristic one, but, in which, components of this may be handled by mathematical programming. Thus, for example, the machine loading problem of Smith et al. [25], discussed in the Heuristic Programming section (2.8) of Chapter 2, is solved by an heuristic which gives rise to a possible mathematical programming form of the travelling salesman problem, which may, however, need to be solved by a sub-heuristic programming method. Another example arises in Exercise 6 of the Heuristic Programming Exercises of Chapter 2, which is an example of the classical bin-packing problem (see Johnson [15]). One heuristic is to load as much as is possible on to the first cassette, and then repeat the procedure for the remaining cassettes in sequence. This may then give rise to a sub-mathematical-programme at each stage as follows. Let T_k be the time available on a cassette k. Let piece of music i take time t_i, $i = 1, 2, \ldots, m$, and let S_k be the set of pieces of music still to be loaded when we reach cassette k. For this sub-problem, let $x_i = 1$ if music i is loaded on to cassette k, $x_i = 0$ otherwise. The problem is then formulated as follows:

$$\text{maximize} \left[f(x) = \sum_{i \in S_k} t_i x_i \right]$$

subject to

$$\sum_{i \in S_k} t_i x_i \leq T_k$$
$$x_i = 0 \text{ or } 1, \quad \forall i \in S_k.$$

This might be solved exactly by some 0–1 mathematical programming method (for example, see Hammer et al. [11]). Alternatively, it might be solved using some sub-heuristic (for example, see Granot [10]). Although the problem is in the knapsack form discussed in the Heuristic Programming section (2.8) of Chapter 2, the application of the greedy heuristic suggested is quite arbitrary for this problem, since it does not discriminate between any two pieces of music.

It is quite possible to replace the heuristic by one which involves loading the first r machines to a maximal amount, and then the next r, and so on, with $r = 2, 3, \ldots$. It is possible to formulate the intermediate steps of the heuristic as mathematical programmes as we did for the case $r = 1$.

Jain $et\ al.$ [14] introduce yet another way in which heuristic and mathematical programming methods may be combined. The problem concerns the determination of a production programme for steel producers over a sequence of months. One set of constraints is as follows:

$$\sum_i p_{ik} x_{ij} \leqslant b_{jk} \quad \forall j, k$$

where x_{ij} is the number of rolls of steel to be shipped in month j
p_{ik} is the time for roll i on machine k
b_{jk} is the time available in month j on machine k.

The complicating features are that one does· not know exactly what $\{b_{jk}\}$ will be, since it is a function of the queueing behaviour of the system, and this is a function of the $\{x_{ij}\}$ as planned. In addition, it is not known which machines will be used, and there will be a choice. It is of course possible to produce a mathematical programme to take care of this but, not only is this complex, but it cannot be guaranteed that particular machines will not be in use for other jobs as the programme actually evolves in practice. Thus an heuristic method for determining $\{b_{jk}\}$ was used, details of which may be found in the paper.

In the Heuristic Programming section (2.8) of Chapter 2, an analytic approach to determining the optimal number and location of warehouses was studied. It is possible to use this as a starting point for a mathematical programming model. Thus let $i = 1, 2, \ldots, N$ be possible locations for a warehouse. Partition the region into a finite number of regions, j, $j = 1, 2, \ldots, M$. Let $x_i = 1$ if a warehouse is located at point i, $x_i = 0$ otherwise, $i = 1, 2, \ldots, m$. Let $i(j, x)$ be the nearest warehouse to j given a location vector $x = (x_1, x_2, \ldots, x_N)$, and γ be the total demand associated with any region j. Then the problem reduces to the following:

$$\text{minimize} \left[f(x) = a \sum_{i=1}^{N} x_i + c\gamma \sum_{j=1}^{M} g_j(x) \right]$$

subject to

$$x_i = 0 \text{ or } 1$$

$$\sum_{i=1}^{N} x_i \geqslant 1$$

where $g_j(x) = d_{i(j,x),j}$, $j = 1, 2, \ldots, M$.

The evaluation of $\{g_j(x)\}$ will pose problems, but some procedure may be developed in which, for example, $\{g_i(x)\}$ may be evaluated as it is required for each x. The heuristic method will give a starting solution which specifies $\{x_i\}$ to begin with, providing the feasible locations are chosen to include the starting solution.

5.7 REFERENCES

1. Barham, A. and Westwood, J. B., A simple heuristic to formulate course timetabling, *Journal of the Operational Research Society*, **29,** 1055–1060, 1979.
2. Bissinger, B. H. and Murty, V. N., Approximate queueing formulae based on consideration of a busy period, *Journal of the Operational Research Society*, **29,** 707–708, 1978.
3. Blum, E. H. and Kolesar, P., Square root laws for fire engine response distances, *Management Science*, **19,** 1368–1378, 1973.
4. Buzacott, J. A. and Callahan, J. R., The pit charging problem in steel production, *Management Science*, **20,** 665–674, 1973.
5. Byrd, J., The value of queueing theory, *Interfaces*, **8,** 22–26, 1978.
6. Chelst, K., Pipis, J. S., and Tilles, A. Z., A coal unloader: a finite queueing system with breakdowns, *Interfaces*, **11,** 12–24, 1981.
7. Cobham, A., Priority assignment in waiting line problems, *Operations Research*, **2,** 70–76, 1954.
8. Cosmetatos, G. P., The value of queueing theory—a case study, *Interfaces*, **9,** 47–51, 1979.
9. Cox, D. R. and Smith, W. L., *Queues*, Chapman & Hall, 1971.
10. Granot, F., Efficient heuristic algorithms for positive 0–1 polynomial programming problems, *Management Science*, **28,** 829–836, 1982.
11. Hammer, P. L. and Rudeanu, S., *Boolean Methods in Operations Research*, Springer-Verlag, 1968.
12. Hu, T. C., *Linear Programming and Network Flows*, Addison-Wesley, 1969.
13. Ignall, E. J., Kolesar, P., and Walker, W. E., Using simulation to develop and validate analytic models: some case studies, *Operations Research*, **26,** 237–253, 1978.
14. Jain, S. K., Stott, K. L., and Vasold, E. G., Order book balancing using a combination of linear programming and heuristic techniques, *Interfaces*, **9,** 55–67, 1978.
15. Johnson, D. S., Fast algorithms for bin packing, *Journal of Computing and Systems Science*, **8,** 272–314, 1974.
16. Kolesar, P., A quick and dirty response to the quick and dirty crowd, particularly to Jack Byrd's 'The value of queueing theory', *Interfaces*, **9,** 77–82, 1979.
17. Marshall, K. T., Some inequalities in queueing, *Operations Research*, **16,** 651–668, 1981.
18. Nickerson, T. B., O'Flaherty, T. G., and Rice, D. W., A simulation model for the evaluation of fishing trawler designs, *Management Science*, **20,** 699–707, 1973.
19. Ornea, J. C. and Stillson, P., On the optimum solution in operations research, *Operations Research*, **8,** 616–629, 1960.
20. Page, E., Tables of waiting times for M/M/n, M/D/n, and D/M/n, and their use to give approximate waiting times in more general queues, *Journal of the operational Research Society*, **33,** 453–473, 1982.
21. Sakasawaga, H., Numerical tables of the queueing system 1: $E_k/E_2/s$, Institute of Statistical Mathematics, Computer Science Monograph, 1978.
22. Sargent, R. G. and Shanthikumar, J. G., A unifying view of hybrid

simulation/analytic models and modelling, *Operations Research*, **31,** 1030–1052, 1983.
23. Shapiro, J. E., *Mathematical Programming, Structures and Algorithms*, Wiley, 1979.
24. Siegel, S. and Torelli, P., The value of queueing theory: a case study, *Interfaces*, **9,** 148–151, 1979.
25. Smith, A. W. and Stinson, J. P., A heuristic programming procedure for sequencing the static flow shop, *International Journal of Production Research*, **20,** 753–764, 1982.
26. Swoveland, C., Uyeno, D., Vertinsky, I., and Vickson, R., Ambulance location: a probabilistic enumeration approach, *Management Science*, **20,** 686–698, 1973.
27. Taha, H. A., Queueing theory in practice, *Interfaces*, **11,** 43–49, 1981.
28. Tipathy, A., A Lagrangean relaxation approach to course timetabling, *Journal of the Operational Research Society*, **31,** 599–603, 1980.
29. Vazsonyi, A., To queue or not to queue: a rejoinder, *Interfaces*, **9,** 83–86, 1979.

CHAPTER 6

Measurement in Operational Research

6.1 INTRODUCTION

In this chapter we will explore the concept of measurement in the context of Operational Research. It is not intended that this chapter will provide a full understanding of the fundamental foundations, but merely to provide an examination of some of the issues. For those readers seeking a complete grasp of the foundations the texts by Roberts [68], Pfanzagl [63], Krantz *et al.* [54], Rapoport [67], Ross [70], and Torgerson [81], and the papers by Suppes *et al.* [79], Bevan [7], and Adams [2], will be useful. For a foundation of measurement as it applies to value (or utility) and probability theory the text by Fishburn [27] will be useful.

Let us first begin with a few quotations which will set the scene for a study of the motives and hurdles as they apply to measurement and Operational Research.

When you cannot measure what you are speaking of and express it in numbers, your knowledge is of a very meagre and unsatisfactory kind.

Kelvin (see Mellen [61])

There is no idea or proposition in the field which cannot be put into mathematical language, although the utility of doing so can very well be doubted.

Brand [8]

It is true enough that not every complex human situation can be fully reduced to lines on a graph or to percentage points on a chart. But all reality can be reasoned about and not to quantify what can be quantified is only to be content with something less than the full range of reason.

McNamara [60]

There is no rational reason why every adjective by which a system may be described (i.e. maintainable, flexible, ...) should be capable of quantification.

Kazanowski [46]

An argument which is only convincing if it is precise loses all its force if the assumptions on which it is based are slightly changed, while an argument which is convincing but imprecise may well be stable under small perturbations of its underlying axioms.

Schwartz [76]

Not all the consequences of the 2DCP (2-dimensional cutting problems) are easily formulated into scales of numerical values.

Harrison [39]

These quotations illustrate the different stands which individuals can take on the measurement issue, ranging from those who believe in its complete essentially for scientific study, to those who have doubts either about this necessity for scientific study or who, if they do accept this necessity, implicitly rule out scientific study.

Brand uses the term mathematics and this text will take the stand that measurement is essentially a mathematical concept. Kelvin makes no reference to the value of measurement whereas Brand does, a point which is perhaps much more relevant in Operational Research than in physics as a pure science. Kazanowski rejects the idea of all adjectives being capable of measurement, in principle, a point with which we will disagree as a matter of principle, although the meaning or use of such measures may well be in doubt. Schwartz raises a slightly different point to the others which relates to the deductive content of an argument and to sensitivity, or error, analysis, a point to which we will return later on and have discussed in Chapter 3. Harrison is partly referring to the complexity issue to which we will return later on.

To add to these diverse views, Hayward [40] gives other quotations which indicate, in particular, the contra-measurement views taken by individuals in situations covering: military effectiveness [43], [25]; multi-dimensional indenture criteria [25]; measurement of safety, growth potential, spill-over effects, [25]; vision, foresight, intuition, wisdom [82]; multiplicity, incommensurability, non-measurability [41]. There may well be sound reasons for not trying to measure such properties, but this is not the same as saying that, in principle, they are not subject to measurement.

On the other hand we have the other side of the coin where incautious enthusiasm for measurement has led to suggestions for the measurement of such things as fuzziness, flexibility, productivity, and of uncertainty in terms of surprise or entropy, which do not match up to the rigorous requirements for measurement, and we will discuss these a little later on.

In Chapter 1 we referred to wartime studies and to Blackett's remark on the need for measurement. The roles played by this will be discussed later on and, in particular, we will refer to the judgement to be made on this need. At this point it is worth again linking our thinking with the origins of

Operational Research with the following quotation:

> The scientist in considering an operational problem very often comes to the conclusion that the common sense view is the correct one. But he can back the view by numerical proof, and thus give added confidence to the tactics employed. Or when two alternative qualitative views 'A is best' and 'B is best' are in dispute, he can often resolve this numerically into some such statement as that 'A is $x\%$ better than B in January and $y\%$ worse in June'. In fact the scientist can encourage numerical thinking on operational matters, and so can help to avoid running the war by gusts of emotion. (Waddington [87])

What then is measurement? In its simplest terms it is the assignment of a real number to a property of an element (object, or situation) in such a way that the ordering of the property over a set of elements is maintained by the order of its associated real numbers. Thus if A is the set of elements and if R is a binary relation between pairs $\{a, b\} \subseteq A$, which is transitive, reflexive, and comparable (R is a total order) then m is a measurement of property R when:

$a\ R\ b$ if and only if $m(a) \geqslant m(b)$.

Thus R might have the interpretations:

$a\ R\ b$ means a is at least as good as b

$a\ R\ b$ means a is at least as flexible as b

$a\ R\ b$ means a is at least as likely as b

$a\ R\ b$ means a is at least as safe as b

and so on.

It is to be noted that the terms flexible, likely, safe, may not be pre-defined, and the subject involved in assessing such properties may be expected to interpret these terms subjectively. In some cases such things as flexibility are explicitly defined in terms of computational routines (Phanzagl [63] uses the term fiat) and the question then is one of whether such measures are valid for particular purposes, a point to which we will return. We will call these measurements derived measurements.

Phanzagl has a much broader definition of measurement, which allows for properties of more than two elements of A, but we will confine ourselves to the binary case.

So far there is little of a contentious nature, and, indeed, the ability to measure properties is beyond question, given that R is a total order. For example, if A is a set of people and someone is asked to rank these in terms of their vision capacity for foreseeing future events or trends (again no definition of vision is given), then vision is certainly susceptible to measurement relative to the situation prescribed. This is not, of course, the same as being able to pre-define vision for specified purposes.

Such measurement is known as ordinal measurement (see Phanzagl [63]) and is unique up to strictly monotonic transformations. Conditions for the existence of such measurements to exist are extremely weak, involving topological housekeeping requirements (see Phanzagl). For example if A is finite, or even countable, measurements will exist.

However, this is insufficient to be of any use. To know that $m(a) > m(b)$ is to merely know that a P b (a P b is the same as a R b, b not R a), and, if we know whether or not R is true for all $\{a, b\} \leqslant A$, in advance, measurement adds nothing. For measurement to be useful we must get more from the measurement process than we put into it. To quote Phanzagl [63]:

> The general aim of measurement is to map a set A on the set of real numbers in such a way that — to the greatest possible extent — conclusions concerning the relations between elements of M can be drawn from corresponding relations between their assigned numbers.

This refers not only to a single binary relation with which we began, but to a set of relations, representing properties, which may exist simultaneously for the same set M. Thus we may have simultaneous properties of preference, cost (usually a derived measurement), flexibility, safety, and so on and we may wish to study the inter-relationship between each of these, and ultimately express preference as a numerical measurement in terms of the numerical representation of the other properties. This is known as conjoint measurement (see Krantz et al. [54]).

We will examine Phanzagl's statement in a broader context to allow, for example, for the communication aspect of measurement, an aspect which is relevant to the quotations of Kelvin and of McNamara. The points we will cover are as follows:

   (i) Conjoint Measurement
  (ii) Structural Measurement
 (iii) Testability of the Axioms
 (iv) Prediction and Surrogate Measurement
  (v) Communication and Meaning of Measurement
 (vi) Sensitivity Analysis and Approximation and Errors
(vii) Open and Closed Forms of Analysis
(viii) Operational Procedures.

In the following sections, A will be a set of conceivable actions and any theory will be relative to such a set A. For a given problem situation, the actual set of actions, X, open to the decision maker, may be a subset of A, or equivalent to a subset of A. Thus if (for example see the utility theory of Morgenstern et al. [62]) A is a set of actions specified in terms, possibly, of probability distributions of outcomes, the physical problem may be defined in terms of a set X of investment possibilities, each of which is equivalent to an action in A.

6.2   CONJOINT MEASUREMENT

Conjoint measurement is concerned with the numerical representation of relationships between a set of properties. Thus, suppose R, R_1, R_2, are three total orders over A, representing three distinct properties of any element of A. Then, for our purposes, a monotone decomposable measurement structure will exist if there are real valued functions m, m_1, m_2, g such that, for $a \in A$:

$$m(a) = g(m_1(a), m_2(a))$$

where m, m_1, m_2, are ordinal measurements for R, R_1, R_2, respectively and g is strictly monotonic increasing in its arguments m_1, m_2, respectively (see Krantz *et al.* [54]).

This can easily be generalized to more than three properties and naturally also applies to the case of two properties, trivially so. For this case, with total orders R, R_1, we require:

$$m(a) = g(m_1(a)).$$

Conditions for the existence of such measurements exist. For the simple case above it is quite clear that, for finite or countable A, the necessary and sufficient condition is that R and R_1 are equivalent, i.e.

$$\{a, b\} \subseteq A, \qquad a \text{ R } b \quad \text{if and only if} \quad a \text{ R}_1 b.$$

To avoid unnecessary topological conditions, for the general case we will assume A is finite or coutable. The following condition is necessary and sufficient when we have a total order R, and N other total orders $\{R_i\}$, and we assume that, for each set of indifference classes induced by $\{R_i\}$, there exists an $a \in A$. If $\{R_i\}$ are given by derived measurements, so that $(R_1, R_2, \ldots, R_N)$ is initially represented by, say, $z = (z_1, z_2, \ldots, z_N)$, an N-dimensional vector, then this is equivalent to saying that for each realizable z_i, $i = 1, 2, \ldots, N$, there is an $a \in A$ such that $z_i = z_i(a)$, $i = 1, 2, \ldots, N$. This latter is the usual form discussed in conjoint measurement (see Krantz *et al.*), but we wish to allow for the $\{R_i\}$ to be the primitive information used.

Now define $\{I_i\}$ as follows for $i = 1, 2, \ldots, N$:

$$\{a, b\} \subseteq A, \quad a \text{ I}_i b \quad \text{if and only if} \quad a \text{ R}_i b, b \text{ R}_i a.$$

Then a necessary and sufficient condition for a monotone decomposable measurement to exist is as follows, where, to generalize our simple case, a monotone decomposable measurement is defined as a set of real valued functions m, $\{m_i\}$, $i = 1, 2, \ldots, N$, g such that, for $a \in A$:

$m(a) = g(m_1(a), m_2(a), \ldots, m_N(a))$, where m, $\{m_i\}$ are ordinal measurements for R, $\{R_i\}$ respectively, and g is strictly monotonic increasing in its arguments $\{m_i\}$.

C.M.

The following is to hold for each $i = 1, 2, \ldots, N$.

Let $\{a, b\} \subseteq A$, $\{a^1, b^1\} \subseteq A$ be such that

$$a \; I_j \; b, \qquad a^1 \; I_j \; b^1, \quad \text{for all} \quad j \neq i$$
$$a \; I_i \; a^1, \qquad b \; I_i \; b^1.$$

Then:

$$a \; R \; b \quad \text{if and only if} \quad a^1 \; R \; b^1.$$

This is the independence condition which, in effect, says that the ordering of $\{a, b\} \subseteq A$ depends only on the ordering of the ith component order R_i when the $\{a, b\}$ are indifferent with respect to the remaining components.

Although, for this result to apply, A has to be rich enough, it is arguable that artificially enhancing the original A to include hypothetical possibilities should not be objected to. For the case of incomplete products, a corresponding theory exists (see Fishburn [27]), but we will not pursue this.

Now let us look at the significance of this result. Let us quote Baecher [3].

For scales of evaluation to be meaningful, one must know how numbers behave when combined by simple rules; any scaling and combinations of impacts and their associated desirabilities must be firmly grounded in the theory of measurement.

Thus, to return to our simple example, with $N = 2$, the measurements for R, R_1, R_2, must be related, and condition C.M. must hold. The $\{m_i\}$ are only unique up to strictly monotone transformations, and the choice of $\{m_i\}$ will determine g uniquely up to strictly monotone transformations.

In order to illustrate this, let us return to our queueing theory and let us assume, for the moment, that (see Exercise 1 of the Sensitivity Analysis Exercises of Chapter 3) it is known that the determinants of choice are the cost, c, and the expected waiting time of an individual, $\hat{w}$. Let A contain the set of decisions X, and then $c = c(x)$, $\hat{w} = w(x)$ may be calculated. They are derived measures, so we may take $z_1 = c$, $z_2 = \hat{w}$, with:

$$z_1 \; R_1 \; z_1^1 \quad \text{if and only if} \quad z_1 \leq z_1^1$$
$$z_2 \; R_2 \; z_2^1 \quad \text{if and only if} \quad z_2 \leq z_2^1.$$

The total order R will be the preference order over X, or equivalently over the pairs $\{c(x), w(x)\}$, $x \in X$.

If we now wish to construct a value function (see Chapter 4) for X, we need to determine m, m_1, m_2, g so that (with m replacing v)

$$m(x) = g(m_1(c(x)), m_2(w(x)))$$

and $\{m, g, m_1, m_2\}$ have the requisite ordering properties, and this will require that condition C.M. be checked. It is not permissible to use independent scoring systems (such as weighting factors as discussed in Chapter 4) for the factors $\{c, \hat{w}\}$ and to combine them in any particular way, unless this is done in conformity with the theory.

Let us now take this a little further. We have assumed that $\{c, \hat{w}\}$ are the determinants of choice. However, $\hat{w}$ is obtained from a probability distribution of waiting times in reality. In Chapter 4 we did raise the question (see Form of Statement of Objectives in section 4.2.3) as to whether the use of expected levels is really adequate. This is a derived measurement and, given the whole probability distribution, the decision maker may well choose in a manner inconsistent with the use of expectations. If p is the probability distribution of waiting time we will have $z_1 = c$, $z_2 = p$ and then, if the requisite conditions hold, we may obtain $\{m, m_1, \tilde{m}_2, g\}$, which are somewhat different to the original $\{m, m_1, m_2, g\}$ where $\tilde{m}_2$ is now a function of p, a probability distribution.

It is of course true that it can be extremely difficult to identify the m, $\{m_i\}$, g. As Wiener [97] says:

Things do not, in general, run around with measures stamped on them like the capacity of a freight car. It requires a certain amount of investigation to discover what their measures are. What most experimenters take for granted before they begin their experiments is infinitely more interesting than any results to which their experiments lead!

Given a particular situation, very often it is required to determine derived measurements for particular properties, such as those of safety, complexity, and so on, but such derived measurements must still conform to the theoretical requirements governing their use. We will return to some of these properties later on.

Before we move on to look at more structured measurements, it is worth saying a little bit about conjoint measurement in relationship to preference, probability, and value (or utility), since these are related concepts and any measurements must also be related via the appropriate theory. The reader may find it helpful to go back to Chapter 3, section 3.9. In order to simplify matters let us assume that we have a set of events α, with $\mathcal{S}$ as the set of all subsets of α, A the set of actions (required for the theory, although the actual set X may be a subset of A), and $\theta(x, \alpha)$ the outcome if action x is taken and event α materializes. Let H be the set of outcomes.

We may, if we wish, determine ordinal measurements for the concepts of subjective probability over $\mathcal{S}$, and of value over H.

316

We may obtain values u over H by some method of ranking and scoring. We may obtain probabilities over $\mathcal{S}$, providing the decision maker is able to order the members of $\mathcal{S}$ in such a way that certain conditions hold (see Fishburn [27]). In Fishburn the decision maker is assumed to have a qualitative probability order relation R_2 over $\mathcal{S}$, which we will assume to be total, where a qualitative probability is defined as one which satisfies the following conditions, where

$Y \in \mathcal{S}, \qquad Z \in S, \qquad Z\,P_2\,Y \qquad$ if and only if $\qquad Z\,R_2\,Y, \qquad Y$ not $R_2 Z$:

Q.1. $Z \in \mathcal{S}$ implies $\varnothing$ not $P_2\,Z$
Q.2. $\alpha\,P_2\,\varnothing$
Q.3. $Z \cap Y = W \cap Y = \varnothing$ implies
$\qquad W\,P_2\,Z \quad$ if and only if $\quad (W \cup Y)\,P_2\,(Z \cup Y)$

where $\varnothing$ is the empty set.

These axioms are not, in themselves, sufficient for the existence of a probability measurement p for R_2, but, with an extra housekeeping axiom, which requires that $\mathcal{S}$ be rich enough, one does exist, and it is unique. However, one cannot draw the conclusion from this alone that such a p and u are conjoint measurements for choice in X. To achieve the latter one must treat the preference order R over X, the preference order R_1 over H, and the qualitative probability order R_2 over $\mathcal{S}$ as a triple. This is not to say that finding p separately would not give an adequate approximation, and then finding u using the utility theory of Morgenstern et al. [62] would not then give an adequate choice from X, but, strictly speaking, unless evidence exists that empirically this is so, the conjoint approach is necessary. Savage [74] gives just such an approach. In effect, if R is a total preference order over actions of the form $x = \{f$ if $\alpha \in Z,\ g$ if $\alpha \notin Z\}$, $Z \in \mathcal{S}$, with $f\,R\,g$, then we require that R is equivalent to R_2, i.e. if, in addition, $y = \{f$ if $\alpha \in Y,\ g$ if $\alpha \notin Y\}$, then

$$x\,R\,y \quad \text{if and only if} \quad Z\,R_2\,Y$$

and this is a requisite condition, which may be plausible, but it is not automatically true.

Typical situations in which the subjective probability and value ideas would be relevant would be, for example, in the capacity installation problem in the Mathematical and Dynamic Programming section (2.5) of Chapter 2 (see Exercise 15 of that section) where the demand for service may require a subjective probability representation, and where the value of costs and failure to meet demand may need to be determined or, similarly, in the Inventory section 2.2 of Chapter 2, where demand is for a relatively new product, and again subjective probabilities and values for costs and shortages will be required. Such probabilities and values should, in principle, be determined conjointly.

It should also be pointed out that, strictly speaking, the events should be sequences of demands, and the outcomes should be sequences of costs and shortages, and that it must not, for example, be automatically assumed that we may add these over each time interval, which our simple models assume.

Let us now turn to decomposable measurements for more structured situations.

6.3 STRUCTURAL MEASUREMENT

In the previous section we dealt with the issue of the existence of a monotone decomposable ordinal measurement (i.e. unique up to strictly monotone transformations). As has been indicated, this is rather a weak form of measurement and, in order to get more out of the measurement procedure than we put into it, we really require some further structure (see Fischer [29]). In the following, we will again assume that A is at most countable and that A is rich enough to give all the requisite indifference class combinations, as we assumed for the existence of a decomposable measurement. The countability condition may easily be relaxed if we assume that all the ordinal measurements exist in the first place.

The simplest form of a structured decomposable value function is the weakly additive one (see White [96] or Fishburn [27] for a much deeper treatment), i.e. ones for which:

$$m(a) = \sum_{i=1}^{N} m_i(a).$$

For $N \geq 3$, the following condition, W.A.M.1, is necessary and sufficient, under the condition that condition W.A.M.2 holds.

W.A.M.1

The following is to hold for each subset $J \subseteq K$, where $K = \{1, 2, \ldots, N\}$, and let $\tilde{J} = K \backslash J$.

Let $\{a, b\}, \{a^1, b^1\} \subseteq A$ be such that:

$$a \, I_j \, b, \qquad a^1 \, I_j \, b^1, \quad \forall j \in J$$
$$a \, I_j \, a^1, \qquad b \, I_j \, b^1, \quad \forall j \in \tilde{J}.$$

Then:

$$a \, R \, b \quad \text{if and only if} \quad a^1 \, R \, b^1.$$

W.A.M.2

For each $i \in K$, there exist $\{a^i, b^i\} \subseteq A$ for which:

$$a^i \, I_j \, b^i, \quad \forall j \neq i$$

and

$$a^i \, P \, b^i$$

318

where

$$a \, P \, b \quad \text{if and only if} \quad a \, R \, b, \quad b \text{ not } R \, a.$$

It is easy to verify that condition W.A.M.1 is necessary, with or without the condition W.A.M.2. It is trivially true that condition W.A.M.2 is not necessary, although it is also clear that, under our assumption about the richness of A, we could remove attribute i if the property did not hold.

Conditions for the case $N = 2$ are given in Fishburn [27].

As a simple illustration of this, let us return to the nursery location problem in the Mathematical and Dynamic Programming section (2.5) of Chapter 2, and also in section 4.3 of the Problem Formulation Chapter 4. There, we have three objectives, and our set A is the set of vectors $\{f\} = \{(f^1, f^2, f^3)\}$. Although only a limited set of such f may be achievable, it is not objectionable that we should cover all conceivable vectors of this form, rational or otherwise. For this problem:

$f^1(x) =$ total distance associated with a specific location–allocation plan x
$f^2(x) =$ total cost associated with a specific location–allocation plan x
$f^3(x) =$ total weighted deficit of all children for whom a place is not available, given a specific location–allocation plan x.

Note that these are derived measurements to begin with and, in particular, f^3 already reflects preferences for combinations of deficits in each region. Strictly speaking, the objective f^3 should be replaced by a vector

$$f^3 = (f^{31}, f^{32}, \ldots, f^{3n})$$

where $f^{3l} =$ the deficit in area l.

There is no guarantee that the f^3, as defined earlier, will give the same results as the derived f^3. However, let us proceed.

If the appropriate conditions hold we will have a value function (see the Problem Formulation Chapter 4) of the form:

$$m(f) = \sum_{i=1}^{3} m_i(f^i)$$

with m_i depending only on f^i.

The weakly additive value function arises when we are adding up the component costs for any action in a given problem situation. For example, in the simple economic batch quantity problem of the Inventory section (2.2) of Chapter 2, we have ordering costs and stock level costs. Now, in general, companies handle many items, and it is not easy to associate an order cost with an individual item since items share resources which control the ordering process. Similarly, not only do stock-holding costs derive from shared resources, it can be very difficult to assess capital costs anyhow. If we add in shortages, we also have difficulties in assessment. Conceptually, one would like to think of each component cost adding to a total cost, and, indeed, as we suggested in Chapter 4, section 4.3, we can at least try an efficient solution approach, or even go further and find appropriate subjective weighting factors for a weakly additive value function. However, the interaction between the many items can make this no more than an heuristic approach to the problem, and a larger model integrating all items is, conceptually, needed, although very difficult to handle. Gardner [32] discusses this problem.

Furthermore, returning to the general case, we may assume $\{m_i\}$ to be continuous, and any other weakly additive value function m^1 must satisfy:

$$m^1 = \lambda m + \mu$$

for some $\lambda > 0$.

This form of measurement is known as interval measurement (see Phanzagl [63]) and is particularly important in measurement theory, a point to which we return later on. It means, in essence, that if $\{f, g\} \subseteq A$, then:

$$m^1(f) - m^1(g) = \lambda(m(f) - m(g))$$

i.e. the difference in measurements is independent of the scale used up to a constant multiplying factor.

Again we stress that the above analysis applies essentially to sufficiently rich A, and theories exist for finite A (e.g. see Fishburn [27]) which are perhaps not really relevant to our theme.

We may take the search for specific structural forms yet further, and seek special forms of the $\{m_i\}$ components. For example we may enquire of conditions for which an m of the following form exists:

$$m(a) = \sum_{i=1}^{N} m_i a_i$$

with $\sum_{i=1}^{N} m_i = 1$, $m_i \geq 0$, $i = 1, 2, \ldots, N$. In this case a is represented by N derived measurements $\{a_1, a_2, \ldots, a_N\}$ in the first instance, for example see the location example where $a_i = f^i$, $i = 1, 2, 3$. Thus $a \in \mathbb{R}^N$, and the special structure is now that we can add two members, i.e. if

$$a = (a_1, a_2, \ldots, a_N)$$
$$b = (b_1, b_2, \ldots, b_N)$$

then:

$$a \oplus b = (a_1 + b_1, a_2 + b_2, \ldots, a_N + b_N).$$

If the appropriate m does exist, we will clearly have:

$$m(a \oplus b) = m(a) + m(b).$$

This is known as strongly additive measurement (see White [96]).

Given the same initial assumptions we made for weakly additive measurement, the following conditions are necessary and sufficient for a strongly additive measurement to exist. It is assumed that the requisite members exist in A.

S.A.M.1

Let $\{a, b, c\} \subseteq A$. Then:

$$a \mathrel{R} b \quad \text{if and only if} \quad a \oplus c \mathrel{R} b \oplus c.$$

S.A.M.2

Let $\{a, b\} \subseteq A$, $0 \in A$ and $a \mathrel{P} 0$, $b \mathrel{P} 0$. Then there exists an integer k such that:

$$k \, a \mathrel{P} b.$$

By $k\,a$ we mean $a \oplus a \oplus a \oplus \ldots \oplus a$, k times.

It is easily seen that, providing A is rich enough, the conditions are necessary. The condition S.A.M.2 is known as an Archimedean condition (see Fishburn [27]), although more properly Eudoxian, and merely requires that elements do not have too high an individual measurement implicitly.

If m, m^1 are any two strongly additive measurements, then there exists a $\lambda > 0$ such that:

$$m^1 = \lambda m.$$

This form of measurement is known as ratio measurement (see Phanzagl [63]), again an important aspect to which we will ruturn. It means, in essence, that if $\{f, g\} \subseteq A$, and $m(f) \neq 0$, $m(g) \neq 0$, then

$$m(f)/m(g) = m^1(f)/m^1(g).$$

This was a requirement made by Epstein (see Chapter 4, section 4.2.4) for the measures of value of engineering designs.

The forms we have chosen are fairly simple. A more general study of measurement forms may be found in Krantz *et al.* [54] in a deterministic context, and in Keeney *et al.* [47] in a probabilistic context.

Let us now turn to probabilistic problems. We could take as a framework the situation in which we have N outcomes, $i = 1, 2, \ldots, N$, and each action a results in a probability vector $(a_1, a_2, \ldots, a_N)$ where a_i is the given probability of outcome i. Again the $\{a_i\}$ and derived measures. There is some similarity to the previous development and, given certain conditions, we may deduce the existence of a strongly additive measurement where m_i is the utility of outcome i and m is then the expected utility measurement. However, the standard, more general approach, is that of Morgenstern *et al.* [62] which we will now briefly describe, and which was mentioned at the end of Chapter 4, section 4.5 (e.g. see White [96]). We begin with a set A. If $\{a, b\} \subseteq A$, $0 \leqslant p \leqslant 1$, $a \mathrel{p} b$ is the same as having a with probability p and b with probability $1 - p$. A mixture space A is a space for which, whenever $\{a, b\} \subseteq A$, and $0 \leqslant p \leqslant 1$, then $a \mathrel{p} b \in A$. We will assume, as usual, that we have a total order over A. The conditions required are as follows:

E.U.M.1

A is a mixture space.

E.U.M.2
a p b is the same as $b(1-p)a$ for $\{a, b\} \subseteq A$ (i.e. the order of presentation does not matter).

E.U.M.3
If $p \neq 0$ of $q \neq 0$, and $\{a, b, c\} \subseteq A$, a p $(b$ q $c)$ is the same as $d(p+q-pq)c$ where $d = a(p/(p+q-pq))b$.

E.U.M.4
If $\{a, b\} \subseteq A$, $0 \leqslant p < 1$, a P b, then:

$(b$ p $a)$ P b

a P $(a$ p $b)$.

E.U.M.5
If $\{a, b, c\} \subseteq A$ and a P b P c then there is a p, $0 \leqslant p < 1$ such that:

$$b \, P \, (a \, p \, c)$$

and there is a q, $0 \leqslant q < 1$ such that:

$$(a \, q \, c) \, P \, b.$$

Given these conditions, there exists a measurement m satisfying:

$$m(a \, p \, b) = p \, m(a) + (1-p) \, m(b)$$

for $\{a, b\} \subseteq A$, $0 \leqslant p \leqslant 1$.

This is the expected utility measurement. It is an interval measurement providing we restrict ourselves to those measurements which satisfy the expected utility rule.

As an example, let us return to our inventory control problems of section 2.2 of Chapter 2 where we assume that, over the finite set of K intervals, the determinants of choice are the total identifiable costs a_1 (order plus purchase plus stockholding) and shortages a_2. Thus (see the Mathematical and Dynamic Programming formulation of section 2.5 of Chapter 2) instead of assuming a shortage cost of r per unit, we retain the primitive shortage amounts. In this problem the distribution of a is determined by a policy, i.e. a sequence of decision rules. In this case A may be the set of all probability distributions over the vectors $\{a\} = \{(a_1, a_2)\}$. If the conditions hold then we will have an expected utility measurement over A.

This example may be used to illustrate two points. First of all it does not necessarily follow that a decomposable monotone measurement will exist, nor, if it does, that it will have a strongly additive form. The models used in the inventory section all assume strong additivity and, if this does not hold, even in the weak form, the models must be modified and new solution methods found.

Secondly, given the requisite conditions, it will be possible to find m either by using the conditions W.A.M.1 and W.A.M.2, or the conditions

E.U.M.1–5. However, if m is found in the non-probabilistic case using W.A.M.1 and W.A.M.2 and the associated procedure to which we will return later on, it is not necessarily valid to use this in the expected utility calculations.

Thus, suppose $\tilde{A}$ is all the vectors of the form $\{a\} = \{(a_1, a_2)\}$, rich enough for our purposes, and A is the mixture space generated by $\tilde{A}$. Let $\tilde{R}$, R be the total orders over $\tilde{A}$, A respectively, where clearly $\tilde{R}$ and R are identical on A.

Let $\tilde{m} \geqslant 0$ be any measurement for $\tilde{R}$ on $\tilde{A}$. Let R on A be defined, *a priori*, by the expected utility form as follows. Each a in A will be a probability combination of members of $\tilde{A}$. Let $\tilde{A}$ be countable, in order to simplify matters, and let $a \in A$ be equivalent to a probability distribution p_a over A.

Define:

$$\{a, b\} \subseteq A, \qquad a \text{ R } b \quad \text{if and only if} \quad \sum_{c \in \tilde{A}} p_a(c)\tilde{m}^2(c) \geqslant \sum_{c \in \tilde{A}} p_b(c)\tilde{m}^2(c).$$

This is a perfectly permissible R, which, by its definition, will automatically satisfy the E.U.M. conditions, and automatically agrees with R on A. However, R is not equivalent to using the expected utility measurement based on $\tilde{m}$, or on any positive affine transformation of this.

This once again emphasizes Baecher's [3] point about the need to understand the basis of the measurement used. Also see Fischer [29].

The structural utility forms may be taken a little further if we add further conditions. In Chapter 4, section 4.2.5, for example, the work of Markowitz [59] was mentioned, where, given certain conditions, if a decision maker is choosing between actions whose outcomes are a scalar variable r (e.g. cash), then there is a utility function of the form (using m in place of u):

$$m(r) = \sum_{i=1}^{m} \lambda_i r^i$$

and expected utility will be the appropriate criterion for making choices in such cases.

If x is a specific action, or policy, and if $v(x)$ is the induced expected utility of x with $\mu(x)$, $\sigma^2(x)$ being the mean and variance of r, then:

$$v(x) = \lambda_1 \mu + \lambda_2 \mu^2 + \lambda_2 \sigma^2.$$

Thus, if the decision maker prefers higher values of μ for a given σ^2, we must have $\lambda_2 \geqslant 0$, and, if $\lambda_2 \neq 0$, he must prefer higher variances for a given value of μ. This is incompatible with much behaviour but the theory, as a theory, still remains.

Another area in which structure is important is in the area of subjective probability and utility. Conditions exist (e.g. see Savage [74]) for which the expected utility measurement exists, and from which both the subjective probabilities and the utilities may be derived. Again it is an interval scale (for the utilities) and again any measurements should, strictly speaking, come from within the theory and not from outside.

Finally let us return to the use of discounted values, or present worth, as has been discussed in the context of dynamic problems in Chapter 2, sections 2.1–2.4, and in the context of problem formulation in Chapter 4, section 4.1. We will slightly change the notation of Chapter 4 to conform with this chapter so that, given a set A, with $a \in A$ represented by an infinite dimensional vector $\{a_t\}_{t=1}^{\infty}$, a present worth measurement takes the form:

$$m(a) = \sum_{t=1}^{\infty} \alpha^{t-1} a_t$$

for some α, $0 \leq \alpha < 1$.

Although the representation of a is similar, for example, to the strongly additive case, for this problem we have an infinite set of components and a special approach is required. Koopmans [52] provides conditions for which a related present worth measure exists, viz.

$$m(a) = \sum_{t=1}^{\infty} \alpha^{t-1} q(a_t)$$

for some monotone measurement q. In order to reduce $q(a_t)$ to a_t we will need extra conditions similar to those of the S.A.M.1 and S.A.M.2 kind, which we will not pursue. The first steps in Koopmans' proof require the following conditions, where A is the set of all infinite-dimensional vectors.

D.M.1
D.M.2, D.M.3, D.M.4, apply also to time series commencing at any time t, i.e. we need only consider the form of $a \in A$, not when it commences in reality.

This is a stationarity condition.

D.M.2
There exists an ordinal measurement over A for the total order R.

D.M.3
For all (a_1, a_2), (a_1^1, a_2^1), $(a_2, a_3, \ldots, a_t, \ldots)$, $(a_2^1, a_3^1, \ldots, a_t^1, \ldots)$ we have:

implies
$(a_1, a_2, a_3, \ldots, a_t, \ldots)\, \mathrm{R}\, (a_1^1, a_2^1, a_3, \ldots, a_t, \ldots)$
$(a_1, a_2, a_3^1, \ldots, a_t^1, \ldots)\, \mathrm{R}\, (a_1^1, a_2^1, a_3^1, \ldots, a_t^1, \ldots)$

implies
$(a_1, a_2, a_3, \ldots, a_t, \ldots)\, \mathrm{R}\, (a_1^1, a_2, a_3, \ldots, a_t^1, \ldots)$
$(a_1, a_2^1, a_3, \ldots, a_t, \ldots)\, \mathrm{R}\, (a_1^1, a_2^1, a_3^1, \ldots, a_t^1, \ldots)$.

This is a decomposability condition similar to condition C.M. and, indeed, could be stated in terms of the primitive orders $\{R_i\}$, but we will not do so here.

324

D.M.4

Let $\{a, b\} \subseteq A$, with $a_1 = b_1$. Then, if $a^1 = (a_2, a_3, \ldots, a_t, \ldots)$, $b^1 = (b_2, b_3, \ldots, b_t, \ldots)$ we have:

$$a \, \mathbf{R} \, b \quad \text{if and only if} \quad a^1 \mathbf{R} \, b^1.$$

These conditions are necessary and sufficient for the existence of the discounted measurement of the form given by Koopmans given certain other housekeeping conditions. The necessity is easily demonstrated.

For finite series (for example, see the use of finite discounting in Chapter 2, sections 2.1–2.4) Fishburn gives a corresponding result. In each case, q is an interval measurement for the order over each component for the class of all discounted measurements.

The above treatment produces discounted measurements based on a preference order R over A as the primitive concept. It is, of course, possible to produce a discounted measurement as a derived measurement using various arguments. Cash productivity measurements may be used. Thus suppose, to return to our notation in Chapter 4, sections 4.1 and 4.2.3, r_t is the normal cash payment in interval t, and such cash could be invested at a rate of interest i per unit time interval up to some final point in time of N time units. The total cash at the end would be:

$$c(r) = \sum_{t=1}^{N} r_t (1+i)^{N-t+1}$$

if we assume the cash is available at the beginning of each time interval.

We then have, with $\alpha = (1+i)^{-1}$

$$\alpha^N c(r) = \sum_{t=1}^{N} \alpha^{t-1} r_t$$

and we may, if this cash argument is accepted, set

$$m(r) = \sum_{t=1}^{N} \alpha^{t-1} r_t.$$

This measurement is a ratio measurement, since the only changes which may be made relate to the scales of the cash payments which are ratio measurements.

It is to be noted that the original order relation based measurement may not be interchangeable with the derived measurement.

If we wish to introduce probabilistic elements into the problem where, for example, $\{a_t\}$ may be random variables, then a discounted expected utility result will apply, given certain conditions (e.g. see White [96]), and a probabilistic counterpart of the derived cash based measurement also exists (see White [89]).

Let us return to the specification of $a \in A$. It is quite possible that each a_t is itself a vector or, in the primitive form, a is to be evaluated by several properties at each point in time. In the multi-objective problems of Chapter 4, sections 4.2.4, 4.3 and 4.5, we may have to look at time series of various objectives, for example see the nursery location problem of section 4.3 where the number of children involved may change over time and, instead of $\{(f^1, f^2, f^3)\}$, we may need to look at $\{(f_t^1, f_t^2, f_t^3)\}_{t=1}^N$. Some of the previous results may apply and a discounted measurement may exist with the same discount factor for each objective. This may not be the case. Cretin *et al.* [15] discuss a problem with two objectives, cost and (life-saving) benefits, say $\{(c_t, b_t)\}_{t=1}^\infty$. The paper implicitly assumes that an ordinal measurement exists of a decomposable monotonic form, where $a = ((c_1, b_1), (c_2, b_2), \ldots, (c_t, b_t), \ldots)$:

$$m(a) = g(m_1(c), m_2(b))$$

where

$$m_1(c) = \sum_{t=1}^{\infty} \alpha^{t-1} c_t$$

$$m_2(c) = \sum_{t=1}^{\infty} \beta^{t-1} c_t.$$

m_1, m_2, are essentially derived measurements, for, otherwise, the above form would require prior justification. The problem tackled is to find conditions for which $\alpha = \beta$.

Finally, let us look at the discounted measurements from the point of view of our dynamic programming models of Chapter 2, sections 2.1–2.5, and the principle of optimality.

First of all, with a slightly weaker version of D.M.3, a decomposable measurement exists which takes the form, in the infinite time series case (a corresponding result exists in the finite case):

$$m(a) = g(q(a_1), m(\tilde{a}))$$

where $\tilde{a} = (a_2, a_3, \ldots, a_t, \ldots)$.

From this it is clear that the principle of optimality applies in that, at each stage, we lose nothing by choosing subsequent decisions in an optimal manner for the residual problem. Thus, subject to the limitations placed upon a by the choice of a_1 (note $a_t = a_t(x)$, where x is the decision), we make $m(a)$ as large as is possible.

In the finite case (refer back to Chapter 2 for interval numbering notation) we will have:

$$m_k(a) = g_k(q_k(a_1), m_{k-1}(\tilde{a}))$$

and a similar argument applies.

It is clear that the discounted measurements will give the requisite results for dynamic programming.

Providing the appropriate conditions hold, similar results, in terms of expected utility measurements, will exist for probabilistic problems.

6.4 TESTABILITY OF THE CONDITIONS FOR SPECIFIC STRUCTURES

It is clear that the testability of the various conditions used in developing structural measurement does raise difficulties, especially when the set A of objects is large or, in some cases, infinite (see condition E.U.M.1, for example). Any testing must be based on a finite sample, and an inference made as to the extrapolation, or interpolation, as the case may be, to the remainder of the set A. However, to set this in perspective, this feature is, in essence, no different to the application of scientific method on a much broader front (see Krantz *et al.* [54]) and it is important to see this in the context of the role which measurement plays in Operational Research.

Krantz *et al.* [54] indicate, however, that the testing of particular conditions may involve different considerations. We have assumed, for our modest purposes, that we have total orders R, $\{R_i\}$. The testing of this condition will involve testing, for example, the transitivity condition, viz.

$$\{a, b, c\} \subseteq A, \qquad a \text{ R } b, \qquad b \text{ R } c \quad \text{implies} \quad a \text{ R } c.$$

One failure is enough to refute this condition.

On the other hand the Archimedean (or Eudoxian) condition, S.A.M.2, might appear to be refuted by its not being possible to find, on the basis of a finite sample, the appropriate k, and yet, with a larger sample, may be seen to be true. Naturally we may feel it appropriate to refute the condition on an inferential basis, but it may only be inferential.

Phanzagl [63] discusses the testability of conditions, and divides them into two categories, viz. testable and objectionable. A condition is testable if it is possible, in principle, to falsify, in a finite number of steps, a false condition. The other conditions are objectionable. Providing selection rules exist to identify particular members of A, a total order requirement is testable, whereas, for infinite A, the Archimedean condition is objectionable.

These remarks are made merely to warn the reader of potential hazards but, in the end analysis, an inferential process will be needed, as in the general application of scientific method, and such difficulties should not be considered as a barrier to the application of the ideas. The reader may wish to examine the other conditions for testability features.

There is, of course, another form of testability, viz. the ethical imperative, or normative, test. This requires that the conditions be examined in terms of whether they ought reasonably to hold. The E.M.U. conditions are essentially intended to fall into this category, despite the fact that they tend to be violated in some instances (e.g. see Fischer [29]). The transitivity condition of a total order falls into this category. We will not debate the issues of the applicability of such conditions, but merely point our the essential orientation. Other conditions are not really of this kind, and are, in essence, specially identifiable consequences of the proposed structural form of the measurement. They are a means of checking on the validity of the proposed structure. Condition W.A.M.1 is of this type. The reader may wish to examine the other conditions.

There is another feature of the exhaustive testing of the conditions which is important. As has been indicated, we must get more from the measurement process than we actually put into it. Phanzagl's [63] statement, given in section 6.1, is related to this. If we did actually validate all of the conditions of each possible realization in A, then what have we actually gained? Let us take the location problem of section 6.3, and let us assume that A is the set of actions available. If we manage to validate the conditions for all possible realizations we will, in effect, have solved our problem, viz. to find the best action, or actions, in A. The derivation of the additive measurement structure would be irrelevant for this problem. Only if we can infer structure about a larger set than the one we actually examine, can we actually add something to the problem. If we are not allowed to do this then we are merely left with ethical imperatives whose role is to rationalize the measurement rather to represent the various properties by measurements.

We have indicated, in section 6.3, a distinction between finite A and sufficiently rich infinite A. If A is finite and no justification is felt to extend A, even hypothetically, to a larger set, then, as has been indicated, finite set conditions for given structures exist. This avoids the infinity problem, but is no less subject to the point made about getting more from the analysis than is put into it. An inferential process is still needed, and the fact that we can actually cover all realizations is of no significance. It is also true that extending A weakens the conditions required, as one would expect. It is also clear that, if we are dealing with ethical imperatives, then this should apply to as large a set as possible, even though the actual choices may, quite incorrectly, be restricted to the original A.

Having made all these deliberations, there is the question of where to start when seeking structural measurements. There are many possibilities facing us as, for example, a glance at Keeney et al. [47] will reveal. Popularly, in multi-objective problems (see Chapter 4, sections 4.2.4, 4.3, and 4.5), a start is sought with linearly weighted objective functions, or strongly additive as we have used the term. This may, or may not, be appropriate, and checks must be made. However, the point is that simple structures ought first to be considered and, indeed, Fischer [29] indicates that empirical evidence exists to support the frequent existence of simple structural measurements in practice. Even if exact simple representations do not exist, approximations may be reasonable, although a theory of approximations in this area has yet to be developed. Fishburn [28] discusses this.

Finally, as in all scientific endeavour, there is the question of error in measurement. Again this is a largely unexplored topic and we leave the reader to look at the brief comments made by Krantz et al. [54] and Luce [57], and refer to Chapter 3, section 3.9.

6.5 PREDICTION AND SURROGATE MEASUREMENT

In any decision making situation, there may arise many properties of a proposed action which one may wish to take into account. The following list is a small selection from a very large range:

safety (Raisbeck [66], Watson [88], Baecher [3], Dick [17], Brown *et al.* [9], Green [36], Golabi [33])
uncertainty (Shackle [77], Zadeh [102])
service (Shilton [78])
flexibility (Hansmann [38])
complexity (Harrison [39], White [94])
productivity (Eilon [22], Easterfield [21])
spread (Harrison [39])
value of life (Schachtman *et al.* [75])
accessibility (White [94])
anxiety (Krantz *et al.* [54])
intelligence (Phanzagl [63])
simplicity (White [94])
decisionary effort (Good [35])
quality (White [94], Golabi *et al.* [33])
noise (Keighly [48])
authority (White [94])
value of travel time (Buzelius [10]).

This list is given to indicate that individuals have, from time to time, tried to grapple with the measurement problems associated with these factors. Later on we will look a little more enquiringly at some of these, viz. uncertainty (with specific reference to fuzziness—despite the claims that this is not a measure of uncertainty, it has similarities—and entropy) and flexibility. In this section our purposes are somewhat more general. It is clear that the essential purpose of measurement is prediction of measurement is prediction of one or more properties of a situation, on the basis of knowledge of other properties of the situation, although it does this through real number representations. There are, however, some difficulties of a practical kind which arise in attempting to measure particular properties which, in effect, lead to surrogate measurements, a topic discussed in the problem formulation Chapter 4, section 4.2.3.

Let us consider a few examples, beginning with the depthcharge problem of Chapter 1. In that problem the concept of damage was introduced. In the extreme case, damage might merely take two values, sunk or not sunk. Clearly this is not acceptable, since many other configurations might also be significant to the effectiveness of operations. The question is then one of how we can describe the various possibilities, for the purposes of decision making, in such a way that damage may be related to the distance between the U-boat and the depth charge. It is possible that such a description could be obtained, and that a conjoint measurement, subjective or objective, might be derived. However, this may not be thought to be really feasible, and a natural thing to do is to let distance act as a surrogate for damage. In effect, this would replace the damage function $d(z)$ by the distance z. The question which arises is now one of what should the objective be? It is no longer true that it should be to minimize the expected distance between U-boat and depth charge at time of explosion, i.e. (using the discrete form):

$$\sum_{s=0}^{\infty} |z| \, p(s) = \sum_{s=0}^{\infty} |x - s| \, p(s)$$

although this would be the case if $d(z) = k_0 - k \, |z|$ as suggested in Chapter 1.

In principle, if the analysis is to be carried out using distances only, some such theory as the expected utility theory should be used as suggested in Chapter 4, section 4.2.4. It should also be borne in mind that, if a conjoint measurement is obtained relating damage to distance, then, again, a proper theoretical foundation relating choice and damage would be necessary.

Let us turn to another example, viz. complexity. This factor figures in decisions, in various ways, as something which will influence such things as work content and time (e.g. in welding in ship construction, and in production processes, where pieces have to be cut from larger stock sizes of material, and where the complexity of the patterns of cutting—referred to in the Heuristics section (2.8) of Chapter 2—will influence these factors). The question is one of how complexity should be measured in order to act as a predictor of the work and time factors. In this case, it is possible to present those in charge of production with a set of patterns, and ask them to rank them in terms of complexity at a subjective level. However, this has no predictive content other than the obvious one that one would expect work and time to be monotone in the ranking. In order to have a non-trivial predictive content, some derived measurement (Phanzagl [63] uses the term fiat) is needed, which is an explicit function of appropriate parameters of the situation. It may not be possible to produce a single scalar measurement of complexity giving good predictive power, despite the fact that such single-dimensional concepts are freely used. In addition, if the decisions are made in the context of such complexity representations, they will be surrogates for the real properties of interest (work, time) and may not give the same answers as ones derived on the basis of work and time representations.

The use of surrogates is quite common, and arises essentially from Wiener's [97] observation that measurements are very often not self-evident, and considerable thought may be needed to identify possibilities. Sometimes the surrogates are needed because the property of prime interest defies direct measurement in the first instance. For example, intelligence is measured by (derived, fiat) measurement procedures based on specific tasks (Phanzagl [63]), anxiety is measured by skin resistance (Krantz et al. [54]), and so on. It avoids having to think too hard about the primitive concepts but, in the final analysis, it is the predictive power, for specific purposes, which is the essential requirement. In the case of safety, for example, (see

330

Brown *et al.* [9]) there is the question of thinking about the concept of safety but (see Riasbeck [66]) some people describe decision making in terms of surrogates for safety (in car safety) such as brake imbalance, light direction and intensity, horn function, play in steering linkage and so on, to arrive at an overall safety ranking. Watson [88] also queries the attempts made, in the context of nuclear safety, to reduce safety to a single measurement in terms of Sieverts, or equivalent doses of radiation. Some of the features listed relate to earlier work in this text. Service arises, not only in the context of queueing (should service be in terms of expected waiting time as a derived measure?), inventory (should service be seen in terms of expected shortage as a derived measure?), and in, for example, some of our mathematical programming material (what is service in the context of bus scheduling?—Shilton [78] discusses service on the railways). Quality arises in our defective production problems since items may really have a level of quality, inducing different values, and not simply be defective or non-defective. Quality is also important to our maintenance problems, although not directly introduced in that section, since different conditions of the equipment (not simply breakdown or no breakdown) will influence the quality of the product. Golabi *et al.* [33] discuss the maintenance of roads, where the conditions of the roads (skid number, ride index) are surrogates, to some extent, for safety and quality of driving. Such factors introduce non-explicitly cost-oriented features as distinct from the frameworks we have studied. Complexity is certainly relevant to our trim loss problems in a situation when a wider range of cut patterns is permissible. In each of those cases, it will be seen how essential some form of measurement is, if comparable models are to be used, a point to which we will turn in due course. The measurements must also be conjoint measurements, and not independent measurements.

6.6 COMMUNICATIONS

Let us begin with a quotation:

> We live in a world of semantic pollution.... Entity, item, name, element, value, instance and occurrence (to name a few) come readily equipped with meaning, yet they are used in different ways. We must be precise and are thus forced to make exact definitions for those words which we must use consistently. (Vazsonyi [86])

Vazsonyi is not talking about measurement, but rather about ambiguities in statements, and the use of mathematical logic to unravel the situation and to produce unambiguous meanings. However, his general tenor is very much applicable to measurement in the context of its role in communication.

Although we have been concentrating on measurement for various modelling and prediction purposes, it also has a role in communicating the assessment, by experts, of various features of a situation to a decision maker, and it also has a role in dialogue between individuals.

One example is the communication of an expert to a decision maker concerning his probabilities of certain events, e.g. demand for a new product, reliability of a new component and so on, aspects which are inputs to some of our models in Chapters 1 and 2. It is very important that the decision maker knows exactly what such measurements mean. They have no natural link with such things as frequencies or logical probabilities (see White [93] for a discussion of these) and mean no more than the fact that the expert would act in some way consistent with these probabilities if the expert were making decisions (see Savage [74]). In using such probabilities, the decision maker would be transferring characteristics of one individual to himself—no more and no less—as if they were his own, and then acting on this basis. Despite this rather tight description of the situation, dialogues involving probability statements are commonly accepted as being useful and almost unavoidable. At the very least, it is meaningful to translate such probability statements into equivalent events with the same logical, or frequentist, probability, such as drawing balls from urns and so on, on the basis of which, perhaps erroneously, the decision maker can at least continue a sensible dialogue.

There are, however, other cases where far less can be said in support of the measurements. Dyson [20] studies different policies relating to peat bog operations. Because data was unavailable to determine what the effects of the options would be, a subjective assessment in terms of high, fairly high, medium, and low were used. Such terms have no communication value other than, effectively, to rank the effects. For a single effect, in terms of which options may be ranked, we will have an ordinal scale simply by associating particular numbers with the grades, but this has no use. For multiple effects we need conjoint measurement and, for decision purposes, the individual measurements must be related. However, how is high on one factor related to high or low for another factor? Conjoint measurement theory requires that the measurements all be derived from the decision making behaviour—they cannot be independent inputs without some justification.

Let us return to the question of safety. Decision makers rely on experts to assess the safety of structures (see Dick [17]), of vehicles (Raisbeck [66], Green [36]), and of nuclear plant (see Watson [88]).

Green [36] is concerned with the measurement of perceived safety by individuals and, for cars, produces the formula:

$$\text{perceived safety} = 200(P(D))^{0.17}$$

where $P(D)$ is the probability of death per 10^8 manhours exposure. However, exactly what is the communication value of this? In order to understand this one would need to know exactly how this formula was arrived at, and exactly how it assumed the status of a conjoint measurement in the context of other factors of the situations being considered, e.g. in the case of cars, safety is only one factor, others are cost, speed, and so on.

Watson [88], in the nuclear hazard case, also queries the measurements in units of Sieverts of safety. Sieverts attempt to aggregate the effects of α, β, and γ ray radiation and neutron radiation in terms of their health effects; but no communicable interpretation by the layman seems possible. Each Sievert unit is supposed to represent the same health effects, but does this help? Again one could argue that the actual health effects should be communicated, and that decisions, if at all possible based upon cost and Sieverts, may be somewhat different to those based on cost and direct health measurements.

Finally we again mention complexity and flexibility, very often used in judging the worth of options, and with the same question mark against them. If decision makers are to be advised on such factors, they must be interpretable in a manner compatible with decision making. If they are fiats, or derived measures, the measurement process must be specified.

6.7 ERRORS, SENSITIVITY ANALYSIS, AND APPROXIMATIONS

The question of error analysis, and its foundations, is a subtle one, and what we will have to say will be very limited, but enough, perhaps, to indicate the role of measurement in this issue. We will concentrate on the issue from the point of view of decision making, and hence the essential issue is one of how good or bad is a particular decision in the light of possible uncertainties in certain features of the problem.

In the introductory section, 6.1, we quoted Schwartz [76], who queries the need for precision (we will use the term accuracy, although the two terms are not essentially the same, since this is what is intended). The argument is almost a supporting argument for the sort of approach Dyson [20] uses, which we have mentioned in the previous section. However, the significant thing is Schwartz's use of the phrases 'slightly changed' and 'small perturbations', and this automatically raises the issue of whether such phrases are meaningful, in the context of this chapter, without some measurement scale against which to assess this, although, as we shall see, the answer is not quite so easy as might at first seem.

Let us return to Chapter 3 on Sensitivity Analysis, and examine the issue in this context. We began with the simple inventory control problem for which the objective was:

$$f(x) = as/x + \tfrac{1}{2}hx$$

We demonstrated that if, for example, we made a proportional error ε in the assessment of the parameter a, then the proportional loss of optimality was:

$$\Delta = \tfrac{1}{8}\varepsilon^2.$$

Now a is a cost parameter and its measurement is a ratio measurement. Thus, no matter what units we use, ε will remain unchanged, and hence Δ will remain unchanged. The measurement is a meaningful one under the allowed transformations (see Phanzagl [63]) for the proposed purposes.

Although we have used the proportional loss Δ, rather than the absolute loss, the latter is not invariant under these transformations of a, but, whatever the measurement scale, the numbers obtained are interpretable by the decision maker in an unambiguous way if he has to decide, for example, whether or not an accurate value of a should be sought.

For such situations, and others where objectives such as cost, time, distance, are involved, there is no real contention on the measurement issue and the relevance of error analysis for each objective separately. Empirically derived probabilities provide even a better foundation since they are actually unique, under rich enough conditions, being a special case of Phanzagl's difference measurements, i.e. unique up to shifts (or translations) with zero shifts being the only possibility in this case. However, when we consider situations where conjoint measurement is needed, we do face some difficulty which arises from the freedom which exists in the measurement procedure. Let us look at the extreme case where we have simple ordinal measurements of the decomposable form:

$$m(a) = g(m_1(a), m_2(a)), \qquad a \in A$$

which we introduced in section 6.2. Let us assume, by whatever method is used to determine $\{m_1, m_2, m, g\}$, that m_1 is subject to an error ε_1. This will induce an error ε in $m(a)$ via the specified g. However, any strictly monotonic transformation of g will suffice for ordinal measurement purposes, and thus there is a great deal of choice in size of the induced error, and even in the proportional error, and this raises serious doubts about the usefulness of this sort of error analysis. In order to resolve this, we must ask why we wish to consider error analysis at all and, in Chapter 3, we tried to resolve this by focusing on other, secondary, decisions which might depend upon the size of the error. In Chapter 3 we focused on the expected utility area and argued that, in reality, the decisions as to what to do on the basis of error analysis ought really to be included in the problem in the first instance. Although in such cases we have an interval scale, quite different errors, and error ratios, will be obtained, depending on the choice of base points. Thus let m be an expected utility measurement, and let ε be an error in m induced by an error in some component of the problem. Then $\lambda m + \mu$ is also an expected utility measurement, with error $\lambda \varepsilon$, and may be radically different and, even if we used proportional errors, we find that:

$$\frac{\varepsilon}{m} \quad \text{and} \quad \frac{\lambda \varepsilon}{\lambda m + \mu}$$

may be quite different. Indeed it is even possible to have

$$\frac{\varepsilon}{m} > \frac{\varepsilon^1}{m^1} \quad \text{but} \quad \frac{\lambda \varepsilon}{\lambda m + \mu} < \frac{\lambda \varepsilon^1}{\lambda m^1 + \mu}$$

where (ε, m), (ε^1, m^1) are realizations of the same measurement process, perhaps for different $a \in A$, although, if we also have $\varepsilon \geqslant \varepsilon^1$, this is not possible, i.e. if errors are monotonic increasing in the level of m.

An alternative procedure for a given action set X (which may be a subset of the conceivable set underlying the utility theory) is to find the lowest utility, $\underline{m}$, and highest utility, $\bar{m}$, achievable over X (we assume these exist for simplicity), and then to define the loss of optimality function, for $x \in X$, by:

$$\Delta(x) = (\bar{m} - v(x))/(\bar{m} - \underline{m})$$

where $v(x)$ is the utility induced by action x. Such a Δ is clearly invariant under positive affine transformations, but, nonetheless, such an approach lacks substantive meaning. Thus, for example, by enhancing X to include an action $y \notin X$, such that $v(y) < \underline{m}$, $\Delta(x)$ will change. In addition, there seems to be no reason why any strictly monotone increasing function of Δ should not be used. The approach is somewhat arbitrary.

The essential problem in direct error analysis, prior to considering what should be done on the basis of the results, lies in the interpretation of this error, especially if it is not unique. The cost, distance, time, probability examples pose no problem, but conjoint measurement, including expected utility, does. In Chapter 3 it was shown how one model might be built and also how the direct approach might be justified in some cases.

It is possible to think in terms of differences in measurements of properties being obtainable directly from the responses of the system being studied (see Krantz *et al.* [54], Phanzagl [63], and Sarin [73], the latter being specifically concerned with utility assessments of measurable value, as he terms it). In such cases the process involves orderings, not of the set of individual members of A, but of all pairs of members $\{(a, b)\} \subseteq A$. If the ordering is based on choice:

$$(a, b) \, \text{R}^* \, (c, d)$$

is interpreted as b is preferred to a at least as much as c is preferred to d.

It is arguable that this means anything except a statement about differences between measurements, and it is the view of this author that individuals cannot really do this, and that m derived on the basis of the earlier sections does no more than represent the ordering over A, with differences merely being arithmetical operations on m. In addition, as has been indicated in section 6.2, if $\tilde{A}$ is extended to a mixture space, A, it is quite possible for there to be no relationship between measurements on $\tilde{A}$ and on A, except to maintain the same ordering on $\tilde{A}$, and differences in the measurements on $\tilde{A}$ may depend substantially on the procedure used, while at the same time being quite compatible with the order over $\tilde{A}$, and being interval orders at the same time, i.e. relatively unique.

If (a, b) could be given some physical meaning such as 'what you would be prepared to pay (or be paid) to move from a to b', then the situation is different, but this does not, except in special cases, produce differences in value, or utility.

The original idea behind such comparisons arose really in the context of such things as measurement of length using rods, so that (a, b) might be interpreted (if a is deemed to be larger than b) as an equivalent rod c added to rod a to make a plus c of equal length to b, but this clearly acceptable meaning does not carry over to value and utility.

Nonetheless, if it is accepted that comparisons between (a, b) and (c, d) are meaningful, and certain conditions do hold, then there will exist a measurement m on A such that:

$$\{a, b, c, d\} \subseteq A \qquad (a, b) \, \mathrm{R}^* \, (c, d)$$

if and only if

$$m(b) - m(a) \geqslant m(d) - m(c)$$

and, at the same time, in the usual sense:

$$\{a, b\} \subseteq A, \qquad a \, \mathrm{R} \, b \quad \text{if and only if} \quad m(a) \geqslant m(b).$$

If, on this basis, it may be inferred that R^* is identical with statements about differences $m(b) - m(a)$, then error analysis may conceivably be a little easier than at first seems and, in the context of sensitivity analysis, ε (the error in m) may have a self-evident meaning for the decision maker, but the reader should carefully examine this for himself. In addition, the various conditions may lead to interval, ratio, or difference (Phanzagl's definition) measurements, in which case the previous remarks hold.

Finally in our discussion in section 6.4 we have discussed the possibility of approximations, so obviously important in practical applications. For example, the use of linear approximations in the multi-objective problems of Chapter 4 is appealing. The issues arising in this are precisely the same as those we have discussed in the context of errors, the difference being that approximations are deliberately introduced errors.

6.8 OPERATIONAL PROCEDURES

Let us now look at operational procedures for carrying out the requisite measurement. We will consider only situations where we have structural measurements since, as has been indicated, ordinal measurements are of little use. For the record, for a single total order R over A, it is easy to see that, if A is countable, an ordinal measurement is possible. Thus if we identify $A = (a^1, a^2, a^3, \ldots, a^n, \ldots)$, we begin with $m(a^1) = 0$. If $a^2 \, \mathrm{P} \, a^1$, set $m(a^2) = 1$. If $a^2 \, \mathrm{I} \, a^1$ set $m(a^2) = 0$. If $a^1 \, \mathrm{P} \, a^2$ set $m(a^2) = -1$. Then consider a^3 and so on. If we have determined $m(a^i)$, $i = 1, 2, \ldots, n-1$, it is easy to determine $m(a^n)$ in a manner compatible with R. As has been indicated, such a procedure really adds nothing to R. We can carry out a similar exercise for conjoint measurement for total orders R, $\{R_i\}$. Given certain conditions we can go beyond countable sets.

Consider now the strongly additive case, assuming that we are satisfied that this is an appropriate measurement structure. We then have with respect to total orders R, $\{R_i\}$:

$$m(a) = \sum_{i=1}^{N} m_i a_i.$$

If we may assume that a_1 is relevant (i.e. its level will be important in some instance) we may set $m_1 = 1$. If we then assume that A is rich enough, we can find m_i, $i \neq 1$ by finding a_i so that:

$$(1, 0, 0, 0, \ldots, 0) \, \mathrm{I} \, (0, 0, 0, \ldots, a_i, 0, \ldots, 0).$$

Then:

$$m_1 = m_i a_i$$

i.e.

$$m_i = a_i^{-1}.$$

We will return to this point later on.

Consider now the weakly additive case where:

$$m(a) = \sum_{i=1}^{N} m_i(a_i).$$

We have actually taken a very special case of the weakly additive one, in which we assume that $m_i(a) = m_i(a_i)$ merely to simplify matters. Again we assume that A is rich enough for our purposes.

To begin with, we set $m_i(a_i) = 0$ for all i. Then select $a_1 = \theta$, and set $m_1(\theta) = 0$ (we assume that $(\theta, 0, 0, \ldots, 0) \, \mathrm{P} \, (0, 0, 0, \ldots, 0)$). Then find a_2^1 so that:

$$(0, a_2^1, 0, 0, \ldots, 0) \, \mathrm{I} \, (\theta, 0, 0, 0, \ldots).$$

We have:

$$m_2(a_2^1) = m_1(\theta) = \delta.$$

Then select a_2^2 so that:

$$(\theta, a_2^1, 0, 0, \ldots, 0) \, \mathrm{I} \, (0, a_2^2, 0, 0, 0, \ldots, 0).$$

Then:

$$m_2(a_2^2) = m_1(\theta) + m_2(a_2^1) = 2\delta.$$

This procedure is repeated so that, eventually, points $\{a_2^t\}$, on the a_2 dimension, are determined with:

$$m_2(a_2^t) = t\delta.$$

The same may be done for the a_i dimension so that points $\{a_{i}^t\}$ on the a_i dimension are determined with:

$$m_i(a_i^t) = t\delta.$$

This, in effect, requires that a_i are allowed to be large enough and that an Archimedean (Eudoxian) type condition holds similar to condition S.A.M.2. However, if A is bounded, this may not be so, and the size of θ may need reducing to obtain the requisite result.

We may now return to the a_1 dimension and find a_2^2 so that:

$$(a_1^2, 0, 0, \ldots, 0) \, \mathrm{I} \, (0, a_2^2, 0, 0, \ldots, 0)$$

so that:

$$m_1(a_1^2) = m_2(a_2^2) = 2\delta.$$

The procedure may be repeated to obtain points $\{a_1^t\}$ on the a_1 dimension such that:

$$m_1(a_1^t) = t\delta.$$

We are free to select δ. The procedure will give the m measurement level for points on a grid in A determined by $\{a_{i}^t\}$. The m level for other points may be interpolated, or extrapolated, as the case may be, and δ made smaller if further refinements are desired.

For the expected utility case, let us assume that $a \in A$ is equivalent to a probability distribution over a set of outcomes H. H might be restricted to cash incomes, but it may also be multi-objective, involving several components. In order to keep things simple, suppose that the best, $\bar{\theta}$, and worst, $\underline{\theta}$, members of H are known. Set $m(\underline{\theta}) = 0$, $m(\bar{\theta}) = 1$ (assuming $\bar{\theta} \, \mathrm{P} \, \underline{\theta}$). For each $\theta \in H$ find p such that:

$$(\bar{\theta} \, \mathrm{p} \, \underline{\theta}) \, \mathrm{I} \, \theta$$

Then

$$m(\theta) = p.$$

This is deceptively simple in principle, but if H is multi-dimensional, further structure is needed to facilitate the measurement process. Thus if (see Keeney et al. [47] for conditions), still in the context of an expected utility framework, m is known to be linear, quadratic and so on, then the parameters may be calculated from the knowledge of $m(\theta)$ at selected points $\{\theta^t\}$. If it is known that $m(\theta)$ is weakly or strongly additive, then the previous method may be used.

Finally we have made mention of subjective probabilities for the set of subsets, $\mathcal{S}$, of a set of events, or states, $\boldsymbol{\alpha}$.

338

If the subjective probabilities are based on a qualitative order over $\mathscr{S}$, then the procedure requires a comparison of subsets in order to set bounds on the probabilities, and a continual refinement until the requisite accuracy is achieved.

Thus, given $u \in \mathscr{S}$, if $u \mathrm{P} \tilde{u}$ ($\tilde{u}$ is the complement of u in $\boldsymbol{\alpha}$) we have:

$$p(u) > \tfrac{1}{2}, \qquad p(\tilde{u}) < \tfrac{1}{2}.$$

If $\boldsymbol{\alpha} = \{\alpha_k\}$ is finite, we may compare various combinations of $\{\alpha_k\}$ and obtain equalities, or inequalities, in $\{p_k\}$, (p_k = probability of α_k) and obtain bounds on the p_k this way. There are other ways of doing this.

If the subjective probabilities are choice based (see Savage [74]), the procedure is somewhat different, involving the determination of both utilities and probabilities.

Details of these procedures may be found in White [96] and Fishburn [26], and the above merely illustrate the sort of methods which may be used.

In practice, one may wish to resort to more direct methods. For example (see Saaty [72], Laotsma [55]), where it is accepted that a weakly additive measurement exists, individuals are asked to say how important the ith factor is in relationship to the jth factor, giving a number r_{ij} as an estimate of the ratio m_i/m_j. In some instances (see White [94]) individuals are asked to give numbers to represent the importance of certain features of a problem. In probabilistic situations individuals are asked to state the probabilities, or bound on, of various events. In Sarin's measurable value, individuals are asked to state differences in value. And so on.

These are all appealing because they are simple, and even meaningful to the individuals, but they may not accord with the underlying theory from which the proper use derives. It may well be that such procedures give adequate measurements, and, indeed, Fischer [29] suggests that this may be the case. Nonetheless, the reader should be aware of the need to find justification for such short-cut procedures.

6.9 ENTROPY, FLEXIBILITY, AND FUZZY SETS

Three topics to be found frequently in the literature relating to the measurement of certain properties of situations are those of entropy, flexibility, and fuzzy sets. In the view of the author these provide extremely good examples of erroneous measurement, at least for some of the purposes attributed to them. It would be a salutary exercise for readers to examine the original material in the context of measurement. We will only briefly discuss the topics and will provide references for a more thorough study.

Entropy

The following references will provide a useful source of reading for a thorough study, viz. Khinchin [49, 50], White [90, 91, 95], Danskin [16],

Drechsler [18], Wilson [99], Philippatos *et al.* [64], Abodunde *et al.* [1], Zeleny [103], and Hwang *et al.* [42].

Each of these uses the concept of entropy with different purposes in mind, with the exception of the papers by White which are critiques on which this section is based.

First of all, let us be clear about the formal definition of the entropy measurement. The original measure (see Khinchin [49, 50]) is a derived measure representing the overall state of uncertainty in some system. The question for us is one of the relevance of such measures in decision making.

We will, initially, consider a simple framework in which a system may be in one of m states, $i = 1, 2, \ldots, m$. If P_i is the probability of being in state i, then the entropy of the system is formally defined as:

$$e(P) = -\sum_{i=1}^{N} P_i \log P_i$$

where $P = (P_1, P_2, \ldots, P_N)$.

For systems which are made up of a collection of items, each of which may be in any state i, P_i may be taken to be the proportion of items in state i (e.g. see Wilson [99] and Abodundie *et al.* [1]).

The fact that H is, somehow, a measure of uncertainty in the system, is evident from the fact that $H = 0$ if $P_i = 1$ for some i, $P_j = 0$, for all $i \neq j$.

Let us now look at the governing conditions specified by Khinchin. Let m be any measure of uncertainty which is a function of P. The conditions are as follows.

E.1
$$m(P) = m(\sigma(P))$$

where $\sigma(P)$ is any permutation of P.

E.2
$$\max[m(P)]$$
$$\text{subject to } \sum_{i=1}^{N} P_i = 1, \qquad P_i \geq 0 \quad \text{for all } i$$

occurs when $P_i = 1/N$ for all i.

E.3
Suppose we have two finite sets $\{i\}$, $\{j\}$, $i = 1, 2, \ldots, N$, $j = 1, 2, \ldots, M$. If $Q = \{P_{ij}\}$, P_{ij} being the probability of i and j, $Q_i = (Q_{i1}, Q_{i2}, \ldots, Q_{iM})$, being the probability vector for $\{j\}$ given i, and $P = (P_1, P_2, \ldots, P_N)$, then:

$$m(Q) = m(P) + \sum_{i=1}^{N} P_i m(Q_i).$$

E.4
If $Q = (P, 0)$ (i.e. $Q_i = P_i$, $i = 1, 2, \ldots, N$, $Q_{N+1} = 0$) then:
$$m(Q) = m(P).$$

340

E.5

$$m(P) \text{ is a continuous function of } P.$$

E.6

$$\min[m(P)]$$

$$\text{subject to } \sum_{i=1}^{N} P_i = 1, \qquad P_i \geqslant 0 \quad \text{for all } i,$$

occurs when $P_i = 1$ for some i.

Conditions E.1–E.5 are only satisfied by measurements m which are positive multiples of e (the trivial case of $m(P) = 0$, for all P is excluded). Condition E.6, the one we mentioned initially, is a consequence of conditions E.1–E.5.

Now why should we seek measurements to satisfy these properties? What role does such a measurement play in decision making? Before looking at the attempts to use such a measurement, it is worth noting that other measurements exist which, for example, satisfy many of the plausible requirements for uncertainty in a context-free situation, for example

$$m(P) = \min_{i}[(1 - P_i)]$$

satisfies E.1, E.2, E.4, E.5, E.6, but not E.3, the conditional entropy expression.

Let us first of all look at Danskin's papers. The reader may wish to look back at Chapter 1 where we discuss search problems. Danskin's problem is to determine a best reconnaissance policy, x, for the detection of enemy installations, units, and so on. The states $\{i\}$ are the true states of the enemy installations and P_i is the prior probability of state i. The results of the reconnaissance are $\{j\}$, being data obtained from the reconnaissance, with $S_j(x)$ being the probability of getting j given x. $P_{ij}(x)$ is the probability of getting j given i, x, so that:

$$S_j(x) = \sum_{i=1}^{N} P_i P_{ij}(x), \qquad j = 1, 2, \ldots, M.$$

The posterior probability of state i given x and j is, using usual conditional probabilities;

$$S_{ij}(x) = P_i P_{ij}(x) \bigg/ \sum_{s=1}^{N} P_s P_{sj}(x), \qquad i = 1, 2, \ldots, N, \qquad j = 1, 2, \ldots, M.$$

The suggestion of Danskin is that the measurement of the value of the policy x should be the pre-posterior entropy, i.e.

$$m(x) = -\sum_{j=1}^{M} S_j(x) \sum_{i=1}^{N} S_{ij}(x) \log(S_{ij}(x)).$$

However, how can this be justified without deriving this in the context of a conjoint measurement involving choice, uncertainty, and outcomes, as a collective triple? Entropy is justified by the conditions E.1–E.5 (and perhaps E.6) and its use cannot be extended beyond this framework without proper justification. If it so happened that, by confronting the decision maker with all the probabilities for each x, the decision maker's choice can actually be represented this way, then one might accept this on the basis that the analysis would produce what the decision maker wanted. However, the crucial aspect of entropy is that it treats all states as equals, apart from their probabilities (see E.1). One might argue, in terms of a choice-oriented measurement, that an expected utility measurement is appropriate, viz.

$$m(x) = \sum_{j=1}^{M} S_j(x) \max_y \left[\sum_{i=1}^{N} S_{ij}(x)u(i, y) \right]$$

where $u(i, y)$ is the utility of taking action y for the true state i, and $m(x)$ is the pre-posterior expected utility for policy x. Clearly the subsequent actions, y, contingent on j, must be important, otherwise there would be no point in the reconnaissance. Clearly, also, the optimal xs obtained from the entropy and utility models would differ in general.

Let us now look at Drechsler's paper [18]. He deals with inventory control problems and the state i of the system is the stock level. The entropy of the stock levels is studied and it is recommended that the re-order point should be based upon entropy calculations. Again, how does this relate to the underlying characterizations of entropy and how does this arise in the context of conjoint measurement involving choice? Again also, a crucial factor in inventory control is that different stock levels have different economic significances (see Chapter 2, section 2.2), whereas entropy, via condition E.1, makes no distinction.

The reader will find it valuable to read the papers cited since, whether they agree or not, entropy provides a very interesting testing ground for measurement and its relevance to particular issues. Before moving to the next topic, it is also useful to look at a proposed approach to multi-objective decision making, a topic of some importance in this text. To fix our ideas let us use the nursery location–allocation problem of Chapter 4 section 4.3 where $\{f^i(x)\}$ are the three objective functions, and x is the location–allocation decision. Zeleny [103] discusses the problem of finding appropriate weighting factors $\{\lambda_i\}$ for the objective $\{f^i\}$. A finite set X of actions, $\{x^i\}$, is assumed, and a closeness index d_{ij} is calculated by:

$$d_{ij} = \frac{f^i(x^i) - \min_t[f^i(x^t)]}{\max_t[f^i(x^t)] - \min_t[f^i(x^t)]}, \qquad j = 1, 2, \ldots, l$$

d_{ij} is an index of the closeness of x^j to its optimal value for the ith objective function.

For the ith objective function an entropy measurement is specified, viz.

$$m(d_i) = -K \sum_{j=1}^{l} (d_{ij}/D_i)\log(d_{ij}/D_i) \qquad i = 1, 2, 3$$

where $D_i = \sum_{j=1}^{l} d_{ij}$, $i = 1, 2, 3$.

The suggested weighting factors $\{\lambda_i\}$ are given by:

$$\lambda_i = \alpha(1 - m(d_i)), \qquad i = 1, 2, 3$$

where α is a constant.

Why should such a procedure produce an appropriate conjoint measurement in the context of choice? Since, in any event, no uncertainty is involved, why use entropy at all? In what manner does the problem relate to the characterizing conditions of entropy?

Zeleny's [103] justification is as follows, to quote:

A weight, assigned to the ith attribute as a measure of its relative importance for a given decision problem, is directly related to the average intrinsic information, generated by a given set of alternatives through the ith attribute, as well as to its subjective assessment.

Flexibility

The following references will provide a useful source of reading for a thorough study, viz. Mandelbaum [58], Elton *et al.* [24], Rosenhead [69], White [92], Pye [65], Bayliss [6], Koopmans [53], and Lieb *et al.* [56].

Let us again begin with a few quotations.

We must certainly define, as exactly as possible, what is meant by flexibility, if only because we want the man to be flexible in the right sort of way.

Bayliss [6]

A problem that remains outside these replacement models is that of flexibility. For example, minimisation of cost during the horizon may require the use of a machine with a relatively long economic life. Therefore the solution may prevent us from making the best use of future technological alternatives that may become available after the horizon. In our present treatment flexibility should be considered as an intangible that must be weighted against the economic evaluations obtained from the replacement model.

Hansmann [38]

The concept of flexibility is commonly used in everyday discussion and, in essence, refers to the extent of freedom of action which is available on future occasions, which may be dependent on current decisions. The difference between the two points of view is that Bayliss feels that any measurement of flexibility must be tightly defined, dependent on how it is to be used, whereas Hansmann, at least in the context of his article, considers it to be an intangible.

In the final analysis, flexibility is an action-based concept. With the exception of Mandelbaum, independent measurements of flexibility are sought, which are not considered within a conjoint measurement framework with choice. Several such measurements are as follows.

Action Flexibility (Elton *et al.* [24])

Suppose we have to make a decision now and, later on, to make a second and subsequent decisions at specific points in time, for example if we buy a house, the location of the house might limit the available schools, public transport, etc.

Let X be the set of initial possible actions and $S(x)$ be the set of possible subsequent single, or sequences of, actions once x has been chosen from X. Let $n(Z)$ be the number of elements in any set Z. Then action flexibility may be formally defined, with no reference to the utility or probability of actions and outcomes, by:

$$m(x) = n(S(x)) \quad \text{or alternatively by} \quad m(x) = n(S(x))/n(U_x(S(x))).$$

The first definition relates to the number of options left open for subsequent decisions, or series of decisions, and the second definition standardizes this as a proportion lying between 0 and 1, allowing comparabilities between different situations.

In the Elton *et al.* paper [24], authors are concerned with locating five warehouses, each in one of 21 locations, in sequence over a period of years. From the possible subsets of five locations, 31 subsets were chosen as giving good sequences. It is required to locate the first warehouse now, and it is suggested that the choice be made to maximize flexibility (in this case, action flexibility). There are nine subsets in the chosen 31 which contain location A. If A is chosen as the first location there are $9 \times 4!$ possible sequences for the remaining four location decisions. The total number of subsequent sequences is $31 \times 4!$ (approximately). Hence the measure of flexibility of A is approximately 9/31. The nine subsets are (A, B, M, N, S), (A, B, M, N, T), (A, B, M, N, Z), (A, B, L, N, R), (A, B, D, L, N), (A, B, I, L, N), (A, B, L, M, N), (A, B, N, R, Z), (A, B, H, M, S). The reason why the total number of subsequent sequences is not exactly $31 \times 4!$ can be seen from the above where, if we begin with T or Z in the second and third subsets, we have exactly the same subsequence set (A, B, M, N) for the remaining four location decisions. If we do the same for locations B (which occurs in 30 subsets) and N (which occurs in 30 subsets) we obtain $m(B) = m(N) = 30/31$. These are the maximal flexibilities over all initial locations and one of these is to be chosen.

This measure of flexibility ignores certain important points.

(i) Each sequence will have a different worth in general. If the subsets chosen are of equal worth, then it does no harm to choose the initial location to be the one with maximal flexibility. If they are not of equal worth, then flexibility is not really useful since, by definition, we really want to choose sequences of maximal worth.

(ii) In assessing the worth of a sequence we need to look at all the events which can take place after the first location decision, and their probabilities (e.g. probabilities of possible demand patterns). For sequences to be equally good they have to be equally good for all such events which have a non-zero (non-small) probability. This seems quite unlikely to be the case, in which case the initial decision should not be taken to maximize the flexibility given, but to take into account the worth of subsequent sequences dependent on events which transpire. It is really a dynamic programming type situation, similar to the capacity installation problem of Chapter 2, section 2.5 although incorporating uncertainties (see Exercise 15 of the Mathematical and Dynamic Programming Exercises).

We will make these ideas explicit later on with a simpler problem.

Action-Postponement Flexibility (Mandelbaum [58])

Sometimes, if we are not sure about subsequent events or conditions, we might wish to postpone a decision, which might leave a wider choice of options open to us later on. Again the measure of flexibility might be the number of subsequent actions left open to us by doing so and this becomes a special case of action flexibility. Thus we might postpone buying a house until questions of proposed new roads, new schools, have been decided upon. However, postponing a decision is not always costless, for example if one has to rent a house in the meantime.

State (Environmental) Flexibility

A system is state flexible if it is designed to perform well under a range of environmental conditions without re-design. The measure of flexibility is in terms of the environmental variety it can cope with, and not in terms of the actions which are taken in coping with the environment, although it will influence these, for example a job shop is designed to cope with a high variety of operations, as distinct from a specialized chemical industry, and a general hospital can cope with a wide range of patients, as distinct from a specialized cancer hospital.

The above measurements are derived measurements in the sense that they measure flexibility without considering the worth of the actions. Maximizing flexibility is not necessarily the same as maximizing worth. Let us look at the problem formally and let us assume that we may use expected utility theory.

Consider a two-stage problem $\{X, J, S(x)\}$, in which an initial action x is chosen within X, and where, after some subsequent event or condition $j \in J$ materializes, some action $y \in S(x)$ is to be taken. Let $u(x, j, y)$ be the utility of taking decisions $x \in X$ when j materializes and then decision y is taken. If y is no longer possible when (x, j) are given, we set $u(x, j, y) = -\infty$. As before, let $n(S(x))$ be the number of options in $S(x)$. Let p_j be the probability of j occurring. If we wish to maximize expected utility we should solve the problem:

$$\max_{x \in X} \left[\sum_{j \in J} p_j \max_{y \in S(x)} [u(x, j, y)] \right] = \max_{x \in X} [v(x)],$$

say. This is not the same, in general, as the problem:

$$\max_{x \in X} [m(S(x))]$$

For example, consider the warehouse location problem where we wish to locate two warehouses only. Let $X = \{A, B\}$, $S(A) = \{B, C\}$, $S(B) = \{D\}$. Let $J = \{1, 2\}$, $p_1 = p_2 = 0.5$, and the utilities be given as in Table 6.1.

Table 6.1

$\underline{x}$	$\underline{y}$	j 1	2	
A	B	0.1	0.2	
	C	0.2	0.1	$u(x, j, y)$
B	D	1	1	

The expected utility of A is $0.5 \times 0.2 + 0.5 \times 0.2 = 0.2$.

The expected utility of B is $0.5 \times 1 + 0.5 \times 1 = 1$.

Also $m(S(A)) = 2$, $m(S(B)) = 1$, which gives A higher flexibility but lower expected utility.

Only in very special cases will the choices of initial actions based upon flexibility and expected utility give the same results. For example, if $S(x) \subseteq S(x^1)$, then $m(x^1) \geqslant m(x)$ and $v(x^1) \geqslant v(x)$. However, this is very unlikely to be the case in general.

In the case of Hansmann [38], an attempt is made to allow for other options open to the decision maker at subsequent points in time, arising from technological change, but which are not incorporated in the original model. One might argue that, if it is at all possible to take them into account anywhere, it ought to be possible to model them in the first instance.

It is of course possible to use an open form of analysis. Thus, suppose we are selecting a machine now from among a set X. We may be able to determine the capital cost $c(x)$, for each $x \in X$. It may well be that the machine will be called upon to do various jobs in due course, but that it is not easy to identify which jobs. Thus the machine may also be judged upon its capability of being able to cope with many jobs, or in terms of the ability to convert at specified cost to do whatever job turns up. We might obtain a derived measure for flexibility on this basis, and present the decision maker with this measure and the capital costs for a range of machines, and leave him to choose. He is quite free to do so. One might even determine a conjoint measurement structure so that the choice between many options may be facilitated. However, in doing so, the decision maker has to realize that the flexibility measure communicated to him simply represents the extent of the options open to him and not the effectiveness of these options in dealing with future contingencies. Alternatively, as with Hansmann [38], the identifiable economic aspects of each option may be presented, and the decision maker expected to superimpose some personal assessment of flexibility entirely.

To date, no satisfactory treatment of measurement of flexibility, in a conjoint context, exists. Koopmans [53] did make the beginnings of such a treatment but no progress has been made since.

Finally, to return once again to multi-objective decision making, Lieb *et al.* [56] attempt to introduce flexibility into the problem of selecting a solution from within the set of efficient extreme points. The flexibility of any such point is measured by its closeness to other solutions, on the basis that, if the decision maker changes his mind about certain factors (e.g. about the importance he gives to the various objectives), the decision maker may be able to modify his decision at relatively little cost. Similar arguments apply to this approach as to those already discussed.

Fuzzy Sets

The following references will provide a useful source of reading for a thorough study, viz. Zadeh [101], [102], Zimmermann [104, 105], Shackle [77], French [30], Kandel *et al.* [45], Gaines *et al.* [31], Carlson [11, 12], Wynne [100], Dubois [19], and Jacquet-Lagreze [44].

The seminal paper on fuzzy sets is that of Zadeh [101]. The essential idea behind this is that certain entities belong to a specified set S to a lesser or greater degree. The extent to which a is a member of S is called its degree of membership, denoted by $m(a)$. S is said to be a fuzzy set and $0 \leqslant m(a) \leqslant 1$, where $m(a) = 0$ is interpreted to mean a is definitely not in S, and $m(a) = 1$ is interpreted as a is definitely in S.

If S, T are two fuzzy sets, then if m_S, m_T are fuzzy membership functions, the conjunctive and disjunctive membership functions are defined as follows, viz.

$$m_{S \cap T}(a) = \min[m_S(a), m_T(a)]$$
$$m_{S \cup T}(a) = \max[m_S(a), m_T(a)].$$

For the normal two-valued logic, where $m(a) = 0$ or 1, this calculus is trivially true. The particular calculus of fuzzy sets is, however, not the only one which will give the appropriate results in this special case. The following will also work:

$$m_{S \cap T}(a) = m_S(a) m_T(a)$$
$$m_{S \cup T}(a) = m_s(a) + m_T(a) - m_S(a) m_T(a).$$

There are no underlying conditions setting the fuzzy measurement in the context of conjoint measurement. The measure is not a derived measure, although it has its structural aspects allowing fuzzy measurements of complex entities to be calculated once the basic values have been determined. The basic measurements are obtained by asking the individual what the degree of membership is. It can be given no external meaning and has no communication value.

Let us consider an example given by Wynne [100]. A set of options A is evaluated in terms of the extent to which it is satisfactory on sales and profitability margins. The satisfactory sales options constitute the fuzzy set S, and the satisfactory profitable margin options constitute the fuzzy set T. The individuals are asked to specify the values $(m_S(a), m_T(a))$ for each $a \in A$ and then $m_{S \cap T}(a)$ is calculated. The solution recommended is the one which maximizes $m_{S \cap T}(a)$, $a \in A$.

The big question is why should this procedure lead to the best choice? The measurement procedure is not derived from a choice basis, and must therefore be quite arbitrary, unless empirical evidence exists to substantiate this. Thus, one might ask the decision maker to rank the options initially and then see if the ranking is consistent with the ranking given by the fuzzy set procedure. If there is evidence to believe that this is true for general classes of problem outside the specific one being considered, then, purely as a descriptive and computational device, such a procedure may be used. Without evidence of the universality of such predictive value one would not know when to use it. In addition, returning to the communication issue, if the membership functions were supplied by experts, distinct from the decision maker, such tests would be meaningless. Nor would it be meaningful to test the structural rules if different assessors were used for each fuzzy set.

A similar development is given by Carlson [12] for multi-objective problems. Fuzzy goals $\{g_i\}$ are postulated for each objective function $\{f^i\}$, $i = 1, 2, \ldots, m$, and, in addition, fuzzy constraints $\{C_j\}$, $j = 1, 2, \ldots, p$ are postulated. If $\{m_{G_i}\}$, $\{m_{C_j}\}$ are the respective membership functions, and if X is the set of actions, it is recommended that the optimal x is chosen by:

$$\underset{x \in X}{\text{maximizing}}[\underset{i}{\min}[\min[m_{G_i}(x)], \underset{j}{\min}[m_{C_j}]]].$$

Exactly the same objections may be made to this as to the suggestions of Wynne [100].

Zadeh [102] develops the concept of fuzzy probabilities and also, briefly, introduces the idea of fuzzy utilities, as a step towards producing a fuzzy expected utility theory, but again the fuzzy probabilities and fuzzy utilities are not developed within a theory of conjoint measurement involving choice.

Finally, it is worth making reference to the work of Shackle [77] which predates the fuzzy set developments. Shackle introduces the concept of degrees of surprise of an event. The calculus for determining the degrees of surprise for disjunctions and conjunctions is identical to that of fuzzy sets, prompted probably by the need to obtain conformity with the 0–1 case of two valued logic. Whereas Shackle's work is intended as a substitute for probability, fuzzy sets are not intended to represent uncertainty. It is difficult to tell, in the latter case, whether this is true or not, since the membership idea is meaningless except in the two-valued logic case. However, Shackle's development is as much subject to the critique as is the fuzzy set measurement.

6.10 OPEN AND CLOSED FORMS OF ANALYSIS

Let us, finally, turn to the main reason for measurement, viz. to increase the power of the Operational Research study. Before we do this it is useful to refer to the paper by Kilmann et al. [51], who examine the qualitative–quantitative issue, to which Schwartz's [76] statement, given in section 6.1, is relevant, and, within which, the work of Dyson [20], mentioned in Section 6.6, fits.

Kilmann et al. [51] identity four types of personality in terms of their problem solving approaches, viz.

  (i) sensation–thinking (S.T.)
 (ii) sensation–feeling (S.F.)
(iii) intuition–thinking (N.T.)
 (iv) intuition–feeling (N.F.).

Broadly speaking the S.T. type requires the most quantitative inputs, and uses the most logical processing, and, at the other extreme, the N.F. type requires the least quantitative input and logical processing.

The question of which type makes the best decision maker is an important one. It may be that the N.F. type is the best. This in itself might pose a very interesting Operational Research study. However, the point of view taken in this text is that Operational Research has, as its central objective, the provision of a logical, data-based, framework for arriving at decisions, subject to limitations imposed on the study by resource availabilities, time availabilities, and the general context of the situation. In this sense it will clearly appeal to the S.T. types and not to the N.F. types.

In looking at the role of measurement we have examined such things as communication, and errors, each of which is important in problem solving and, at least at first glance, it would seem that both issues, and hence measurement, should be important to all types. The additional issue is the power of analysis given by additional structural properties of the factors with which we are dealing. In Chapter 4, section 4.3, we dealt with open and closed forms of analysis.

The open form is less demanding, less powerful, and in many instances the measurement issue is perhaps non-existent. Thus if we have a relatively small number of options, and the objectives have clearly specified measurements such as cost, distance, time, and so on, no further refinement is needed. However, as has been shown in section 6.5, many objectives do pose measurement problems, even if we do not go so far as to produce a complete conjoint measurement framework in a choice context. Even in our fairly simple queueing, inventory, and other problems, there is a hidden measurement problem as has been mentioned earlier, viz. the systems have a probabilistic behaviour and it has to be demonstrated that the use of expected levels of variables such as waiting time, shortages, and so on, is the appropriate measurement of these features for decision making purposes. Thus, even the open form of analysis is not without its measurement problems.

The closed form of analysis is the most demanding and the most powerful. Without a structured conjoint measurement framework it would be practically impossible to cover more than a small number of options actually open to a decision maker (see, also, Chapter 2, section 2.10). Bailey [4], in the first volume of Operations Research, makes this point very clearly, and it is as true now as it was then. No decision maker could evaluate all the conceivable possibilities available. Nor could they do any error analysis and consequential sensitivity analysis.

If we return to Chapter 2, sections 2.1–2.4, where we discussed queueing problems, inventory problems, and so on, where the options are very numerous, it is clear that, without some conjoint choice-based measurement, very little could be done, in many instances, to cater for all these options. It is, of course, true that such things as efficient solution approaches can help, but, for many problems, even with two objectives, obtaining the efficient set is extremely demanding. For problems with more than two objectives the situation is much worse.

6.11 EXERCISES

1. In the second year of your present degree you are required to select five courses. You will choose these courses with certain purposes in mind in relationship to subsequent third-year courses, which reflect flexibility of choices open to you in the third year, the utilities of classes in your second and third year, the possibilities of failure in classes in the second year, and the possibility that the utilities (or values) you give to classes now may change. How would you define an *a priori* measure of flexibility? Then examine this definition in the context of other features of your choice mentioned above.

2. A company has certain types of manpower, j, $j = 1, 2, \ldots, n$ and certain types of jobs i, $i = 1, 2, \ldots, m$, to be done. At any point in time, as a result of any production policy, π, there is a probability p_i that a job type i needs to be done, and a probability q_j that manpower type j is available to do the job, where $p_i = p_i(\pi)$, $q_j = q_j(\pi)$, depending on π. In principle, job type i may be done by any type of manpower, and some agreed flexible working arrangement is desired.

How would you define, *a priori*, two measures of flexibility? Examine the properties of these in the context of a utility approach to the problem, where u_{ij} is the utility of doing job type i using labour type j at the time the job is required.

3. In section 6.5 a list of properties discussed by some authors is given. Examine these in the context of the various aspects of measurement introduced in this chapter.

4. Do the same for the following properties: job security, job stability, wage security, wage stability, skill, responsibility, development potential (see Van den Mayzenberg [83]).

5. Productivity measurement is geared to determining the ratio of certain outputs to certain inputs. Discuss the following productivity measures:

(1) added value per year/per employee (added value is the monetary value added to materials by the process of production from which wages, salaries, rent, tax reserves and dividends, selling, distribution, and advertising costs have to be met)
(2) profit per unit of capital employed
(3) profit per unit of sales
(4) sales per unit of capital
(5) sales per unit of fixed assets
(6) sales per unit of stock held
(7) sales per employee
(8) profit per employee
(9) total output per unit of summed input of labour, capital, raw material and purchased parts, miscellaneous goods and services, all measured in suitable units (see Wild [98]; see also Cosmatatos *et al.* [14], Eilon [22], Eilon *et al.* [23], Gold [34], and Easterfield [21] for discussions of productivity measurement, where the second referenced paper discusses the dangers in productivity measurement).

6. Performance measurements of individuals, or groups, may be obtained by trying to separate off, from total performance, that part which is outside the control of those concerned (for example, if total profit is used, that part of the profit due to controllable factors is removed but the same may apply for production output, accident levels, and so on). Examine the question of

performance measurements in the context of the material of this chapter (see Cloot [13]).

7. Discuss the question of the measurement of a state of health in the context of the material of this chapter (see Rosser *et al.* [71]).

8. In the Queueing Theory section (2.1) of Chapter 2, we discussed priority queues. Suppose now that we now have m streams of customer (you may think in terms of different categories of hospital patients, discussed in the Mathematical and Dynamic Programming section (2.5) of Chapter 2) and that you wish to maximize the fairness (or equitability) of handling patient admissions. Examine the problem of measuring the fairness of any procedure for admissions (Bar-Hillel *et al.* [5] give a useful analysis of the fairness problem, and Varian [84] is a useful text on the subject).

9. Do the same as in Exercise 8 for the school location–allocation problem discussed in the Mathematical and Dynamic Programming section (2.5) of Chapter 2, in Chapter 4, section 4.3, and in this chapter (section 6.3).

6.12 REFERENCES

1. Abodunde, T. and McClean, S., Entropy as a measure of stability in a manpower system, *Journal of Operational Research Society*, **29**, 885–890, 1978.
2. Adams, E. W., Elements of a theory of inexact measurement, *Philosophy of Science*, **32,** 1965.
3. Baecher, G. B., Gros, J. G., and McCusker, K., Methodologies for facility siting decisions, in *Formal Methods in Policy formulation*, D. W. Bunn and H. Thomas (Eds.), Birkhauser, 1978.
4. Bailey, R. A., Application of operations research techniques to airborne weapon systems planning, *Operations Research*, **1,** 187–199, 1953.
5. Bar-Hillel, M. and Yaari, M. E., On dividing justly, *Social Choice and Welfare*, **1,** 1–24, 1984.
6. Bayliss, R., A contribution to the application of systems analysis to manpower planning with a naive model, Department of Econometrics, Southampton University, 1970.
7. Bevan, R. G., Measurement for evaluation, *Omega*, **8,** 311–321, 1980.
8. Brand, H. W., *The Fecundity of Mathematical Models*, D. Reidel, 1961.
9. Brown, R. A. and Green, C. H., Precepts of safety assessment, *Journal of the Operational Research Society*, **31,** 563–571, 1980.
10. Buzelius, N., *The Value of Travel Time*, Croom Helm, 1979.
11. Carlson, C., Fuzzy sets and management science methodology, Department of Business Administration, Åbo Academy, Finland, 1981.
12. Carlson, C., Tackling an MCDM problem with the help of some results from fuzzy set theory, *European Journal of Operational Research*, **10,** 271–281, 1982.
13. Cloot, P. L., Objective measurement of branch performance, paper given to Euro-Banking Group, 1981.
14. Cosmetatos, G. P. and Eilon, S., Effects of productivity definition and measurement on performance evaluation, *European Journal of Operational Research*, **14,** 31–35, 1983.

352

15. Cretin, S. and Keeler, E. B., Discounting of life-saving and other non-monetary effects, *Management Science*, **29**, 300–306, 1983.
16. Danskin, J. M., Reconnaissance I & II, *Operations Research*, **10**, 285–309, 1962.
17. Dick, J. B., A study of the effectiveness of some recent research at the building research station, UK, United Kingdom Government Paper 87/68, 1968.
18. Drechsler, F. S., Decision trees and the second law, *Operational Research Quarterly*, **19**, 409, 1969.
19. Dubois, D. and Prade, H., *Fuzzy Sets and Systems Theory and Applications*, Academic Press, 1980.
20. Dyson, R. G., Operational research on a peat bog: a case for qualitative Modelling, *Journal of the Operational Research Society*, **34**, 127–136, 1983.
21. Easterfield, T., Productivity—target or conceptual tool, *Operational Research Quarterly*, **16**, 177–187, 1965.
22. Eilon, S., The use of index numbers for measuring output of multi-product systems, *Journal of the Operational Research Society*, **34**, 671–695, 1983.
23. Eilon, S., Gold, B., and Soesan, J., *Applied Productivity Analysis for Industry*, Pergamon, 1976.
24. Elton, M., Gupta, S., and Rosenhead, J., Robustness and optimality as criteria for strategic decisions, *Operational Research Quarterly*, **23**, 413–431, 1972.
25. English, J. M., (Ed.), *Cost Effectiveness*, Wiley, 1968.
26. Fishburn, P., *Decision and Value Theory*, Wiley, 1964.
27. Fishburn, P., *Utility Theory for Decision Making*, Wiley, 1970.
28. Fishburn, P., Multi-attribute utilities in expected utility theory, in *Conflicting Objectives in Decisions*, D. E. Bell, R. L. Keeney and H. Raiffa (Eds.), Wiley, 1977.
29. Fischer, G. W., Utility models for multiple objective decisions: do they accurately represent human preferences?, *Decision Sciences*, **10**, 451–479, 1979.
30. French, S., Fuzzy decision analysis: some criticisms, Department of Decision Theory, Manchester University, 1981.
31. Gaines, B. R. and Kohaut L. J., The fuzzy decade: a bibliography of fuzzy systems and closely related topics, *International Journal of Man–Machine Studies*, **9**, 1–68, 1977.
32. Gardner, E. S. Jr., Inventory theory and the gods of the Olympus, *Interfaces*, **10**, 42–45, 1980.
33. Golabi, K., Kulkarni, R. B., and Way, G. B., A statewide pavement management system, *Interfaces*, **12**, 5–21, 1982.
34. Gold, B., Productivity analysis and system coherence, *Operational Research Quarterly*, **16**, 287–307, 1965.
35. Good, I., Deciding and decisionary effort, *Information & Control*, **4**, 271–281, 1961.
36. Green, C. H., Risk, beliefs and attitudes, in *Behaviour in Fire*, D. V. Carter (Ed.), Wiley, 1980.
37. Hansmann, F., *Operations Research in Production and Inventory Control*, Wiley, 1962.
38. Hansmann, F., *Operations Research Techniques for Capital Investment*, Wiley, 1968.
39. Harrison, P., A multi-objective decision problem: the furniture manufacturer's two-dimensional cutting or trim problem, in *Multi-Objective Decision Making* S. French, R. Hartley, L. C. Thomas, and D. J. White (Eds.), Academic Press, 1983.
40. Hayward, P., When is a property measurable? *Operations Research Society of America National Meeting*, 1970.

353

41. Hitch, C. J. and McKean, R. N., *The Economics of Defense in the Nuclear Age*, Athenum, 1966.
42. Hwang, C. L. and Yoon, K., *Multiple Attribute Decision Making*, Springer, 1981.
43. Industrial College of the Armed Forces, Modern design for defense decision, Washington D.C., 1966.
44. Jacquet-Lagreze, E., Modelling preferences among distributions using fuzzy relations, in *Decision Making and Change in Human Affairs*, H. Jungermann and G. de Zeeuw (Eds.), D. Reidel, 1977.
45. Kandel, A. and Yager, R. R., A 1979 bibliography on fuzzy sets, their applications and related topics, in Gupta, M. M., Ragade, R. K., and Yager, R. R. (Eds.), *Advances in Fuzzy Set Theory and Applications*, North-Holland, 1979.
46. Kazanowski, A., Cost effectiveness fallacies and misconceptions revisted, *29th Operation Research Society of America National Meeting*, 1966.
47. Keeney, R. L. and Raiffa, H., *Decisions with Multiple Objectives*, Wiley, 1976.
48. Keighley, E. C., Acceptability criteria for noise in larger offices, Building Research Station, Current Paper 15/70, 1970.
49. Khinchin, A. I., The entropy concept in probability theory, *Uspekhi Mathematicheskikh*, **VIII**, 3–20, 1953.
50. Khinchin, A. I., *Mathematical Foundations of Information Theory*, Dover Publications, 1957.
51. Kilman, R. and Mitroff, I., Qualitative vs. quantitative analysis for management science, *Interfaces*, **6**, 17–27, 1976.
52. Koopmans, T., Stationary ordinal utility and impatience, *Econometrica*, **28**, 287–309, 1960.
53. Koopmans, T., On the flexibility of future preference, in M. Shelley and G. Bryan (Eds.), *Human Judgements and Optimality*, Wiley, 1964.
54. Krantz, D. H., Luce, R. D., Suppes, P., and Tversky, A., *Foundations of Measurement*, Vol. 1, Academic Press, 1971.
55. Laotsma, F. A., Saaty's priority theory and the nomination of a senior professor in operations research, *European Journal of Operational Research*, **4**, 380–388, 1980.
56. Leib, E. B. and Morse, J. N., Flexibility and rigidity in multiple criteria decision making: theory and application, G. Fandel and T. Gal (Eds.), Springer, 1980.
57. Luce, R. D., Conjoint measurement, a brief survey, in D. E. Bell, R. L. Keeney and H. Raiffa (Eds.), *Conflicting Objectives in Decisions*, Wiley, 1977.
58. Mandelbaum, M., Flexibility in decision making, an exploration and unification, Ph.D. thesis, University of Toronto, 1978.
59. Markowitz, H., *Protfolio Selection*, Wiley, 1959.
60. McNamara, R. S., *The Essence of Security*, Hodder & Stoughton, 1968.
61. Mellen, T., Operational research in the gas industry, Research Communication G. C. 140, The Gas Council, 1967.
62. Morgenstern, O. and von Neumann, J., *Theory of Games and Economic Behaviour*, Princeton University Press, 1947.
63. Phanzagl, J., A general theory of measurement: applications to utility, *Naval Research Logistics Quarterly*, **6**, 283–294, 1959.
64. Philippatos, G. C. and Wilson, C. J., Entropy, market risk and selection of efficient portfolios, *Applied Economics*, **4**, 209–220, 1972.
65. Pye, R., A formal decision theoretic approach to flexibility and robustness, *Operational Research Quarterly*, **29**, 215–227, 1978.
66. Raisbeck, G., How the choice of measures of effectiveness constrains operational analysis, *Interfaces*, **9**, 85–93, 1979.
67. Rapoport, A., *Operational Philosophy*, Harper Brothers, New York, 1953.

354

68. Roberts, F. S., *Measurement Theory*, Addison–Wesley, 1979.
69. Rosenhead, J., An education in robustness, *Operational Research Quarterly*, **29,** 105–111, 1978.
70. Ross, S., *Logical Foundations of Psychological Measurement, A Study in the Philosophy of Science*, Mannsgoord, Copenhagen, 1964.
71. Rosser, R. and Watts, V., The measurement of illness, *Journal of The Operational Research Society*, **29,** 529–540, 1978.
72. Saaty, T. L., A scaling method for priorities in hierarchical structures, *Journal of Mathematical Psychology*, **15,** 234–281, 1977.
73. Sarin, R. K., Strength of preferences and risky choice, *Operations Research*, **30,** 982–997, 1982.
74. Savage, L. J., *The Foundation of Statistics*, Wiley, 1954.
75. Schachtman, R. H. and Zalkind, D., A method to determine a non-economic personal value of life, *Journal of the Operational Research Society*, **34,** 145–153, 1983.
76. Schwartz, J., The pernicious influence of mathematics, in *Science, Logic, Methodology and Philosophy of Science*, E. Nagel, P. Suppes and A. Tarski (Eds.), Standford University Press, 1962.
77. Shackle, G. L., *Decision Order and Time in Human Affairs*, Cambridge University Press, 1961.
78. Shilton, D., Modelling demand for high speed train services, *Journal of the Operational Research Society*, **33,** 713–722, 1982.
79. Suppes, P. and Zinnes, J. L., Basic measurement theory, in *Handbook of Mathematical Psychology*, R. D. Luu, R. R. Buch, and E. Galanter (Eds.), pp. 1–76, Wiley 1963.
80. Tarski, A., *Introduction to Logic*, Oxford University Press, 1965.
81. Torgerson, W. S., *Theory and Methods of Scaling*, New York, 1958.
82. United States of America Senate, Inquiry of the Sub-Committee on National Security and Industrial Operation, Planning Programming Budgeting, 1970.
83. Van den Mayzenberg, L., Production systems Today, in *The Director's Handbook*, G. Bull (Ed.), McGraw-Hill, 1977.
84. Varian, H. R., Distributive justice, welfare economics and the theory of fairness, *Philosophy of Public Affairs*, **4,** 223–247, 1975.
85. Vazsonyi, A., Through the looking glass to data bank management, *Interfaces*, **9,** 99–104, 1979.
86. Vazsonyi, A., Predicate calculus and data base management system, *Interfaces*, **10,** 64–71, 1980.
87. Waddington, C. H., *O.R. In World War II: Operational Research against the U-boat*, Elek Science, 1973.
88. Watson, S. R., Multi-attribute utility theory for measuring safety, *European Journal of Operational Research*, **10,** 77–81, 1982.
89. White, D. J., *Dynamic Programming*, Oliver & Boyd, 1969.
90. White, D. J., Operational research and entropy, *Operational Research Quarterly*, **20,** 126–127, 1969.
91. White, D. J., The use of the concept of entropy in system modelling, *Operational Research Quarterly*, **21,** 279–281, 1970.
92. White, D. J., Comments on a paper by Elton, Gupta and Rosenhead, *Operational Research Quarterly*, **24,** 311–313, 1973.
93. White, D. J., *Decision Theory*, Allen & Unwin, 1969.
94. White, D. J., *Decision Methodology*, Wiley, 1975.
95. White, D. J., Entropy and decision, *Operational Research Society Quarterly*, **26,** 15–23, 1975.
96. White, D. J., *Fundamentals of Decision Theory*, North-Holland, 1976.

97. Wiener, N., A new theory of measurement, a study in the logic of mathematics, *Proceedings of the London Mathematical Society Series 2*, **19,** 181–205, 1920.

98. Wild, R., Productivity: measurement and incentive, in *The Director's Handbook*, G. Bull, (Ed.) McGraw-Hill, 1977.

99. Wilson, A. G., The use of the concept of entropy in system modelling, *Operational Research Quarterly*, **21,** 247–266, 1970.

100. Wynne, B., Qualitative modelling, a beginning, *Interfaces*, **12,** 34–36, 1982.

101. Zadeh, L. A., Fuzzy sets, *Information and Control*, **8,** 338–353, 1965.

102. Zadeh, L. A., Fuzzy probabilities and their role in decision analysis, in *Theory and Application of Digital Control*, A. K. Mahalanabis (Ed.), Pergamon, 1982.

103. Zeleny, M., *Linear Multiobjective Programming*, Springer, 1974.

104. Zimmermann, H. J., Theory and applications of fuzzy sets, in *Operational Research 1978*, K. B. Haley (Ed.), North-Holland, 1979.

105. Zimmermann, H. J., Using fuzzy sets in operational research, *European Journal of Operational Research*, **13,** 201–216, 1983.

B0 1 787 772 X

Index

surrogate, 122, 235, 238, 312, 328, 329
symbolic, 25

tardiness, 173
teaching, 156, 171, 304
team, 216
technological, 222, 304
testability, 312, 326
testing and controlling the solution, 21
testing the model, 21
thickness of a coin, 278
throughput rate, 239
topological, 312
transient behaviour, 43
transitive, 311, 326
transport, 219
transport optimization method, 83
travelling salesman, 23, 70, 159
trawler, 300
trimloss, 70, 124, 330
trucks, 295
types of action, 220

uncertainty, 310, 328, 339
utility, 192, 204, 244, 248, 309, 320, 341

validate, 327
value, 192, 243, 309, 314
value of life, 328
value of travel time, 328
variance reduction, 89, 99
vehicle, 114, 278
verification, 298
virtual work, 86
vision, 310
Vogel's method, 170
volume, 237, 244

wage security, 350
wage stability, 350
waiting time, 39, 216
warehouse, 85, 343
weakly additive, 317, 336
Weber problem, 73, 85
weighting factor, 217
well-defined, 211
well-structured, 109, 211
wisdom, 310
worst case, 108, 169